The Memoirs of Lord Gladwyn

The Memoirs of Lord Gladwyn

Weidenfeld and Nicolson
5 Winsley Street London W1

'Moi qui tremblais, sentant geindre a cinquante lieues,
Le rut des Béhemoths et les Maelstroms épais,
Fileur éternel des immobilités bleues,
Je regrette l'Europe aux anciens parapets.'

Arthur Rimbaud, 'Bateau Ivre'

ISBN 0 297 99415 8

Printed by C. Tinling & Co. Ltd
London and Prescot

Acknowledgments

For the production of my MS my thanks are chiefly due to my inimitable part-time secretary, Irene Hunter, who (as Irene Durlacher) was with me in New York and, briefly, in Paris, and one of whose many virtues is an ability to read my script when I myself cannot do so! I am also very grateful, in this respect, to my researcher, Helen Pickthorn, who has spent much time, which she could ill afford, in the Public Record Office and in various libraries: to Mr J. H. Wormald and Mrs E. C. Woulfe of the Foreign and Commonwealth Library and Records Department for their unfailing assistance and courtesy; and to all those in the Foreign and Commonwealth Office and the Cabinet Office whose perusal of the original script must have added considerably to their normal work but who, happily, found hardly anything in it to which they could take exception. The actual production of the book was admirably supervised by Gila Curtis.

On the composition side I am greatly indebted to Professor Sir Isaiah Berlin and to my son-in-law, Professor Hugh Thomas, both of whom read the original text (some thirty per cent longer than the present version) and made invaluable suggestions on cutting and presentation, as well as to Anthony Godwin of Messrs Weidenfeld and Nicolson who, by suggesting various ways of fitting the book into his Procrustes bed, undoubtedly much improved it in the process.

Finally, I am above all grateful to my wife not only for refreshing my inadequate memory, but also for much sage advice, nearly all of which I have accepted.

Contents

Foreword

I have only kept a diary for very short periods and unless you are a born diarist it is best not to depend on one for memoirs, or even for confessions! A diary is like a photograph: it reflects the mood of the moment, but quite often not the essential truth. If poetry is emotion recollected in tranquillity, memoirs should represent the past seen through the telescope of time. So these recollections are based chiefly on simple memory assisted by a great mass of documents. What happened was that whenever I abandoned one job for another I simply asked the Registry to take away my accumulation of 'personal' papers which were mostly copies of minutes, memoranda and letters which I had composed during my occupation of that particular room and thought no more about it. What was my surprise, therefore, a few years ago when I asked if the Foreign Office had any material which I could consult, to be told that all these documents, beginning as far back as 1931, had all been bound, classified and indexed.

I have, naturally, not been able to quote from such documents as are within the 'closed' period of thirty years, though I have certainly used them to refresh my own memory. But reading through the millions of words has brought back the past to me as nothing else could and I only hope that I shall in some way be able to communicate to the patient reader the atmosphere of political excitement in which I spent so much of my time.

This book was already in page-proof form when the astonishing diaries of Sir Alec Cadogan appeared. In respect of these all I would say is that, in spite of the closest and friendliest daily contact with Cadogan over the two and a half terrible years that preceded the War, and thereafter working in almost as close an association with him for a further two years and a half, I had no inkling of the volcano that lay beneath that cool and calm exterior; that the vivid account which he gives of his 'conversion'

ix

after Hitler's Godesberg ultimatum, to which I also refer shortly on p. 80, shows that he had not in contradistinction (though I say it) to myself, misguided though I may have been, really worked out in his own mind a politically consistent philosophy or equated ends and means; and, finally, that if it had not been for the system which I initiated and which is described on p. 72, I can scarcely imagine what might have happened to my unfortunate Chief.

There is, so far as my own book is concerned, one rather revealing passage in Cadogan's diary when he says (p. 458) that in 1942 he 'found a little draft circular on my table this morning which, in a parenthesis, seemed to throw all future foreign policy into the new Department. (Now I know why G.J. is so pleased with his new appointment!) This won't do, and after all my consultations I think I see a way out.' I have forgotten – if I ever knew – what the 'way out' was. All I do know is that the PUS's apprehensions were largely justified in the event! (see p. 109).

Introduction

I began this autobiography three years ago partly through 'désœuvre-ment', in other words, for the purpose of occupying myself. Not that I was then unoccupied. I had, and still have, an interest in politics. I was active in journalism, in lecturing, and in the production of books. I had various other interests. But after leaving the City in 1967 I had no very regular employment and the idea of putting in so many hours a day with some definite object appealed to me. I therefore thought I might record the chief events of a life which has been fairly eventful, not so much because I imagined it would be of vast public interest, as because it would be diverting to write and lead to a self-appraisal that might at least be of considerable interest to the author.

At first I thought that the chief object might be to discover, by burrowing into such papers as were available to me, how my own political judgments and values changed during the period I was in the service of the Crown and thus in a position to influence, however slightly, the progress of events. And it seemed to me then – perhaps it still seems to me now – that these attitudes might best be depicted against the background of a British Raj, splendid and almost unchallenged when I was born during the Boer War, but gradually, and in the end rapidly, disintegrating as the years went by.

But as I now put down my pen (and perhaps I should say that it really is a pen, since I find that dictating produces a text that is much too discursive and a genuine autobiography can hardly be written by 'ghosts') and look through what I have written, I discover, rather to my surprise, that what I primarily seem to have been is a purveyor, if not sometimes even an originator, of political ideas. However misguided, these ideas often corresponded, a little later, to the line pursued by the government of the day. I am not so foolish as to maintain that this necessarily represented cause and effect. It is quite possible that I was simply very receptive to a political atmosphere that was forming itself quite irrespective of any conscious effort on my part. Nor do I presume to say that I had anything like the influence on events of powerful statesmen or even of highly trained and politically minded writers and columnists.

But it is nevertheless true that in my back room in the Foreign Office – and from 1935–8 and 1942–4 it was a garret! – I did pour out proposals for long term projects and policies that were, quite frequently, adopted in the event. For example, the European Advisory Commission (which, after doing wonderful work under Lord Strang's direction more or less evolved into the High Commission for Germany) was, in varying forms, first advocated by me. The famous 'Four Power Plan' (which ended up with the United Nations) was originated by myself. It was I who first prepared drafts for an 'Atlantic Treaty' which blossomed out eventually into NATO. The German Occupation Zones (which, for good or evil, largely shaped the whole post-war development of Europe) were at any rate prepared in the committee of which I was the chairman. And, above all perhaps, suggestions for some kind of 'Western Union' (which ended up in the Brussels Treaty Organization and in the Western European Union) were, so far as I know, first formulated in that dark back room.

Later, it was always the theory of the thing rather than the practice which attracted me. What I really loved in New York were talks with, for instance, Hammarskjöld or Ham Armstrong, or George Kennan on the correct role of the United Nations. When I was in Paris nothing gave me greater satisfaction than discussions on great political issues with such people as Jean Laloy, or Mendès-France, or, above all, with that champion, if wrong-headed, ideas-merchant, Charles de Gaulle. And if there has been any idea to which I have been exceptionally faithful over the years it has been 'Europe' – '*durchaus studiert*' as Goethe makes Faust say, '*mit heissem Bemühn*'. That is something which I feel I really do know something about and the chances are that I shall see it accomplished before I die. How 'Europe' – or rather Western Europe – can be formed; why it should be formed; what it will be like; the part that it could play in the world; the necessity of its being associated with some wider Western, or 'Atlantic' community; on all these great issues I have put forward proposals which now at last have some prospect of gaining general consent. The reasons which led me to these conclusions are summarized shortly in this work and I hope the reader will find them interesting.

I trust he will not also think that I am self-satisfied or conceited. As a matter of fact the strange thing, as the reader will discover, is that for many years I never believed I was much good at anything. Nor have I ever been 'satisfied' with myself – very much the reverse. My principal failing is not taking enough trouble and being insufficiently aware of practical difficulties – to say nothing of other people's feelings. As Lord Home once remarked in the House of Lords, I fear I have often given the impression of a man who has been a success in diplomacy without ever really trying.

I should hope, therefore, that this work will not be regarded entirely as a diplomatic 'memoir' ('at this point I could hardly refrain from reminding His Excellency') but rather an account in what might otherwise have been a quite conventional career, of various political conceptions, one of which gradually came to overshadow all others and often seemed to take possession of me whether I wished it to do so or not. Certainly it is odd, how for many years events* seemed to conspire to put me in positions where I had both the time and the opportunity to advance this idea, and this in spite of frequent and fruitless efforts to take on large administrative jobs, which I had no doubt of my own ability to conduct successfully but which would have necessarily implied less concentration on the European cause.

I did not plan it that way, but when I look at the life that is now laid out before me I realize that from the earliest moment, that is to say when I became primarily interested in history at Eton and at Oxford, and with the exception of two and a half happy years in Persia and four years in New York (though this last period was only a partial exception), my whole background and my enduring interest have been the politics, and the relations between themselves, of the small and medium states of our Western European peninsula. I say that my time with the United Nations was only a partial exception because in the first place Manhattan is, or at least was when I lived there, a semi-European island anchored off the coast of America, and in the second place because I was, all that time, in a sense representing Europe in the Security Council, Britain still being, in 1950, by far the most important power in Western Europe and with European leadership in her grasp if only she had cared to take it.

I imagine, too, that the fact that I have a reasonable knowledge of the art, the history, and the literature of France, Italy and Germany and can speak all three languages with varying degrees of fluency, has made me especially aware of a common culture and of the need for preserving this by common action in a common cause. And yet I feel that I am almost exceptionally English, not only by descent, but also by reason of my out-

---

* And, indirectly, the Government, too, who since my retirement have only conferred on me one – most enjoyable but not very time-consuming – job, namely the chairmanship of the Government Hospitality Wine Committee.

look on the world. Besides, of my seventy-one years only about fifteen have been spent abroad, holidays included, of which about seven in Europe. And England is certainly the land of my choice as well as of my birth, and the only one in which I desire to end my days whatever may happen to the country in the interval.

Looking backward, I must confess, is something which I have rarely done. Nor, though this is perhaps rather less true, do I think that I have ever idealized the future. That might indeed be difficult at the present time. I have lived, therefore, largely in the present – '*le vierge, le vivace et le bel aujourd'hui*'. But what I have always felt an urge to do is to think out what is likely to happen if, as a nation, we pursue the one course or the other. It is not, therefore, because I believe that we shall necessarily all be better off if we succeed in forming some democratic entity in Western Europe that I have for so long advocated this – though I do think that we probably shall be: it is rather because of doubts concerning the maintenance of a free and orderly society if we do not. By the time this book appears the die will no doubt have been cast.

'Europe' apart, I see on reflection that, in the light of what actually happened, I was often only doubtfully right and sometimes clearly wrong. Perhaps most people who attempt to apply theory to politics are as often as not disowned and repudiated by events. This does not mean that they were not right to advance their theses. Look at Gladstone and Home Rule, and what would have been the future of Ireland if he had had his way. It is arguable that politics is a game best played by those who, subject to certain rules of conduct, are, like my ancestor Hal Dundas, only guided by their sense of personal advantage. But occasionally it may happen that one idea, long held and constantly pursued, does prevail. After all, this happened regarding the abolition of slavery, the Great Reform Bill, the social reforms of the Liberal Government of 1906, and what one might call, in general, the philosophy of the Welfare State. So, with these few remarks I embark hopefully on what I believe is an unvarnished account of my life, beginning at the earliest age and as near the truth as I can get it.

I

A Shy Young Man
(1900-24)

Perhaps the person most responsible for my background was Fanny Jebb, the only daughter of Joshua Jebb of Walton, who died in 1845. The Jebbs were an old and distinguished Derbyshire family, which can be traced back to Francis Jeppe, born in 1490, of whom I am the fourteenth descendant in the direct male line. Legend has it that they originally came from Scandinavia, 'Jeppe' being a common Danish or Norwegian name. They came 'armigerous', i.e. members of the gentry, or what on the Continent, but not in England, corresponded to the minor nobility, at the end of the seventeenth century. Samuel Jebb, who achieved this distinction, married Elizabeth Gilliver, 'in right of descent from whom Dr Jebb claimed to be the heir-at-law of John de Witt, Pensionary of Holland'. How exactly this claim was justified I have not been able to discover though it seems that she was probably the daughter of de Witt's niece. But we do still have two excellent portraits of the famous de Witt brothers by Mytens, so I suppose there was something in it, and I like to think that I may have some drop of blood of the family of the great Dutch democrat who was so unfortunately torn to pieces by the mob. The Jebbs subsequently had a tradition of nonconformism and were mostly squires, soldiers, physicians, scholars and divines. They never had very much money or hung on to it for long. One was a celebrated 'non-juror', another a friend of Swift's.

The elder branch emigrated to Ireland and produced a bishop and eventually Sir Richard Jebb, the famous Greek scholar. Joshua Jebb, the grandson of a centenarian Joshua, who was an alderman of Chesterfield, married in 1792 a Miss Gladwyn (or Gladwin), described as a 'co-heiress', the daughter of General Gladwyn whose distinguished role in the American War of Independence is still remembered in the United States. The name is certainly of Welsh origin and Mr Lloyd George once told me that it could properly be rendered as 'White, or Bright Sword'; but the family had lived in Derbyshire since the reign of Queen Elizabeth, so the amount of actual Welsh blood in my veins must be very small. Subsequently most of the male members of my branch of the family, including Jack Jebb the explorer and great friend of Rider Haggard's, bore this name before their own. Joshua's eldest son, my great-grandfather, a very good-looking man, was accordingly named Joshua Gladwyn Jebb and he was Fanny's favourite brother.

Judging by her picture by Samuel Lawrence RA, Fanny must have been ravishing. Not surprisingly, she soon attracted a rich and charming Bristol merchant called William Miles and they got married in 1829. As a sort of wedding-present Miles bought the Firbeck estate in South Yorkshire – including a large grey stone mansion with, as so often, a park laid out by Capability Brown. The house (now a miners' home) had been built by a rich late eighteenth-century romantic called Galley Knight whose ambition it was to construct something as large as the neighbouring Welbeck Abbey, but who luckily lost his money before this could be achieved. We have a print of him in Arabian fancy dress. Firbeck was beautiful. A little clear trout stream (long since polluted) came down through the property from Maltby by the glorious Cistercian ruin of Roche Abbey and blossomed out into two lakes, joining which was the celebrated 'dark walk' of yews. Family legend has it that it was Tennyson's famous 'Brook'. The drive of Spanish chestnuts was also justly famous, as was the huge Gothic conservatory. The neighbourhood was very grand. Next door was Sandbeck, the seat of Lord Scarbrough. Not far off were the 'Dukeries'. To the north lay the properties of the Earls of Halifax and Fitzwilliam. The Park Hill pheasants on the property were some of the highest thereabouts. The gently rolling stone-walled countryside was the happy hunting ground of the pack known as the Grove.

Miles soon died: there had been no children so Aunt Fanny stayed on as a rich widow for many years. Joshua was a frequent guest and progressed steadily in the Army, ending up as Major-General Sir Joshua Jebb KCB, Director of HM Prisons, and thus responsible for the reformed penal establishments such as Pentonville, which was certainly a great improvement on the old dungeons. In this he was assisted by the celebrated Elizabeth Fry, and I believe Florence Nightingale (a neighbour) consulted him on nursing matters. I have a paper written by him in 1855 in which he suggests that, since the country was then practically defenceless, and might be occupied by the French at any moment, we might do well to mobilize his convicts as a kind of Home Guard. No doubt there might have been something to be said for the scheme, but it was rejected by the wretched bureaucrats in Whitehall. Anyhow, during these years Firbeck must have been the centre of considerable intellectual activity. Joshua was popular locally and was, I believe, trustee of the neighbouring Sitwell family at Renishaw, and we have a charming water-colour of him which Osbert Sitwell presented to us long ago. Aunt Fanny's taste, unfortunately, was not impeccable. Most of the Old Masters she diligently collected were subsequently shown to be bogus. But at least she was an admirer of the arts and Firbeck must have been an enjoyable rendezvous for all the Jebb family.

By his first wife, Mary Legh Thomas (his second being Lady Rose Pelham), Joshua had a number of daughters and my grandfather, whom nobody seems to have liked very much. Judging from his portrait, indeed, he cannot have been a very attractive character. Certainly he was unpopular with Aunt Fanny. But in 1867 he succeeded in marrying the beautiful and eligible Alice Dundas, grand-daughter of the famous Hal Dundas, first Viscount Melville, the intimate friend and adviser of the younger Pitt. By her he had three sons and a daughter, Aunt Mabel, the eldest son, Sydney Gladwyn Jebb, being my father. Young Sydney, who must have been a delightful and rather brilliant boy, won the heart of Aunt Fanny and on her death in 1877 she left a remarkable will, whereby the entire property went for his life to another nephew, the Reverend Henry Jebb, and on his death to my father, avoiding Foxy Grandpa altogether.

After what must have been a rather unhappy childhood, Sydney was sent to Eton and would have wished to go on to Oxford but was prevented by his father who insisted on his going into the Army. So he got into Woolwich, passed well out of there and joined the Royal Garrison Artillery, or 'Gunners'. Six foot five, left handed, and a very fine figure of a man, he might have been thought to have been cut out for a successful military career had it not been for a tendency to get exasperated with authority and thus to be dejected and slightly unco-operative, referring to all those in authority as 'They'. Still, he started off as a soldier very well and was shortly sent to India, where, in the middle of shooting mouflon during a period of leave from his garrison activities (he was a first-class shot with any kind of weapon and was once reputed to have had three pheasants in the air at the same time – 'You must shoot them in the beak, my dear boy, so that they come spinning down slowly, and not just plummet down as they do if you simply fill " 'em up with lead" '), he got a telegram at the end of 1897 saying that the Reverend Henry had unexpectedly died and that he had come into the property.

Immediately resigning his commission, my father boarded the first available P and O steamship and arrived back in England in 1898. It was clearly desirable for him to get married and at a Hunt Ball in Barnstaple, North Devon, he met my mother, a younger daughter of Major-General Chichester of Pilton, himself a younger son of Robert Chichester of Hall, a very old family of squires who had concentrated since the early Middle Ages on preserving their extensive properties and playing a valuable part in the affairs of the County. She had at the time only a very small fortune, but she was an Edwardian beauty: fair hair, blue eyes and a romantic expression. On her mother's side she was a Longman and thus connected with the ancient publishing firm of Longmans, Green and Co. Perhaps at this point I should say that, with the exception of my Scottish grandmother and conceivably my Dutch forebear, there is no evidence in any of my ancestors as far back as they can be traced, of anything save English blood.

All seemed to point to a splendid future for my father as a country gentleman and perhaps even as a Member of Parliament. I arrived in 1900, it seems with some difficulty, so my mother said, owing to the complete ignorance among girls in those days of the 'facts of life'. Two daughters, Molly and Marjorie, quickly followed. But clouds soon appeared, perhaps partly occasioned by the fact that my mother was warned not to have any more children and birth control was not then exactly easy. Besides, my father, in spite of joining the Yorkshire Dragoons, did not really hit it off with the local nobility and gentry, quite a few of whom would, in the unforgettable words of Sir Thomas More, have 'snored through the Sermon on the Mount'. He bitterly regretted his lack of a University education and consequently, like Sir Willoughby Patterne in *The Egoist*, hired a certain Professor Burrows of Cambridge (at least we believe him to be a professor) to perfect his Latin and Greek. With this formidable bearded character he spent months on end, and eventually succeeded in reading most of the classics with ease in the original, an accomplishment which did not in itself endear him to his immediate neighbours. Then, a horse having once run away with him, he abandoned hunting, while, in spite, as I say, of being a superb shot, he had a habit on an off day – all good shots have off days – and even if he were the host, of chucking his gun to his loader and striding off to the house to polish up his Sophocles, leaving his guests to fend for themselves as best they might. He also had a certain interest in natural history, and I remember being taken in to see him in his study where (to my mother's horror) he was engaged in pulling out the gossamer from a large spider in order to establish exactly how long it was. All this was a matter of great sorrow to his wife who longed to be a successful hostess. The situation was not improved by her constantly inviting her Chichester relations to stay, some of whom were, frankly, not my father's type. The influence of Mr Burrows, therefore, continued to extend and was perhaps partly responsible for the ensuing disaster.

Sydney in any case never took much interest in his offspring, so we were brought up by nice nannies under the general supervision of my conventionally minded, and at that time very religious mother who endeavoured to instil into us the basic elements of the Christian faith, rather unsuccessfully in my case. I was, I think, always a little sceptical of official views, nor was I particularly obedient. When told – probably about the age of six – that I must not be angry, I remember well replying that in my case anger was always 'righteous anger', a phrase which I had presumably picked up from some pharisaical grown-up. But on the whole I think I was a normal and quite manageable little boy.

Since 1904 my father had been prospective Conservative candidate for the Holmfirth division of the West Riding of Yorkshire, a seat which had been held by the Liberals for many years. The prospects of success were diminished by the fact that he was both a strong Free-Trader and an anti-Chamberlainite, which irritated many of his Conservative supporters, and a tremendous Imperialist and powerful advocate of the use of indentured Chinese labour in South Africa as well, which by no means endeared him to the already largely Socialist workers of the West Riding. He was also for the principle that a Member of Parliament should be, as Burke maintained, a senator rather than a delegate. Judging from the *Sheffield Daily Telegraph*, his general line was that he would say what he thought and that if his prospective constituents did not like it they could lump it. Anyhow the result was scarcely encouraging. After nearly three years of obviously energetic campaigning, my father fell a victim to the Liberal tidal wave and was defeated by 6,850 votes to 2,677. It was a disaster. His relations with his wife got steadily worse. He became the obvious prey of any clever and designing woman. Late in 1907 she appeared and the family simply broke up, my mother indignantly carrying off the three children to Montagu Square. For the next ten years my family background was entirely female, my father chiefly occupying himself in fishing in Lake Taupo or exploring the Upper Parana.

The trouble was that in the circumstances I lost confidence in myself. It was from about then, I think, that I got the impression that I was not much good at anything, and that other boys were anyhow far better at everything than I. Always they were grander, or stronger, or brighter. I myself was only moderately good at work or at play, and though I tried hard enough I could never excel. I can't say that I was terribly unhappy; but the entirely female background resulted in my becoming uneasy and quite insecure. Besides I tired fairly easily and probably for that reason became rather easily dispirited. Probably I was just overgrowing my strength. You must therefore picture a rather solitary, preoccupied and conventional little boy, going first to Mr Gibb's pre-preparatory school in London, whence we used to go and play football in Barnes in one of the first steam motor-buses, then to Sandroyd and finally (in 1913) to Eton.

Sandroyd was a good school and the joint-Headmaster, Mr Hornby, was an excellent teacher of the top form, and producer of plays, though he did have a tendency to beat rather hard. I need hardly say that the general atmosphere was immensely Conservative. In the 1910 election we spent much time sticking little blue stamps on the Observer map of Great Britain to show Tory victories (in those days election results only came in gradually) and when the preponderant Liberal and Radical red was much diminished there was great rejoicing. We even read the great Mr Garvin's editorial fulminations. It was, after all, the heyday of the British Empire and we were Imperialists almost to a boy. Cricket was taken very seriously and I suffered agonies by being no good at the game (on which I wasted about two thousand hours between the ages of nine and seventeen) though I was better at football, and even scraped into the First Eleven as outside left, a place I often think I later tended to fill in the British 'Establishment'.

I was happier when I got to Eton at the end of 1913, though I had done badly in the entrance exam and had only taken 'middle Fourth' (then one class from the bottom save for the small 'Third Form' which was a byword for bone-headedness). At the end of the half I was, it is true, pushed up to 'Lower Remove', but I never caught up with my abler 'Oppidan' friends – such as Jock Cranbrook*– who had taken that division on arrival. This made me feel that I was not very clever and increased an already considerable inferiority complex. I don't think, however, that sex – that modern obsession – had any particularly terrible effect on me, though naturally finding out about it took up a good deal of my time and I am on the whole very glad that it was never my privilege to have it explained to me at an early age by pedagogues with diagrams and films. Such official information as I got was pretty rudimentary but was supplemented by other boys and a vivid imagination. Strangely enough I never associated it, even remotely, with physical love between males. 'So insipid' as Harold

* The Earl of Cranbrook.

Nicolson, while we were riding together over the Persian *biaban*, once told me, rather surprisingly, it had been declared to be by his housekeeper. The housekeeper's views were mine. What other people did was their affair, but for my part I simply was not tempted. And, strange though it may seem, I was never invited to do anything of the kind during the whole time I was at Eton; still less did I invite anybody. Judging by the experience of others this must have been something of a record!

On the whole, Eton was tremendous fun, though to paraphrase Gray, it was, alas, unconscious of our fate that we little victims played. Doom duly came, however, a few months later and a great many of those who had arrived a little before me were killed in the massacres of Passchendaele and the Somme. A little later there was a dawning consciousness among some of us that all might not be well with our own social system. The initiator of this movement was Buck De La Warr★ and he recruited, among others, myself and Clive Burt – a Scholar – who was responsible for our magazine. We had prominent Socialists and Trades Union Leaders down to address us – Albert Mansbridge, the founder of the Workers' Educational Association was our first speaker, I think – and I suppose it was from about then that I began to understand how divided England was and on what a precarious basis our system of immense privilege really rested. It was also our privilege, we recognized, to be the first to die in war. 'Glaucus', says Sarpedon in the *Iliad*,† 'why is it that we are especially honoured in Lycia and all the people look up to us as Gods?' And the answer, broadly speaking, is 'because we fight in the front line of the battle'. Indeed, in those far off days of 1916 we still lived in a Homeric Age. We were still brought up on the classics, and though we were nominally Christians, I think that the majority of us, consciously or unconsciously, were much more Stoic in outlook, if we were not, frankly, Epicurean.

Anyway, the effort of reconciling Christianity with the war was one which most of us did not face, and personally I found the whole ceremony of Confirmation and First Communion highly embarrassing. I knew that I was expected to undergo an emotional, even a mystical experience; but nothing of the kind occurred. It was true that I appreciated the Gospel stories and loved the glorious language of the Book of Common Prayer, the recent suppression of which is one of the greatest indictments of our modern society. For a long time I blamed myself for the lack of 'Love', because that, I suppose, was what it was. It was much in the same way that I tended to blame myself for my lack of love for my devoted mother. But

★ The Earl De La Warr, subsequently Lord Privy Seal and President of the Board of Education.

† *Iliad* XII, 310.

THE MEMOIRS OF LORD GLADWYN

over the years the sense of guilt got less acute and eventually the 'trailing clouds of glory' pretty well vanished. I still recollected the main sayings of Christ; I still tried, I still try, to live up to them as much as possible; I still said, I still say (if I am permitted to do so), the General Confession and feel the better for it; but the miraculous content of the Christian religion gradually seemed to me to be less important. It was not long before I could not repeat, without inner reserve, most of the Apostle's Creed.

The process was probably assisted by the fact that in the autumn of 1917 I had no less a person for a tutor than Aldous Huxley. This splendid man, who remained a friend, had been roped in as a 'dug-out' master, his eyesight having failed him and most of the other masters having joined up. He addressed us 'history specialists' as if we were undergraduates, a mistake, because he was not capable of maintaining much order. But when we went to him to discuss our weekly essay he was wonderful. The boredom which he underwent in coping with these essays must have been prodigious, and is graphically described in *Antic Hay*. I remember that he took very little notice of my own. But quite soon we were off on a discussion of almost anything, philosophy, politics, French literature (more particularly, perhaps, French literature), biology, goodness knows what. My eyes were opened, my zest for knowledge was quickened, the slow, beautifully modulated voice went on and on. It was the real beginning of my education. The barbarism of much of Sandroyd, the philistinism of much of Eton fell away. For a space I lived in Arcady and walked on air.

During this period I was induced to compete for the Royal Asiatic Society's Gold Medal Prize Essay, open to all public schools, on the subject of the Mogul Emperor Aurangzib and, to my amazement, won it. Glancing at this first effort again, I must say that it has the first, faint glimmerings of a style. But it never occurred to me that I could compete in this field with the scholars – the 'KS.s' or 'OS.s' as they were called. The mere fact that they *were* Kings or Oppidan Scholars seemed proof positive that they were much cleverer than I. I was quick enough, but not really solid – not 'gründlich' as the Germans say. Nor was I ever any good at ordinary IQ tests. Even today, I doubt if I could pass the simplest. For that matter crossword puzzles have always left me completely floored. I just have not got the scholar's type of mind. Still, when I went up for a Christ Church History scholarship in 1918 I didn't do so badly and was subsequently offered an 'Exhibition' – a kind of minor scholarship – at Magdalen College, Oxford which I accepted. By that time I had become a member of the celebrated Eton society ('Pop'), but here again I couldn't understand quite why. 'Pop' is supposed to make you feel grand for life, but it certainly didn't have this effect on me. In any case I was only a member for one half, at the end of which I joined the Army and was sent to the Household Brigade Officers' Battalion in Bushey Park.

I rather enjoyed the Army and I am sure it did me good. The life was pretty tough, but I didn't mind the discipline nor being bellowed at by Sergeant-Majors. My physique improved, but I was never very strong physically and the one thing I could never get right was bayonet practice. You had to lunge at and impale a dummy and then, withdrawing, give it 'one with the butt in the orchestral stalls'. In any hand-to-hand encounter of this kind with a member of the Prussian Guard I had no doubt whatever who would come off second best. Blood lust was, I felt, the last emotion I should ever experience and lectures on 'the spirit of the bayonet' left me singularly cold. However, in spite of this disability I was a good soldier and passed out with flying colours among the top two or three. Again, I was extremely surprised. Perhaps my general assiduity and good humour and the fact that I was a reasonably good long-distance runner appealed to the officers, who were splendid.

Demobilized after nearly dying of Spanish flu, I arrived at Magdalen in January 1919. In my rooms in the 'New Buildings' looking on to the Deer Park I felt on top of the world. Other young men included my Etonian friends, John Strachey (a cousin of Aldous Huxley's), David Balniel, Ivor Churchill, Buck De La Warr, Bob Boothby, Edward Majoribanks, and Chris Hussey, together with Charles Peake, and a very nice Communist called Ralph Fox, the son of a wealthy northern industrialist and a Conscientious Objector during the war who was subsequently killed in Spain. Another Communist acquaintance was Wogan Philipps, now the solitary Communist member of the House of Lords; but I must say I was never attracted to Communism at all, largely, I suspect, because, rightly or wrongly, I had absolutely no sense of guilt. Like many others I duly wrestled with Marx, though I must confess I never wrestled very hard. Also among my intimates were Peter, the nephew of the famous President Warren (of Magdalen), Jocelyn Proby and Richard Rees, the author of an excellent appreciation of his friend and my own subsequent acquaintance, George Orwell (Eric Blair) who, along with Cyril Connolly, was an Etonian about four years junior to me. One of the advantages of going up in January 1919 was that there were undergraduates who had been right through the war, such as George Gage, Roger Lumley and Victor Cazalet – we even had a Brigadier-General, to say nothing of T. E. Lawrence, then meditating in All Souls, to whom, I regret to say, I took an instant dislike. All this made the atmosphere much more adult and responsible, and when I joined the Canning Club in 1920 there were several future MP.s and ministers to be found in it, including John Strachey himself who was a sort of Left-wing Tory at that stage in his career, as indeed he was at its end.

Looking back, I must say that I enjoyed Oxford very much. I worked at my History very hard; and I actually rowed during my first term in the winning 'Torpid' eight, but promptly abandoned this exhausting form of exercise, preferring beagling, and an occasional hunt with the Heythrop on a hired animal. I did all the conventional things, too, and must, I suppose, by modern standards, have been remarkably 'square'. I liked the company of the successful and the gay, but I still did not consider myself to be either gay or successful. I still had no particular girl-friend, nor did I at that time miss this greatly. In spite of devouring many of the great French novels, love for me was something to come. It was concerned with 'the not impossible She'. Edward Majoribanks wrote once that he was going to lampoon me as 'the man with the marble heart'. Poor Edward. He was, in spite of his lampoon, a great friend of mine and I was desolated when he later shot himself as the result of an unhappy love affair. Had he lived, he could well have been the leader of the Tory Party and Prime Minister of Great Britain. His heart was the reverse of marble. I suppose, in a way, I was idealistic. Certainly I was very shy. A slow developer, if ever there was one, from the intellectual point of view largely, from the emotional point of view wholly. When I submitted my essay which got me one of the University prizes the name had to be disguised under a phrase or quotation and mine was 'Plants of slow growth endure the longest'. The reference was to something said about the subject of the essay, namely 'The Policy of Federation in South Africa'; but it might have applied – indeed I trust it will apply – to the author too!

Generally speaking, I think I was inclined to be quite irreverent and highly critical of authority and the 'Establishment'. At the same time I took this Establishment very much for granted. I was no rebel as such. It just seemed to me that it only needed the new enlightened generation to come to the top for England to cast off its nineteenth-century shackles and become a better and a happier place. The war was over, we had won, and there were not many clouds on the horizon in 1920. Even Ralph Fox, though he often lectured me on Marxist lines, was unable to shake my natural meliorism. I remember telling him in one session that a British Communist was like a man getting into a train in Paddington Station knowing that there was bound to be a crash. No doubt I should have done better to have got to grips with some difficult philosophical thesis and thus at least sharpened my mind. But apart from some Aristotle and Plato – with a strong preference for the former – I did not really absorb any particular philosophy in an intellectual way.

However, I was once again fortunate in my tutors and it was really they who drew me out and set me up, in particular, perhaps, the famous 'Sligger' Urquhart at whose chalet in Savoy I spent some very happy weeks. But there was a grimmer and less mundane don who did bring me much nearer to realities. This was the great Lewis Namier, the son of a Christianized Jewish landowner in Eastern Galicia called Bernstein who came at an early age to an adored England in the tremendous moral and intellectual qualities of which he, alas, very largely ceased to believe after the Second World War. Perhaps this was partly due to the fact that his genius was inadequately appreciated in Britain during his life. It was undoubtedly chiefly due to his patient and indefatigable coaching that I became thoroughly versed in such things as the relationship between Napoleon and the Tsar Alexander, the Austro-Hungarian *Ausgleich*, or the reasons for the Revolution of 1848, and thus managed to get a First in History in 1922. It must have been, because during my last two years I never went to lectures at all. I have, indeed, always preferred learning by visual rather than by aural means, and most of the lectures seemed to me to be an almost total waste of time.

Typically, when I heard the news of my First I was living by myself in a rather gloomy pension in Siena patiently studying Sienese art. Why I had not asked my friends to provide the names of Italians whom I might have visited or at least made friends, I cannot imagine. Coming back, I went down to the cottage which my mother had on Exmoor – and from which from about 1916 onwards I had been in the habit of hunting, quite dashingly, with the Devon and Somerset Staghounds – and read Gibbon's *Decline and Fall*. Then I decided to try for a Fellowship of All Souls, which I failed to get. The obvious thing then seemed to be to try for the Diplomatic Service, but though I was supposed to know French quite well I did not know a single word of German and you had to qualify well in both languages in those days and indeed to be able to 'offer' another language as well. As the exam was to be in July I obviously did not have much time. So I rushed off to, of all places, Rostock-in-Mecklenburg, on the shores of the Baltic, the reason being that there lived my mother's old German governess, Fräulein Gärtner. I enrolled in the university and the first book I ever read (and mastered) in German was, believe it or not, Spengler's *Untergang des Abendlandes*. Like Enoch Powell, therefore, I at least heard the great German voices but, unlike him, I was never completely dominated by them or underwent a sort of *Rausch*. Faust, and indeed Beethoven – in spite of my lack of musical understanding – were both magical. I read and heard with delight, too, many of the great plays of Goethe and Schiller. I loved Heine. But with Wagner I became uneasy, and Nietzsche I could never abide. There seemed, indeed, to be a strain of madness running through the tremendous web of German culture, or at any rate a marked lack of measure. I was thus perhaps less surprised than Enoch apparently was when 'Satan' (as he calls him) was enthroned in Germany. And perhaps also less inclined to see in that horrible character a sort of Lucifer, who surely should have gone down fighting at the head of his satanic troops and not just poisoned himself in a bunker. 'How art thou fallen from Heaven, O Lucifer, Son of the Morning'!

The University itself was violently *Deutsch-national*, and there was a brilliant young professor who usually concluded his harangues with such a phrase as 'We could have been the Lords of the World, and what are we – the slaves of the Entente!' So it was even then – in 1923 – that I first heard the clarion call of '*Deutschland, erwache!*' Certainly it was not I who was surprised when, some ten years later, that cry rang out loud and bold.

So prepared, I qualified in the July exam for the Diplomatic Service with distinction in that most difficult of languages, but to my disgust failed by a few marks to make the grade in French, in which I had always regarded myself as fairly proficient. Thus the whole ordeal had to be undergone once more the following year, and in order to perfect my French I got myself the post of Honorary Attaché in our Paris Embassy of which, just over thirty years later, I was destined to become the head.

In the autumn of 1923, the British and the French were, as usual, quarrelling, this time about German reparations and the French occupation of the Ruhr. Since the Americans had just retired into splendid isolation, Germany was down and out, and the Russians had only just emerged from their Civil War, the whole world political centre of gravity – Japan not yet being a really great nation – was in Paris, or, occasionally, in Geneva at the newly created League of Nations which was at that time entirely dominated by the two major Western European Powers. Italy, in fact, was not taken very seriously at that time by the French, or indeed, I suppose, by ourselves. I remember hearing of a meeting, just after the march on Rome, attended by a rather scruffy Fascist diplomat. After a while he disappeared and somebody suggested that he had gone to change into his *chemise noire*. '*Ce serait également intéressant*', observed the impeccable representative of the Quai d'Orsay, '*de le voir dans une chemise blanche.*'

I am afraid that this fundamental contempt of modern Italy was responsible for much subsequent trouble, and I was myself only freed from it by my subsequent four years in Rome which we will come to later.

Anyhow the 'Ambassadors' conference' – a relic of the Paris Peace Conference – was still functioning and we had a special representative, Orme Sargent, installed in the Rue d'Aguesseau, close to the Embassy, whose reports to the Foreign Office and the way it conducted its business was therefore of very great importance. It was at that time presided over with dignity by Lord Crewe and on the staff were some of our ablest diplomats such as Eric Phipps (subsequently Ambassador), Hughe Knatchbull-Hugessen, an excellent 'career' man, Ralph Wigram* probably the ablest of all, whom we shall come across later, Tom Spring Rice, Bill Cavendish-Bentinck and that celebrated link with both the politicians and the *monde*, Charles Mendl, who was particularly kind to younger members of the staff. There were also the other Honorary Attachés whose functions were chiefly decorative, one being, strangely enough, the father of Duncan Sandys.

It was quite clear to me that there was no real job for me to do as Honorary Attaché. But it was useful to be able to read the telegrams and the 'print' and to learn what was going on. So for the most part I concentrated on brushing up my French and penetrating, to some slight extent, French society. I was not particularly successful in this last direction, partly because of my shyness (Sargent subsequently told a friend that at that time I was one of the shyest young men he had ever met), and partly because I was not in the Embassy for long. Besides I was engaged in discovering other aspects of life. Paris is, I have always thought, the most beautiful city in the world. It is thus, for young people, the best city for love, or perhaps it was, because it may not only be advancing years which make me think that no modern city is ideal for love-making any more. But in 1922 it had not changed much from the days of *L'Education Sentimentale* and the surrounding countryside very little from those of *Le Grand Meaulnes*. You could still get on a horse at the Embassy and ride out to the Bois.

It will not surprise the reader, therefore, to learn that it was in Paris at the age of twenty-three that I had my first experience both of love and of sex. Both were happy experiences. Perhaps neither was very profound. It was much later that I discovered that true love was 'a durable fire, in the mind ever burning, never sick, never dead, never cold, from itself never turning'. And was sex 'but the vulgar tune, which all that breathe

* Counsellor in the Foreign Office. Head of Central Department when he died in 1936.

beneath the moon, so accurately learn so soon'? A vulgar tune perhaps, but in my case, I must confess, most enjoyable. No doubt I was lucky! During this process of growing up I had left the Embassy and was staying at the Hotel des Grands Hommes in the Place du Panthéon having meals with a professor's family and attending lectures at the Sorbonne. The Hotel, which was full of foreign students, was quite incredibly cheap – £1 a *week*, I see from my notes, 'including bed, breakfast, tea, washing and extras'. The meals with the professor's family in a little street round the corner called the Rue de l'Estrapade were a bit of a bind. There was a son, rather older than I was, whose motto was *'tout est relatif'* and who used to get a rise out of me by running down Rolls-Royces: *'Evidemment, c'est une très belle voiture, mais peut-être un peu lourde?'* etc. He told me afterwards that this gambit never failed to arouse the inherent patriotism of the Englishman. Would it still?

But it was now time to brush up my German, so clutching my Baedeker and my German grammar I boarded the Arlberg Express and arrived in the then 'sterbende Kaiserstadt' of Vienna, finding, at the end of a long tram-line, the rather gloomy apartment, in Döbling, of the Professor with whom for two months I was to lodge. I have no very vivid recollection of this period. I do remember the *Rosenkavalier* at the Opera and a Mahler concert by which I was, in my ignorance, terribly bored. Of course I did all the sights religiously and even today I could say a good deal about the splendid Fischer von Erlach churches and the contents of the great museums and picture galleries. There were jolly and attractive people at the Embassy and in business, who found Vienna at that time one of the most romantic places in the world; and so it might even have been for me had I not been absolutely intent on polishing up my German and on practically nothing else.

Really, looking back, it does seem as if I was at that time a slightly in-human young man, and a bit priggish too, I am afraid. Anyway I was so *'zielbewusst'*, as the Germans say, that when I returned to London a month or two before the second exam, I was absolutely stuffed with all the information necessary for success; and it hardly needed two months with the famous French crammer Monsieur Turquet ('Monsieur, il faut un *verbe*!') to enable me to pass first into the Diplomatic Service after which I found myself in the Communications Department of the Foreign Office being initiated into the mysteries of cyphering. Soon I received a summons to the Assistant Private Secretary to the Foreign Secretary, at that time responsible for all minor appointments. Conscious of the fact that I had after all passed in first and seemed, on the face of it, to have every possible qualification, Hugh Lloyd-Thomas★ asked me whether I had ever thought of Washington as a post? On the spur of the moment I replied that I had not, but that as a matter of fact I would rather like to be sent to Persia. 'What, *Persia*?' said the Private Secretary, uncomprehendingly. 'Yes,' I replied, 'Persia.' And half an hour later I got a chit saying that he had happily been able to arrange this. (I afterwards learnt that three other people had asked to be excused!) My place in Washington was taken by the Number Two in the exam, the faultless Henry Hopkinson,† now Lord Colyton. And in November 1924 an entirely new chapter in my life began.

★ Minister in Paris during Chamberlain's government, 1935–8. Killed in a steeple-chasing accident, 1938.
† Later Conservative MP and Minister of State for Colonial Affairs.

2

A Shaky Start
(1924-7)

It was with a light heart, therefore, and a new uniform, a Persian Grammar, Lord Curzon's and Sir P. Sykes's classic works on Persia, and the then obligatory solar topee, that, in the company of the Counsellor, Edmund Monson, I set out, nearly half a century ago, for Tehran. The journey now takes nine hours. Then it took well over a fortnight. You got a boat to Alexandria, thence to Cairo and on to Haifa by train. Car to Beirut and Damascus where you formed up in a 'Nairn Convoy' in order to cross – at some risk – the Syrian desert. Again the train to Khaniqin and eventually a three-day car drive over appalling roads to the Persian capital. We had to take a 'bag' so the shorter route through Russia was out.

I have never been one of those Englishmen who regard the Middle East from a romantic point of view, and my first brief experience of it – more especially, perhaps, my experiences of Baghdad – did nothing to alter my outlook. But when I got into the Buick at Khaniqin and bumped up into the foothills of the Persian mountains and then up and down the high snow-covered pass to Kermanshah I felt that I was leaving the difficult Arabs well behind and was entering a totally different civilization. As we approached Hamadan, indeed, the whole aspect of the country changed. It was not only the lovely desolate mountains, it was the nature of the villages with their clumps of poplars and willows, and the appearance of the inhabitants, the men in their (now, I believe, vanished) blue, bulbous *kulahs*, or brimless hats, the women in their black *chadars*, which effectively concealed everything except the eyes, the children pretty and vivacious, even if still often suffering from terrible eye-diseases. Besides, with the Persians, or, more especially with the Persian-speaking inhabitants of Iran, cheerfulness, whatever the circumstances, keeps on breaking through. They are a civilized nation with a history two or three times as long as the Arab and though converted to Islam have always manifested their nationalism by practising the Shiá heresy.

In 1924 Tehran was an almost completely medieval town, surrounded by a deep ditch and large mud walls, or ramparts, in which were set a number of lovely gates, with two or four minaret-like towers, covered with blue and yellow tiles, fairly modern in themselves but in the old Persian tradition. Practically nothing had been changed since the days of Queen Victoria's friend, Shah Nasreddin. The streets were unpaved and alongside each of them was a little runlet of clear flowing water which had come down from the melting snows of the Elburz mountains in underground channels, or *qanats*, a system of irrigation introduced thousands of years previously, no doubt when the land, previously afforested, was gradually deprived altogether of trees. The whole centre of the high plateau was desert, the Dasht-i-Kavir and the Dasht-i-Lut, once inland seas which had dried up. Round it were chains of great barren mountains, of which the ridge of the Elburz, going up to 14,000 feet, was one. Not quite barren because in the high valleys there were streams, some perennial, some winterborn, and even on the slopes themselves there was a pale flush of vegetation in the spring, enough for sheep and goats on the lower levels and for the mouflon and the ibex up above. The whole immediate effect of Persia on me was, indeed, magical, if nostalgic.

The inside of the town was like a vast garden, or rather a collection of gardens, centring round the bazaar, a huge rabbit-warren of a place, whose dark tunnels were properly roofed in, not covered with tin, as in Baghdad, and in which you could still buy reasonably good carpets, to say nothing of an occasional lovely tile or pot coming from the ruins of the old medieval town of Rhages or Rayy a few miles to the south. The whole area had a wonderful aromatic smell which seemed to derive basically from pistachio nuts, the Persian nougat, known as *gaz*, charcoal fires, the local flat bread or *nan*, sherbet, recently worked leather, saffron, peaches, hemp and tobacco, which, once smelt, was unforgettable, as indeed, once tasted, is the delicious Persian food. Near the bazaar there was a tumble-down palace and a central square or *Maidan*, surrounded by rather unimpressive nineteenth-century buildings of which the most imposing were those of the Imperial Bank of Persia, then firmly under British control, and of the Anglo-Persian Oil Company which was practically an *imperium in imperio*.

So it was not unnatural that the real centre was the hard-by *Sifarat-i-Ingliz*, the British Legation, in the street known as the *Lalezar*, a series of late nineteenth-century yellow brick Office of Works structures, set in a magnificent garden with many water-tanks and huge *chenars*, or oriental planes. Here lived what was still in many ways the real power in the land, the Vazir Mukhtar himself, nobly personified by the proconsular figure of

Sir Percy Loraine. Round the Residence (which also comprised the Chancery wing) were villas housing the Counsellor, the Oriental Secretary, the Military Attaché, the Consul-General, the doctor and the secretaries, of whom I was the junior. Behind were vast mews in which lived the *gholams* – red-coated mounted messengers – and a whole troop of the Central India Horse, comprising about forty Arab and country-bred horses and ponies, of great incidental use, because they provided mounts for polo and steeple-chasing for the younger and more sporting members of the staff. When the Minister paid visits in his dashing yellow Vauxhall tourer he was usually accompanied by at least some of these colourful protectors. After all, we were the top power, and it was considered right to show that we were more important than the Russians, whose influence, once enormous in the north, had, since the revolution six years previously, noticeably declined.

Such was the land of my election when I arrived and it might have been thought that I should have had, as it were, the ball at my feet. Besides, I pick up languages easily and with the aid of a charming Bahai Persian instructor, the Dabir-i-Moayyahad, or 'Felicitous Writer', I was soon chatting away in that fairly easy, and basically Aryan, language. Three things conspired to encourage my natural diffidence. In the first place my stable companion, the First Secretary, was an enormous demon of energy called Bob Hadow, a senior prefect at Harrow, I believe, but born and largely bred in Kashmir, and hence an acknowledged expert on 'the East'. Hadow was kindness itself, but quite overpowering. His colloquial Persian, I need hardly say, was as brilliant as his Hindustani, but he had a certain contempt for the Persians, most of whom he believed were suffering from incurable diseases, chiefly venereal. He was also a great expert on the dreadful ravages among the unfortunate population of drugs, above all opium, but also hashish, then in vogue, it seemed, in certain much frequented gardens in the capital. Hadow not only insisted on doing all the available Chancery work himself but, devout Christian as he was, spent hours and hours befriending 'lame dogs' – often obvious ne'er-do-wells. The intervals were spent in cursing the Persian staff and the Registrar and in organizing the British colony in the rather gloomy local club. I therefore had to concentrate on typing out interminable dispatches for the Bag, in helping the cypher clerk to decypher and encypher telegrams, and in comforting the Munshi Bashi, and Assistant Munshi – the Persians employed chiefly to translate our communications to the Persian Government and theirs to us – after they had been verbally assaulted by the head of the Chancery. The advantages were that I did learn to type and had more time to concentrate on my Persian; the disadvantage was that I became rather disheartened and in no way encouraged to progress in my new profession. Besides, my predecessor, Michael Huxley (cousin of Aldous), a very brilliant and good-looking academic, was always held up to me as a model whom I could scarcely aspire to emulate. There was nothing that I could do about this but the circumstance depressed me even further.

But above all there was the brooding presence of the all-powerful Minister with whom I never really got on. As a quasi vice-regal figure, Sir Percy was impeccable. Fine-looking and of old family, rich, speaking beautiful, if rather academic, French, highly industrious and pretty shrewd, he had been Curzon's own nominee for the job which he had obtained at the unusually early age of forty-two. When I arrived he had moreover just married Louise Stuart-Wortley, who was both beautiful and charming and not yet a victim to the arthritis which subsequently confined her all too often to her room. His only defect, if it was a defect, given the great office that he held, was a rather ponderous manner and perhaps a certain lack of sense of humour. What was, however, apparent from the start was that Sir Percy did not altogether appreciate the new arrival. I should be all right, of course; I had everything in the way of background which would normally recommend me to him. And yet I had a distressing habit of not appearing to accept what he said with sufficient deference; of answering questions straight away without sufficient reflection; of putting up drafts on minor matters which were insufficiently thought out; in a word, of seeming to be rather superficial, if not, indeed, callow, a judgment which, I must admit, was at that time largely justified. After a little while I received a rebuke in the shape of a minute to the effect that 'Mr Jebb would be well advised to cultivate habits of accuracy'. All this was good for me and I did indeed improve slightly as a bureaucrat. It was true that the Minister took the Vice-Consul with him instead of me on an official tour, which was rather wounding, but no doubt that could be explained by his knowledge of Persian.

I nevertheless earned good marks by soon going off into the mountains by myself with a retinue of servants and mules on a shooting and fishing expedition during which I scaled some large mountains, secured good specimens of ibex and *mouflon*, investigated the conditions of the mountain villagers and, generally kept the flag flying in some outlandish parts. I also earned even better marks by dealing with our suspicious French colleague, Monsieur Lucien Bonzon, with whom our relations were rather similar to those between the two Missions described by Evelyn Waugh in *Black Mischief*. But disaster was near.

Beavering away at decyphering telegrams, and not, perhaps, sufficiently developing those 'habits of accuracy' which had been enjoined on me (it was a great crime to 'guess at the meanings' of dud groups without employing every other means of verification), I came on a simple communication, in the non-confidential code, which said that, on the occasion of the New Year's Honours of 1925, His Majesty had been pleased to confer the honour of the CMG on our excellent Oriental Secretary, Godfrey Havard.* Innocently enough I rushed down the passage to convey this good news to my colleague, who seemed quite gratified. He was the hatchet man of His Excellency and wielded very considerable power. The Persians knew, or thought they knew, that if they really came up against him something quite unfortunate might occur in the large areas to the south virtually controlled at that time by the often rebellious, and fairly pro-British tribes of the Bakhtiari or the Qashqai. Or the attitude towards the representative of the Central Government of the still largely autonomous Sheikh of Mohammera, in close contact with the Anglo-Persian Oil Company, might suffer a curious change. Or perhaps our Resident in the Persian Gulf himself – then even more under the authority of the Government of India than of HMG – might make difficulties in his virtual satrapy of Bushire. Certainly Havard was an influential man.

Nothing happened until the telegram itself went up to the Minister who, with great joy, promptly sent for Havard. Apparently Sir Percy had for long been angling for this decoration, which, after all, added to the lustre not merely of Havard but of the whole Embassy, and hence of the Minister himself. Havard appeared and the great news was solemnly imparted, whereupon my slightly embarrassed colleague said 'That's all right, Sir, as a matter of fact Jebb told me about it a little while ago.' The thunderstorm broke. I received an 'official reprimand', which, the Minister said, would be 'entered in my file'. It was outrageous, the long document continued, for a Third Secretary to be so ignorant of procedure as not to know that *all* incoming telegrams were the property of the head of the mission and could not be acted on without his express consent. In this case the mistake was all the more unpardonable since the telegram began with the words 'Following from the Private Secretary', which clearly meant that it was a confidential communication destined for the Minister himself and for no one else. I should, of course, have communicated it directly to him for such action as he considered necessary, and so on.

Dismayed though I was, I was not prepared to take this, as it seemed to

* Diplomat; HM Vice-Consul in Tehran, 1922 and then Oriental Secretary Tehran, 1923–31.

me, rather preposterous ticking-off lying down. I replied that, while I quite understood that it would have been better for me to have acted as suggested, and apologized for my mistake, I did not see that any real harm had been done, and in any case was not the castigation a little ponderous? The effect of this communication was electrical. How was I to know that some time previously a kind friend had told the head of the mission that his nickname was Ponderous Percy? I was, I need hardly say, informed that I was impertinent and that the sentence already pronounced would be confirmed, only more so, or words to that effect. I must say I thought my career was practically finished. Not that I minded all that because I still was not sure that diplomacy was the right career for me. I had just received information that I could, if I wanted to, become a don at Christ Church and join, presumably, my friend and contemporary Roy Harrod* in this entrancing branch of Academe. Who knows? I suppose I could have been a kind of minor, iconoclastic A. J. P. Taylor if I had really tried. And, after all, there were worse fates than living at Oxford, then producing a particularly gifted and attractive generation of undergraduates. Eventually the Minister and I got on to much better terms and when he left I sent him an agreeable letter. Within his limits he certainly was a model diplomat.

I decided however to soldier on until I was replaced in 1927 and I was encouraged to do so by the departure of 'Old Mon' for Bogota ('I always knew it,' he said mournfully when I imparted the news that the Foreign Office wanted a really good man for this important post) and his replacement by the highly civilized Harold Nicolson, with whom I at once got on. After his spectacular efforts at the Paris Peace Conference of 1919 when he had hobnobbed with all the great, Harold had, it seemed, been going from strength to strength in the Foreign Office under Sir Eyre Crowe but had subsequently fallen foul of Sir William Tyrrell who had insisted on his taking up the job of Counsellor in some remote spot in order – so it was darkly hinted – to get him out of the way. Anyhow there he was, a dazzlingly urbane and already quite famous character, an example of what you might become if you pegged away in the Service. His fabulous wife, Vita, the poetess, who would have been Lord Sackville, the owner of Knole, had she been a man, was said to be joining him shortly, travelling through Russia.

It was shortly after the arrival of the new Counsellor that the row over Havard took place, and a few days later he was rather taken aback – as

* The well-known economist; a member of Churchill's private statistical staff at the Admiralty, 1940 and adviser in the Prime Minister's office 1940–2.

indeed we all were – by instructions to parade in full uniform in His Excellency's office for an important ceremony. We all did so, and after a bit the great door was flung open by two *gholams* and Sir Percy, ablaze with gold braid and his KCMG, appeared, stood to attention and said, 'Godfrey Thomas Havard. I have it in command from His Majesty the King, to bestow on you, not by way of investiture, but in a formal and ceremonious manner, the insignia of a Companion of the Most Distinguished Order of St Michael and St George.' He then hung the CMG round Havard and we thought he might be going to embrace him, but he did not. There followed a slight pause after which we all congratulated the recipient and had a drink. Harold always pretended he never really recovered from this his first experience of Diplomacy in Action. Anyway from then on we became firm friends and when some six months later the Vazir Mukhtar was transferred to Turkey, I believe he used his period as Chargé d'Affaires to put in to the Office a report on my progress rather different from that which had previously been submitted. But he also insisted that my own efforts should be written in good and clear English and that I should get out of the all too easy and lazy habit of writing in officialese. Things brightened up for me too with the departure of Hadow and his replacement by a Magdalen friend in the shape of Christopher Warner, while the new Ambassador was a much more genial, if admittedly less able and imposing, figure, called Sir Robert Clive.

The subsequent six months were very satisfactory. Iran is beautiful in all seasons, but chiefly in the spring when the Judas trees are out, about the time of *No Ruz*, the Persian New Year (in March). The summer Embassy at Gulhak, up towards the mountains, had a large pool and the Secretary's house a large verandah and a little pool, into which the water gurgled all day long. We played tennis and bathed and rode and played polo and in the intervals I did a certain amount of work, having been promoted, under the Nicolson régime and after the departure of Hadow, to be acting head of Chancery. Another awful thing then happened. Perhaps my only really responsible function was to see that papers were not 'put away' until the action on them had been completed. Drowsily ticking them off one evening I 'put away' a highly important telegram from the Government of Iraq in which we were desired to inform the Persian Government that a rebellion, led by the notorious Salah el Dowleh, was impending on the Kurdish border. Only a few days later, when a chaser came in, was this error discovered, whereupon Harold nobly insisted on putting on a white sheet and informing Baghdad that the paper had been disregarded entirely through his own fault. Luckily the rebellion never took place, but I had

had a great lesson (a) in the development of 'habits of accuracy' and (b) in the duty of any senior to assume responsibility for the misdeeds of his junior. These are the sort of things one does not easily forget.

Though the Persians had small reason to love foreigners, I never in my travels came across anything like xenophobia. You were advised not to try to penetrate a mosque, but that was all. Sometimes there were rumours of bandits, but I must say I never met any, nor was I even attacked when, with the Secretary of the US Embassy, Copley Amory, I travelled north from the oilfields through the wild mountains of Luristan, a district then said to be largely outside the control of the central Government. Perhaps it was partly because the country was so treeless and open that the *Ammieh*, or police, were able to keep all the long main roads passable. Bandits had usually nowhere to hide. At intervals of so many *farsakhs*, the '*parasang*' of Herodotus – a notional measure of distance, being, in theory, the amount of road that a well-laden mule would be likely to cover in an hour – there was a mud-walled caravanserai where you could usually get a little bread and tea, but that was the only visible shelter for miles and miles.

Whether it was necessary for this medieval country to be dominated by a dictator of the type of Reza Khan in order to become a modern state is something which some of us doubted, but it is quite arguable that it was. In the early twenties it was still supposed that when and if the British Raj ever withdrew it would be because some efficient democracy had been installed which could act as an effective bastion for the Indian Empire. Whatever might be said about the tough Turkish-speaking trooper who eventually turned out the effete Qajars, he could hardly be thought to be a democrat. But the majority view in the Legation certainly was that he was the only person calculated to modernize a country which at that time was still virtually in the Middle Ages, and on reflection I believe the majority opinion was right. Nearly twenty years later he was, under war-time stresses, exiled to the Seychelles but there is no doubt that his able son has done even better than his father in bringing Persia into the modern world. So the long paper I wrote recommending that we might suitably give more encouragement to the *Tudeh*, or Socialist Party, was, no doubt rightly, consigned to the waste-paper basket. It was not a very good paper anyway, being rather amateurish and based on newspaper cuttings rather than on actual observation of the *Majliss* or local parliament.

What I certainly had, I think, looking back, was what might be called a Left- rather than a Right-wing bias. There was no wireless connection with home – we could not hear the BBC that is – and the papers arrived ten days late: in point of fact we only saw the weekly edition of *The Times*.

But letters which I then wrote show that I was very much on the side of the miners in their long and agonizing struggle in 1926 and had I been in London about then I am not sure that I should have responded very energetically to the call of duty during the General Strike. Though I didn't know much about it, I well remember, too, being instinctively horrified by Churchill's return to the Gold Standard. Even then I suppose I was something of a Keynesian of whose economic, but not of whose foreign policy I thoroughly approved. The remark with which he is credited, 'Civilization progresses on a series of gigantic debt repudiations', seemed to me to be indisputable. I have never been deeply attached to property. It is not that I dislike or disapprove of property as such but it should be regarded as something fortuitous and evanescent. We brought nothing into this world and it is certain that we shall take nothing out. I am not therefore acquisitive nor am I any good at making money. I remember expressing such views to Copley Amory who was horrified and said they were most un-British.

It may seem as if I had a perpetually enjoyable time, and so I did on the whole. On winter week-ends I often went snipe shooting in the marshes or organized partridge drives on the foothills of the Elburz. In the summer there was polo, played, incidentally, on a gravel ground which was uncomfortable if you ever crashed, as I once did, refusing, perhaps out of deference to my father's prejudice, a horrible anti-tetanus injection. But often in Tehran a young foreigner felt bored in the evenings and the local club was not very diverting. Once when the Minister had sent back a dispatch asking that the discomforts of our life should be taken into consideration when determining our allowances he had spoken of 'the almost entire absence of social intercourse' and the typist had made the obvious Freudian slip. It was indeed true that the bachelors were not catered for domestically at all. Persian women were *tabu* and there were few others who were either tempting or available. The story of how not so long ago one of the secretaries induced the Oriental Secretary to dress him up as a *Mullah* or religious leader, and take him to a home of ill fame, as a result of which he was promptly discovered and sacked from the Service, was an awful warning, as was Hadow's constant insistence on the frightful dangers of disease. So, not unnaturally perhaps, I led a monastic life the entire two and a half years that I was there though towards the end I very nearly broke this dismal record.

At a fancy-dress party at the Club, to which I had gone in a magnificent Zoroastrian costume, I met a most ravishing creature. Snow-white skin, jet-black hair, blue eyes, red cheeks, perfect figure, this young Georgian was discovered to be the wife of a Soviet official called Golubiatnikoff. How she had made the Club at all was a mystery, but though we could only converse in Persian and inadequate French, we got on very well and I dropped her afterwards at her home not far from the Russian Embassy. Though I knew it was appallingly risky, I also made a date with her a week ahead when she said her husband would be away. But though she let me in that night, she would only agree to talk on very hard chairs in her bleak sitting room: it seemed that her children were asleep next door. So I felt I could not take risks for nothing and abandoned the siege. What the Minister would have put on my file had I in fact been caught *in flagrante delicto* with the wife of a Soviet official I can hardly imagine. It would have no doubt been considered even worse than being discovered disguised as a priest in a Tehran brothel. I did try later to get her to come to a hotel but she failed to turn up. I can only think that I was specially protected by Providence.

And so, in the spring of 1927, I left Tehran to return to the Foreign Office, this time via the Soviet Union. I had conceived the grandiose plan of going eastward through Soviet Turkestan to Kashgar then turning south and gaining India via the Gilgit Gap, the Hunza country and the High Pamirs. But the Soviet Government would not give me a visa so I was deprived of the opportunity of seeing Tashkent and Bokhara and Samarkand, then legendary towns difficult of access, but now, I believe, ordinary tourist attractions. I suppose that motor-bus loads of 'processed' tourists will shortly also be careering through the Hunza country and the Gilgit Gap. Soon there will be 'nothing left remarkable beneath the visiting moon'. Even the moon itself has been discovered to be a mass of grey plasticine. Anyhow there was nothing for it except to take the car to Enzeli, now rebaptized Pahlewi, the boat to Baku and the train to Moscow which I duly did, accompanied, pleasant surprise, by Hilda Arfa, the English wife of a half-Russian Persian General, who was taking her child to England on a holiday, her husband, who was under orders to fight the Turkomans, being left behind. Hilda, a niece of the Lord Cromwell of the day and a former member of the Diaghilev Ballet, was one of those remarkable Englishwomen who seem to flourish from time to time in the Middle East. Later she became a great friend of the Imperial Family, a prominent Ambassadress and had a very considerable influence on the progress of events.

We meandered through the Caucasus and the Ukraine at twenty miles an hour for what seemed a very long time, during which we got used to having the main meal of the day – horrible by Persian standards – at 3.30

in the afternoon. Hilda's perfect Russian was very useful. The great plains were quite impressive and I recalled the astonishment of one of Shah Nasreddin's staff on his way to England on the Shah's State Visit. After a lifetime spent in the barren plateau he said in astonishment at Russia, 'the whole place is a garden' – *hamisheh bagh*. Eventually we arrived at the capital of the garden but to our dismay found that we could not see any of the sights. During our journey the Russians had broken off relations with us as a result of Joynson-Hicks's descent on the Soviet Trade Mission – the 'Arcos Raid'. Our own mission in Moscow was consequently packing up and could not help us in any way. The sooner we cleared out too the better, the Minister, Sir Robert Hodgson, said. I did just manage to spend an evening at the Bolshoi and saw *Swan Lake*, identical, I need hardly say, so far as production and choreography were concerned, with one I saw nearly a quarter of a century later in London, but still lovely. Revolution, it always seems to me, tends for a period to fossilize taste. The bulbous orange lamp-shade, designed for oil lamps under the Tsars, is still, I understand, the principal adornment of a Soviet sitting-room (if the Communist family living-room of the more fortunate citizens can thus be described); while the ultimate refinement of vice is still believed to be drinking champagne out of the slipper of a ballerina. But in 1927, as I say, we had no time to investigate these paradoxes. At Nyegoreloye on the Polish frontier we changed trains and entered what was still, then, Europe. It was certainly not due to propaganda alone that I discerned a complete change in the atmosphere. It was just that my previous impression, derived simply from what I had read, was at once confirmed: Russia is not 'Europe'. The difference between her type of civilization and that of the West is fundamental. It is not that human nature is different one side of the Russian frontier to the other; it is not as if Russia and the West do not share much cultural heritage; it is simply that the attitude of mind of the ordinary citizen, and notably the attitude of the Russian towards the central power, or *vlast*, is of a different order.

You may say, what was the attitude of, for instance, the bulk of the Germans towards their own *vlast* between 1932 and 1945? Perhaps the answer is that there was, indeed, a certain affinity between the two regimes, but it is possible to believe that the 'culture' in which that horror, a Police State, thrives has, over the years, been much more evident in Moscow than in Berlin. After all, Germany has been, from time to time, perfectly 'democratic': Russia never. It is not my intention to suggest that the Germans are morally 'better' than the Russians; I am not indeed seeking here to establish any moral values; all I am saying is that the Russian society is, and for the foreseeable future will remain, different in kind from any European society, even European dictatorships. I just do not see, therefore, the Russians becoming democratic in the Western sense, any more than I should think it possible for them to impose indefinitely a Russian type of society over other European countries.

Reflecting on these matters I arrived in London at the end of May, 1927, anxious to penetrate the mysteries of the 'Office' and to decide whether or not I really should stay on in the Diplomatic Service or try my luck in some quite different career.

3

Making a Mark
(1927-35)

Returning to a London of Bloomsbury intellectuals, dreary politicians, sullen workers and bright young things, I had, detached though I was, a vague feeling that all was not well. But I still had little doubt about the order of society. Two years before the great slump young people with any money, and many of those who had little or none, could still enjoy themselves madly without the aid of drugs or, indeed, of too much alcohol. Evelyn Waugh had not yet published his first work; and even when it did appear *Decline and Fall* just seemed to us to be terribly funny and not the bitter satire on a decaying social order that it actually was. Nor indeed did I know Evelyn then, though I did come across him quite often just before and after the war. I must have been lucky, too, for I never witnessed or was the subject of the great man's frequent and celebrated rows. Besides, there was enough work in the Eastern Department, to which I was assigned, to keep me quite busy, even though a lot of it consisted of rather fruitless correspondence with the Colonial Office, still in those days a considerable power in the land. The Eastern Department was presided over by Lord Monteagle – Tom Spring-Rice – who was fine in many ways, but a great fuss-pot. So was his Number Two and ultimately his successor, George Rendel, who nevertheless was also an excellent Civil Servant and a champion composer of learned 'minutes'. Both in any case were devoted to 'habits of accuracy' and for a year and a half my often wandering thoughts were once again canalized to some extent by, quite rightly, meticulous superiors. The most meticulous of all was Sir Lancelot Oliphant, then the Under-Secretary in charge of the department, who for years had, as it were, been the final Foreign Office arbiter as regards the whole of the Middle East. Sir Lancelot was immensely English, a fine figure of a man, pale face, piercing blue eyes, long blonde moustache and all. He also had an elaborate and rather devastating manner. It was quite an experience to be summoned to the presence in order to explain a possibly rather ambiguous phrase in one's long and lucid 'minute' on (for instance) a report from our Consul in Hodeidah on the pilgrim traffic across the Red Sea, or the quarantine station on the island of Kamaran.

I must say that in my heart of hearts I did not take my duties altogether seriously. It was more like a game which one played as well as one could but without great enthusiasm. I still did not imagine that I was ever likely to become a considerable figure in the Service. Indeed I don't think such ideas at that time crossed my mind at all. I was much more intent on discovering life – '*faisant de frisson en frisson la découverte de la vie*'. There was one member of the Department who helped in this direction – D'Arcy Osborne, subsequently 'The Prisoner in the Vatican' during the war, and alas, only shortly before his death (because he would have been a notable duke) the Duke of Leeds. D'Arcy was inhibited and shy, but he had enormous charm. Whatever the disappointments which resulted in his becoming a bit of a recluse, he was very kind to younger colleagues. To me he recommended a book that had just come out called *Time and Western Man* by Wyndham Lewis. Just as, five years previously, I had swallowed Spengler whole, so now I devoured this enthralling work which seemed to throw a new light on many puzzling political problems. Nor did I then perceive the Fascist tendency, or rather the tendency towards what subsequently turned out to be Fascism, in the presentation. At the time I was under the spell. What I think Lewis finally did for me was to increase my scepticism about the likelihood that our democracies, as they were then organized, would cope successfully with the social problems of our time.

This sort of scepticism was shared in many of the Bloomsbury circles to which my friendship with Harold Nicolson now admitted me. Harold himself was only a sort of honorary member of the inner circle so graphically described in Holroyd's excellent work on Lytton Strachey.★ But his wife Vita's great friendship with Virginia Woolf had, as it were, given him the *entrée*. Of course 'Bloomsbury' was largely a figment of the imagination in so far as it was conceived to be a band of entirely like-minded intellectual iconoclasts all busily intent, under the leadership of Lytton, in reversing accepted Victorian conventions and in advocating the most absolute licence in all personal relationships. But there was something in it. The group was essentially a coterie of brilliant Cambridge undergraduates engendered by the philosopher Moore with the assistance of Lowes Dickinson out of the decayed romanticism of the 'Apostles'. They had a kind of 'in' language, the main feature of which was heavy accentuation of

★ Michael Holroyd: *Lytton Strachey* (London 1969).

inessential words. They were also very much of a mutual admiration society.

Looking back on 'Bloomsbury', I have myself little doubt that, however civilizing its influence, it was, politically speaking, a liability. It did indeed produce some works of art, notably certain novels of Virginia Woolf and some pictures by Duncan Grant. Also, I suppose, some notable additions to the corpus of English literature, such as various works by Strachey, novels by E.M. Forster, to say nothing of one or two books by Vita Nicolson and even *Some People* by Nicolson himself. It also added to the gaiety of London. It did stand, generally speaking, for basic human values, though how far it would have been useful in actually confronting Fascism if that had ever made its appearance in England is perhaps open to doubt, even if some members would have fought like lions. But its contempt of all existing politicians and its tendency to retreat into an ivory tower was, I believe, partly responsible for many talented and potentially politically minded younger people coming to the conclusion that some form of Communism was England's only hope. Perhaps this is too severe a judgment. Admittedly, I did not form it at the time. But I am sure that this school of thought represented the beginnings of the failure of the British will to govern. '*Tu regere imperio populos Romane memento*' – all that became a ridiculous conception. I am not arguing whether this tendency was inevitable or not, nor whether it was desirable. I merely observe that the retreat from Empire was vigorously fostered and assisted by the Bloomsbury set.

The great bulk of my new friends were on the Left, and some of them, no doubt, were Communists, which in those days was considered an unorthodox, but still not a totally reprehensible thing to be. But I myself had at least heard of the disadvantages of the totalitarian system as practised in Russia. I had even read the prophetic work of Karl Kautsky explaining what would happen in the USSR if democracy really was abandoned and I had considerable sympathy with the unsuccessful Mensheviks, to say nothing of the Arch-Fiend, Trotsky. I was certain that the Webbs, and indeed Bernard Shaw, had been completely taken in by Stalin. If it really was to be a question of some collapse of our democratic social order in the West – which appeared to me to be most unlikely – then I would greatly prefer to have some kind of authoritarianism which would at least preserve some of our Western values – a 'benevolent despotism' as they used to call it some centuries ago. On the whole, however, I think I then subscribed to many of the social ideas of *The Nation*, though not always approving of its foreign policy. When the *New Statesman* absorbed the old Liberal periodical, I had the same sort of attitude towards it. But I was never moved to enter politics myself during my diplomatic career, and I certainly never belonged to any political party. It never seemed to me that I had any of the qualifications necessary. In particular I was for long convinced that I could not possibly attempt a public speech.

It was at this point in time that I formed a great friendship with Cyril Connolly, whom I had already met at Urquhart's famous châlet. Though he had been at Eton with me he was four years younger, and in College. During the winter of 1927–8 we saw a lot of each other and I found him a fascinating companion with a soft voice that I have always found most attractive. In the spring of 1928 we decided to go and visit Harold Nicolson, then Counsellor at the Embassy in Berlin whither he had gone on appointment from Persia. With him we found Lord Berners* and Ivor Novello, an incongruous pair. Gerald Berners was brilliant, rich and un-predictable: a sort of eccentric eighteenth-century English peer. Novello, then at the height of his career, was rather sentimental and not my type. We visited the usual horrible Berlin night clubs which were most unappealing to me.

Cyril and I left Berlin in my blue Darracq and did a tour embracing Dresden, Prague, Bavaria, the Neckar valley and the Rhineland, finishing at Düsseldorf where we parted. I am glad I once saw Dresden, that most European of towns, in all its glory. The Zwinger, I thought, was one of the wonders of the world. I revisited it nine years later with my wife and Sam Courtauld when it was drowned in swastikas, and now, after being blotted out by us, it is, though carefully rebuilt, presumably as anonymous as any other town in a 'popular democracy'. Prague, I thought, was most lovely, particularly, perhaps, the Jewish cemetery. We also visited there a *Nachtlokale* where we fraternized with the local ladies, largely consisting of Russian *emigrées*. Cyril seemed particularly attracted by a (to me) rather hideous woman and, when I reproached him, said in a loud voice which, let us hope was not understood, 'We needs must love the lowest when we see it!' At breakfast in the hotel the next day he did not, however, seem the worse for wear. We proceeded to Nördlingen, where we sat, this time unaccompanied, in a rather gloomy bar and by way of cheering things up subjected each other to a 'questionnaire' – Cyril's favourite parlour game. My own questions (dictated by Cyril) and answers ran as follows –

Favourite Place	Wherever I happen to be feeling well.
Favourite Emotion	Fear.

* Musician, painter and writer; honorary attaché to the Diplomatic Service 1909–20.

Religion	C. of E. i.e. complete eighteenth-century sceptical.
Greatest Ambition	To be thought 'able'; in other words to be a reasonably successful man of action with literary leanings and friends.
Greatest Fear	To be thought ineffective and inefficient.
Pet Vice	Lack of ambition.
Aim of Life in One Word	Adventure.
Views on Constancy and Chastity	One can only be constant to a friend or an idea. If one is constant to an idea one's brain becomes rigid, in other words *on cesse d'aimer et d'être aimable*. Therefore constancy to a friend is the only desirable sort of constancy, and this kind of constancy is as beautiful as it is rare. Only fools and invertebrates are sexually constant. Chastity is a male illusion. G. chose, for the end of the world, to be in an English country house with friends.

I did one myself for Cyril, but he denies its existence and in any case it was lost. My recollection is that he said that his 'ambition' was to 'create a work of art', and that he thought that my own 'ambition' was dreadful.

By the Rhine we sat drinking hock on a lovely evening and an old man came by with an accordion and sang a charming song, of which the refrain was, '*Und der Onkel Peter weiss schon was er tut*'. It was in the days before Germany went mad, and I explained to Cyril, who never took the trouble to learn German, that the song meant that we might still look forward to a happy old age. I think we were certainly both happy on that trip, so much so that we agreed that, if we did not get married, we might share a flat when we got back to London. What would have happened if we had set up house together I cannot imagine. Cyril indeed actually wrote a dream piece in which that highly dubious character, Congoly, was accused by the Public Prosecutor of the Establishment of corrupting a well-known member of the Foreign Service by inducing him to send home a copy of the banned work *Ulysses* in the Diplomatic Bag. But I expect we should have been happy enough for a year or so. However, that summer I was more and more occupied in the serious and more engaging process of trying to get married.

During the summer of 1928 I was invited to dine with Vera Bowen in her house in Spanish Place. Vera was a Russian and I had been introduced to her by Hilda Arfa. On a stool in front of the fire was sitting the most beautiful girl that I had ever seen. Of this simple fact I was not then, nor indeed have I ever been, seriously in doubt. My view was also shared by others. Cynthia Noble was known to many as the 'pocket Venus' and she had intelligence and energy as well. After a few months' pursuit she agreed to marry me, though I think she had some doubts. But I never had any doubts at all and I suppose that this confidence was not without its importance. Anyway, we announced our engagement in November and got married at the end of January 1929.

Back in London after a Moroccan honeymoon we moved into 14 Royal Avenue, Chelsea, then a lovely, quiet, double road with plane trees and gravel in the middle and tiny Georgian houses on each side. (It was originally designed to be the main approach to the Royal Hospital.) At the corner no 'drug store' but a respectable pub. Forty years ago Chelsea was, by modern standards, rather square. Apart from the (genuine) artists in Tite Street and thereabouts and the well-disciplined students in the Polytechnic, the bourgeoisie reigned supreme. They gave decorous musical parties in St Leonard's Terrace and The Vale. We even gave one ourselves at which Adila Fachiri* played. They gathered chez Ethel Sands and Nan Hudson† to hear the witticisms of Logan Pearsall Smith and the less unconventional occasionally flocked to the huge house of St John Hornby on the Embankment, along which, of course, the unemployed usually slept out on hard benches, the Welfare State not having come into operation yet. Syrie Maugham was still queening it in Argyll House and had not yet made way for the intensive entertainment of the famous and rich inaugurated by Sybil and Arthur Colefax. In a word, Chelsea, rivalled only by Bloomsbury, could then claim to be the cultural centre of London.

Having done up our little house which we had acquired from the architect, Clough Williams-Ellis, we began, as all newly marrieds begin, to entertain – successfully, I think, for my wife was, and has remained, a born *animatrice*. On our small income we could afford a couple, a lady's maid and a motor car. Nor did we ever overdraw. Soon the friends arrived: diplomats and Foreign Office types, of course, but also politicians, artists and what would now be called socialites. I remember one rather unfortunate occasion on which we had invited Arnold Bennett and Gerry Wellesley‡. The former was much put out at only being offered an inferior cigar. '*Cela ne me dit rien*' he observed as he waved it away. Though with some pain he had acquired a reasonable prose style, he was never noted for his manners. It was always the boy from the Potteries who

* Celebrated Hungarian violinist.
† Two charming and talented American ladies who did much to promote the Arts.
‡ Subsequently the seventh Duke of Wellington.

had made good. Our other guest was horrified that, in speaking to the French maid, I had mistaken a gender. 'I thought' he remarked 'that you had passed first into the Diplomatic Service?' Being trampled on by Gerry was something which during the ensuing forty years I have never minded, and indeed enjoyed, for he is not only invariably right, but also very funny.

Our son Miles was now on the way, which meant employing a Nanny. But that was all. Two things upset this Arcadian existence: the advent of the second Labour Government and the subsequent slump. Neither, as a matter of fact, affected us personally very much. For our small income, derived largely from gilt-edged securities, was not greatly reduced. And, in any case, the change of government resulted in my getting an exciting new job.

Sitting at my desk one July day immersed in the difficulties of the Sheikh of Mohammera, I received a summons to see the second Private Secretary, Nigel Ronald. It appeared that the incoming Parliamentary Under-Secretary of State, Dr Dalton,* was being very difficult and was refusing point-blank to accept any of the various blameless candidates put up by the Office for the post of Private Secretary. Ronald thought that as a last resort I might have a shot. Luckily, I had no idea of what I was up against. I did not know much about the Labour Party, and in any case was unconscious of the background of the Doctor. Advancing into the room I observed a large, bald-headed, middle-aged, rather clerical-looking figure seated at his desk and peering at me over half-closed, light-blue eyes. He motioned to me to sit down and then put some harmless questions after which he said suddenly and rather fiercely 'Are you a Catholic?' To which I replied, equally fiercely, 'No: are you?' Dalton was delighted and said 'You'll do'. It was the end of the interview. I afterwards discovered that he had been labouring under the impression that all members of the Service were Catholics or homosexuals, or both. This was, however, not so. Neither category, it subsequently turned out, was above the national average. Anyway Dalton got what he wanted.

Though at that time the system was that practically no important policy papers (other than the distribution of telegrams and the 'print' – i.e. dispatches) came through the Parliamentary Under-Secretary, either on their way up or down, the Doctor threw his weight about as much as possible. He began by circulating to all Under-Secretaries and heads of departments a copy of the Labour Party foreign policy pamphlet called *Labour and the*

* Labour MP who rose to prominence in Churchill's wartime coalition government; Minister for Economic Warfare (1940); President of the Board of Trade (1942); Chancellor of the Exchequer (1945). He was forced to resign as a result of a budget leak in 1947.

Nation, suggesting that this would be of great use to all officials concerned as 'guidance'. In any case, he observed, no answers to Parliamentary Questions should be composed which went contrary to the views expressed in the policy paper. Nobody paid undue attention to this injunction, but I remember Moley Sargent coming into my room one day with a PQ on some fearfully esoteric question and saying he couldn't answer it because he had lost his copy of *Labour and the Nation*. Would I therefore have a shot at drafting an answer myself? Apart from such pleasantries, there were occasional rows, Dalton rightly suspecting that the majority of the hard-working officials, even if not Catholics or homosexuals, were after all irredeemably bourgeois in their outlook on the world. But, generally speaking, we got on very well, more particularly as I myself quickly invented the right technique of drafting answers to PQs.

Clearly it was impossible, in the general interest, always to tell the plain truth in answer to a question on foreign affairs. To do so might result in a perfectly unnecessary deterioration of our relations with a friendly foreign power. On the other hand it was not only against the rules but clearly counter-productive ever to give expression to anything resembling a lie. The right solution as often as not therefore was to compose in crisp and convincing English some answer which was not untrue. The departments, by whom the answer had in the first instance to be prepared, were often not alive to this necessity, and I frequently therefore had to re-draft the answer myself, square the Under-Secretary concerned, and somehow get the result through the Doctor. Quite often both he and I were then summoned into the august presence of 'Uncle Arthur' Henderson, the Secretary of State.* It was quite a good training in certain of the more elementary techniques of diplomacy.

'Uncle Arthur' was in my view a very good Foreign Secretary. He hardly ever wrote anything; he did not read a very great deal; he relied very largely on his officials; but he knew what his colleagues in the Labour movement were thinking all right, and he also had some clever and devoted intellectuals like Philip Noel-Baker† about him who could stand up to the foreign equivalents and knew all about burning subjects like disarmament (burning in 1929 and burning ever since, except during the war). There was the celebrated story of how, when the negotiations with Egypt had reached a sticking point and the Egyptian Prime Minister,

* Foreign Secretary in the second Labour Government (1929). Presided over the World Disarmament Conference in 1932.

† Secretary of State for Air 1946–7; for Commonwealth Relations 1947–50; Minister of Fuel and Power 1950–1. On British delegation to UN 1946–7; leading advocate of disarmament.

Nahas Pasha, was being exceptionally difficult, Mr Henderson observed that he proposed to see the Prime Minister alone. As Nahas could only talk Arabic and French and the Secretary of State only English, the suggestion caused surprise, if not dismay. But the two great men retired into a small separate room; a few shouts were heard; and Mr Henderson emerged, rather red in the face, announcing that Nahas Pasha had 'agreed'.

Perhaps high-level negotiations were rather easier then than now. But Mr Henderson really did have enormous common sense. It is also said that when after the crash of the Labour Government in 1931, he was succeeded at one remove by Sir John Simon, that great lawyer, anxious to prove his worth, sent for all the back papers on all the files submitted to him during one morning. About lunch time he had thoroughly mastered two huge dossiers on unfamiliar subjects. The remaining six or seven lay about the floor. Turning to his Private Secretary in despair Sir John said, 'And how on earth did Mr Henderson manage? After all, he was a very *stupid* man.' It is, however, generally alleged in the Foreign Office that Sir John, whom I scarcely ever met myself, so I cannot judge, was a terrible Foreign Secretary, often going back on his decisions, not really trusted by his own or by the other side. It only shows that in the conduct of foreign policy what really counts is knowledge of men rather than of things. The officials ought to have knowledge of things – if they have knowledge of men too, so much the better – but the people who take the decisions must be primarily successful politicians who know instinctively the sort of people they can trust.

1929 also saw my first exposure to international diplomacy in the shape of the Assembly of the League of Nations. Dalton was, of course, on our delegation, the secretary to which, and head of the League of Nations Department, was Alec Cadogan assisted by the irreproachable, if somewhat unapproachable William Strang* (it only shows how far we are from 1929 when I say that I was an original member of the club, founded by Horace Seymour, called 'The William Strang Society', the qualification for which was to have dared to have called Strang William to his face). Lord Robert Cecil, who bore the same sort of relationship to the League as Monsieur Monnet subsequently bore to 'Europe', was naturally also a delegate and he spent most of his time working with Phil Noel-Baker on disarmament questions and making speeches about universal peace. It was the heyday of the League. In spite of having quarrelled violently over the right policy to pursue as regards Germany, Britain and France were really

* Diplomat. First Secretary at the Foreign Office (1925); Permanent Under-Secretary of State at the Foreign Office (1949–53).

the only two powers that counted, so when they did get together some-thing could occasionally be done. Italy was still digesting Fascism, Japan was preoccupied with Manchuria but had not yet kicked over the traces, Russia was an uneasy and suspected partner, America was in total isolation, Germany was present, but the cry of 'Gleichberechtigung' was beginning to be heard. If the victors would not, or could not disarm, what right had they to say that Germany should be disarmed for ever?

The real trouble was the lack of a common Anglo-French policy. The great Briand was about to put forward his plan for a sort of Western European Customs Union within which many Anglo-French differences might have been ironed out with Germany in a wider European context. But the first to turn down the idea had been the British, and Briand was now old and tired. I heard him make one speech but it was not terribly impressive. The magic was no longer there. I do not think that the British delegation were then very conscious of all the clouds on the horizon. There was even a certain optimism in the air. The talk was of 'closing the gap in the Covenant', which had something to do, I think, with a legal difficulty about defining the famous 'aggressor', and about the tremendous improve-ment that would take place in international relations generally if only we would sign the so-called 'Optional Clause', whereby we undertook to refer any justiciable disputes with foreign countries to the International Court at The Hague. It was not only the heyday of the League but of the international lawyers. Never since have they been held in such respect by the politicians who now, I fear, tend to regard them rather as hired assas-sins whose job is to make out the best possible legal case for what the politicians are in any case resolved to do.

While we pursued the millennium in Switzerland, the state of the nation went from bad to worse. Unemployment shot up to record heights and the Treasury officials were almost unanimous in declaring that any expenditure on public works to relieve the situation would be a disaster for the pound, for the country, and for the City of London. Nobody accepted this strange thesis more whole-heartedly than Philip Snowden, the Chancellor of the Exchequer. Nobody understood its evil conse-quences better than Sir Oswald Mosley, appointed a special assistant to the Rt. Hon. Jimmy Thomas,* who was supposed to submit plans for coping with the ill. What Mosley says about his chief in his recent book is entirely true: the trouble was that, instead of staying in the Labour Party

* Trade union leader and Labour politician. 1924 Colonial Secretary; stayed with Mac-donald in National Government – ostracized by his union and Labour party as a result; public career ended in 1936 when a tribunal found him guilty of leaking budget secrets.

in order to get a majority on his side with a view eventually to taking it over, he chose to try to start a movement of his own which more and more came to resemble the Italian type of fascism. The British are essentially a gentle people and do not take kindly to thuggery. They would always rather go on pegging away in their own traditional social forms than combine to change their lot for the better. It needs a real crisis to induce them to contemplate real reforms, and even when these occur they must always be represented by the politicians as being a natural development of national institutions. All through 1930, with unemployment rising month after month, the debate within the Government continued. Finally in May Mosley chucked his hand in and began to found the New Party, dragging my old friends, John Strachey, and Harold Nicolson with him. I myself never met Mosley during this period, though I did so some three years later on a cross-Channel boat. When I asked him what should be done to put the nation straight he said that the first thing was 'to get our politicians out of skirts'. Having by that time founded the British Union of Fascists what he presumably meant was to get them into shirts. I never took to this arrogant, if very able, man. He may well have mellowed with the years, but I shudder to think what might have happened if Hitler had won the war and he had become *Gauleiter* of Britain.

Dalton was not directly involved in this particular row. He suspected that (Tom) Mosley was right; he despised Jim Thomas;* but he was certainly not prepared to go out on a political limb. In September 1930 we set off again for Geneva, this time in my small Hillman motor car which also contained Willie Henderson, his father's PPS, and a good deal of luggage. It is remarkable, and shows how things have changed in forty years, that when Harold Nicolson drew attention to this reversal of the normal order of things in the 'Londoners' Diary' that he had just begun to edit, I was furious at what I believed to be a breach of confidence, and apprehensive lest the publicity should get me into trouble with the authorities. In 1930 most regular members of the Service had as little to do with the press as possible. They were usually regarded with deep suspicion and it would never then have occurred to me to hint, even to Harold, at what was actually going on. Our political bosses could, of course, see the press if they wished to do so, but even they were immensely cautious. Talking 'off the record' had not yet been invented; terms like 'not for attribution' were unknown. There was indeed a Press Section in the FO under a certain Mr Koppel; but it spent most of its time simply fobbing people off.

Since our political bosses, and notably my own, were thus playing the Foreign Office game so loyally, it did not occur to us, or at any rate it did not occur to me, to be other than completely loyal to them. Some of my colleagues were indeed inclined to regard the Labour Government's, and notably Phil Baker's and Dalton's enthusiasm for the League as a kind of harmless eccentricity, but this had never been Nicolson's view when he was in the Service nor indeed was it my own. I do not think, in other words, that my assiduity in carrying out Dalton's wishes was primarily due to a desire to curry favour and paddle my own canoe: I really felt that the new team, in foreign policy at any rate, were on the right lines and that it was up to me to do all I could to help.

The second Labour Government was however staggering towards its end. The vain and harassed Ramsay Macdonald was successfully persuaded by the Treasury and the bankers that the only cure for our vast unemployment and general misery was increased deflation, involving even less government expenditure and a reduction in the exiguous 'dole'. Only so, it seemed, could the pound look the dollar in the face, and the PM feel comfortable in the presence of Lady Londonderry. The May Committee was created and proposed even more 'economies'. The Cabinet split, the majority, including 'Uncle Arthur' and Dalton resigning. A 'National Government' was installed and an enormous majority of the British people subsequently voted for the maintenance of a policy of stagnation at home and muted jingoism abroad. Nobody can deny that it was the British themselves who were responsible for the ensuing disasters.

Shortly before he left the Office, Dalton, on the assumption that I was due for a spell abroad, had asked me where I should like to go to and I had replied Rome or Berlin. At one time he had apparently thought that I might be well qualified to act as one of the secretaries to the King. But quite apart from the fact that I did not happen myself to regard this as my destiny, any influence that he might possibly have exercised would undoubtedly have been counter-productive. Even as a very small boy he had apparently succeeded in insulting Queen Victoria. Anyway it was arranged that I should go to Rome at the end of the year and I did so after working for a week or two with the new Parliamentary Under-Secretary of State, Anthony Eden.

Our Ambassador to Italy was Sir Ronald Graham, a sensible diplomat of the old school with a beautiful and charming wife called Lady Sybil who could well have been the heroine of a novel by Somerset Maugham. Both, in their way, were more than kind to the new arrivals. Sir Ronald got on well with a still sane Mussolini. Since our second child, Vanessa, was about to arrive I had set out with my sister, Marjorie, who shortly got engaged to an Italian banker called Enrico Scaretti, and I now have an Italian nephew and niece.

The Fascist regime, which, most people believed, had at least prevented a collapse of the existing social order in 1922, had settled down and there did not seem to be a great deal of discontent and certainly no organized resistance. The *fuorusciti*, voluntary and involuntary exiles, denounced the tyrant from abroad but seemed to have little effect in the country. The economy was working reasonably well. Serious efforts were being made to recuperate the South and the programme of land reclamation was at least being started in the draining of the Pontine Marshes – the first show-piece of *Fascismo*. The doctrine of the 'Corporative State' was being slowly elaborated by competent lawyers under the encouraging eye of the Duce. Anybody might have been pardoned for imagining that a fairly successful effort was in progress to remedy some of the acknowledged ills of the old democratic regime and to substitute for it one more capable of furthering the industrial process without the hideous inhumanities of Communism. It was not only Mussolini's celebrated achievement in getting the trains to run on time. A great programme of construction and development was being undertaken. And there was some reason to suppose that, as a result of the 1929 concordat, the Italian Government might be able in its pro-jected reforms to enlist the co-operation of that ancient opponent of liberal 'progress', the Holy Catholic Church.

The circle in which we moved was, however, rather restricted to Rome. Besides, Rome's treasures, artistic, architectural and literary, were so spec-tacular and so numerous that it was difficult not to spend most of one's spare time exploring them. And towns and villages within easy reach were entirely fascinating as well. Nor was it possible, even if we had wished, to ignore 'Roman Society', who would certainly have spread rather ugly rumours about us if we had. Besides, some of them, such as the Gaetani family, or the Dorias, were people of great culture and intelligence. Others, it is true, though often significant to look at, seemed to behave at times rather like spoilt children, and in any case we were never drawn towards the gambling set or to what subsequently became known as 'cafe society'. The phrase '*dolce vita*' had not, I think, as yet been invented as a description of Roman life; but there was a good deal of it around even in 1932.

However we did get about the country as much as we could, one month in each spring being devoted to a tour round one of the four corners of the country. In one of these tours we set off in our Ford for the South, the famous Mezzogiorno, supposedly sunk in apathy and misery under the regime of 'latifundi', or huge undeveloped agricultural estates belonging to absentee landlords and, in the case of Sicily, the secret rule of the Mafia.

This time we were accompanied by Zanotti-Bianco, the Founder President of the great Mezzogiorno Association which even then was most active in social reform. Zanotti was a well-known and acknowledged anti-Fascist, though not, presumably, engaged in any attempt to overthrow the regime: otherwise he would certainly have found himself in *confino* on one of the islands. A sort of Italian Parsifal, he was also said to be a friend of the Princess of Piedmont which may have protected him to some slight extent. But between Naples and Eboli (where, it will be remembered, 'Christ stopped' in the celebrated work of Carlo Levi) we were pursued by a police car which reappeared at intervals during our trip. There was no doubt at all that the Italy of Mussolini was a police state, but at all events in the early thirties it was not comparable to the police states of Eastern Europe as they exist to this very day.

As a newly arrived Second Secretary I was considered by Sir R. Graham a suitable person to investigate the famous 'Corporative State' then being actively promoted by Mussolini. After all, it might possibly provide some lessons for the ailing British economic system with its millions of un-employed. After a few months in the Commercial Department I produced some material, the first dispatch prepared by me being signed by Sir Ronald in June 1933. Mussolini had by then exercised absolute power for about ten years and was precisely in mid-career. Perhaps the well-known effects on him of absolute power were beginning to show themselves, but there is no doubt that by then he had a good deal to his credit. It was not only that the trains ran on time and that a considerable start had been made with *bonifica*, or land reclamation, and with the great arterial roads or *autostrade*. It was also a fact that a stable regime had resulted in a consider-able increase in productivity and indeed, in spite of the dreadful slump which had hit all industrial Europe since 1930, in some increase in the standard of living of the industrial workers – that is, if the State-run *Assistenza*, or social service programme, was also taken into account. Strikes and lockouts were, of course, forbidden by law, and the whole system was paternal rather than democratic, in that it was, effectively, run by the Party, which was predominantly lower middle class. But it could not be denied that, even if the Italian régime was basically vicious, it could at least bear comparison with 'free' regimes which nevertheless tolerated millions of unemployed on a bare subsistence level – a sort of cancer which was only partially cured (for the effects persisted), not by any act of policy, but simply by preparation for war.

Though I had arrived in Rome full of contempt for the Fascist 'boy-scouts' with their castor-oil and rejection of democratic values I was gradually affected by such considerations. I never did, as a matter of fact, fall for Fascism as such, which was far too brutal in its general philosophy for my liking, but after a time I discovered that there were Fascists who were by no means contemptible, such as the veteran economist, De Stefani, and the much younger Bottai, who resigned soon after I arrived in Rome, his rather Left-wing theses having been rejected by the Government. Besides, the Duce himself, an ex-Marxist journalist after all, was at that time making highly interesting and, as I thought, intelligent speeches about the decay of capitalism, the evils of State Socialism and the necessity, in the interests of the entire people, of discovering some middle way. Nor could I help, even in 1932, suspecting that there was something in his criticism of the League of Nations and in his suggestion that it might be preferable to constitute a 'Europe', based on Four Power co-operation, rather than to rely on an organization which, weakened as it was by the absence of its inventor, America, and of Russia, had by then been thrown out of gear by the defection of Germany and Japan. Before the final triumph of Nazism in Germany, all this seemed to make pretty good sense.

As I went on studying the 'Corporative State' in the light of the Italian attitudes so well described by Luigi Barzini* (and I find that, over the years, I produced almost the equivalent of a small book on the subject), it seemed to me that it was a little doubtful whether it could be said to exist at all. The 'National Council of Corporations', for example, had existed for some time before there were in fact any 'corporations', the latter only being officially established in February 1934, and not functioning in any way until much later. But there was really no 'State' in existence other than that which had existed since the Fascist Revolution in 1922, and all the Duce's assertions that he had set up something between the 'New Deal' of Roosevelt and the 'reforms' of Stalin – had to be accepted with considerable reserve. What had unquestionably been established was a machine for producing 'collective contracts' governing wages and social conditions that was efficient and, as it seemed, generally acceptable. Industrially, too, there had been very valuable reforms not unlike, I said, those suggested by Harold Macmillan in his recently published work called *Reconstruction*.† For the rest, no real compromise had been found between a free and a 'planned' economy except that from time to time solutions were imposed from above, in other words by the Party, as epitomized in the Duce. 'All that can be said with certainty' the investigation concluded 'is that corpora-

* Luigi Barzini: *The Italians* (London, 1965).
† Harold Macmillan: *Reconstruction* (London, 1933).

tiveness in Italy, though largely opportunist up to now, does contain a substantial kernel of reality, and that it would be unwise to hold that it will not eventually produce a new form of economy, from which the Italian nation may draw considerable advantages.' 'Unwise', perhaps. But only a year from the date of this judgment the nation was caught up in preparation for the Abyssinian War; the Duce became increasingly paranoaic; and all prospect of creating a new form of society had to be postponed until after the revolution of 1943. Unfortunately, it has not yet been accomplished.

By this time, indeed, supreme power was having its deplorable effect on the Italian dictator and the necessity of some spectacular success in foreign affairs in order to maintain enthusiasm for his regime preyed more and more on his mind. Though I was never drawn towards Mussolini personally, believing him to be theatrical and even at times rather absurd (the great placards that then began to cover Italy asserting that '*Mussolini ha sempre ragione*', which must presumably have been set up with his consent, were ludicrous), I was influenced by the general propaganda of the regime to the effect that Italy, a modern and reformed European industrial state, should have some 'outlet' for her energies and her exports comparable to that of Britain or France. So when it became clear that the Italians were obviously intending to extend their 'sphere of influence' from their existing colonies of Eritrea and Italian Somaliland over the neighbouring Abyssinia I was not as shocked as no doubt I should have been, though I hardly then imagined that Mussolini was actually contemplating an aggressive war. After all if the Italians had been able to establish in 1934 the sort of relationship with Ethiopia as we then ourselves enjoyed with Egypt, it might not necessarily have been to the general disadvantage. In view of our own record it did not, to say the least, seem to me to be very seemly that we should prevent them from having a try. As time went on, however, it was more and more obvious that the Italians were seriously bent on something that amounted to a military conquest.

This was indeed serious, since it was apparent that no conquest and occupation of the country could possibly be squared with Italy's obligations under the Covenant of the League of Nations which we, too, were pledged to support. And any successful violation of the Covenant would, in its turn, imply a collapse of the whole system of European security that had been laboriously built up since the war. On the other hand if such a collapse, involving terrible opportunities for an aggressive Germany, were to be avoided, the willing participation of Italy in a security system along with France and Britain was equally essential. It was the greatest dilemma of the time. With this background, the Heads of Government and Foreign Ministers of the three Western countries met at Stresa in April 1935, our own representatives being Mr Ramsay Macdonald and Sir John Simon (accompanied by the Permanent Under-Secretary at the FO, Sir Robert Vansittart), Lord Perth and the Head of the Chancery, Phil Nichols, joining them from Rome. Much time was taken up discussing the German problem, disarmament and so on, with no very remarkable result.

On the return of our party to Rome I asked Nichols what had happened about Ethiopia? It had not been mentioned, he said. I was astounded, and deeply worried. I was in no sense aware of what was happening behind the scenes in London, but I could only conclude that His Majesty's Government had taken some secret decision to let Mussolini go ahead. Otherwise the policy made no sense. There were two alternatives: you could tip Mussolini the wink – which was Laval's policy – or you could tell him that if he violated the Covenant you would mobilize all your resources against him and even, in the last resort, not shrink from war. To do neither was simply to ask for trouble. I suppose it was the fact that neither of the alternatives was at all pleasant that induced Sir John Simon to follow his lifelong inclination to sit on the fence. This was a disaster.

Certainly Mussolini believed that the Western Powers, by their silence, had implicitly given their consent at Stresa to his projects. And when it turned out that the British in any case had done nothing of the sort, but on the contrary were set on applying sanctions until he relinquished his prey, his fury was perfectly genuine. What is more, it was shared by a considerable majority of the Italian people. We therefore had the worst of both worlds. It is true, you can argue that it would have been both impossible and undesirable for us to have tipped him the wink. But in that case we should at least have told him that we could not answer for the consequences if he violated the Covenant. It is therefore impossible to avoid the conclusion that we did want to have it both ways, in other words allow Mussolini to carry on and then, having gone through the motions of protest, including some innocuous sanctions, patch up the quarrel by recognizing the new Emperor and by receiving the errant 'aggressor' back into the fold. Or, better still, arrange some sort of deal which would result in his getting his way without going to the full extent of a complete occupation of the country. And this was, in fact, the solution recommended by Samuel Hoare who had succeeded Sir John Simon as Foreign Secretary following on a General Election in which support for the League as against Mussolini had played a most important part.

It was chiefly because I had little confidence in our ability, more especially in view of the pro-Fascist tendencies of the French Government and the green light to German expansion which such a policy would provide, to galvanize the League into any really effective action against Italy, that I tended, on balance, to favour the policy of 'tipping the wink'. The other policy was certainly possible given sufficient determination, but if it were followed it seemed essential, in order to keep Italy in the anti-Nazi fold, to consider means of giving some satisfaction to Mussolini other than in Ethiopia, e.g. by transferring British Somaliland, changing the regime in Tunisia, giving Italy due representation on the Suez Canal Board, considering economic concessions of various kinds and so on. And all this would admittedly have been pretty difficult, for Mussolini would have remained a dictator, even if he had never been an aggressor. Nevertheless it would certainly have been preferable to a policy of masterly inaction and hoping for the best. We shall see what happened as a result of that in the next chapter.

So we said good-bye to Rome about six weeks after war had broken out and the Italians had already avenged their great defeat at Adowa under Crispi nearly forty years before. Many of our Italian friends refused to speak to us because of our attitude on sanctions which, naturally, we defended. Some remained faithful, and even went out of their way to be nice. Among these were Fulvio Suvich, then Under-Secretary for Foreign Affairs, and his charming wife. And in the train the great Marconi himself came up and lamented the state of our relations as a result of Mussolini's action, which it was pretty obvious he much deplored.

We had been happy in Rome, where our last child, Stella, was born in December 1933. The regime of the Drummonds had been rather cosier than that of the Grahams, but I had the impression that Sir Ronald was an abler man than Lord Perth (as Drummond became while we were there). Both, naturally, made the best case for Mussolini, but Perth was, I believe, almost an apologist for the Duce, whose judgment was rapidly becoming more and more erratic, even during the period when I was in Rome. Be that as it may, it was surely wrong to appoint the Secretary-General of the League of Nations to a national diplomat's post immediately after he had left the international organization. It was particularly unfortunate that this post was Italy, but in almost any post the ex-Secretary-General ran the risk of being criticized by one side or the other for his attitude towards any international problem in which the League might be involved. I believe that under United Nations rules the Secretary-General is debarred from entering national employment for some time after his resignation, which is a distinct improvement.

In any case, everything that Lord Perth reported to the Foreign Office was at once made known to the Italian Ministry of Foreign Affairs. There was an excellent butler, called Barbero, whose role was subsequently suspected to have been equivalent to that of the famous 'Cicero', valet to our Ambassador to Turkey during the war. What is now known is that one of the Chancery servants, Secondo by name, was in the pay of the Italians and he used to open the Chancery in the small hours of the morning to the agents of Mussolini who penetrated into the office, photographed the telegrams and dispatches and put them on the Duce's desk almost before they appeared on that of the British Secretary of State. This state of affairs persisted I believe right up to the rupture of relations in 1940. Its discovery led to a revolution in 'security' generally.

4
Band of Brothers
(1935-8)

On our return from Rome we lived, until the outbreak of the 'real' war, on the top floor of my parents-in-law's large mansion in Knightsbridge, now a synagogue. My mother-in-law, Celia Noble, with whom I got on very well, was a beautiful and rather brilliant woman. A talented musician, she was also a notable hostess, and the book about her grandfather, the great Isambard Kingdom Brunel, which she wrote after the war, was a considerable literary achievement. I also got on with my father-in-law, Saxton Noble, who was a tremendous balletomane and a constant frequenter of the Garrick Club. So what with his theatrical and business, and Celia's musical, artistic, political and even occasionally 'minor Royal' friends, Kent House was the scene of much entertaining. The long ballroom was decorated with black and gold murals by Sert, depicting extraordinary goings-on at what appeared to be some jamboree at the Court of the King of Siam. The parties, however, were nothing like so abandoned as the oriental revels by which they were surrounded. Mostly formal dinners, musical evenings and receptions, smart luncheons and so on.

No – or perhaps I had better say, very few – dipsomaniacs, no drug fiends, no bankrupts, no cinema or television stars, no pop singers, no noisy young people in unorthodox costumes, by modern standards it must have all seemed quite incredibly square. But it was certainly gay and interesting, and, when very late after the ballet (because being famished they had usually had to gobble something first) the great dancers such as Tchernicheva, Danilova, Voyzikovski, Markova, Lopokowa, Baronova, and often Karsavina herself came charging in (usually shepherded by their London bear-leader. Florrie Grenfell, later St Just), they could usually be induced to have a second champagne supper. I remember, too (but that must surely have been earlier in 1930 or so), a large formal lunch at Florrie's in honour of Diaghilev, who failed to turn up. At about 1.45 we sat down without him, whereupon he arrived, unexpectedly dragging behind him a shy young man called Lifar, then being 'groomed for stardom', as they say. He was generally thought to be not a patch on Nijinsky.

I was still at this time inclined to be rather shy and remote, and was usually quite unconscious of producing – as I am now told I often did – an unfortunate impression of coldness and 'effortless superiority'. But, due no doubt to the charm of my wife, we were invited often enough to fairly important week-ends. One that I remember (though it was later) was to Stoke D'Abernon Manor as the guest of Lord and Lady D'Abernon, he then being partially paralysed but still very much all there. At this party there was no less a person than Winston Churchill, then on the point of publishing his book on *Great Contemporaries* and deeply disturbed about the possibility of General Franco's seizing Gibraltar by a *coup de main*. After we had listened to him reading aloud his famous chapter on Lord Curzon, we listened, for an even longer time, to the dreadful possibility of losing our most famous fortress as a result of an insidious Spanish attack. It seemed that General Franco was building caves in the mountains round Gibraltar into which he would insert guns that would bombard the fortress and were not capable of being knocked out from the air. During this horror story, Winston gave a discourse about our strategy in the Mediterranean generally, explaining that there was also Malta, in an exposed position, five hundred miles from Gibraltar and five hundred miles from Alexandria. At this point, greatly daring, I observed that my impression was that it was one thousand miles from both points mentioned. 'Nonsense, my boy. I was mobilizing the Fleet in 1914 and I know these things.' But he agreed that a map might be sought and eventually one was found in the middle of his book *The Gathering Storm*★ from which it conclusively emerged that the Mediterranean was, in fact, 2,000 miles long. Much disgruntled, Winston retired to his room while an elderly Liberal Peer advanced on me on the way up and said 'Well, that is something. If he is wrong about the length of the Mediterranean, he may be wrong about guns on Gibraltar !'

But still I was not sure that I had much to give the Service or the Service me. Certainly, I had no suspicions that I was destined to remain in the Office (or in close association with it) for no less than fifteen years. The job allotted was Number Two in the recently formed Economic Section of the Western Department, the head of which was Frank Ashton-Gwatkin,† a man of intelligence, charm, distinction and considerable

★ W. S. Churchill: *The Gathering Storm* (London, 1948).

† Diplomat, member of the Runciman Mission to Czechoslovakia 1938. Chief Clerk at the end of the War.

pertinacity. He had emerged from the Far Eastern Consular Service, having served in Japan. about which he wrote some excellent novels under an assumed name. His main political contention was that the economic reasons behind the evidently expansionist policy of Germany since the advent to power of the Nazis had been insufficiently understood, and that something should, if possible, be done to remedy this situation. This belief caused him, no doubt, to dismiss too lightly the counter-argument that it was rather the Nazis themselves who demanded 'expansion' for their own horrid purposes of conquest, and not so much because they were driven on by sheer economic necessity. The truth, as ever, was probably between the two. We were, however, in the period preceding the publication of such works as Rauschning's *Die Revolution des Nihilismus*.

I myself had just spent four years in a country which, however much you might criticize the Fascist regime, had at any rate put itself on the diplomatic map in a way which had not happened since Cavour. Though I detested the German Nazis, I disliked, for the reasons previously described, the Italian Fascists much less and was, under the influence of Gwatkin, to some extent persuaded that 'expansion' in both countries had a largely economic background. Looking back I must admit that I did not then recognize the inherent difficulty of making a deal with any form of totalitarianism, even if it had a fairly attractive outward appearance. In other words, I neglected the likelihood that the Italian dictator could hardly avoid, in the last resort, siding with the more powerful Hitler.

What in any case I felt strongly was that, whatever the reason, the League system of 'collective security', based as it had been up till then on the hegemony of only two members, namely Britain and France, just could not go on for much longer. Nor did I ever think that there was at that time any particular chance of making some 'regional' security scheme work in Europe under the general aegis of the League of Nations. Since America had thrown her hand in and retired into political isolation, and since the Soviet Union was only waiting for the 'capitalist' powers to fall out so that it could draw some Communist chestnuts out of the ensuing fire, it seemed to me that the discontented powers, namely Germany, Italy and Japan were almost bound to come together in the long run to reverse the *status quo*, and by force if need be. The one hope of avoiding this, I thought, was that by their policies the democracies should beat them, so to speak, at their own game of *Machtpolitik*. Thus we might avert the formation of a potential alliance which, incidentally, the Chiefs-of-Staff kept on saying that we and the French alone might well be unable to defeat in war, at any rate if we failed to re-arm at a much faster rate than that which seemed possible in 1935 even under the spur of Italy's Abyssinian adventure.

My belief that the League could not by itself maintain the peace, which had been strengthened by the Japanese aggression in Manchuria, was strengthened further by the evident failure of the 'sanctions' policy against Italy. Before leaving Rome I had in fact been appointed Foreign Office representative on a Geneva sub-committee which was engaged in tidying up the minor implications of the Sanctions Order of the League of Nations. It was largely as a result of mild exasperation with the absurdities inherent in the operation of 'sanctions' that I then formed the view, never subsequently abandoned, that economic sanctions were worse than useless unless the sanctioneers were prepared to use physical force in the event of their sanctions not being effective. I remember that when asked at the end of 1963 to associate myself with the International Conference on Economic Sanctions against South Africa (to consider measures in relation to 'apartheid'), I refused on the grounds stated. I had on that occasion a friendly letter from Harold Wilson who said that I was perfectly right.

It occurred to me then that, seeing that the two giants were outside a security system, and likely to remain there, or rather that one was quite outside it and the other was not prepared to co-operate except in conditions which would favour its objective of world revolution, the sensible thing would be for the four great European powers to get together and try to agree on a common world policy. However, if the Germans were impossible – and all the signs seemed to show that they would be – then the next best thing would be to split Italy off from Germany by offering her certain concessions that might be negotiable; recognizing, however, that, short of war, or the threat of war, Germany was not going to be deterred from re-occupying the Rhineland, absorbing Austria, and establishing some economic superiority over Czechoslovakia and South-East Europe generally; but recognizing also that, if she really went about establishing her '*Mitteleuropa* outlet' by force of arms she would be bound one day to seek further 'outlets' in the Ukraine, in other words that she would eventually come up against the Soviet Union, in which case the West would do what it seemed in its best interests to do, having by that time accumulated heavy armaments, more especially in the air. The shorthand for this policy was 'the Stresa Front'. The policy may appear to be immoral to some. It may well be thought by others to have been impossible of achievement. But it was a view inspired chiefly by a strong desire not to risk a war until (a) we had a cause which would rally the support of the entire nation, and (b) we had rearmed enough to make our influence felt. The cynical may say it was the policy of 'deflecting the pistol', afterwards pursued by the Russians. I never myself conceived of it in such terms. It was rather designed, rightly or wrongly, to achieve some balance of power which in the long run might make any war entirely unprofitable.

So far so good: and it must be remembered that, as my notes show, I had more or less arrived at these conclusions before the re-occupation of the Rhineland in March 1936, so in any case it cannot be said that I was not looking quite far ahead. I must confess that my notes also show that I was, as I now think, unduly impressed by the danger of chaos in Germany if the Nazis were overthrown, or, in a general way, if both dictators were successfully opposed by the democracies. But as it seemed to me then, the economic situation in Germany would be so unfavourable in such an event that the USSR would be able to fish in troubled waters, and the end result might very well therefore be a semi-Communist Germany in alliance with a Communist Russia, which would represent, ultimately, a force capable of extending its influence over the whole of Western Europe, and might even do so before America, abandoning isolation, was prepared to re-enter the European ring. In other words, I shared apprehensions which have often been ascribed to the more palsied of the French and British *bourgeoisie*; though to do myself justice I do not think that this was so much, if indeed at all, due to a fear of losing precious possessions as to a genuine fear for our freedom in the event of a triumph of *Brauner Bolschewismus*.

Even now, looking back, I do not think that my general thesis was necessarily discredited by events. The trouble is, of course, that you can never demonstrate what effects a policy, not pursued, would have had if it had been pursued. It is just as fruitless to consider what would have happened if Napoleon had won Waterloo or if General Mason-Macfarlane* had shot Hitler. Besides, we all felt in our bones that war was probably coming – it hung all the time like a black cloud at the back of my own consciousness – and that all means of avoiding it must at least be considered, however unorthodox they might be thought to be. Oddly enough, I have never had this feeling since 1945, not even at the time of Korea and Cuba; and I certainly do not have it now.

So, with the encouragement of Ashton-Gwatkin, I really began my career in the Economic Department at the beginning of 1936 by starting up an off-the-record discussion on whether we would be well advised to arrange for some kind of economic 'outlet' for Germany and, if so, what

* British military attaché in Berlin in the 1930s.

it might conceivably be. The effect of the abandonment of 'most favoured nation treatment' in certain areas was explored in detail, as was the advantage and disadvantage of creating economic blocs: the possibility of a Customs Union between the United Kingdom and Germany (and thus between Germany and the colonial Empire) was next examined, as was the possibility of transferring the ex-German-mandated territories to German mandate; and the general conclusion was that if, as postulated, German 'expansion', in the sense of increased export markets, was essential, the 'natural' direction for this to take was towards Central and South-East Europe; and that 'subsidiary outlets' could be found in the return of the ex-German colonies. The whole operation, of course, would be part of a political deal involving disarmament, a return of Germany to the League and so on.

The paper had a good run for its money. Even the great Ralph Wigram said he did not dissent in principle, but that it was going to be very difficult, in practice, to get these sort of ideas accepted unless the Board of Trade and Treasury agreed. He himself believed they would make considerable difficulties. But 'Wigs' was at that moment failing, and at the end of 1936 the disease with which he had been wrestling for nearly ten years finally got him down. It was a tragedy for the Office, of which, had he lived, he might well have become the head soon after the war, in the great tradition of his hero, Sir Eyre Crowe. The Service had no more lucid mind or indefatigable worker, and he invariably said what he thought – I mean inside the Office. I myself had known him well before the war (his family being friends of my mother's family in North Devon) when he was engaged in running a boy's club in Wapping, and was delighted when in 1925 he married the brilliant Ava Bodley, who has remained a lifelong friend. He himself, as is known, had a great influence on Churchill's thinking and was able from time to time, possibly irregularly, to supply him with important statistical information. So when I came back to the Office I should have had someone on whom I could have tried out my ideas in the first instance and at whose house in Lord North Street we might have met more of the politicians than we otherwise did.

I should like to say at this point that in 1936 the Foreign Office contained a number of intelligent middle-rank officials concerned in one way or another with the Central European issue. Like all human beings these men often differed widely in their approach to the great problem, but all were responsible characters who, in their various ways, thought they had something to contribute, even though they well knew that it was not they who took the decisions; they could only try their best to influence those who did. What, I think, did distinguish the Office at that time was an intellectual liveliness and complete liberty, inside the machine, to say what you thought and to press your own point of view, provided that outside you were reasonably discreet about the official line whatever it might be. After all, I myself was then only a quite junior First Secretary. Thus many views were exchanged off the record as well as on it, and it would not be becoming for me to quote things said or written in confidence and in the belief that they would not be exposed to outside criticism. More especially must this rule apply to people who are still living and who, like myself, regarded themselves as a band of brothers who trusted each other and were, by and large, above considerations of personal advantage, and petty intrigue. On the other hand the so-called 'entered' papers are now public property up till well after the outbreak of the war so until then there can be no secret about the general attitude during this period of the various officials.

Maybe I am an innocent, but I must at all events say that I never detected among my own contemporaries any back-biting or efforts to paddle their own canoes and the great thing was that all, however junior, would express an individual view which, if it was intelligently voiced and to the point, might come up to the Secretary of State himself. I really don't think, indeed, that any Secretary of State could have had a more devoted body of advisers. Perhaps, collectively speaking, their defect was that they were too conscious of their special position as the possessors of all known intelligence on their own subject, and thus tended to think themselves superior to journalists – or at least some of them did forty years ago – and to disregard the works of the academics and even, I fear, the speeches of the politicians who sometimes, however, had a greater knowledge of the real background than they had. But, as I say, among themselves they were about as agreeable, intelligent and hard-working a group as you could wish to have.

I was proud to be a member of the group and flattered that my own views should apparently be taken seriously. Perhaps my rather rash tendency to put my thoughts on paper as soon as I have any, resulted in my being a reasonably good adviser even if a poor diplomat. A successful professional diplomat is surely a well-informed, agreeable and socially-minded character with a profound knowledge of his fellow men and a certain natural cunning, who knows exactly when to slip a word in edge-ways that will influence the mind either of his own chief or that of the foreigner with whom he is negotiating. To be successful he need not have any fixed political principles and indeed he is likely to operate more successfully if he has none. To be sure, he should be honest and capable, if only because, as Harold Nicolson repeatedly pointed out, honesty in diplomacy is in the long run the best policy, with some instinctive understanding of the mentality of his opposite number. But his chief function is to be an operator or *entremetteur*, in other words, a tough, sensible man of the world. In this category I would myself place men (and I only instance them as types) like Lord Stratford de Redcliffe, Lord Bertie, Lord D'Abernon, Lord Tyrrell – who hardly ever recorded his views on paper!, Sir Horace Rumbold, and, among my own contemporaries, Christopher Soames.

Among the 'advisers', that is to say those of the Foreign Service who chiefly sought to sway their chiefs by the exercise of the written word, I would rank above all Sir Eyre Crowe, Parliamentary Under-Secretary from 1920 to 1925, and the author of the famous memorandum on the principles governing British foreign policy that did so much to influence the actions of our rulers immediately before the First World War. But in this class I would also put such outstanding figures as Cadogan, Orme Sargent, Ralph Wigram, and, if he had asserted himself more strongly, William Strang. In principle, the operator ought to be in the field and the advisers in the Office, and this, as will be observed, has usually been the case in the past. Perhaps the original division, before the unification of the Service after the First World War, between the Foreign Office 'grubs' and Diplomatic 'butterflies' was not so reprehensible. Of course the 'grubs' ought to have had some experience of foreign countries and the 'butterflies' to have been in close contact from time to time with the central administrative machine: but what is certain is that it is the 'operator' type that should preferably be employed abroad. The trouble is that the tough, self-confident operator, sure of himself and preferably pluri-lingual, is not now being produced in such quantity as formerly.

At the head of the official machine in 1936 was Robert Vansittart, who had taken over from Ronald Lindsay some six years previously. 'Van' was a legendary figure for most of us. His French was so good that he had been able to compose a drama in that language which was actually produced at the Odéon. He had married a rich and beautiful woman whose sister was married to Sir Eric Phipps, Ambassador in Berlin and later in Paris. Sir Eric was splendidly anti-Nazi then, and when Goering, returning from one of his shooting parties, boasted of a bag of several thousand, inquired gently 'Animals, I hope?' Van had a superb Queen Anne mansion at Denham and a large and luxurious house in Mayfair where he and his wife entertained on an almost regal scale. Politically he was always represented as being madly pro-French and anti-German; and it is true that in his published works he did expose himself to the criticism that he believed there was an inherent and incurable bellicosity in the German race. But in private life he was kind and very well mannered, and even in a curious way rather simple. It was not, I think, very difficult to take him in. On the great issues he was also vehement to a degree on paper, but when you really got down to it and said, 'But what would you actually do about it, Van, declare war?' he was often disconcertingly vague. What nobody could possibly deny, however, was that he had from the first been right about the fell intentions of Hitler and his Nazis. The only trouble was that he often denounced them in such unmeasured if elliptical terms that he failed to get his message across to the denser of those influential Tory politicians whom it was essential for his own purpose to convince. Generally speaking he sometimes gave one the curious impression of a man fighting vigorously without ever using his arms. Certainly in personal contact he was much less violent than he was on paper, and even on paper he was much too long-winded.

Apart from Van, Wigram and Gwatkin, the other officials with whom, looking back, I was chiefly in touch at that time were Edward Carr, William Strang, Ralph Stephenson, Owen O'Malley, Orme Sargent, Rex Leeper, Frank Roberts and Roger Makins (Oliver Harvey came a little later into my life). All of these have long since retired and some are dead. One (Ted Carr) abandoned us before the war and became a most distinguished professor whose general *Weltanschauung* is known to all. So perhaps I can say without indiscretion that some, broadly speaking, favoured the 'classical' policy of a close alliance with France based on common action in the League of Nations and absolute resistance to all Axis pretensions while others had doubts and thought that, before it was too late, some serious effort should be made to come to terms with the one or the other of the two Fascist powers and perhaps also with Japan. Differing views between ourselves and the French as regards the correct treatment of Italy, to say nothing of the right policy to pursue in Spain, had put some of the 'classicists' in a rather difficult position. Van himself, for instance, though not in favour of consciously 'diverting the pistol', was a strong 'Stresa Front' man who would have forgiven Mussolini much, if not everything, had it been possible to prise him loose from his German allies. Wigram, I think, was inclined to despair of the 'Stresa Front' by early 1936. But if it were not possible, then how best to stand up to Germany?

The problem of the Russian alliance was already raising its highly contentious head. What none of us, I think, would have then disputed (save
one perhaps) was the absolute necessity of Britain's rearming far more
quickly – more particularly in the air – than seemed likely *sub consule*
Baldwin, already the 'Man of Peace,' even more so, perhaps, than his
immediate successor, Chamberlain.

It was with this background in any case that I also approached the
current issue of what to do about sanctions against Italy. Towards the end
of April it was pretty clear that economic sanctions had not prevented the
Italians from occupying Ethiopia and setting up their own administration,
thus flagrantly defying the League of Nations, which meant, in practice,
Britain and France. The vital question was whether to increase sanctions
or whether to call them off. Everyone agreed that the one effective way of
increasing them would be to close the Suez Canal to the Italian troopships.
This could only be accomplished by an act of war. It was recommended by
some of us; but others, including Wigram, Ashton-Gwatkin and Rex
Leeper disapproved of it and I have no doubt that they were backed up by
Sargent and Van, who, true to his 'Stresa Front' ideas, had always been
critical of sanctions and who, echoing the famous words of Robert
Walpole, had said to me, prophetically enough, at the time of the famous
'Hoare-Laval Plan' of November 1935 – a repudiation of which was to
result in the departure of Sam Hoare and the advent of Eden – 'they are
ringing their bells, but soon they will be wringing their hands'!

In lapidary language Wigram and his colleagues observed that 'the
League can only render war unprofitable and unlikely by securing that
those of its members who intend to keep the peace are strong enough and –
because they are strong enough – ready and able to enforce it'. France in
any case would not support a closure of the Canal and war would thus run
the risk of 'a general conflagration' for which, in our disarmed state, we
were quite unprepared.

Indeed, we consider that in the present state of Europe the physical danger to
our own existence of a break with France to the point of real animosity, cannot
be exaggerated; and there are already disquieting symptoms on both sides of the
Channel which cannot be ignored.

As for the argument that a combination between Italy and Germany was
improbable,

It is not in the least necessary for the two countries to combine in order that
Germany should seize Austria. All that is required is that Italy should be deeply
involved elsewhere. As to dealing with the smaller bully first, that would be

sound if it were safe. But it is not safe now, although the proposition was certainly arguable six months ago.

And, finally,

We do not consider that the argument that we should fight Italy in order to be able to raise our armaments more quickly to the German level is a valid one. It could not be used in public, and opinion would be rightly shocked if it was thought that it was used in private.

The proposal to close the Canal was not, however, immediately killed; anyhow I find that about that time I committed my own thoughts to paper in an effort to estimate what the ultimate results of any such action were likely to be. As it seemed to me, and here at least I think I was right, we could hardly avoid an Anglo–Italian war (France being neutral) which might, at the start at least, have certain unpleasant consequences owing chiefly to the terrible unpreparedness of our existing military and naval dispositions. As I understood it, the position then (late May 1936) was that the Italians had about twenty times the number of troops in Africa that we had. On the face of it, therefore, there seemed every likelihood that they would be able to take Khartoum and even advance on Cairo. In the existing state of our Navy (which we were assured had very little ammunition) they might further be able to block the straits between Sicily and Africa, to say nothing of the mouth of the Red Sea at the Bab-el Mandeb, and possibly bomb Alexandria and the Suez Canal Zone generally. We should be prepared to lose certain major units of the Fleet, and there was little reason, too, why the Italians should not mount an offensive against Egypt from Cyrenaica. If all this happened, and even if we continued to hold Egypt, we should have to rely on a blockade of Italy while we built up our strength. This would no doubt result in eventual Italian capitulation but only after the lapse of many months and a general weakening of our position in the Middle East.

But what would the additional consequences be? In the first place Germany would certainly seize Austria, for any hope of roping in the Italians to prevent this would have disappeared. Further, the longer the Anglo-Italian struggle went on the more impossible it would be to prevent Germany from consolidating her position in South-East Europe and France would not, and indeed could not be expected to do anything about this in the circumstances. As for the USSR, it would be difficult for her to intervene to prevent this development since various countries stood in her way, and anyhow, if she did, she would be forced to strengthen her position in the West by withdrawing troops from the Far East. Japan would be strongly tempted to profit by our weakness by breaking out in the Pacific area, and if she did there would be little to prevent her from taking Singapore – even threatening India. The elimination of Mussolini would, therefore, in the circumstances of 1936, hardly be expected to be to our general advantage.

On the other hand, if we failed to shut the Canal, the Italians would obviously triumph in Abyssinia; the League system would be completely discredited; continuing sanctions would just have to be called off; and normal relations with Italy restored. It seemed probable, however, that Italy, though weakened economically and financially, would, as it were, 'return to Europe' and become once more conscious of the danger of an expanding Germany to the north. Nevertheless, the resulting situation would be very dangerous for us unless we played such cards as we had with great intelligence. If we all (French, Italians and Russians, perhaps with our support) decided to resist the *Anschluss* by force of arms, it still seemed that a total collapse of the Germans, which might then be achieved, could only result in a Russian absorption of Poland and the probable extension of Russian power westwards in alliance with some Russophile government in Germany. This might well be the case even if the French had seized the Rhineland and possibly the Ruhr and had succeeded in setting up some pro-western government in Bavaria.

On these, it must be confessed, rather doubtful, if sustainable, premises I proceeded to argue that we should no longer oppose the *Anschluss* if it were carried out by 'peaceful' means; that we should make it plain that we did not oppose German economic expansion in Central and South-East Europe; that Germany should, however, be warned that she could not rely on British neutrality if she attacked Czechoslovakia thus bringing the French pledge of support into operation; that the Russians should be told that if they were subsequently attacked by the Germans they would have our support and that if they were attacked by the Japanese we should at least be benevolently neutral. In other words it was a proposal for a kind of regional security system.

All this was not, on the face of it, unreasonable; the weak point was that I entirely ruled out the possibility of any action on the part of the USA. But when one recalls that it required the supreme folly of Pearl Harbour to bring America into the eventual war, perhaps the omission was pardonable. It is true that by the time of Munich public opinion in America had become much more alive to the danger presented by Nazi aggression, but in 1936 there were small signs of any kind of American intervention unless the USA itself was directly attacked. It was therefore surely right at that time to base all our plans on the assumption that, in the event of war with what later came to be known as the Axis, we could only count on American neutrality and perhaps not even a very benevolent neutrality at that.

Meanwhile the 'outlet' hare was let loose and started running, giving rise to more official correspondence. Soon there was a come-back from Berlin. The Ambassador there (Eric Phipps) said that he thought the real issue was, did we want a fat Germany or a lean one? He himself preferred a 'lean' Germany. Indeed this might well be the only way of preventing her from organizing a 'war à la Bismarck'. He was quite right; that *was* the essential issue, and there *was* certainly a good deal to be said for the 'lean' argument. After all, if the Nazis were going to commit atrocities they might find it easier to commit them if they were well off and had no economic worries, whereas if they were kept really lean it might be that the situation would get out of hand and the leadership would simply not be in a position to carry out its nefarious schemes. The debate went on, often in an informal way, sometimes involving itself in the most complicated calculations. An unofficial committee was set up on the initiative of Frank McDougall of Australia House. McDougall was a fascinating and brilliant man who, to a great extent, used Lord Bruce, ex-Prime Minister of Australia, as a vehicle for his own ideas. One of his chief claims to fame was an ability to recite from memory all the Collects in the Book of Common Prayer, an accomplishment equalled by few other economists, I should imagine, and even less likely after the recent virtual suppression of perhaps the greatest monument of the English language.

Rex Leeper and I were the FO observers on this committee which chiefly concerned itself with the ideas of Professor Noel Hall of University College. Other members of this group included Barrington Ward of *The Times*, Mike Pearson of Canada House, George Schuster and Alfred Zimmern. It was agreed that encouragement of a 'fat' Germany only made sense if it was part and parcel of some much wider scheme involving such matters as the Ottawa agreements of 1932 establishing the regime of Imperial Preferences, the role of sterling and some revision of the whole policy of His Majesty's Government towards the dependent territories. Generally speaking the Economic Section were not convinced by the 'keep Germany lean' argument. But how exactly you arranged for Germany to get 'fat' and what safeguards you could possibly secure if you did, remained unanswered questions. In July 1936, the Secretary of State (Anthony Eden, who had succeeded Samuel Hoare six months previously) was understood to have summed up the dilemma very well by recording that he did not admit that we were to blame for Germany's economic weakness; that we could nevertheless certainly agree to offer Germany economic and financial help in return for, and subsequent to, a general political settlement; that it was better to have a reasonably fat Germany with a political settlement than a desperately lean one; but that, until she had given proof to the contrary, Germany was a nation that would 'need watching' and that we should not be serving the cause of peace either by handing over her weaker neighbours into her economic clutches or by weakening ourselves.

But the question of what sort of economic and financial help we could give, in the circumstances and subject to the conditions postulated, remained on the agenda and continued to give rise to long debates inside Whitehall notably with Sigi Waley of the Treasury and Quintin Hill of the Board of Trade. Always in the background was the impressive figure of Sir Frederick Leith-Ross ('Leithers') who was then Economic Adviser to the Government and in some ways a power in his own right. Leithers was a 'keep Germany fat' man in principle and I, with whom he got on, was attached to him with the object of keeping him on what the Foreign Office would suppose to be the rails. Together we went out to the Economic Committee of the League and subsequently motored up to Berlin where we saw, among others, Schacht and Goering. In September 1936 the Section was asked to submit a short considered note on the possible ways and means of assisting Germany in the event of the latter's agreeing to participate in the political settlement of Europe. This we did to the best of our ability, and we ended by saying that, failing any move on our part, or on that of other people, it remained our view that in all probability the Germans would rearm until the 'blockade' forced them to call a halt to rearmament, and then embark on some military adventure, the success of which seemed to be considerably less doubtful than it previously did, owing to their improved relations with Italy and Japan and to the course of events in Spain. In a way this was prophetic.

Later we thought it might pay us to meet some of the Germans' economic demands. In some ways we were like a passenger in a sledge pursued by wolves. It might be a good thing to throw something out to them to eat while you were able to get your gun. The real question, as it seemed to us, was whether or not we were going to oppose the apparently inevitable *Anschluss* (which duly took place, of course, two years later). If we were *not* prepared to resist this, by force if need be, then one way out would be to say that we could take no action if a plebiscite in Austria declared in favour. But this, in any case, really was the key point. From the beginning of 1937 onwards, however, the drive to get what McDougall had called the policy of 'Economic Appeasement' began to peter out. (Incidentally I think this was about the first time that the famous word 'appeasement' gained any currency and it certainly did not then connote a policy of giving the Nazis everything they wanted; merely a possible means of achieving a 'peaceful solution'.) In any case it was obvious that the powers that be, for one reason or another, were just not going to play. Gwatkin said gloomily that 'for the moment it seems to serve no useful purpose for the Foreign Office to wail Cassandra-like at the doors of the Treasury and Board of Trade' though he believed that 'sooner or later events will force us to play our part'.

My own frame of mind during this period has already been described at the beginning of this chapter. One thing I can say to my own credit. Even more than some of my colleagues, I constantly maintained that, unless we rearmed hard and soon, we should be unable to conduct any foreign policy and might just have to wait until the German dictator thought that the moment was ripe to strike, no threats of ours being then able to deter him. Disarmament had failed: the League, after the Abyssinian War, was likewise discredited. Whether we liked it or not we were in the middle of an international jungle from which we could only emerge unscathed if we became much stronger than we were and in the meantime made the best use of our wits. When, therefore, the Rhineland was occupied by the Nazis in March 1936, the reader will not be surprised to hear that, in common with the great majority of the British people, and indeed of the House of Commons, I was on what, in the light of subsequent evidence, was no doubt the wrong side, unless what follows should in any way affect the judgment.

For my own satisfaction I then wrote a short paper called 'Locarno and London'. In this paper – which was only put up as a basis for discussion and was in no way an official submission – I suggested that there were three possible courses of action. The Germans could be pushed back out of the Rhineland; there could be a formal condemnation of Hitler's deed but no action, and no notice should be taken either of his 'olive branch' (return of Germany to the League, conclusion of non-aggression pacts, etc.), Germany remaining the black sheep of Europe; or the 'olive branch', subject to certain amendments of a 'delaying' character, could be accepted and an effort made to keep Germany, if not Russia, in the 'polite society' of the League. The 'first course', I suggested, would result in a war in which Germany would no doubt be defeated, but only after she had occupied Austria and possibly also Czechoslovakia. Such a defeat would result in chaos in Germany, the resulting economic distress would eventually produce a government under the influence of the Soviet Union, which would naturally remain Communist and hence anti-Western in tendency. This could be a disaster for the entire West. The 'second course' would almost undoubtedly result in a war in two years' time, that is to say at a time when Hitler would probably have reached his rearmament peak and we should certainly not have reached ours, with the result that there was no certainty that we and the French could win. Indeed we might well be defeated. The 'third course' would have the advantage both of buying time and of holding out the possibility of Germany's obtaining her 'outlet' in South-Eastern Europe by means not necessarily involving war. Once she had established such an outlet then it might be that she would become a 'satisfied' power. But if she was mad enough to seek further expansion towards the Ukraine – and this would then be the only direction in which she could expand further physically – then we should at least have free hands and join up with the Russians if we so decided.

It is obvious, in the light of hindsight, that this analysis neglected the possibility that, if Hitler had been pushed out of the Rhineland, his government might have at once collapsed and another, less hostile to the West, could have taken its place. The likelihood was, in other words, there would then have been no war, for the war party in Germany would have been ousted. On the other hand there would indeed have been some prospect of grave civil disturbances in Germany. The desperadoes of the SS and the Hitler *Jugend* could have provoked some kind of civil war, and how the successor government could have coped with the ensuing economic situation is anybody's guess. The emergence of a new Rosa Luxemburg was not to be excluded. We cannot, in fact, say what would have happened because we just do not know. But that a contented, peaceful, unaggressive Fatherland could have emerged is, I fear, open to considerable doubt. Czechoslovakia and even Austria would probably not, as I suggested, have been successfully invaded; but the influence of the Soviet Union would most likely have been advanced. Besides the French once more in physical occupation of the Rhineland, or even the Ruhr, might very well have been tempted to stay there, or at any rate to institute a separatist regime, and this in itself might have led to long-term difficulties with Great Britain.

Nevertheless there is little doubt that the right thing for us to have done would have been to encourage the French to turn Hitler out of, as it was always said, 'his own back-garden' and to have declared that we would back them if they did so (though whether they would have accepted our advice is by no means certain, for their Chiefs of Staff and their Minister of

War were resolutely opposed to any such thing). And having done that we could both of us have seen to it that the legitimate government of Spain got the better of the rebel Franco and that Mussolini was consequently also put in his place. Perhaps sanctions could then have been replaced by physical action and the Italian dictator overturned by the same sort of forces as eventually emerged some nine years later in the wake of the Allied victory. The Emperor of Ethiopia would have been restored. The whole cause of Fascism could have been shattered. The Japanese at that stage would perhaps not have dared to break out. In other words, we might have won the Second World War without ever really fighting it. And yet, one still wonders. Would it really have all worked out like this?

In the first place it was clear that the great weight of British public opinion, for whatever reasons – and most of them no doubt bad reasons – would have been at that time totally opposed to any such vigorous policy. This did not excuse a minor Foreign Office official for sharing views that may well have been wrong in principle; but it did mean that no British Government could, in practice, have acted as suggested. The thing was out. Sixteen years of reliance on 'collective security' and neglect of armaments; a severe guilt complex in connection with the Peace of Versailles so savagely attacked by Maynard Keynes; a strong pacifist element dating from the massacres of Passchendaele and the Somme; all these factors combined to persuade the British that the Dictators must at least be given the benefit of the doubt. Even if they had had to assume the responsibility for pushing back Hitler they might well have had an even greater sense of guilt if things in Germany had gone really wrong economically. Nor were we in March 1936 in a much better condition, from the point of view of the state of our armed forces, for even taking on Mussolini in the Mediterranean. For example, the Mediterranean Fleet had hardly any reserves of ammunition at that time, nor any air cover for that matter. And radar, the chief reason for our subsequent defeat of the efficient Italian fleet, had not then been invented.

In the second place, the hypothetical Second World War, won by the West, without America, might well in practice have ended up in the same way as the real Second World War, that is to say in a great extension westwards of the power and influence of the Soviet Union. For even a bloodless victory over Hitler, and perhaps, over Mussolini, would not, in itself, have solved the problems presented by the 'hungry' and 'dissatisfied' Powers. If it had been possible, as it was possible nearly a quarter of a century later, for us all to contemplate something like the European Economic Community – and to do them justice the Front Populaire

Government of France was, as we have seen, apparently so disposed – then things would have been very different. But as things were, the play of forces among the various great European Powers would have resulted in some new problems for which war might well once again have provided the only possible solution.

In the third place it is possible that the policy of 'deflecting the pistol' might have worked, provided only that we and the French had really gone all out for rearmament and had succeeded in roping in the Belgians too within an effective defence system. After all it was employed very effectively three years later by the Russians against us even though the British Government had not, and never had had, any real intention of employing it against them. (The subsequent British guarantee of Poland must presumably have been proof positive of that.) Nor even under my own 'third course' would it have been a question of our encouraging the Germans to attack the Russians. It was only suggested that if they were mad enough to do so after having obtained some 'outlet' in SE Europe, a heavily rearmed West would have their hands free to take such action as they thought best. And perhaps I might add that I see that I resumed my thought as follows: 'Failing such a solution (the 'third course') there will, I fear, be no choice but A or B, and of these A (i.e. turning Hitler out of the Rhineland at once) is greatly to be preferred.' Incidentally my little paper was written only six days after Hitler's invasion so possibly I was not entirely unregenerate and misguided.

The general situation continued to deteriorate in 1937 and I became increasingly exasperated with the Nazis. The Government having apparently opted for what I thought was a fatal 'course' in the matter of the Rhineland (just doing nothing) my pessimism as regards the avoidance of war slowly increased. Thus in February I reported to Van that I had heard from Patrick Buchan-Hepburn that Lady Maureen Stanley, the wife of the brilliant Oliver Stanley, had had an odd experience while in Berlin about Christmas time. It seemed that Goering – jokingly it is true, but with a serious undertone – had said to her 'You know, of course, what we are going to do? First we shall overrun Czechoslovakia, and then Danzig, and then we shall fight the Russians. What I can't understand is why you British should object to this. Clearly, from your point of view, the more Germans and Russians that are killed the better!' It seemed that this suggestion for leaving Hitler a free hand in the East has made a certain impression on Lady Maureen. Van replied that Goering had been flying the kite quite a lot of late, partly in earnest and partly to produce exactly the effect that he appeared to have produced on Lady Maureen. It was not quite evident why. Perhaps he was counting on a 'yellow streak' ! But was it the 'yellow streak' in Molotov which caused him to sign the Ribbentrop-Molotov Pact? It seemed to me that a difference of opinion on such matters concerning national survival was not necessarily one between the pure and the impure as imagined by the slightly Manichaean Van. In any case, I was myself, gradually becoming more and more apprehensive of the Nazis' taking violent action. The only question was what, in our disarmed state, could we be expected to do about it, and how could we best put it off until we had effectively re-armed.

In September 1937 there took place the Conference of Nyon, the object of which was to regulate the assistance given by all outside powers to the two sides in Spain. And after it was over I once again voiced my fear that we might be getting into a position in which we would risk a clash with Italy before we were ready for it. Certainly the position was better now than it had been in late 1935 and the advantages of 'humiliating' Mussolini (which I listed) were considerable and by no means to be ignored. We might indeed consolidate our position in the Mediterranean; be assisted by the Front Populaire Government in France; ensure the victory of the legitimate government of Spain and generally win respect all round and notably in Germany. On the whole it still seemed preferable to try to get him on our side rather than to attempt to confront him. In 1938, however, things might well be different. But I was now about to leave the Economic Section for a position in which I would probably have greater opportunity to influence the thinking and the decisions of the great. Up till now I had just been skirmishing about on the fringe and throwing out provocative ideas. From now on it would presumably be more serious.

5
Munich
(1938)

Vansittart had differed seriously from Eden over Italian policy in 1935–6, and now there was a prime minister to whom his ideas about Germany were even more suspect. It was pretty evident, therefore, at the end of 1937 that his position was difficult, but I do not think that he expected to be deprived of his job, or, to be exact, to be pushed upstairs as 'Chief Diplomatic Adviser'. If he had, I doubt whether he would have asked me to take the place of his existing Private Secretary, the trusted Clifford Norton,* less than a month before the elevation. Naturally I was pleased at being chosen – perhaps on the advice of Clifford – for the post was an important one, usually leading to higher things later on.

I had, however, very little time with my new chief before we both went on leave and at the New Year I got a telephone message from him telling me of the new arrangement and that the new Permanent Under-Secretary was to be Alec Cadogan, to whom, therefore, giving me no option, he announced that I would be transferred. I was staggered but could hardly have disputed the transfer, even if I had so wished. Besides, I knew and liked Alec Cadogan who was however the antithesis of Van. Careful, cautious, reserved, conventional, clearly shy, clearly repressed emotionally, he was nevertheless a man of quiet charm and native intelligence. He was also usually fair in his judgments about people and sensible in his judgments about things. Everybody trusted, and most liked, him. At Eton he had – so it was whispered with amazement – had the reputation of being an exuberent character with a passion (like that of Lord Halifax) for practical jokes. Anyway he had been President of Pop and, as the son of an Earl, he did not have to worry about his place in the scheme of things. Nobody could have been more typical of British authority. You could be quite certain that, however tiresome the natives were, he would never be in danger of losing his head. In some ways, however, he was rather old-fashioned. He dictated little and his minutes were usually

* Later HM Ambassador to Athens 1946–51.

written out in his beautifully legible hand. Nor had he read as much as had, for instance, Van, His great strength (I thought) was his calm and his commonsense.

In my new capacity, with only one lady shorthand typist, I had, among many other duties, that of co-ordinating a mass of unofficial reports that came into the Foreign Office from all sorts of channels. They were often not particularly 'secret' except that it was essential to 'protect the source', usually categorized as 'unimpeachable', 'highly reliable', 'usually reliable' and so on. The reports were, indeed, really gossip, some much better authenticated than others, about what important people had said without knowing that their words would be repeated to foreigners. But I remember even then thinking that many of the reports we got in the FO were not terribly valuable as such, and could hardly be so in the circumstances. After all, the position was constantly changing and even the greatest statesmen were known quite often, and quite suddenly, to change their minds. Of course at that time all devices, such as those successfully deve- loped by the Russians, for actually listening in to what the adversary was saying were in their infancy.

Finally established, then, in the room next to Cadogan, with Miss Thomas, our devoted amanuensis, in the room beyond that, with some- times another girl to help her out, and coping alone – no doubt quite inadequately – with matters which now, I believe, occupy several depart- ments, I began for the first time to observe the actual formation of policy. It was a fascinating experience. At that time the rule that all papers of importance should come up to the Secretary of State through the Perman- ent Under-Secretary and the Private Secretaries was still pretty well observed. It may be still, for all I know. Of course the two Parliamentary Under-Secretaries of State – there were only three Foreign Office ministers then (up till the early 'thirties there had only been two) compared to seven now – had the right of direct access to their chief, and this was more especially the right of Lord Cranborne,* an old friend and ally of Anthony Eden's. But even he would, I think, have consulted the head of the Office before putting in any considered papers on policy. This did not mean the Secretary of State could not send for the heads of departments and discuss things with them alone, or at meetings – he often did; but the *result* of such confabulations had normally to come down through the Permanent Under-Secretary, who would then intervene if he chose to.

This system not unnaturally resulted in a terrible bottle-neck. As the war approached during 1938 and the work became more feverish, the

---

* Secretary of State at the Foreign Office under Eden 1938. Secretary of State for Dominion Affairs 1940–2 and 1943–5. Succeeded as fifth Marquess of Salisbury 1947.

congestion grave. Alec Cadogan was a tremendous worker and most methodical; but the red-labelled red boxes piled up on his desk like mountains and often seemed to get him down. Something had to be done. I therefore took it on myself to go through the boxes before the PUS arrived, or during the lunch hour, and transferred most of them to one box, making the pile at any rate *look* less daunting. Then I took to taking back one or two papers to the Department explaining (which was true) that my chief was overwhelmed, and could not the Under-Secretary concerned cope with the paper himself? Then, having found my feet, I regret to say that I had a special stamp made marked 'Seen by Sir A. Cadogan', which I used to initial myself, explaining to my chief later in two words what the paper was about. And finally, greatly daring, I had another stamp made which said 'Sir A. Cadogan agrees'. This was a bit dangerous, but I knew my boss's mind pretty well, and anyhow I never got caught out. When war actually broke out I did get some assistance in the shape of the excellent Godfrey Thomas, until then Secretary to the Duke of Gloucester, but he never used the stamps!

In February 1938 – only a month after I had taken up my new job – Eden resigned and was replaced by Halifax whose mind was, as it were, more attuned to Cadogan's, though he certainly did not always agree with Halifax's political attitudes. Should Eden have resigned? Nobody who reads his book can deny that his position had become impossible. Chamberlain was resolved to negotiate with both dictators, if necessary behind his back; and Eden very rightly felt that nothing would come of this, though he could hardly oppose, in principle, the effort to come to some agreement. The trouble was that Chamberlain at that time undoubtedly represented the general feeling in the country and in the House of Commons. Besides, a policy of merely 'standing up to the dictators' did not make much sense unless it were accompanied by serious rearmament and a vigorous effort in addition to 'mobilize all our resources', whether financial or diplomatic. Should Eden then have tried to form a third party in order to accomplish this? Personally, I think it might in some ways have been better if he had. But he would have had to have been a different sort of man to attempt it, and he could not have rallied more than about ten per cent of the vast Tory majority in the Commons. Even Churchill, who shared his views on foreign policy generally, would probably have remained in the Tory Party. At least I do not suppose that he would have cared to serve under Eden in a separate group.

Eden was, after all, potentially the leader of the younger and more vigorous elements in our pre-war society. He was both courageous and careful and, though not eloquent, he could make a very effective House of Commons speech. He was also a first-class negotiator. However, to break through the prevailing mood of the time something different was necessary. A man more ruthless, perhaps and, in a way, less conventionally minded and no doubt stronger physically, was required. For this we had to wait for Churchill, and it needed a national disaster before even Churchill could come into power. Moreover Eden did not take readily to new ideas. Few politicians do. The theory of the thing interests them less than what we are going to do about it tomorrow. I myself have always been to some extent a theoretician, and for that reason I was aware that I had no particular influence on Eden's mind. Some may feel that what follows proves that he was well-advised not to take me entirely into his confidence! For that I would never reproach him, and we have, I think, always been friends. Besides, for his major negotiations I have nothing but admiration. But I do think that he was the 'Lost Leader', nor can there be much doubt that, as has already been said, I believe compared to Churchill, he was always a 'secondary figure'.

Whether they were acceptable or not, I was, at the beginning of 1938 in any case in a position to air my own views. This may have been irregular, but I never had the sensation that my colleagues in the Departments objected to my interventions. Certainly, Sargent, then the Under-Secretary in charge of European matters, would have been the last to object to my weighing in with ideas of my own. This brilliant and rather passionate character had for long been a friend of mine and I had enormous respect for his intelligence and knowledge. A bachelor, who had never left the Foreign Office except for a brief excursion to the Ambassadors' Conference in Paris, he was basically of the 'Van' school of thought, but with (as I felt) a sharper cutting-edge to his mind. He was realistic and thus inclined to be pessimistic in his general outlook, and nobody could 'debunk' some high-falutin' theory better than he. At the same time he was a tiger when it was a matter of the defence of British interests and the maintenance of British security. His only defect was his health, which was poor, so that he could only with difficulty keep long hours or go to late parties. Before his untimely death in 1961 he made it clear that he thoroughly approved of my 'European' activities, which we will come to later.

By March, then, I recall that I was taking part in a high-level inquest on the *Anschluss*, which, as the reader will remember, I had myself thought would almost certainly come in the spring of 1938. There were three considered papers, one by Sargent, one by William Strang and one by me, together with a note on the juridical aspect by the Legal Adviser, William

Malkin, and a covering paper by the head of the Office. Sargent's was a classic statement of the consequences that we might expect to flow from the rape of Austria. It seemed certain to him that Hitler would now advance on his career of conquest. The way was open to the Nazis to impose their will in the whole Danube basin; the object being to reduce its component parts to the position of vassal states, Czechoslovakia being, in addition, dismantled. If the Western Powers did nothing the whole of Central Europe would be lost to us and France. In any future war, not only would they not be allies, they would not even be neutral. As for Italy, since Germany was now firmly established on her northern frontier, she would be compelled, in the last resort, to side with the stronger Power. And, as compensation, Hitler might well arrange for her to get the upper hand in Spain. In Eastern Europe there was likely to be a stalemate until such time as Hitler might decide to attack; the Low Countries might well just run for safety; and France was likely to concentrate on an insistence that Britain should declare precisely how she proposed to restore and maintain the shattered balance of power. If all was not yet lost, it shortly might be.

Conclusion: we should 'mobilize all our diplomatic resources'. This should include staff conversations with France and Belgium; elaboration of a common policy as regards Central and SE Europe; strengthening of our ties with Greece and Turkey; the 'cultivation' of Poland and Russia; restoration of good relations with Japan; a revival of Pitt's policy of subsidies to our friends and possible friends; and above all a serious attempt to cultivate, interest and educate the people of the USA.

Strang's paper, devoted to what we might do to avert German action in Czechoslovakia, was a wise and careful analysis of all apparent ways of halting Hitler's advance, given the obvious fact that the position of the Western Powers and of Czechoslovakia itself had been seriously weakened. It was brought out that the actual defence of Czechoslovakia might now be impossible; nor was it clear how, given the fortification of the Rhineland and the great superiority of Germany in the air, the French in spite of their declared intention to abide by their obligations, would actually propose to conduct any ensuing war. Strang therefore very forcefully emphasized that the undertaking of any new commitment on our part would only be justified if we increased our military preparations in every sphere, took measures for the reorganization of our national life for war purposes and mobilized all our resources (as suggested by Sargent). He himself still thought we might best work to this last end in the League of Nations. The general conclusion was that the best thing (subject to the Chiefs of

Staff being satisfied that we could face the military implications, which seemed rather doubtful) would be to give an indirect commitment to Czechoslovakia by undertaking to assist France if the latter were attacked by Germany as a result of fulfilling her own obligations towards Czecho-slovakia, which, apart from the League of Nations aspect, did not exist in our own case. But the commitment should be subject to two conditions: (1) that the Czech Government had satisfied us of their treatment of the *Sudetendeutschen* and (2) that the French Government had sought our approval before going to the Czechs' assistance. In order to prepare for (1) an Anglo-French, or perhaps even a purely British mission might be sent to Prague. It will be seen that some kind of negotiated settlement was even then contemplated.

My own paper said that we might have to follow the line suggested by Sargent, but that before giving any indirect commitment about Czecho-slovakia, we might be well-advised to make an all-out attempt to break the Axis by getting the Italians on our side. Possible concessions to the latter were outlined, including an eventual joint Franco-British guarantee of their northern frontier. In return the Italians might agree to withdraw from Spain and not to maintain troops in Libya. It would follow that while attempts to negotiate this, or something like it, were under way no assurances would be given as regards our support of Czechoslovakia if attacked. As it still seemed to me, indeed, we were not at that time in a position to give any such assurance, even an indirect one, without running a grave risk of being involved in a war with Germany, Italy and Japan in which we might be defeated. Cadogan agreed that the reconstitution of the 'Stresa Front' if it could be achieved, would be the best hope. But thought the means suggested were too crude. If two wayfarers were fallen upon by two highwaymen it was not much good the two former offering the two latter to guarantee the one against the other!

I do not recall exactly what happened as a result of this symposium. If the Sargent thesis was at least understood by Halifax I have no doubt that it was anathema to No. 10, Mr Chamberlain, powerfully assisted by Sir Horace Wilson and Sir Joseph Ball of the Conservative Research Associa-tion, then being more than ever convinced that some general and lasting arrangement with both dictators – as opposed to a sort of 'holding opera-tion' as regards the Nazis which was certainly the most that even I was prepared to contemplate – was not only desirable but possible without any very exceptional rearmament effort on our part. Though we had our differences inside the Office, there was hardly a Foreign Office official who could swallow this preposterous theory, and we watched, therefore, with some dismay the goings on in No. 10 and heard with trepidation the rumours regarding the missions of mysterious emissaries (and notably the self-appointed one of Ivy Chamberlain to Mussolini) who might, for all we knew, be about to conclude some bargain which could weaken the whole diplomatic position of the country. Whatever may be said about Munich, however much some of us in the Foreign Office may have sympathized with some of the Prime Minister's efforts to achieve 'economic appeasement', granted freely that Chamberlain was a good and sincere man animated by noble motives; it cannot be denied that his attitude of mind, fostered as it was by the equally sincere and industrious Wilson, was thoroughly wrong and that, finally, it brought us very near to disaster. Never perhaps, has the way to Hell been paved with better intentions.

Perhaps this is the point at which some specific mention should be made of Horace Wilson. In many ways Wilson was the ideal civil servant, and his career in the Ministry of Labour had been spectacular. He was discreet, intelligent, self-effacing, and absolutely devoted to his chief. It was not his fault that more and more Chamberlain leant on him for advice on foreign policy. The theories about how best to get on with the Dictators, though they were no doubt shared by the adviser, really did originate in the Prime Minister's mind. Since it was obvious that, generally speaking, they were not shared by the Foreign Office, their chief political critic was therefore shortly eased out of the Government, and the chief official one removed from the levers of power in the Foreign Office. All this was no doubt legitimate in the sense that a Prime Minister who really believes his ideas are correct and that he represents the country must have the right to find colleagues and subordinates with whom he can work. What cannot be justified is the installation in No. 10 of a small machine which acts completely independently of, and quite often at variance with, the official machine, including its representative in the Cabinet. Halifax should never have consented to such a system. A Prime Minister running foreign policy through the medium of an *éminence grise* is a recipe for disaster. It may have worked in the days of Richelieu, but, to say the least, it is incompatible with the successful operation of a modern democracy. Nor should I have thought that the example of America was very encouraging.

The debate in the Foreign Office, however, continued. Believing, rightly or wrongly, that my own thesis had been imperfectly understood, I composed (on my own typewriter) an immensely long memo which bore the date of my thirty-eighth birthday (25 April). In this paper I, rashly, sought to justify my attitude on theoretical and even on philosophical grounds. I began by outlining our presumed objective, namely the formation of a defensive alliance of the UK, France and Italy so far as possible in co-operation with Spain and Portugal and with a 'Balkan bloc' to include Yugoslavia, Roumania, Greece and Turkey. The Low Countries would be armed neutrals and the Soviet Union would have a sort of conditional guarantee against attack, i.e. it would be conveyed to them that no aggressor would have any certainty that he would not find himself at war with the Western Powers as well. Japan would be offered certain facilities in China but told that if she attacked any of the possessions of any member of the group in Asia she would be at war with all of them. Everything should be done to enlist the sympathy of the USA but no support from the latter should be expected. In this way the 'dissatisfied Powers' would all be largely satisfied, but if they pursued 'expansion' beyond a certain point they could call into being forces which might in the long run destroy them. More especially would this be the case if one of them was so mad as to get bogged down in Russia and another in China.

The whole theory was, however, based on the conception that perpetual peace was an unprofitable dream, embodying the fallacy that the Kingdom of Heaven was realizable in this world instead of in the next – or possibly 'within oneself'. What was called 'aggression' was consequently likely to be in some degree a permanent factor in international affairs, or, in other words, tension of some kind was a condition of all life. If it were not then obviously the oysters would soon cover the globe. Even the Roman Empire, which was founded on the exhaustion produced by prolonged warfare, was only kept in being by the permanent 'aggression' of the barbarians – and much more in this vein. This did not however mean that we were condemned to a series of devastating wars. It merely meant that change was inevitable, and that change was invariably promoted by some kind of force. The task of the statesmen was to see to it that such force was properly harnessed and directed. '*In der Beschränkung zeigt sich erst der Meister, und das Gesetz nur kann uns Freiheit geben.*'*

There were various 'fears' which might stand in the way of successful pursuit of such a policy. One was that any abandonment of Czechoslovakia would result in a Russo-German alliance. This, I thought, was an undoubted danger, but also unlikely. After all, if Germany got control of Central Europe she would be, as it were, nearer to the Ukraine and the Russians could hardly rely on paper assurances by Germany that she would never expand in that direction. Nor would a policy of 'deflecting the pistol' seem to be very profitable for the USSR or for Germany. For

---

* The Master first shows himself in limitations, and only the Law can give us liberty.

77

if Germany profited by an alliance with Russia to attack the West and was completely successful in knocking the West out, the USSR would be at the mercy of the Nazis: whereas if the attack was unsuccessful then the Nazis for their part would be at the mercy of a war on two fronts and an all-European coalition. Only on the assumption that a German attack on the West would result in an inconclusive war in the West would a Nazi-Soviet pact seem to be in the interests of Russia. If such a pact was not possible the Russians could, admittedly, attempt to buy the Nazis off by supplying them, on easy terms, with some raw materials that they wanted; but this in itself would be unlikely to appease Nazi appetites. Finally, they could simply prepare to defend themselves against any possible Nazi attack and hope that in that event they would have the support of the West. It was this that they were most likely to do. How wrong I was in the event! But it all seemed quite sensible then. Nations are not always guided by what appears to a rational observer to be their interests.

Even so, there were those who said that in the event of their gobbling up Czechoslovakia, the Nazis would be able eventually to dominate the world. This fear might indeed be justified, but if it were it would be a reason for our striving to put off an inevitable war by means which would not only give us time to prepare for it physically but also to build up some system of alliances based more on expediency than principle. Even if it were justified, too, it would mean that Germany would have to fight, among others, Russia, and if that happened there was reason to suppose that she would eventually be destroyed by 'pursuing the will-o'-the-wisp of expansion into the bogs of the Ukraine'. (A rather better effort at prediction.)

The paper attracted some attention in our little circle. In the light of hindsight was there anything to be said for it? The reader will judge. Clearly it was an effort to think out what might happen if something else happened – a sort of game of chess. Clearly also, though I touched on it, I did not predict one very important thing that could happen in the event of an 'abandonment' of Czechoslovakia, namely a Nazi-Soviet pact coupled with an agreement for the division of Poland. It can well be argued, and many do argue, that if we had ignored Poland, as suggested by Litvinov in Geneva in the spring of 1938 before his replacement by Molotov, and simply plumped for a defensive alliance with France and Russia we should have been better off. But in that case Poland would no doubt have come to terms with Germany and joined the Axis. Nobody, as the French kept on telling us, could really depend on Colonel Beck.

Faced with the certainty of a real war on two fronts in the event of an attack on Czechoslovakia or even with the prospect of war with France and Britain only, the suggestion nevertheless is that the German generals, led by Halder, would have deposed Hitler and seized power. Indeed General Halder is said to have had the whole plan worked out and was only prevented from putting it into operation by the journey of Chamberlain to Berchtesgaden. But even supposing he had deposed Hitler, we should still have had to negotiate with a German Nationalist government which, while continuing no doubt with the rearmament programme, would have done their best to absorb the *Sudetendeutschen* by 'peaceful' means, thus achieving Germany's obvious national objectives by more devious means. Unless indeed the removal of Hitler had resulted in a sort of civil war and a revolutionary situation from which only the Russians could have profited. Actually I still doubt whether the *coup d'etat* would have taken place if Chamberlain had not gone to Canossa. Nor do I think that Hitler, if confronted with an ultimatum, would still have invaded Czechoslovakia in defiance of Britain and France. Much more likely he would have changed his line at the last minute and merely settled for a plebiscite in the Sudetenland which would probably have given him most of what he wanted anyhow. For the fact was that the critical concession had already been made some time before the Berchtesgaden conference. Both Britain and France, and an overwhelming majority in both countries, had already agreed that there must be at least some autonomy for the *Sudetendeutschen*.

Anyhow, the assumption that a policy of 'deflecting the pistol' would not necessarily be in the interests of Russia was, I think, justified in the event. Just as any effort by the West to give Germany a completely free hand in the East would not have been in the long-term interests of France or Britain either. If the paper had any effect – and perhaps it did – it was in the direction of confirming in their view those who thought that, given the report of the Chiefs-of-Staff, it would be unwise for us to give any absolutely definite undertaking to defend Czechoslovakia, whether directly or indirectly, by force of arms, against Nazi aggression; and I freely confess that I did not have any greater sense of guilt in so believing than I had some ten and some thirty years later in believing that we could not, in practice, defend that country by force of arms against almost equally unpardonable aggression by another Power. For, if 'the master of Bohemia is the master of Europe', as Bismarck said, I believe, then a declaration of war on Germany in 1938 by ourselves and the French might well have resulted in the Russians becoming the 'masters of Europe' much earlier and more completely than they did. Though of course in the years that have elapsed since Munich the whole face of European politics has been changed by the nuclear balance of terror.

By this time the FO was caught up in the great wave that took Chamberlain to Berchtesgaden, to Bad Godesberg and, finally, to Munich. I do not propose to examine the details of that celebrated crisis. This is, after all, only a record of how my own personal attitude developed. So I will only say that, as the reader will have seen, I was myself reconciled, on purely rational grounds, to the dire necessity of coming to some arrangement with Hitler about the *Sudetendeutschen*, in the knowledge that whatever this arrangement was, it could hardly, in the nature of things, be such as to prevent the Germans from getting virtual control of Czechoslovakia and of much of South-East Europe as well. It also seemed to me that we could hardly invoke Russia at this point for the purpose of restraining Hitler without a danger of bringing Russia right into Europe and prejudicing the possibility of eventually, after we had ourselves rearmed, restraining him without such an unfortunate result. I was not, therefore, anti-Soviet in the sense of preferring the Nazis to the Communists. Both regimes appeared to me to be horrible, though the Nazi system was undoubtedly the worse. I was simply sceptical of the possibility of then and there forming the defensive alliance of France, Britain and Russia which a year later and after the Nazis had proved that they were not going to expand peacefully within their alloted sphere, we were, after many hesitations, to attempt.

Wrong though I may have been, troubled though I was in my own mind, this was a line which I personally stuck to, for having seen all the papers, I believed that at that time we had no better alternative. In one conclusion I was confirmed by the frightful attitude of the Führer during that terrible fortnight: this was that any kind of long-term deal with him was henceforward out of the question. So long as he was in unchallenged command, Germany could only be restrained, if restrained at all, by force or the threat of force. We would no doubt have to go on trying to reach some settlement and perhaps Goering or some general would eventually emerge with whom we could do business. Cadogan, on the other hand, had one moment (after the presentation to Chamberlain by Hitler of the famous Godesberg 'ultimatum') when he believed that Chamberlain should abandon the attempt to reach any agreement and come home simply saying that if Hitler by his action caused the French to abide by their obligations and assist Czechoslovakia by force of arms, he would also find himself at war with us. If the reader should think that Cadogan was right, I should not object. Though I still believe myself that it was an open question.

Basically, my own thought can be summed up in a paper composed on 23 August of that agonizing year.

The alternative policy of making it clear that we shall come into a war has much to recommend it. It is not the intention of this memorandum to argue against such a policy if we feel that we have both the strength and the determination to carry it out. But it is precisely because I personally feel that we have not, as a nation, at present such strength and determination that I have endeavoured to examine the situation on the assumption that, when the crisis comes, we shall, in effect, allow Hitler to swallow the Czechs. If the assumption is held to be false, the entire memorandum need not be read.

The assumption, however, was not false. I repeat that I do not believe that there was ever any prospect that either France or Britain would have gone to war to protect Czechoslovakia. Whether they should have is another question. In the light of hindsight, and in spite of relative British unpreparedness, particularly in the air, most people would probably hold that they should. But what would have happened had they done so nobody can possibly say.

In any case I cannot admit that I personally took part in the general rejoicing that accompanied the return of the Prime Minister from Munich, or that I heard him utter the famous phrase of 'Peace in our Time' from the window of No. 10 with anything but a sinking heart. Along with Sargent and Hugh Dalton I witnessed the scene from a first floor Foreign Office room overlooking Downing Street. The street, I seem to remember, was full of happy, cheering people and just before the PM appeared his athletic PPS, Geoffrey Lloyd, climbed up the lamp-post. As I have said, I felt depressed myself, even though I had always thought that the sort of arrangement he had achieved was at any rate better than a war which, as I believed, would not have saved the Czechs' skins, even if we had saved our own. But the Deputy Under-Secretary after a time said that he couldn't stand it any more and went off to do a bit of work in his room along the corridor.

6

The Foreign Office
on the Eve of War
(1938-9)

After Munich there was another Office inquest, just as there had been after
the occupation of the Rhineland. Cadogan thought on 19 October 1938,
that in our existing state of 'inferiority in military strength' it was 'difficult
to have or to pursue a foreign policy'. Our first need, therefore, was 'to
get on equal terms'; and since disarmament was clearly impossible the only
thing to do was to increase the armed strength of the democracies relative
to that of Germany. We ourselves could not hope alone to equal Germany's
military effort – even we and France together could probably only hope
to achieve equality – because 'Germany was far more self-sufficient than
were we, who, in order to keep alive, had to import the bulk of our food
and maintain the value of the pound'. We also had to make provision for
the defence of our various possessions overseas, to which, incidentally, the
Dominions ought to contribute more. It all amounted to an absolute
necessity to increase our armaments. Nor could Hitler legitimately object
to this. We might even announce that 'our defencelessness had left us
practically helpless in the recent crisis'. This might, conceivably, 'galvanize'
our own people.

His proposals for what should actually be done were not, however, very
inspiring, and did not get much further than saying we should cultivate
good relations with everybody who was prepared to have them with us
but should avoid the 'encirclement' of Germany. At the end there was a
suggestion for a conference but also an admission that it was probably too
late for this kind of thing. Indeed it was. The Permanent Under-Secretary
himself was, I fear, suffering from the remains of the British bad conscience
about Versailles and still did not quite appreciate what he was up against.
He was, at heart, always a revisionist rather than an appeaser.

My own assessment of the effects of Munich was volunteered in a memorandum which I submitted on 19 October after talking to a large number of politicians, journalists and so forth. The great majority of intelligent people, I said, seemed to think that Munich represented something much more like a defeat than a victory. About half thought it was a 'necessary' defeat, in other words that we could not have gone to war with a prospect of achieving any success that was not entirely Pyrrhic. About a quarter felt (like the P M) that it was in a way a 'victory' owing to the possibility afforded of arriving at some 'permanent settlement' with Germany and Italy. The remainder were filled with despair and stoutly maintained that, confronted by the legendary 'firm stand', the walls of Jericho would have fallen. These were those most bitterly critical of the P M. Nearly all, however, of whatever school of thought, blamed the Government for having apparently neglected our defences and nearly all, in addition, had the sensation that, wherever the fault might be, we now had our backs to the wall. Nearly all were consequently in favour of some kind of rearmament spurt here and now. Though intent on rearming, few would object to an effort being made, if such a thing was possible, to arrive at some arms limitation deal with Hitler and to a renewed attempt to come to terms with Mussolini. But as for Germany all we could now do was to keep our weather eye open and not offer any concessions except in return for some genuine settlement.

I urged, therefore, that the Foreign Office should press for really drastic measures such as the creation of a Ministry of National Defence and another of National Service and indeed for the formation of state-run arms factories, however much such measures might interfere with our 'way of life' and irrespective of any possible inflation. I was appalled by the rumours reaching us that, in the weeks following Munich, the PM was actually thinking in terms of some reduction of existing British armaments rather than of rapid and vigorous rearmament.

In a subsequent paper I see I was critical of a suggestion of Cadogan's that we might make and broadcast some kind of offer to the German people. It was rather a question of holding the fort while we recovered, and the 'period of our defence weakness' was likely, I was told by the experts, to last until about May 1940. Generally speaking, I believed that the time had come for us to adopt a pretty strong attitude on the lines 'You have got what you said you wanted, and so far as we are concerned you are not going to get anything more unless you change your policy radically'. By taking up such a line we should be far more likely to encourage the moderates in Germany than if we adopted a sweetly reasonable attitude. This line was incidentally in harmony with the bulk of the secret reports we had been receiving: nothing, it was alleged, would have a greater effect than British adoption of compulsory military service. Cadogan said that he thought it would be a good thing if I could ask the departments concerned in the Office to prepare a commonly agreed policy paper based on various ideas that had been floating around; but for various reasons only an 'Outline Paper' was prepared by me after consulting the people concerned. This never saw the light of day in the sense of becoming an agreed submission. It was to discuss certain ideas such as 'We must give up the idea of policing Europe' and 'The last war placed the whole of Central and SE Europe at the mercy of Germany; the next war may place the whole of Europe at the mercy of Russia' – all the worst scenarios. There was also to be a frank discussion of the pros and cons of a continuing 'Stresa' policy and of the possibility or otherwise of some arrangement with the Russians.

Another less sketchy paper of mine of this period, a little later in date, was entitled 'Paris Visit'. It was submitted to Cadogan, who did not think much of it. This was based on three major assumptions: the first that Germany, according to all our reports, was almost bound to 'move East' sometime in 1939, and that such a move might even be coupled with one against ourselves, France being 'terrified into neutrality'. In France itself a majority favoured resisting all German pressure, anyhow on the West, in close alliance with us, but a minority, perhaps larger than we thought, was in favour of peace at any price and might not even come to our assistance if attacked. The French, though still dreadfully weak in the air, were stronger even than the Germans in some other regards and in any case were themselves more than a match for the Italians, with whom therefore they were in a position to come to terms if they could. The Italians for their part were becoming increasingly alarmed by events in Germany and the great bulk of the people, half the Fascist leaders, the Court and most of the Army would have liked to get out of the 'Pact of Steel'. The conclusion was that the PM and Secretary of State would be well advised during a visit to Rome to make some really tempting offer to Mussolini in return for the recall of his men from Spain. If the French could be squared this might take the form of the two Somalilands, the southern half of Tunisia, large credits and an Italian seat on the Board of the Suez Canal Company. In other words, I was once again displaying my King Charles's Head, and I continued to do so at intervals during the coming months.

On 2 December, for instance, I said I did not want to be a Cassandra, but I thought the coming Rome visit of the Prime Minister and Secretary of State was likely to be a flop, nor had I detected much sense in our post-Munich diplomacy. Our first idea, I understood, or rather the first idea of the Prime Minister, had been to arrive at some 'general settlement' directly with Hitler. If there ever had been anything in this, which I doubted, it was frustrated by the dreadful Pogroms. Faced by this situation the Prime Minister had said, on 14 November, that the only hope lay in making friends with Mussolini. But he could hardly have thought that the Anglo-Italian agreement (signed on 16 April 1938) was in itself a sufficient basis for 'friendship' with the Duce, whose bargaining position it had considerably increased. Seemingly realizing this, he fixed up the Rome visit before leaving for Paris in order, as he had said, 'to have a heart-to-heart talk with Mussolini' and to give the latter 'greater freedom of manoeuvre'. In other words, though he clearly could not officially try to endanger the Axis this must presumably be his first objective. But Italy had hardly been mentioned during the Paris talks, even as a problem to be solved, so we should presumably go to Rome with empty hands, and it seemed to me that it might only increase the general tension that would certainly be mounting in the spring.

Later in December I reverted to the idea. Pertinax, the celebrated French columnist, had published a story about a possible offer of the two Somalilands to Italy. (I thought he might possibly have got this story from No. 10, but Cadogan believed that this was not so.) Could we not in any case do something to lessen the tension in the Mediterranean, not indeed by granting Franco belligerent rights, which would hardly be possible, but by making some reasonable offer to Mussolini on the lines previously suggested in return for his accepting fully the plan of the Non-Intervention Committee? Otherwise the intended visit to Rome of the Prime Minister and the Secretary of State might be profitless and the situation remain dangerous. Cadogan dissented. He was against bribing Mussolini to accept something which he had said he would accept anyway, and the bribe suggested by me was much too large. In view of the subsequent revelations of Mussolini's thinking contained in the Ciano diaries, I have no doubt that Cadogan was right, but the diaries do show that there was considerable opposition to Mussolini's policies in Italy at that moment. Later, commenting on yet another approach, Cadogan said he was no longer interested in any such ideas. 'I have always thought,' he minuted, 'that the time would come when we must put our foot down, and I think it is now'. He clearly meant this to apply to the pretensions of all dictators. It was the last flicker of the 'Stresa Front' idea, and the stage was now set for an eventual guarantee of Poland and Roumania.

Meanwhile the secret reports on Germany came pouring in and at the end of January I summarized them as objectively as I could for the Cabinet. There was no reason, I said, for extreme pessimism, such as for thinking that we should ourselves in the near future be the victims of a German attack. The German people in any case did not want war and it was after all *possible* that anti-war forces might still prevail. Nevertheless there were grounds for serious concern. Before March 1938, all reports had agreed that Hitler intended to bring the Czech crisis to a head before the end of September. After Munich there had been the same curious unanimity on two points: (1) Hitler had been at once encouraged and infuriated by Munich, which had deprived him of his 'quick war' and a military occupation of Prague; (2) his irritation was thenceforward focused on the Prime Minister and the British generally. The Prime Minister was abused in private and Britain was described as 'decadent'. He was also reported as saying that he would 'take for himself what he could not get by negotiation'. On this Ribbentrop had enlarged by saying, 'If no agreement with England can be reached, Hitler is determined not to shrink from war in order to destroy her'. His irritation was fanned by the deteriorating economic situation which Schacht told him was becoming desperate; but when a body of alarmed industrialists had made the same point, Hitler had replied, 'Very well, all that this means is that a vital decision must come at once, and it is coming at once.'

Many of the sources had independently arrived at the conclusion, indeed, that Hitler would be forced to 'explode' during 1939, his chief objects being to direct attention away from the German economy, to suppress his own 'moderates' and to secure supplies of raw materials. But apart from one report (according to which Hitler had said 'Why should I bother about colonies when I can get Holland and Belgium and shortly after that England?') all the evidence was that the 'explosion' would be in the East. Besides, there was evidence of unrest in the Ukraine, the Poles were nervous, and, after all, there was the doctrine of *Mein Kampf*.

Additionally it was alleged that 'everybody in the Party' was convinced that there would be a war 'at the earliest in March, at latest in April' and the persistent advice of Himmler and Ribbentrop was 'simply to get on with it'. In these quarters it was even stated that England would be attacked whether she acquiesced in Germany's Eastern action or not. One (but only one) report spoke of threats by Hitler to promote a 'new Munich' in January or February. Further, the German Chiefs of Staff had been told to give Hitler plans by 15 February for (a) an attack in the East and (b) a combined attack on Holland and Switzerland with simultaneous action against Britain and France (some believed (b) to be a bluff). And, finally, talking to his officers, Hitler had announced that it was not only a question of conquest, but of the destruction of Christianity (which was only another form of Judaism) and the foundation of a new philosophy which would 'crush the democracies and rule the world'. It was scarcely necessary to persevere right to the end to discover that the egregious Ribbentrop had added that the Munich accord was the 'obituary notice of England'.

You did not have to believe all these reports to come to the conclusion that something pretty sinister was afoot, and the total absence of any reports that were remotely reassuring could hardly be ascribed to anti-German bias on the part of the Secret Service. In the light of our subsequent knowledge, there is little reason, indeed, to suppose that they were, generally speaking, anything but accurate, in the sense that Hitler was actively planning hostilities, at all events in the East. Never, in any case, could any government have been more fully warned of the prospective conduct of an adversary. The wonder was that anyone in the Cabinet could have any continuing illusions about Hitler and the Nazis. My own recorded conclusion was that there was 'no definite proof, but it can be said with practical certainty that an "explosion" of Germany is coming in the comparatively near future and that it is necessary for us to take immediate measures to guard against the possibility of its being directed against us'.

In the late spring, six weeks after the occupation of Prague, there was another witness to the dark designs of the Nazis, namely Karl Goerdeler, ex-Mayor of Leipzig, the particular protégé of Ashton-Gwatkin. Goerdeler's first message (at the end of April) concerned the German General Staff. The latter, he assured us, had now come to the conclusion that, given the presumed industrial support of the USA, the Western democracies would prove too much for Hitler who would therefore be restrained 'by force' at the critical moment. If only Britain and France could 'remain strong' and show their determination to resist *any* new aggression, by force if necessary, the whole 'Hitler adventure' might be 'liquidated before the end of June'. They should also 'attack the cruelties of the regime, demand the restoration of Czechoslovakia, introduce conscription and take Churchill into the Government'. I must say I was never really impressed by the earnest and no doubt sincere Goerdeler. If the German General Staff were convinced of the criminal lunacy of Hitler there was nothing to prevent them from overthrowing him – perhaps shortly before any outbreak of war seemed inevitable. After March 1939, indeed, they could hardly have had much doubt that the British this time were going to stand firm; and if they had had any doubts they should have shortly been dissipated by our guarantee to Poland.

Before the war started we had already, as it seemed to me, for some time passed the point at which, thanks to the complete stranglehold which the Nazis had on the administration of Germany, internal German 'resistance' to Hitler was likely to be effective. In the first place no revolt would succeed unless it involved the actual assassination of Hitler, which was a difficult thing to do when he appeared to be on the crest of the wave. In the second place even if the Führer had been assassinated before August 1939, that is to say before the conclusion of the Nazi-Soviet pact – which seemed to promise complete success – it was likely that the successor government, presumably imposed by the Army, would still have been pretty nationalist and militaristic. As such, it is difficult to see how it could willingly have agreed in advance to the terms on which we would no doubt have insisted, namely the evacuation of 'Czechia', a free plebiscite in Austria, and so on. In the third place, even if all this had been possible, and we had come to terms with a reduced and, in principle, a pacific Reich it would have been on the assumption, on the German side, that the resulting combination in Western Europe would have been directed against the Soviet Union, and for that public opinion in France and Britain at any rate would not have been prepared. The only alternative would have been, after the collapse of the Nazi regime, to bring the USSR itself into the ensuing European settlement. But for that public opinion in France and Britain would not then have been prepared either, when it came to the point. For by one means or another it would almost certainly have meant – as the result of the Second World War was to demonstrate – extending Russian influence up to, and even well beyond the Eastern frontiers of Germany.

In other words the few German 'resisters', brave and devoted men though they were, were the victims of an insoluble dilemma, and you have only to read the tragic memoirs of Ulrich von Hassell – a great friend of ours when he was Ambassador in Rome – to understand what this was. For the most part members of the upper class, Hassell and his friends always took the view that, in the circumstances, it was impossible for them to 'act' – by which was meant inducing the apprehensive German generals to use the Army for the purpose of an anti-Hitler *putsch* – unless they could be given at least some assurances that, in so doing, they would not lead their country into total collapse or place her at the mercy of a hostile coalition. Such was certainly the conception, too, of the controversial Adam von Trott (whom I never met) and I strongly suspect that it coloured the thinking of that splendid man, murdered by the Nazis in the last week of the war, Albrecht von Bernstorff.

The trouble was that the assurances needed just could not be given. During the 'phoney war' when Germany was, after all, allied to Russia, it is possible that the assassination of Hitler might have led to peace with the West, Russia then being regarded almost as an enemy. But even so it would have been most unlikely that we could have agreed to call off the war unless Poland had at least been restored as a state with its western frontiers as they were in 1938 and probably unless the new German government had agreed to repudiate the Munich settlement also. Such at any rate was my own thought in 1938–40, and I still believe that, basically, it was correct.

After the collapse of the West it was difficult to imagine that any German generals could be found willing to dispose of the conqueror, and after the Nazis became involved in war with Russia, which *ipso facto* became an ally of Britain, it was obvious that no peace could have been concluded with them except by general consent. And soon we had the doctrine of unconditional surrender also. In desperation, Cadogan's cousin, the courageous Stauffenberg, attempted to blow up Hitler in his East Prussian bunker in August 1944. He failed. But even if he had succeeded it must by then have been apparent, even to the German 'resisters', that all hope of concluding peace except on the basis of an allied occupation of Germany was out of the question. The hope of the 'resisters' – and indeed the secret hope of some Nazis – was then that Germany should be occupied by the Anglo-Saxons only and not by the Russians at all. It follows that the last moment at which the removal of Hitler might have altered the tragic sequence of events was before Munich, and we have already speculated on the possible consequences of such a happening then. In sum, once Hitler had taken over the Reich and embarked on his career of conquest there was in all probability no outcome except Germany's total defeat or that of the other European powers who were not prepared to accept her rule. The seeds of the European tragedy were, in other words, present in the whole vicious system of totally independent European nation-states. That was the real enemy then and, as I believe, it is the real enemy still.

The truth was, as I observed to Cadogan a few days later, that war was almost certainly coming. But as a final effort to avert it could we perhaps instruct Henderson to 'talk frankly' with General Keitel, who seemed to be a friend of his, even though he had the reputation of being rather a lightweight, and tell him straight out that if Hitler provoked a war over

Danzig it would result not only in the destruction of the Nazi regime but also, very probably, in the final collapse of the *Grossdeutsches Reich*. It was true that it would be even better if such language was held to Hitler himself, and failing him, to General Halder who was 'alleged to have views of his own'. There might not be anything in the idea that the German General Staff would have any influence on Hitler at the moment of crisis, but if there was the remotest chance of this it might be that such language would do good. In any case there was not the faintest use in speaking to Ribbentrop or Ciano.

At this point perhaps I should record two conversations which I had about this time with representative Germans. One, in May, was with Theodor Kordt, then Counsellor in the German Embassy, the other the Count von Schwerin, whom I met at lunch with the Director of Naval Intelligence, Admiral Godfrey. With Kordt I started off by saying that, though war seemed to be inevitable, I couldn't help feeling that so great a disaster for all of us would somehow be averted at the last moment, a sentiment which the Counsellor, with a heavy wink, warmly shared. But it quickly became evident that, whereas what I was suggesting was that at the last moment the Nazis would recoil from their projected onslaught on Poland, he was convinced that it would rather be Mr Chamberlain who, at the last moment, would fail to assist the Poles. So I spent a lot of time trying, without much avail, to persuade him of the contrary. Finally he observed that if there was a war, and if we won it – a possibility that he was polite enough to say could not be excluded – one thing was certain, the Empire would disappear and we should be reduced to the status of an American dominion. To which I retorted that if such a choice had to present itself, I would infinitely prefer my country to become an American dominion than a German *Gau*.

A month later, with Schwerin, I was even more explicit. The Count, who seemed to be a brave and sincere man, said that it was obvious that Hitler was going to go for Danzig before September and that we should not only *say* that we would fight in that event, but actually *do* something about it, such as mobilizing the Fleet, or sending squadrons of British aircraft to French airfields, or taking Churchill into the Government. Admiral Godfrey and I naturally emphasized the great unity of purpose that now animated our country. There was absolutely no question of our not assisting Poland. Our strength had increased enormously since Munich and was now very formidable. Our anti-aircraft had been perfected, and we now had conscription. The Director of Naval Intelligence also described all the details of our proposed blockade. I recorded myself as speaking as follows. If the Germans really thought that they were going to conquer the world with the sole assured support of Italy, they were likely to receive an unpleasant surprise. Only by a successful *Blitzkrieg* could they hope to succeed in Europe, and the prospects of success in this line were becoming increasingly remote. Failing such a success the results of a general war, bad though they would be for all of us, would be appalling for Germany. The famous German *Lebensraum* would swiftly be converted into a *Todesraum* and Germany might well be as shattered as she had been by the Thirty Years War. Even if the Germans thought they could win such a war how could it profit them? And were they really prepared to risk the newly won unity of the Reich for the sake of incorporating a small German town the retention of which (if the word had any meaning) was essential to Poland's *Lebensraum*?

Von Schwerin replied that Hitler had nevertheless been genuinely convinced after Munich that it was the British intention to surrender at any rate Central and Eastern Europe to Germany. I retorted that, whatever false assumptions the Führer might have made, the fact remained that the possibilities of a pacific German penetration of the East had been shattered by the German occupation of Prague. This fact, and not our guarantee of Poland, was principally responsible for the present check to German plans of expansion. Nobody feels more deeply about the unfortunate behaviour of an individual or indeed about that of a nation than he who has had illusions about the possibility of avoiding it: and the attentive reader, if he perseveres in these confessions, will perceive that I am by no means exempt from this all too human characteristic.

By this time we had given our guarantees to Poland and Roumania, and it was hardly possible that Hitler should have had any illusions about our giving effect to them if necessary, though the evidence, I think, is that he did. There was opposition to these guarantees – Rab Butler, for one, was opposed – but not, to the best of my recollection, among the Foreign Office officials who after the March occupation of Czechoslovakia had come to the conclusion that any thoughts of an arrangement with the Nazis must now be dismissed from the mind and that a war, for which, after all, we were now much better prepared than we were in 1938, was the only probable outcome. After the conclusion of the Ribbentrop-Molotov pact on 23 August this probability became a certainty, and the question arises: could we have done anything to avoid the Nazi-Soviet deal, for which, in spite of a few warnings, we were certainly unprepared.

I doubt it myself. The only way in which we could have avoided it – as I think the long negotiations in which William Strang wrestled with Molotov and Voroshilov made clear – was by agreeing to a clause in the projected Anglo-French-Soviet treaty whereby we, and the countries immediately concerned, effectively agreed that, in the event of the treaty coming into operation – that is to say in the event of German aggression – there would be no objection to the passage of Russian troops through the countries standing between them and the German Army, namely the Baltic States, Poland and Roumania. If anything is certain it is that, at that time at any rate, the Poles feared the Russians just as much as, perhaps even more than, they feared the Germans. After their experience of the Germans during the war it is probable that the contrary is the case today; but if, in July or August 1939, we had told them that, in the likely event of a Nazi attack, we had agreed that Russian armies should be allowed to come into Eastern Poland – at that time largely populated by people of Ruthenian stock – there is little doubt that they would have preferred to do a deal with the Germans themselves. What might have happened then I have no idea; but in any case having given our guarantee to Poland – which presumably covered her Eastern frontiers – it is difficult to see how we could possibly have done something which would have had the effect of nullifying that guarantee straight away. The alternative policy would have been not to guarantee Poland, or Roumania either for that matter, and make an ordinary defensive alliance with the USSR. It is perfectly arguable that this would have been the wiser thing to do, as I have already said when discussing Munich. But if we had, the Nazis might after all have triumphed for the following reason.

If Poland had, in fact, repudiated our guarantee and relied on her existing Treaty of Friendship with Germany, Hitler would have proceeded to make good his whole position in South-East Europe and the Balkans and he could then either have attacked the West and embarked on a holding operation in the East, or attacked the USSR possibly with the help of Poland and Roumania in the knowledge that it would not require much strength to ward off the French and the British. Then after his conquest of Russia, he could no doubt have proposed peace on terms favouring ultimate German hegemony of the Continent. Unless indeed he decided to knock us out first by force of arms which seemed not at all impossible. No hope, in any case, of averting a war by not guaranteeing Poland. The more or less instinctive reaction of the Government, approved by the Foreign Office, was not therefore unpremeditated panic as suggested by some: it was a calculated defiance, and it was probably right.

Nevertheless we should certainly have been more alive to the possibility of a Nazi-Soviet deal than we were. There were plenty of warnings, though, as I say, I doubt whether, even if they had been heeded, we could have done much about averting it. Curiously enough, one of the earliest to suspect that something was up was Neville Henderson. Writing to Cadogan in May, he said, 'I feel intuitively that the Germans are getting at Stalin. Goering said to me the other day, "Germany and Russia will not always be enemies"; *absit omen*, but if Poland does not talk a little less about her bravery, and think a little more about the realities of her geographical position, we may yet live to see a fourth Partition.'

The war was now very close. But at the end of July there were mysterious rumours that the minister in charge of the Department of Overseas Trade (Rob Hudson★) had hinted that His Majesty's Government might, in certain circumstances, be willing to grant Germany a loan of no less than £1,000 million. Tremendous efforts by the Foreign Office to get to the bottom of this extraordinary story were headed off; but documents seized from the Germans have revealed that Horace Wilson had during the summer been secretly negotiating on this point with Wohltat, the German Trade Commissioner. We suspected this, and also believed that Rob Hudson and perhaps another member of the government were in on this negotiation, though we had no evidence. 'The immediate effect of this piece of super-appeasement', I told Cadogan, who was on leave, 'has been to arouse all the suspicions of the Bolsheviks, dishearten the Poles . . . and encourage the Germans into thinking that we are prepared to buy peace . . . I must say I doubt whether folly could be pushed to a further extreme.'

The whole incident shows how policies which might have had some validity in, say, 1937, provided they had formed part of a coherent attitude towards all the dictators and had accompanied some great British rearmament effort, were pursued relentlessly by No. 10 long after it had become evident to all but the blind that Hitler was only interested in force and could only be restrained, if at all, by the creating of a vast anti-Nazi coalition. But the moment for the dissipation of even Mr Chamberlain's illusions was about to arrive. On 1 September, the Nazi armies swarmed over the Polish frontier, and after a few days of dreadful hesitation on the part of the French, some of whom wanted to organize another Munich – as perhaps did Lord Halifax – the Second World War began.

As the reader will have seen, it was, in my view, almost inevitable, given the determination of the Führer and his Nazi intimates to dominate the Continent by force and the desire of the democracies to avoid such domi-

★ Conservative MP; Parliamentary Secretary to Ministries of Labour 1931–5; Pensions 1935–6, Health 1936–7; Minister of Agriculture and Fisheries 1940–5.

nation if they could, by means other than force. It is probable that had they rearmed seriously sooner and played their cards rather better, the democracies might have over-turned Hitler; but they were inhibited from so doing largely by those to whom rearmament was repugnant on moral grounds. Nor was it ever entirely clear how the principle of democracy in Central and Eastern Europe at any rate could be preserved by a coalition of which the totalitarian Russians might well prove to be the dominant partner.

But that the war was useless or, in the circumstances, evitable, as some now pretend, is a dangerous illusion. Had we really lost our nerve in 1939 there is no doubt that Hitler could have smashed us after coping successfully with the Russians, or vice versa, and what would our present generation have been if Britain had become part of a Nazi Empire? With our élite (of all classes) and our Jews in the salt-mines or the gas-ovens, there would not even have remained an intelligent historian to make an apology for Hitler or the *Drittes Reich*. In a sense, it may seem silly, in the age of the Hydrogen Bomb, to stand up for anything; but it is only those who have ceased to believe in themselves who can reproach their fathers for standing up in 1939. It was not we who were then living in a dream-world. The tragedy is that we may have preserved freedom for so many who cannot appreciate it any more.

7

Special Operations
(1939-42)

When the war finally started, all plans for the future, save winning it, naturally lapsed so far as the Foreign Office was concerned. It is true that a number of excellent intellectuals were cooped up in Balliol under Arnold Toynbee and asked to define War Aims; but it was pretty evident that our only hope was to arm as quickly as possible and mobilize the nation for the impending struggle. Besides, there was quite a lot to do. Mussolini had happily declared his neutrality, but there was much diplomatic activity on the Italian front. The new ministries which had been so carefully planned, such as the Ministry of Economic Warfare and the Ministry of Information had to be put into operation. Even greater liaison with the Chiefs of Staff had to be set on foot (it was here that Bill Bentinck made his great reputation as chairman of the Joint Intelligence Sub-Committee of the Chiefs of Staff): SS activities of all kinds were stepped up and the Service was now allowed almost all the money that it asked for. The flood of work directed into the Parliamentary Under-Secretary's room on the first floor (Van still retaining the traditional room immediately below the Secretary of State) therefore increased still further. Besides, the 'phoney war' was not thought to be such at the beginning of its eight months' existence. Everybody assumed that the first action of the Germans would be to bombard London, and the one thing that really was quite ready was the Government's air-raid shelters. There were even vast plans in existence for moving the whole governmental apparatus, if necessary, to the West Midlands. The FO was not under this scheme to be very near the central dug-out. Goodness knows what might have happened if it had ever been put into operation. Probably our whole defensive effort would have collapsed.

As the first scare died away we all became more confident and even the fearful news from Poland was not too discouraging since it had been more or less expected. What was discouraging, and as it turned out significant, was the extreme reluctance of the French to indulge in aggressive activity of any kind in the West so as to take some of the heat off the unfortunate Poles. Maybe logically this would have not had any great effect; but the whole mentality of our major ally was then entirely defensive. There, the prevailing mood seemed to be that if they could only get rather more aeroplanes they could just sit behind their defences and await developments. If the Germans took the offensive they would be repulsed from the Maginot Line or be held up in the Ardennes: if they attacked Russia, well let them. That would only make us all the stronger, for we could become quite impregnable and they would probably only exhaust themselves. Fuming in the Admiralty, Winston concocted an idea for floating masses of mines down the Moselle and the other tributaries of the Rhine which would result in all the bridges being blown up, thus impeding German communications. The suggestion appalled our allies; and I expect it would not have had the effect intended either.

I suppose in any case that until May 1940, we all more or less subscribed to the famous doctrine 'Nous vaincrons parce que nous sommes les plus forts' and went ahead with our well-laid if rather deliberate plans for mobilizing the nation and training and dispatching our divisions to France. In the FO a great deal of our energies went in trying to think out the right propaganda lines for weakening the German war effort – it all sounds a little unrealistic now. I remember having a controversy with Rex Leeper who refused to accept my 'Christian Civilization versus Paganism' line, for, I have no doubt, on re-reading the correspondence, very valid reasons. But in Whitehall, among officials, there had been an increasing feeling that to say the least, all was not well with the direction of the war and that the PM, able and essentially respectable as he was, had really been so wrong about the motives of the Dictators and so keen, even after Munich, on going slow on rearmament, that he was hardly the man best qualified to lead the country in any life and death struggle. True, he had seemed to undergo a change of heart after the Nazi occupation of Prague; but this in itself scarcely qualified him to be the leader of an eager and embattled nation. There was an irreverent limerick going the rounds which ran as follows:

> An elderly Statesman with gout
> When asked what this War was about,
> In a Written Reply
> Said 'My colleagues and I
> Are doing our best to find out.'

The brilliant and emotional Charles Peake, my contemporary at Magdalen, had been transferred from the News Department under Leeper (this combination being known to the journalists as 'Leak and Peeper') to the Ministry of Information. Charles used to feed me with stories about the dreadful insufficiency of Mr Chamberlain, whom he sincerely hated, as a war leader, and how he felt that No. 10 was still a sort of dead hand on all efforts to mobilize the nation for the revolutionary tasks that clearly awaited it. The new ministry was itself involved in hideous rows about who should do what; and since there was nothing for it to celebrate in the way of victories, the officials had a very difficult time. Duff Cooper was a brave man and a real statesman, but he was no administrator; while his Parliamentary Under-Secretary, my old friend Harold Nicolson, brilliant as he was, had little organizational capacity either and was said to spend a great deal of his time coffee-housing and writing his excellent diary. Luckily the Ministry of Economic Warfare, which had a specific job to do, shook down much more easily; but even here lack of hard experience resulted in much too favourable estimates being produced about, e.g. the effect of the blockade on German industrial production; and one constantly had the impression that, in the ministry's view, all we had to do was to sit tight and the Germans would eventually have to surrender because they would have no more oil, or rubber, or tungsten or whatever it was that they were thought to be incapable of producing or replacing locally.

My own chief memory of this gloomy period was the blackout and a general sense of frustration and unreality. In spite of the Ministry of Economic Warfare it was difficult to see how the war could actually be won and many people seemed to feel in their bones that one day we should have to negotiate some sort of peace. This was certainly the view of the pro-Germans who were still quite numerous in London society, even though they could no longer openly express their feelings. Oswald Mosley had, indeed, been 'detained'; but it was not only his Blackshirts who would have welcomed some kind of patched-up truce. And in the background there was always the American Ambassador, Joe Kennedy, that prophet of pure defeatism, who had considerable influence, I regret to say, in certain sections of the Tory Party. Luckily the working class, generally, was not defeatist at all. If the war had not had any spectacular result so far, it had at least solved the problem of unemployment and in any case their instinct told them that it would be slavery if ever the Nazis looked like getting the upper hand. As for myself, from having felt that I was in the middle of things I now felt that I was on the edge of them. Having missed the First World War I was, it seemed, destined to miss the

Second. The younger members of the Service, in so far as they could, were joining up; but I was nearly forty and would never have been allowed to go. It was a gloomy outlook. The way to get out of the Office and into the Army was only discovered later by Fitzroy Maclean. You resigned in order to stand for Parliament at a by-election. But Fitzroy was much younger than I was and therefore had more chance.

It was in Admiral Godfrey's house near Sevenoaks which we had taken for a brief holiday that we heard the news of the Nazi assault on Denmark and Norway. It was totally unexpected by the Admiralty and everybody else, save, no doubt, Liddell-Hart. I rushed back to London. It looked as if the real trial of strength was about to begin. The ease with which Hitler occupied Norway was, however, depressing. Where was the Navy?* And the withdrawal to Narvik seemed to prove that something was wrong with the leadership. I began seeing more of my Labour friends, and notably Hugh Dalton. They had no doubt at all about who was responsible: it was Chamberlain. They were resolved to turn him out if they possibly could and, as everybody knows, with the aid of many Tory rebels, they very shortly did. There followed the unbelievable fall of France and the evacuation from Dunkirk. I remember sitting one moonlit evening on the terrace of the House of Commons with Rab Butler and his admirable wife, Sidney, the daughter of Sam Courtauld, and my wife's dearest friend. Looking over towards Lambeth I muttered something about 'the doomed city', and was rounded on by Sidney for defeatism. I defended myself by saying that I did not think we should be defeated, only that we were in for a hell of a time. I was, indeed, rather frightened, not so much by what might happen to me as by the assumed immense destruction and loss of life from bombing by an enemy in command of all the Western coasts of France.

Then again, a little later, while watching dog-fights over Kent from the garden of Buck De La Warr's house at Withyham the question came up: Would you, if you had a gun, shoot a Nazi pilot in his parachute? Personally, I said, I would. At the time I just felt enraged by the Nazis. What right had they to come and shoot people up? The real reason, no doubt, was fear. When, later still, we were in fact bombed to bits I no longer felt this way about German pilots. But by that time we knew pretty well that we were not going to lose the war. However, I am not really sure that it would, from the point of view of morality, have been worse to have shot a falling Nazi pilot than it would have been to shoot, as Churchill urged, the crew of an invading tank from behind a hedge when they got out to relieve nature. It is all a question of degree.

* I believe the Germans had cracked its cyphers.

War arouses pretty bestial instincts, admittedly. But it certainly brings out the best in people too, certainly in those who feel their cause is a just one. And when you had a clear conscience, in the sense that, whoever was to blame for the Germans behaving as they did and beating everybody up, it was certainly not we, who had over the years bent over backwards to find excuses for them and to allow them to have an outlet for their national energies, you got a situation in which an extraordinary sense of comradeship and unity developed which no one who experienced it will ever forget. Perhaps the same sort of thing happened in Russia where even the horrors of the Communist regime were disregarded following the sudden and treacherous Nazi attack. Reading Pasternak one gets the impression that it did. I do not think that the lazy British – or should I be more accurate if I said the lazy English? – were ever happier, collectively, than in the weeks following Dunkirk, and indeed during the next few years. An exhilaration seized us, just as, I imagine, it did at other moments of our history: we knew what we were fighting for. No doubts any longer about how the war could possibly be won; it just had to be won, and that was that. Churchill, I believe, was really the symbol of this collective instinct. He was perfect in his role: but if he had not been there, or if he had been killed, we would undoubtedly have produced somebody else. It was indeed our finest hour, and I am sorry for the 'brave Crillons'* who were not in England then.

But one 'brave Crillon' had just arrived in the shape of a little-known Brigadier-General called Charles de Gaulle, and I well remember our first meeting. A few days previously he had delivered his famous BBC broadcast ('L'Appel') to the French nation. A slightly alarmed Government insisted that his next major broadcast, to be delivered at 8.30 p.m. on 26 June, should be vetted by the Foreign Office. (We must remember that it was not until 28 June that he was even recognized as the leader of the Free French.) Seven o'clock and still no script. Cadogan went off, leaving me with strict instructions that any text should conform to certain rules, notably as regards references to Marshal Pétain. Shortly after, it arrived. I found it brilliant, but it did violate several of my rules. Hastily making the minimum changes and even so taking a considerable risk, I rushed round to the Rubens Hotel, only to be told that the General had not yet finished his dinner. Just before 8.00 p.m. he emerged, clearly in a bad temper, and gazing down on me said: 'Qui êtes-vous?' I explained that I was a mere subordinate; that Sir Alec Cadogan himself had been eagerly looking

* Henry IV of France said to one of his barons who had missed a battle, 'Hang yourself, brave Crillon!'.

forward to discussing with the General the draft broadcast, but owing to its late arrival it had fallen to me to propose certain '*legères modifications*'. '*Donnez-les moi.*' Awful pause. '*Je les trouve ridicules*', said the General, '*parfaitement ri-di-cules.*' I felt bound to point out that it was now 8.05, that the delay was not my fault and that, not to put too fine a point on it, if he could not accept the 'modifications' he would not be able to broadcast. The ultimatum worked. One of the General's main characteristics was that if there was absolutely nothing to be done about something he did not kick against the pricks. Like the elephant, he advanced in a straight line through the jungle crushing everything that came along until confronted by the baobab tree, when he executed a detour. '*Eh bien*', he said, '*j'accepte. C'est ridicule, mais j'accepte.*'

Could I come with him to hear what I repeated I thought would be a classical utterance? ' *Si vous voulez.*' In the taxi he thawed a little and I had the impression that he was not bearing me a grudge for having stood up to him. No doubt he thought my 'modifications' were puerile. But he did not cheat, and he read them all out as I had drafted them. I shall never forget the back of his head, as, trembling with emotion, and with that wonderful voice, he started off '*Monsieur le Maréchal, par les ondes, au-dessus de la mer, c'est un soldat français qui vous parle.*' Ah! That was magnificent. In all the subsequent rows with the Free French I always did my best to see things from the General's point of view, even when (according to Charles Peake with whom I was living at the time) he was behaving in an utterly unreasonable way. When I became Ambassador to France I sought him out twice, though at that time it was not a very popular thing to do. Nor did I regret this. When he came into power again I even had the impression that I could influence him very occasionally. On reflection, I fear this was an illusion. Anyhow, I have every reason to suppose that he listened to what I had to say, which was flattering to some extent, for I soon discovered that he could not really understand what was said to him unless it was expressed in '*un impeccable français*'. About this great man's influence on events I shall have much to say later.

So, when a little while after the fall of France, the Prime Minister asked the new Minister of Economic Warfare, my old friend Hugh Dalton, to become responsible for the organization on the Continent of all forms of resistance to the enemy – sabotage, subversion and so on – it was with the greatest joy that I received an invitation to be his chief lieutenant in the task of 'setting Europe ablaze', to use the dramatic phrase of the Churchillian mandate. Technically, Van was to be the chief lieutenant, but nobody really expected the Chief Diplomatic Adviser to leave the Foreign Office and to do anything except give advice. I myself, however, was to get a (temporary) double promotion from First Secretary to Assistant Under-Secretary of State and to be installed next door to the Minister in Berkeley Square House disguised as 'Foreign Policy Adviser', the rumour being put about for security purposes that I had been appointed to keep a sharp Foreign Office eye on the doings of the 'Dynamic Doctor'. It was typical of that not very popular character that when he had to go and see the Lord President of the Council (and lately PM), Neville Chamberlain, for the purpose of taking the oath he should have arrived purposely late, exclaiming 'Sorry I'm late, Lord President, have I missed the bus?'*

The immediate job to be done was to rationalize, so far as possible, the organizations already operating in this field. The so-called 'D' Section of the Secret Service under the impressive but rather theatrical and James-Bondish leadership of Colonel Grand, was a problem because it had already made itself pretty unpopular in Whitehall and spent much of its time conducting subversive operations less against the enemy than against a rather similar outfit operating under the War Office known as MI (R). After some hesitation, for he was an able man who inspired loyalty, the decision was taken to replace Lawrence Grand and to form a totally new body under the immediate command of Frank Nelson, a business man and ex-MP in whom Dalton had great confidence. If I can claim credit for anything in this operation it was also on my recommendation that the decision was also taken to terminate the appointment of Guy Burgess. Not that I had any reason to suspect that Burgess was a Communist, still less a Soviet agent, but having met him once or twice I had formed the opinion that he was quite exceptionally dissolute and indiscreet and certainly un-fitted for any kind of confidential work. Other officers were, however, taken on from 'D' and the new set-up gradually emerged. The real motive force in the machine always seemed to me to be Colin Gubbins, a regular Brigadier recruited in the very early days by Dalton and who eventually became a Major-General. But there were many admirable characters in it, too: I perhaps need only mention George Taylor, a highly intelligent and active Australian historian, and Robin Brook, very able Etonian Kings' Scholar, who was for part of the time my own Private Secretary. All are now big noises in the City of London.

Unfortunately the Doctor, though immensely active, did not himself have any great sense of organization. The original idea was that the Special Operations Executive – as the whole new organization was to be called – was to be divided up into SO 1, Subversive Activities (referred to above)

* Chamberlain had said on 5 April that Hitler had 'missed the bus'.

and SO2 which would take charge of all the 'black propaganda' side including leaflets, rumours and secret radio transmitters. There was also to be another section which was to deal with planning and research for both sections. As originally conceived I was therefore going to be, under the Minister, the man in charge of the whole organization; but unfortunately Dalton was persuaded by Vansittart to appoint Rex Leeper – twelve years my senior – to be the Head of SO1 and it was evident that whatever I might do in theory, I should not in practice be able to 'co-ordinate' this senior Foreign Office official who was, incidentally, a personal friend. In any case the consequences of the decision rapidly made themselves felt and it became more and more apparent when the SO1 headquarters moved in November from London to Woburn. As a result largely of physical separation, subversive propaganda was thus conceived of as something apart from subversive action: separate loyalties followed and whereas SO1 tended to regard their colleagues as rather bungling amateur assassins, SO2, equally unjustly, began to think of SO1 as half-baked theorizers who were not to be trusted for reasons of security. All this did not, of course, prevent most excellent work being done by both sides of the house; nor did it even prevent a certain amount of genuine co-operation; but it certainly did prevent the spreading of the concept of 'subversion'; and indeed SO1 rapidly put up their own counter-concept in the shape of 'Political Warfare' – a concept which incidentally I myself always regarded as bogus since it was never clear whether it really included subversive action or was, on the other hand, simply confined to 'propaganda'.

It was true that the minister himself did make an effort to co-ordinate the activities of the disparate groups under his command but he tended to be bored to distraction by debates on propagandology and political warfare and certainly never appreciated the need for theory as a background for action. Ministerial visits to Woburn, numerous none the less, consequently tended to be occupied by rather dreary discussions on personalities and administrative questions generally. The Doctor was never at his best on such occasions, nor did he ever grasp the inherent delicacy of my official (as opposed to my personal) relations with Rex Leeper. His method of approach was to insist that 'machines and hierarchies don't matter: it's the men that count': admirable sentiments in theory but unfortunately burking the real issue. He would also insist that 'you and Rex can work perfectly well together as equals: I will do the co-ordinating'. As I say, he did try. But this did not compensate for a faulty machine.

While there was therefore a perpetual *équivoque* in my relations with the

Director of Subversive Propaganda, another, and subtler discrepancy grew up in my relations with SO2. Before the new machine had got going, and before the conception of one department for conducting all forms of subversive warfare had even been mooted, it was clear that I would have to establish myself in the same building as the Minister. This might have been workable if indeed I had had the originally suggested machine for research and co-ordination at my disposal, but unfortunately I was unable, for various personal reasons, to get this established properly. I was thus left rather 'in the air'. On the one hand I could hardly leave the immediate presence of the Minister, more especially since he was immensely interested in the SO2 side of the work; on the other hand I was getting out of touch with the machine of which I was supposed to be the head, and loyalties, not unnaturally, began to crystallize round Frank Nelson (known as 'CD'). I tried to meet this situation by presiding from the earliest days over a weekly meeting originally known as the 'D' Board. The great criticism of the old 'D' Organization had been that nobody knew what it was up to and that none of those departments which should have been consulted was consulted. The 'D' Board – later the 'SO' Board – was accordingly an attempt to remedy this situation. In addition to myself and Frank Nelson, Philip Broad and a few senior representatives of SO2, we had the liaison officers with the Service Departments, C's representative, Brigadier Brooks representing SO1 and Commander Fletcher, the nominee of Admiral Sir Roger Keyes. I think this body was responsible for removing much suspicion and some of the decisions which it took on particular projects were wise; but eventually it became quite unwieldy and in March 1942 it was dissolved.

In the nature of things there was bound to be some tension between a body like the Special Operations Executive and the Foreign Office but I certainly think that many members of the FO were quite unduly suspicious of SOE. If, looking back, I blame myself for anything during this period it is for not having succeeded in convincing the critics and the inquirers that, intelligently used, SOE had war-winning potentialities, and further that it was even, on occasions, of positive use to our diplomacy, at all events when we and the Americans were stronger. To be candid, I thought it was a weakness of the FO that it tended to be more critical than constructive; and I often wished that those members of the Service who regarded the Special Operations Executive first of all as a joke and then as a menace could have at least tried to understand what SOE was, however inadequately, attempting to do. In my view what was wanted was for disputes to be fought out fairly, and in an atmosphere of mutual confidence, and to avoid suspicion and recriminations based, usually, on inadequate knowledge by both sides of the facts.

There were thus incidents which stand out during this period. Though propaganda generally was the business of the Ministry of Information and black propaganda that of SOI, SOE proper claimed at one point the right to send agents having some right to be propagandists into neutral countries. At least they did not make themselves out to be propagandists but claimed the right, for their own purposes, to, for instance, finance articles in local newspapers. This resulted in one of the most appalling 'demarcation' disputes that I have ever witnessed. The Minister of Information, Brendan Bracken,* demanded the instant recall of two SOE characters from (I think) the Argentine; and the correspondence which had started with 'Dear Brendan' and 'Dear Hugh' and passed to 'Dear Bracken' and 'Dear Dalton', ended up with communications of pure invective between the 'Dear Minister of Information' and his 'Dear Minister of Economic Warfare'. I can't remember exactly how it all ended, but I rather think that Brendan invoked the support of Churchill and won. I must say I rather hope this interchange has been preserved somewhere as it really is a classic example of the 'Whitehall War' consequent on the establishment for war purposes of large and powerful organizations.

It must also be admitted that Dalton was often the reverse of easy. I have already briefly described this rather passionate and at the same time fundamentally sentimental and profoundly patriotic man who had served with distinction on the Italian front in the First World War. He was fairly simple in his reactions, certainly when compared to the ultra-civilized approach of his clever contemporaries at King's College, Cambridge, such as Maynard Keynes, but nevertheless able at mastering a brief, and a more than adequate speaker in the House of Commons. He admired Churchill immensely and his sorrow was that the feeling never seemed to be reciprocated. Some people found him heavy-handed and a bore and it is true that he had a rather elephantine way of endeavouring to ingratiate himself with people. His eye used to roll round in a rather terrifying way. His voice also was always penetrating and even sometimes deafening. Like W.S. Gilbert's King Boria Bungalee Boo, his 'sigh was a hullabaloo; his whisper a horrible yell'. And in moments of stress, more particularly when the war was going badly, I was often the target of his frustrated energy. The whole of Berkeley Square House occasionally shook with roared

* Politician and publisher; close friend of Winston Churchill; became Minister of Information in 1941.

insults, and on emerging into the adjoining room where Hugh Gaitskell,* then his Private Secretary, presided, I sometimes used to find the entourage in a state of genuine alarm. Not that I ever was myself, since I knew 'big' Hugh well and was fond of him. He had immense energy; he was genuinely kind-hearted; he really believed that it was possible to better the lot of the poorer people of the country by controlling the economy rather than by letting it rip; in fact he was in most ways a worthy and even an admirable politician. Unfortunately, not only his voice but his wildly roving eye tended to prejudice people against him. 'You may be right', Frank McDougall once said to me in 1930 after I had been vigorously defending my chief, 'you may well be right. But the trouble about him is his eye. All I can say is that, if he was a horse, I just wouldn't buy him.'

Apart from the appalling hours we kept – I often worked fifteen hours a day for long stretches – we were all, I need hardly say, under a certain strain. The nearest bomb to my house was, it is true, about three hundred yards away but the nearest to the ministry was only about 150 – a small one, thank goodness. This rocked the building and people rushed out into the corridor and when the lights came on again they revealed the fairest of the typists being consoled by the Doctor with considerable expertise, I thought. But the first blitz happily did not go on for too long, and many of us, I think, were able to sleep through most of it all night. It really was odd that the bombardment, which in our pre-war imaginations had seemed to be so dreadful, did not do any very tremendous damage when it actually happened, and in any case resulted in a general increase in 'national morale'. It was the second bombardment of the V1s and the V2s four years later which was more tiresome, because, I suppose, everybody was then much more exhausted and under-nourished.

Other memories of this exciting, but exceptional, period of my career occur to me. There is that of the one real row we had with the FO over some scheme for sabotage in the Balkans in which I maintained that we had authority to go ahead, this being disputed by the office and particularly by Sargent, with whom my relations were for a little while severely strained, though we eventually made it up. The dispute was in the end settled by Lord Halifax himself in a meeting in his own room and I must say I thought I might have quite blotted my copy-book so far as my own Service was concerned, but I was determined to stick up, when I thought they were right, for my war-time associates who, I need hardly say, tended, quite wrongly, to regard the FO as a collection of timorous

* Labour MP; Chancellor of the Exchequer 1950–1; Leader of the Labour Party in 1955; died in 1962 and was succeeded by Harold Wilson.

officials unaware of the supreme necessity of 'getting on with the war'. There were also local rows connected with such things as the installation of our branch in Cairo designed for work in Greece and the Balkans, and there were the perennial difficulties presented by our relations with the Intelligence Service proper, or 'C', whose basic interests naturally lay in keeping things quiet for the collection of intelligence whereas our whole *raison d'être* was to stir things up. Perhaps, knowing 'C' (a fellow Etonian) so well myself I was of some use in smoothing things over.

At this point I would like to draw attention to a curious fact, namely the extent to which the entire Government machine on the foreign side, out-side No. 10, was at the beginning of the war dominated by Old Etonians. Take Foreign Affairs strictly speaking, Eden, Halifax, Cadogan, Vansittart, Neville Henderson (regrettably), Ronnie Campbell, Percy Loraine, Harold Macmillan, Duff Cooper, almost all the tops, had been at Eton. So were the two Ministers successively responsible for SOE, Dalton and Selborne, together with the Heads of the two Secret Services, Stewart Menzies and (after myself) Charlie Hambro. You might well throw in Edward Bridges, the Secretary of the Cabinet, as well. In fact the only really powerful and significant non-Etonian in the whole foreign affairs apparatus was Horace Wilson, and even he was flanked by Alec Home. I do not say that this was necessarily a good thing. I certainly would not pretend that there was a similarity in the process of thought or in the political affiliations of the characters mentioned. But I do think that the fact that they all had the same start did do something to facilitate relationships and thus promote efficiency. Maybe if they had all happened to be at the LSE the effect would have been similar. But just as the *Polytechniciens* in France do some-how seem to form an inner group, or core, of the society, so the Etonians, in 1940, were a kind of inner fraternity. If this were an abuse, and in a certain sense no doubt it was, I have no doubt whatever that it has now been rectified!

Then there were the visits to the various country houses commandeered by the organization and turned by Gubbins into schools for the training of agents of various kinds. Here I had the honour to meet occasionally some of the bravest men and women in Europe whose exploits have been now recorded in various works and in an excellent film called *Green for Danger*. I must say it made one feel very humble to shake the hands of such people who often returned to the Continent when they knew that their *réseau* might be compromised. *'Atqui sciebat quae sibi barbarus tortor pararet.'** And

---

* Horace on Regulus who, keeping to his pledge and went back to Carthage 'Although he well knew what the foreign torturer had in store for him'.

there were visits, too, to the Polish and Czech armed forces, Dalton being particularly attracted by the Poles and, like most of us, having a bad conscience as regards the Czechs. One of my own visits was to the HQ of the Anti-Aircraft Command at Uxbridge with which we wanted to establish contact for the purpose of evading the German flak directed against the Lysander aircraft carrying our agents. The head of the outfit was a great character called General Sir Frederick Pile who in private life was an accomplished rider to hounds, I believe in Ireland. He had a number of his officers to meet us at lunch and I asked whether, as we did, he had any scientists on his staff, and, if so, did he understand what they said and how could he deal with such professional advice? Of course he did, he replied, quite a number. As for knowing how to cope with them, that really was easy: 'I tell 'em by their cry'. Everyone admitted, however, that the Anti-Aircraft Command was a model of efficiency. Perhaps, even in these days of computers, we might do worse than to have a MFH as Prime Minister?

In April 1942 Dalton was made President of the Board of Trade and his successor, Lord Selborne, soon made it clear that he no longer wanted a Foreign Office man as his principal adviser on SOE matters. He would like, he said, to have a business man, and indicated his preference for Charlie Hambro.* Though I had nothing against my old fag-master I was nevertheless furious. Having presided over the formative period, I wanted to see SOE out until the end of the war. Besides Alec Cadogan said he had no job for me at the moment. But there was nothing for it but to go on leave and to write my own report which is still in the FO archives and was, I thought, a pretty good apologia for my own activities.

As a matter of fact I think I was pushed out at the right moment since I just escaped having to take responsibility for what the Germans have called the *Englandspiel* with the SOE in Holland. What happened there was that in their excitement at finally getting out a suitable master agent for the Netherlands, SOE dropped him after his training with the usual instruction that, if by any evil chance he was arrested on arrival by the Germans, he should, when sending back an account of his landing at the dictation of his captors (which was common form) omit a certain group which would indicate that the communication was bogus. He was captured; he did radio his message back; he did omit the group; but the message sounded so genuine that the section of SOE concerned decided to assume that it was an error and thenceforth for months poured arms and agents into Holland all falling into the hands of the Gestapo. Eventually an

* Banker. Head of British Raw Materials Mission to Washington 1944-5.

agent got out via Gibraltar and revealed the appalling situation. But immense damage had been done and some of the Dutch even thought they had been betrayed by the British. No doubt if I had still been functioning I might not have been aware of the decision of the Section, though I think I should have been, or I might, quite possibly have backed the Section up. But I must say I am glad that I did not in fact bear the responsibility.

When I arrived back in London from leave, Alec Cadogan said he still had nothing to offer me, though he thought he was hopeful. He said it might be a good thing to do a spell in the Treasury. I was not attracted by this, and offered to go to Madagascar, which had then just been 'liberated'. This suggestion was firmly rejected and to the Treasury I duly went for a few weeks to work under Sigi Waley. Then I was sent for and told that it had been decided to set up a new department in the Foreign Office called the Economic and Reconstruction Department which would devote itself to all the subjects then looming on the horizon, such as relief after the war, refugees, civil government in 'liberated' countries, armistices and so on.* Once again an entirely new chapter in my already quite varied career had begun. I was, so to speak, back on the rails. They gave me a couple of attics on the top of the aged Foreign Office building; Sammy Hood (Viscount Hood) and Evelyn Baring (now Lord Howick) joined me; and we got down to work.

---

* I was luckier than I knew, for I was afterwards told that the Board had also considered sending me as Counsellor to Buenos Aires!

8

Post-War Planning
(1942-3)

The Economic and Reconstruction Department was not originally supposed to be a sort of 'planning' section, or what is now called, horribly enough, a 'Think Tank'. There were some pressing practical problems, such as relief, wheat supplies, currency questions, colonial options and so on, all affecting foreign policy but not the concern of any particular Foreign Office department, and the Foreign Office high-ups were rather enamoured of the idea that I should concentrate principally on these. I myself was naturally more inclined to let the new department be concerned with 'long-term' political matters and liaison with outside government departments. I thought that 'its essential purpose (should be) to see that the general policy conducted by the Treasury, the Board of Trade, etc. does not conflict with the policy pursued by the Foreign Secretary and, more particularly, to ensure that foreign political considerations are present in the minds of those conducting our economic policy'. In fact it became a machine for thinking out an entire long-term foreign policy.

Nigel Ronald* was the Under-Secretary in charge. He had been at Magdalen and was an old friend of mine, so the going was easy. It did not look to start with as if our activities would greatly bother the Secretary of State, who was spending most of his time coping with high and urgent matters of State, and, incidentally, with a rather wayward Prime Minister. As for Churchill, his interest in foreign affairs was at that time minimal. It was just after the inexplicable surrender of Tobruk, which had followed on the sinking of the *Prince of Wales* and *Repulse* and the fall of Singapore, all of which cast at least some doubt on our fighting reputation. Nor was it at all certain that the Russians would hold the second great Nazi offensive. The ship of State, reeling additionally from the U-boat attacks, was almost on its beam ends. Though our confidence in ultimate victory was still extraordinarily high, it was hardly a time when the Cabinet could

* Assistant Under-Secretary at the Foreign Office 1942. Ambassador to Portugal 1947-54.

think much about the future. Nevertheless from the start this is what the new department had to do.

For a little while, however, we were concerned in the Department with the Cabinet discussions on 'raw materials' and our own discussion with Lord Keynes on the foreign political implications of his 'clearing union' plan. I have a note saying that we inquired of the great man why his plan could not in some way cover relief (to which also our efforts were increasingly directed), receiving the sensible reply that whereas relief could be thought of as a kind of super Red Cross, reconstruction involved the whole future of international exchanges. If his plan was to be a success it ought not in any case to be associated in the public mind with charity on an international scale, but something which was likely to benefit all the powers concerned. The final plan itself, which I circulated in the Office and urged everyone to read, was, of course, after it had been largely emasculated by the American expert Harry White, adopted at Bretton Woods and ended up as the International Monetary Fund.

Maynard was then at the height of his powers and what would have happened if he had lived on into the peace instead of dying in 1946 – exhausted, it was said, by is historic fight with Harry White – is anybody's guess. I shudder to think what might have been the effect if he had written a book on 'The Economic Consequences of San Francisco'! His inherently pro-German and anti-Soviet (though not anti-Russian) tendencies would no doubt have prevailed, the latter strongly encouraged by Lydia Lopokova, the great Russian dancer whom he had married, to all his Bloomsbury friends' great surprise, in 1925. A little later on – in 1944 I think – I remember having a tussle with him on German reparations, I taking the popular, if unintelligent view, that the Germans ought to be made to pay somehow, and he, true to the theory he propounded in 1919, maintaining that they could only pay by delivering goods; that such goods, if accepted by us for no payment, would nevertheless have to be sold on our market; the net result being an inflationary situation at home and no outlet for our own industries in the conquered country. In any case, seeing that Germany would eventually be producing goods in an economy unburdened by arms, it might well be that she would undercut us unless we took suitable counter-measures. For his part he was therefore inclined to favour some annual German subscription to a 'peace-keeping fund'. In point of fact I suppose this would have eventually worked itself out as a German contribution towards the cost of the maintenance of our troops in Germany.

It was, however, chiefly by reason of concentration on 'relief' that the

Department began to find its feet as a formulator of long-term policy. For if this great project then being negotiated on our side in Washington by Sir Frederick Leith-Ross was to be successfully operated it became more and more apparent that it would have, if possible, to be organized by the Allies, more particularly by the major Allies. And if they were to get together for this purpose it would no doubt mean that they would have to get together in all other fields as well. In other words, we soon, and almost unconsciously as it were, came up against the whole problem of the post-war settlement. If, indeed, a certain international set-up was necessary for what afterwards blossomed out as UNRRA (the United Nations Relief and Reconstruction Agency), it was probably also, by analogy, necessary for the negotiations of the Peace Treaties for example, and indeed for the subsequent organization of the world. It was thus obvious that for practical and compelling reasons the Department had to operate on a coherent and generally acceptable political basis of some kind, and there was soon much discussion within the Office as to what this could most suitably be.

As early as July we had had some indication of American thinking on the official level. The United States had only been in the war for six months but already they seemed to have a much more powerful machine than we had for formulating post-war policy. The views of John Foster Dulles were freely quoted but it seemed that already there was a consensus of a sort. This, we understood, contemplated a military occupation of Germany and its possible dismemberment, the Rhineland, the Ruhr and probably Bavaria tending, as separate entities, to associate themselves with the West, and the rest of Germany with some kind of Eastern European Confederation that would look rather towards the Soviet Union. By this means (the record continued)

you might get a situation in which the very *desire* for a powerful Germany would disappear. After all, when Germany is defeated the bulk of the Germans and more particularly of the young Germans, will enter into a period in which they simply cannot achieve what they have been taught to believe, namely the inevitability of a German-controlled Europe. They will therefore tend to catch at any straw which promises them life on reasonably tolerable conditions; if they can be led to suppose, in Western Germany at any rate, that there will be some hope of getting their bread and butter under the aegis of some Western "international authority", then there is some likelihood that they will willingly accept such a system and all that it implies.

I thought that this was very sensible advice and indeed it largely coloured my subsequent thinking. There were other constructive thoughts about a possible world organization.

My first effort at a long-term policy was distributed early in August in the shape of a memorandum entitled 'Relief Machinery, the Political Background'. It was, as I say, considerably influenced by what we believed to be the working of the American official mind. Its general line was that our whole approach should be influenced by political considerations. Should we, in fact, regard the existing tentative scheme for the administration of post-war relief as capable of extension to other spheres, in other words as a prototype of some new and better League of Nations; or should we regard it as a temporary machine designed to cope with certain restricted and technical problems? There was little doubt that the first conception was that favoured by the US administration who seemed to favour a world organization after the war based on the United Nations as a whole and directed by a small 'policy committee' – probably the four Powers only. There might also, it seemed, be regional organizations each led by one Great Power. 'Colonial resources' would be internationalized, and 'technical commissions' could deal on a world-wide scale with communications and transport. The whole rather loose system was clearly designed to be based on immense American sea and air power and (to a secondary degree) on the British Navy and Air Force and on the Russian Army. 'Bases' could be shared, and would serve to represent the power of America in the four continents. By this means there might be constituted a 'concert of the world', which might be expected to keep the peace as it was kept, in Europe, by Britain between the Battle of Waterloo and the beginning of the First World War. In other words we should be approaching the 'American century' or the 'century of the common man' – the terms seemed to be largely identical.

If this should prove to be the American (or New Dealer) Dream, what should be our response? Should we accept it, or try to whittle it down together with the Russians and our European allies, thereby assuring a high measure of autonomy for Western Europe, under our leadership, and for Eastern Europe, under the leadership of Russia? Were we, in any case, to regard the maintenance of the British Empire and Commonwealth as our primary objective? Were we to contemplate the survival of Germany as a Great Power? Were we, finally, bound to restore France and her Empire to the status of a Great Power as well? Whatever the answers to these questions, the four-Power conception, as such, seemed to have much to be said for it, that is, if each Power was regarded as a leader of a certain group of states. Nor would it be inconsistent, however interpreted, with some underlying Anglo-American co-operation. Besides, even if the conception was unacceptable what were the alternatives? They seemed to me to be the following:

(1) A strong and self-sufficient British Empire and Commonwealth capable of pursuing some independent policy of its own. This did not appear to be a tenable thesis. The events of the war had made it inevitable that the Commonwealth should break up as a political entity even if, as we might hope, it retained some value based on mutual goodwill.

(2) An attempt to associate ourselves, if possible in a leading position, with Western Europe and its colonies thus forming some kind of European bloc to act as a counterpoise to America and Russia. There was probably little prospect of achieving this immediately after the war, though certain steps towards it might well be compatible with the 'world system' recommended by the USA. It was just conceivable that some Western European states might agree to our representing them in a World Council.

(3) A revival of the League of Nations, perhaps located in Washington rather than Geneva. This was unlikely, and probably undesirable. The League of Nations might, it is true, have achieved more if the Council had really embraced *all* the Great Powers. If any successor did this it would not be inconsistent with the general 'Four-Power' idea.

Therefore, the best system would probably be one which would give the Americans, the Russians and ourselves all the scope we wanted in our respective spheres. How exactly these spheres would be defined would be a matter for argument in the light of the position existing at the end of the war. What we for our part should seek to avoid above all was a system which would tend to unite the continent of Europe against us. Under German leadership the Continent was no doubt most dangerous; but there was small reason to believe that it could not be united under some other leadership if Germany collapsed. The worst position of all for us would be to face a united Europe without being certain of American support. Consequently our aim should be, if possible with the co-operation of America, to organize some measure of unity in Western Europe, leaving Eastern Europe to be guided either by some association of the West Slavs with Russia in the background, or possibly (if we could not prevent it) by Russia herself. In this way we should avoid the menace of Continental unification, and present ourselves as a real support to Western Europe, rather than appear to them to be ourselves a menace. To this end Germany's frontiers should be 'rearranged' and perhaps the Reich should be dismembered too, a solution which many American planners seemed to favour.* At any rate, the idea that the Rhineland, and possibly the Ruhr and Bavaria, should ultimately join some Western Europe association would not be inconsistent with what we understood to be the American plan for the reorganization of the world.

There were difficulties and dangers. France, for instance, would obviously have to be a member of any world council. But nobody yet knew whether, as de Gaulle asserted, France would be '*présente à la victoire*' or not: and we should just therefore have to wait and see. Accommodating France might well not be all that easy. Then, too, it was impossible to dismiss the possibility that the US might run out of the peace, this resulting either in a revival of a military Germany or in Russia's crossing the Rhine. And when all was said and done, did the general conception make sense? Could the Americans really take the lead? And even if they did, might not the rest of the world regard the system as a sort of anonymous Anglo-Saxon tyranny designed to eliminate all the human individualism still represented by the older civilizations of the world? We should not give the impression that we wanted to transform La Beauce into a sort of Manitoba, and construct another Pittsburgh on the ruins of the Ruhr. Perhaps the best way of avoiding all this would be if Britain could act as a sort of bridge between the civilization of the New World and that of Europe. And my conclusion was that we should willingly accept the underlying conception of the Roosevelt Administration and seek to render it more practicable by an admixture of our own political sense, standing absolutely fast on the Four-Power idea, with possible extension to provide for France. We should also agree to American presidency of any other technical world organization provided a large measure of regional autonomy was accorded.

For a first effort I do not think, in the light of hindsight, that this was too bad. The thoughts of one person are normally better in form, of course, than those of a committee, or those which perforce have to be based on compromises between conflicting points of view; and my own had naturally to run the gauntlet of expert criticism by all the political departments. Some seven years had gone by since the 'band of brothers' had begun exchanging papers on general policy, and now here I was again doing the same thing with another and younger band, though some of the original one had remained. This time it was Frank Roberts who was the

---

* There were divided opinions on this in the Office, and Sargent at one moment declared that he was perfectly certain that Germany would remain a unified state of eighty million! But we all finally agreed that if German separatist tendencies *did* emerge there was no reason why we should discourage them.

chief and also the most constructive critic, though I was to differ with him on the inevitability, and indeed desirability, of early German reunification, even though that country might be temporarily divided. One of my colleagues, Maurice Peterson, thought my views were too theoretical, and even untimely. Another, Christopher Warner, did not altogether share my belief that it would be possible to bring the Russians into the peace settlement, even though we should do our best to try. Neville Butler, head of the American Department,* thought that I originally overestimated American desire to accept widespread obligations after the war. Nor, he believed, would there be a tendency to form the equivalent of an 'American Empire'. This idea was more or less echoed by Ronnie Campbell in Washington, who also introduced the idea that Europe should always be our 'hinterland'. There were other valid criticisms. Dick Law, then Minister of State,† took a keen interest in the whole matter. The essential feature of the scheme, however, which was to survive all subsequent redrafts and modifications, was the desirability of some post-war international organization which would include, and indeed be based on, co-operation between all the Allied Great Powers, or nominally Great Powers. For this reason the proposal came gradually to be known as 'The Four Power Plan'.

During August there was some criticism from higher up in the machine. I see that I said that the *primary* duty of organizing a defence against the German *Drang nach Osten* would presumably, under our plan, rest with the Russians, and in the West, against possible German expansion generally, on ourselves and the French together with the smaller allies, the Americans assisting to the extent to which we could persuade them to go. But even so we would be unlikely to hold down Germany for a very long period unless we could somehow destroy the idea that the Germans, as by far the largest organized nation in Europe, should in the nature of things organize the Continent on their own lines. The least unhopeful way of accomplishing this would be to encourage separatist tendencies and get the Western Germans associated with an Atlantic civilization and the Eastern Germans with some kind of *Mitteleuropa* bloc. Sargent, as I understood it, maintained that Europe must be considered 'as a whole', and therefore favoured an Anglo-French alliance in the West and two large confederations in middle Europe which, rather than Russia herself, would affect a

* A Private Secretary to the Prime Minister 1930–5; Ambassador to Brazil 1947–51; Ambassador to the Netherlands 1952–4.

† Son of the Conservative Prime Minister Andrew Bonar Law; Conservative MP; briefly Minister of Education 1945; subsequently Lord Coleraine.

European balance of power and succeed in keeping a united Germany still under control. Russia should not have any predominating say in these confederations, and in any case no greater influence than we should have.

Personally, I thought this conception was misguided for if we did not propose to split up Germany (and more especially if Austria remained in the Reich) there was really not the faintest hope that the middle Europe confederations could prove any greater barrier to German expansion east-wards than the small states set up under the 1919 settlement. To maintain any balance, indeed, it would, on the assumption that the Reich remained undivided, be necessary for the Russian power to be brought as near to Germany as could be arranged. If, however, Germany were split up there was both more chance that 'confederations' would act as a buffer and that Russia might retire behind her 'glacis', though even in such an event she would insist that the confederations should not have anti-Russian govern-ments. After all, if the war ended with a spreading of Russian armies westward it would be quite possible for Russia to go into a sort of splendid isolation and snap her fingers at the rest of the world. It might equally be possible for her to make an alliance with a defeated Germany, more especially if a unified and potentially strong Germany were left in exist-ence. If on the contrary German unity no longer existed, this would be much more difficult for the Russians to do. Rather later, I argued strongly against the (as it seemed to me) defeatist notion that we should be forced eventually to 'compound' with a united Germany and said that I attached less importance than others to the argument that, if Germany broke up spontaneously or as the result of pressure, the centripetal forces would be so great that we should be placed at an additional disadvantage in our efforts to keep her down. In the event Sargent insisted on my notions being revised so as to assure the continuance of German unity and only to mention the eventual mergers of some Western German states in a Western European bloc as a very dim, and not particularly desirable, possibility.

The final version entitled *The Four Power Plan*, proud product of our collective thought, was a document of some eleven thousand words containing an introduction; a hypothesis, consisting of three major assumptions, a 'Practical Application', a section on 'Doubts', another on 'Possible Alternative Policies', a general conclusion, and a 'Suggested Grand Strategy'. The first assumption was that the three Great Powers would all after the war take account of their world-wide interests and responsibilities and be both able and willing to enter into world-wide commitments in order to prevent any other nation from again troubling the peace. This was followed by a long and frank discussion of whether the UK herself was in fact likely to do anything of the sort. There would be many people who would maintain that it was undesirable, as beyond our powers, and that we ought to 'hand over the torch' to the Americans and the Russians – those over a certain means level tending to favour the first and those under it the second course.

But on the whole it was thought that if we did not 'fulfil our world-wide mission' we would sink to the level of a second-class Power and thus, in the long run, be likely to suffer an agonizing collapse from which we should emerge as a European Soviet state, the penurious outpost of an American pluto-democracy, or a German *Gau*, as forces might dictate. We therefore proceeded to make the assumption for ourselves as, for various reasons, we also did in the case of America and Russia, though with many doubts as regards the latter. China really did not count. We also made a second assumption, namely that the real object of the concert of the Four Powers would be to hold down Germany and Japan for as long a period as possible, for once this objective was abandoned the whole Four-Power conception would clearly lapse. It would be best, if both Germany and Japan would cease to be national entities altogether. But this was impossible in the case of Japan and most unlikely in the case of Germany (the Sargent thesis). The 'Practical Application' dealt largely with the future of France and with the concept of regionalism to which I have already alluded; the 'Doubts' section embodied many of my original ideas; and the 'Possible Alternative Policies' contained a fresh appreciation of, among others, the possibility that the USSR might pursue her own policies on Europe in the Near East without regard to our interests. In that event, we should inevitably be driven into forming some kind of anti-Soviet front, and in doing so we should have eventually to accept the collaboration of Germany – the policy of ostracizing Germany would have to go by the board. It was possible that for a time we should be able to rely on American support, but the US would be equally likely to leave Europe to stew in its own juice and we should have to go to all lengths in our efforts to prevent her from so doing.

The conclusion was simply that the Four-Power idea was the best if we could put it into operation, but that we should not try to do so until and unless the Americans were definitely committed. But the 'Suggested Grand Strategy' had a certain flavour of Niccolo Machiavelli, for which I was no doubt responsible. For the suggestion was that in dealing with the Americans we should, while doing our best to induce them to participate in the scheme, not fail to hint that if they made their terms too stiff, we might be obliged, by the force of things, to make a close working alliance with Soviet Russia; and, when assuring the Russians that we were sincere in asking them to play their full part, and that we had no desire to impose some Anglo-Saxon world hegemony, not hesitate, if they were too grasping, to talk about the necessity of Anglo-American co-operation and the danger that Russia might find herself isolated from the rest of the world. By such means we might achieve 'a real world balance of power'.

Early in October the Secretary of State resolved to consult the Cabinet. There was a procedural difficulty to be overcome in so doing, in that the Paymaster-General (Sir William Jowitt* as he then was) had been made responsible for a committee investigating post-war reconstruction generally and a strict interpretation of his terms of reference (which spoke of the need 'to prepare a scheme for a post-war European and world system . . .') might even be supposed to give him the right to put up papers on post-war political or security matters. The Secretary of State, however, was, happily, very conscious of the need for leaving all such matters within his own sphere and the difficulty – with the additional help of Richard Law – was successfully surmounted. Then it was thought (quite rightly) that the Prime Minister would never even glance at a document of ten thousand words or so, and a short summary was accordingly prepared by me which, shorn of all the closely reasoned argument and colourful phrases, looked to me at any rate, to be quite unconvincing. I must say I doubt whether, what with Monty racing across North Africa and the Russians hanging on at Stalingrad, the Prime Minister found much time to look at that either. The fact was – as we were increasingly to discover – that Churchill was quite allergic to any proposals for post-war action which he had not himself engendered, or at least discussed personally with the President of the United States; and as he was so desperately busy with other matters anyhow it was clearly going to be a difficult matter to get our policy paper through the Cabinet, essential though that was for the purpose of influencing the future action of the American Administration. Though no Cabinet decision was therefore available, the fact that the Cabinet had at least been consulted meant that we were now to come up against tough and intelligent opposition from outside the Foreign Office.

The first to present itself was that of the formidable Leo Amery,†

---

* Attorney-General under Ramsay Macdonald; Paymaster-General 1942; Lord Chancellor 1945–51. Made Earl Jowitt 1951 (d. 1957).

† Statesman and journalist; Conservative MP 1911–45; First Lord of the Admiralty 1922; Colonial Secretary 1924; India Office during the war.

then Colonial Secretary, who argued, with some apparent reason, that there was no 'inherent identity of outlook' between the Four Powers and that alliances did not usually survive the achievements of the objectives for which they were designed. But the essential point of the paper was that *none* of the four Powers should concern itself with 'Europe', which would be left to work out its own destiny and develop what Amery thought was inevitable, namely some sort of European union. Thus, Britain should occupy itself with the British Commonwealth; Soviet Russia would retreat into Asia and America would be chiefly concerned with the American continent (presumably other than Canada) though she might retain a certain interest in the Far East as well. As for Germany, she would apparently be 'contained' by France and some vague Eastern European Confederation.

I denounced this policy in unmeasured terms. Amery was an isolationist – a sort of English Luce. Under his plan, Germany would shortly be in a position to dominate Europe. Perceiving this, the Soviets, unless they were crazy, would by no means 'retreat into Asia'. On the contrary they would advance West and all hope of getting confederations in Europe would vanish into thin air. They would also, if they could, try to establish Communist governments in Western European countries, and seeing that we should take no effective interest in what was happening in Europe, but be spending our time (apparently) knocking Indians on the head, there would be quite a good chance, not of a happy Europe, based on the essential tenets of Western civilization, but of a Sovietized Europe, and of a pretty anti-British one into the bargain.

At this point my indignation seems to have run out. I rather think that the Foreign Secretary was unmoved by the remonstrances of his colleague, for we heard no more from the Colonial Secretary. But soon there was an assault from yet another quarter. On to the scene moved the great Arnold Toynbee,* then head of the Foreign Research and Press Service and shortly to become our Director of Research. Arnold's was a very different approach. He was a great advocate of world government and had Attlee on his side, in principle, to say nothing (at one time) of Stafford Cripps.† I myself had tended to fight shy of his organization which since the beginning of the war had been housed in Balliol College, Oxford, but which was shortly moving up to London. It consisted for the

---

* Historian, renowned for his *A Study of History* (1934); Director of the Research Department at the Foreign Office, 1943–6.

† Economist and Labour MP; succeeded Beaverbrook as Minister of Aircraft Production in November 1942; in 1947 succeeded Dalton as Chancellor of the Exchequer and introduced the austerity policies with which he is always identified. Retired in 1950.

most part of highly intelligent dons, most of whom had had little experience in government, and though they were very useful purveyors of information it did not seem to me that they could really be absorbed into the governmental machine, or that even if they were they would be much good at the tough job of bringing the political departments into line and thus in actually formulating policy.

More especially, I did not believe that someone of our foremost historian's temperament would be very effective in the world of struggling politicians, overworked bureaucrats, and fierce military men whose one idea was to 'get on with the war'. World government was all right as an objective but a belief in it did not, in itself, qualify a man to draw up plans for what should immediately be done in the chaotic situation that would follow the end of hostilities. It seemed to me also – and here I may well have been wrong – that Toynbee's very Christian background might make him too disposed to 'turn the other cheek' to the Germans. He was, too, by nature pacific and non-combative and this side came out at the Peace Conference in 1946 when he tended to see things rather through Russian spectacles.

Still, we did need an intellectual in the new department, more especially one with some knowledge of international organizations; and there was one member of the Research Department who certainly had these qualifications, though I was warned that he was a strong character with whom some people found it difficult to get on. The celebrated Professor Charles Webster, historian, author of classic works on Castlereagh and the Congress of Vienna had, indeed, few inhibitions. From the start he had obviously set his heart on 'penetrating' the Foreign Office, and penetrate it he did, largely by persuading me that he was the right person to take on as Departmental Adviser. In manner rather aggressive, but human and kindly underneath, this tall, Roman-nosed, chinless extrovert, very much a don of pre- First World War vintage (he had been at Liverpool University and King's College, Cambridge), quickly established himself as a pundit in the Economic and Reconstruction Department. His great advantage was an encyclopaedic knowledge not only of what had gone on at the Paris Peace Conference, to say nothing, of course, at the Congress of Vienna, but of the Covenant of the League of Nations as well. Besides he got on with me because, fundamentally, he was a 'Great Power' man.

But the 'Prof', as we called him, was only to join us in the spring, and I shall have more to say about his influence later. In the meantime the 'Four Power Plan' had to survive another and perhaps a more dangerous assault, this time from Stafford Cripps. Cripp's views, though greatly preferable to those of Leo Amery, were, I thought, a little naïve, and perhaps from someone with a rather doctrinaire approach that was only to be expected. His suggestions consisted of a number of *obiter dicta*, the greater part in harmony with the provisions of the Four Power Plan, but others which departed from it considerably. Nor was there any reference to France, to the necessity of some special arrangement for Italy, to the Anglo-Soviet treaty, to the Middle East, to the possibility of Britain's taking the lead in Western Europe, to the desirability of the Great Powers being represented on *all* regional commissions, and so on. There was, however, a proposal for a 'Council of Europe' on which incidentally we and also the Americans would be represented, and this Council would nevertheless itself be represented on a 'Council of the World', along with the Great Powers. There was even a proposal for a 'Council of Asia' in which the lead would be taken by China. How exactly any of these bodies might be expected to function was not made clear, nor even what they would be supposed to do. Some of this did not seem to make much sense; nor would it apparently be easily harmonized with American policy, in so far as we were aware of it. Nevertheless Sir Stafford's views were reported to be not very dissimilar to those of the Prime Minister. The situation consequently was grave. Luckily there came to our assistance a providential man.

The minister's private secretary, who functioned more like a *Chef de Cabinet* in the continental sense, was, in fact, a youngish Welsh socialist called David Owen. He was the only man, I concluded, who could possibly bring Sir Stafford back on to the rails; and so we had a series of long conversations during which I think he himself became more or less converted to our general point of view. One of the difficulties was that Cripps had only been allowed to see the 'short' version of the Four Power Plan and had therefore necessarily remained in ignorance of all the supporting arguments. During my talks with Owen he at one time proposed a new 'tabloid' paper consisting of a series of short points, but eventually this was discarded, since I resolutely maintained that if it were to be approved, it would certainly have to be put up by the Foreign Secretary. The latter then had a word himself with his colleagues, after which we heard no more. It seemed that once Cripps had actually read the longer paper himself he was much more amenable and even confessed that he would never have put forward all his 'points' had he done so.

One final obstacle – a sort of Beecher's Brook – had to be overcome before our policy was more or less adopted. I have already said that the Prime Minister had probably not even read the shorter paper. Nevertheless we were dumbfounded when at the end of February we learnt that he had, at Adana, of all places, in a document called 'Morning Thoughts', confided his own innermost views about a post-war settlement to the Turks! Furthermore they seemed to differ, in most material respects, from the FO policy paper. In commenting rather bitterly on this development I let it be known that 'the only hopeful feature was that where the PM's proposals were vague they were, like the Atlantic Charter, capable of being adapted to almost any scheme for a world system that might eventually be approved by the Cabinet, and where they were specific were so impracticable as hardly to merit serious consideration. A point which I thought was particularly dangerous was the apparent association of the idea of 'unconditional surrender' with an immediate peace conference. If there really was to be an unconditional surrender – and incidentally no surrender could be completely unconditional because some sort of terms would, after all, be imposed – then it would be the business of the victor governments to see that the terms were carried out, and indeed there might well be for some time no German government with which to sign a treaty. Then Russia was singled out as a state particularly in need of relief, something which would hardly be encouraging for the Poles and our other European allies, who were all lumped together – along with Germany – in the phrase 'ruined and starving Europe'. But my chief criticism lay in the Prime Minister's proposals for Europe. As a part of his plan – i.e. a world organization for the preservation of peace which the Prime Minister said he had already agreed upon with President Roosevelt – an 'instrument of European government' was to be established which would 'embody the spirit, but not be subject to the weakness of the former League of Nations'. What could this possibly mean?

To my mind practically nothing. We had already had many discussions with Stafford Cripps on the subject of a unification of Europe. Having apparently convinced the Minister of Aircraft Production of the folly of his original view, it was rather disheartening to see this hoary old hare being let loose over Anatolia by Winston Churchill. Further, it seemed that the units forming this body would be 'the great nations of Europe and Asia Minor as long established'. Was it therefore contemplated that Great Britain and the USSR would both form part of the instrument of European government? Were we really going to have a Turk sitting in the headquarters of the 'instrument', which would no doubt be in Berlin, seeing that the instrument could hardly function without the participation of some German government? It was true that the Prime Minister's conception might not be terribly dangerous because it was obviously impracticable, except possibly in the form of some 'Armistice and Reconstruction

Commission' on the lines of the suggestion recently made by the Foreign Secretary. But that was not all. The Prime Minister had also told the Turks that he favoured forming the smaller European states into 'confederations', specifically a Scandinavian, a Danubian and a Balkan bloc. There were as we knew enormous difficulties in the way of such formation, the least impracticable being, perhaps, the last; but now that the Prime Minister had admitted Turkey into Europe were we to suppose that its eastern limits would be in the neighbourhood of Mosul and Erivan? Even more horrifying, however, was the suggestion that a 'similar instrument with different membership would be formed in the Far East'. Could this be our old friend the 'Council of Asia', presided over by China? Perhaps my feelings were too violent. But I thought I might at least recall a well-known passage in one of the Prime Minister's own works, where he observed that the man who could win a war was practically never the man who was capable of producing a satisfactory peace.

My explosion got no further than Cadogan, who told me that, though I might well be right, it was really much too violent. He did not think the Prime Minister's indiscretion would really do much harm. And so it proved. The main lines of the Four Power Plan, or rather the Five Power Plan, with its attendent recommendation for some kind of regional organization in Western Europe in which we should, if possible, take the lead, was in fact gradually adopted as the basis for all forward thinking on both sides of the Atlantic as we shall see in the next chapter. Perhaps I can best wind up this one by quoting from a letter about my paper which Nigel Ronald received from Lionel Robbins* just after I had fired off my broadside against our national hero. 'As a piece of drafts-manship', said the Professor, 'it reminded me of the great state papers of pre-1914; and with the main and concluding theme that, whatever the details of this final settlement, its general shape can only be satisfactory if we play an initiating and mediating role, I would not be more in agreement.' Having paid this high tribute Robbins proceeded to make some comments which I must say, as editor of the document, were among the most intelligent and far-sighted that I ever received.

In the first place he much doubted whether any economic arrangement covering totalitarian Russia would ever be possible; and if co-operation with the Soviet Union had to be limited to security, the resulting balance might be very precarious. In the second place he did not believe that the 'peoples of Europe' would in the long run be 'content with a subordinate

* Professor of Economics at London University 1929–64; Chairman of the Committee on Higher Education 1961–4. Professor of Economics 1961–4; now Lord Robbins.

role'. Europe really could not become a sort of Latin America. Thus we should not concentrate only on trying to be one of the Big Four but rather build up something in Western Europe. What was said about this in the paper should be expanded. Could we not even think of 'opening the Commonwealth' to the Scandinavian states, the Low Countries and even France? 'How immensely more solid would be the prospects of peace; how immensely more powerful should we be at the meetings of the four Great Powers.' If indeed there was to be regionalism surely Europe should be a region – i.e. a consolidation of 'the western fringe' of Europe with its empires. In the third place, why *not* break up the Reich? Otherwise the continuance of a solid bloc of seventy to eighty million Germans would make the whole situation unstable. If we were to insist on Austria's being detached, why not other portions too? The British had been misled by text-books which had taught them to believe that the unification of Germany by Bismarck was intrinsically good in itself. Economic *Zersplitterung* would admittedly be disastrous. But if the various German states were to be part of a wider economic system under the rules of which members were precluded from policies of economic nationalism, the economic argument against division would vanish altogether. The erection of such a system would surely be desirable in itself, and how much easier to admit the Germans to it if they came in as a group of states and not as one possibly dominating body. It only remains to say that on this document the equally patriotic and European, but occasionally despairing and cynical Sargent had scribbled, 'Mr Robbins is an Imperialist. The British proletariat is not. It is interested in the Beveridge Report, not in international planning. We must fashion our foreign policy accordingly.' One might, I suppose, now say much the same thing about the price of butter. But I would not myself, however, accept the dictum. There is more sense in the British 'proletariat' than we planners sometimes think. However we were shortly to advance from theory to practice.

9

Preparing for Peace
(1943-4)

In March 1943, the Secretary of State wisely decided to get in touch himself with the Americans. The three advisers he took with him, namely Oliver Harvey, his then Private Secretary, the indispensable William Strang, and myself had never been to America before. The idea was to sound out the President and the Administration and to lay the basis for talks about the future which, as a result of Stalingrad and El Alamein, now seemed far more alluring. To assist the Foreign Secretary, the Prime Minister had made available the personal aeroplane, which he had just discarded for a better one, namely a converted Liberator bomber, under the command of Churchill's favourite American pilot, Captain Van der Noot. We took off from Prestwick into the night, bound, at the first hop, for Gander, Newfoundland. There was only one berth, occupied by the Secretary of State. The remainder of us sat around swathed in scarves and overcoats. Two hours out, the heating system failed. Luckily for us, Captain Van der Noot, it seemed, like the Russians, never flew much above three thousand feet. It was another thirteen hours before we touched down in Gander. It appeared that the head wind was stronger than appreciated and we had arrived with practically no petrol in the tank. A RAF crew took over after Washington.

Halifax, exiled from London, presided over the Embassy with great distinction. After an uncertain start, during which his uneaten hot-dog had been photographed under the bench at a Chicago baseball game, and after subsequently surviving some rather unfortunate publicity about his fox-hunting activities in Virginia, he had begun to establish himself as a popular figure, greatly aided by the devoted Charles Peake, whose loyalty to a fellow Anglo-Catholic had overcome any reluctance to serve under a statesman whose desire to appease the Nazis had originally not fallen far short of that of Chamberlain. The Ambassador was also lucky in having acquired the services of the brilliant and then not generally known

Isaiah Berlin.* At first destined for the Soviet Union, Isaiah, a Fellow of All Souls who spoke perfect Russian, eventually found himself in Washington where during 1942 he had already acquired an extraordinary knowledge of the local scene. Not unnaturally he was often of great use in compiling speeches. Assisted by John Foster, Isaiah assembled almost all the known political intelligence and served it up in highly readable reports which, I trust, will shortly be published. On the occasion of the Secretary of State's visit he was called upon to prepare the first draft of Eden's major speech in Maryland – a highly important and successful occasion. It will be remembered that this was the first occasion on which the Foreign Secretary had made any real contact with the American Administration and notably with the President, so he was very much on his mettle.

Meanwhile Strang and I had been having most interesting conversations with the lesser fry, namely Norman Davis, James Dunn and Ray Atherton. Davis did most of the talking. On armaments and disarmament he confessed that the administration was in two minds. The President was now 'not sure' that his famous scheme of denying arms to the minor allies – and indeed, originally, to France – would be practicable. It had been pointed out to him, for instance, that if only the Big Powers were armed – and heavily armed – the smaller powers would reap undue economic advantages. In these circumstances the Americans were toying with the idea of an international police force. He himself agreed that France should be strong so that she could participate. As for disarmament that would indeed be difficult. How would the Allies be able to insist on the necessary inspection?

The Americans seemed to have strong views about Germany. The President, we were told, definitely favoured dismemberment, as did some other high-ups. But Cordell Hull was 'undecided' and the Chiefs of Staff were 'by no means convinced'. Nor apparently, was Davis, Separatist tendencies might be encouraged if they really emerged, but enforced dismemberment might simply encourage centripetal tendencies. In general, the Germans might perhaps be encouraged to look towards 'some rather loosely unified confederation'. As for occupation, he himself favoured three separate zones, but General Strong was in favour of 'mixing up' all the occupying forces – all the Allies occupying 'strategic points' all over Germany. Three zones, General Strong thought, would 'not promote harmony among the Big Three'. It will be observed how sensible and forward-looking Davis was. What would have happened if the US military had really had their way about 'mixing up' is an unpleasant

---

* Distinguished academic; war service at HM Embassy in Washington 1942–5; President of Wolfson College, Oxford since 1966; received the Order of Merit 1971.

thought. We might have had local Communist authorities established in the Rhineland or the Ruhr. Thank God for Norman Davis! He was equally sensible on post-war collaboration with the Russians. The general assumption, he thought, was that we should continue to be friends. Personally, he doubted this but he quite agreed that the greatest possible efforts should be made to bring Russia into the settlement and to work out schemes with her beforehand. He himself appeared to think that Russia would be determined to build a large navy. Maybe they had not as yet made up their minds about their policy. But there was no doubt that, if they wanted to, 'they could play old Harry with their Communist propaganda'.

At the request of Dunn, I raised my own King Charles's Head on which I had been working for some months, namely a 'United Nations Commission for Armistice and Post-Armistice Problems' in Europe, which later, much modified, was to blossom out at the end of the year as the European Advisory Commission in Lancaster House, on which William Strang was the British representative and Winant the American one, the Russian being the extremely dull and obdurate F. T. Gusev. Davis reacted quite favourably to this project, particularly when he grasped that it would consist of civilians rather than soldiers. He said there was a view in Washington 'that the military should be responsible for the occupation and administration of enemy territories' and I replied that this was not at all our view, explaining the relationship, as we saw it, between the Commander-in-Chief and the Armistice Commission and between both and 'any UN body that might be established'. (It will be observed that we had even by then got into the habit of referring to the post-war authority as the United Nations, presumably because Roosevelt had used this term when he tried to rally the Allied Governments in Washington earlier in the year.) It was agreed that this project should be studied further and so it was, constantly, and we will discuss its activities later. All our talk, said Davis, finally, was unofficial and subject to the views of the President who, however, when he saw the Foreign Secretary, was likely to be 'cautious' as he had just received a rocket from the Dutch Foreign Minister, Elcho van Kleffens, about 'Four-Power Dictation'. This proved to be the case. The President, as Eden describes in his book,* raised the disarmament of the Allies point, but did not press it; clearly favoured dismemberment of Germany in principle; was optimistic about Poland in spite of being rather nervous about Soviet intentions; suggested creating a new state called 'Wallonia', out of bits of France, Belgium and Alsace Lorraine, and, in

* *The Reckoning* (London 1965), pp. 372–3.

general, radiated a kind of jauntiness on these great matters which Eden found a little distressing.

After this excursion I was more and more concerned with the whole problem of suitable inter-allied machinery for planning the peace. There was excellent planning for war. The combined Chiefs-of-Staff in Washington, inspired from time to time by joint decisions of the President and the Prime Minister, was an admirable and increasingly efficient instrument: the 'Combined Boards' were working well to achieve the maximum effort on the economic front; even 'relief and rehabilitation' was now taking concrete organizational form; but nothing similar existed for deciding what we were jointly going to do when victory was achieved. We might, indeed, have a glorious military victory and then promptly lose the peace, which was even more important than military victory. We had, it is true, made quite a good beginning since the formation of the E. and R. Department with organizing our own post-war planning machine; but this was only half the battle. Early in May I submitted my views on the main principles which should govern an approach to 'armistices and related problems', one of these principles now being the constitution of a 'United Nations Commission for Europe', the steering committee of which would consist of the three Great Powers plus, no doubt, France. The functions of this body would be to supervise the activities of all the various armistice or control commissions; to cope with civil wars etc. and to co-ordinate the activities of the various international organizations (UNRRA, Transport, etc) on the Continent of Europe. I had also roped in the 'FORD' (Foreign Office Research Department) who were regularly producing good background and information papers. Finally, by late June we arrived at a revised 'United Nations Plan', re-christened 'Suggestions for a Peace Settlement' which again (on 7 July) became 'The United Nations Plan for Organizing Peace' and was, I believe, circulated in the Cabinet. This was, basically, the old Four-Power Plan but it had been much improved as a result of consultation with Professor Webster (still in FORD) and it also took account of the well-known though seldom formulated views of the great man in No. 10 with which, as the reader has seen, I had already had occasion to differ.

Such, then, was the state of play on the home front when, in the middle of July, I suggested that it was essential for someone, and preferably myself, to go to Washington to make contact with the American planners. I pointed out that for the last few months we had been wrestling with problems connected with the Italian armistice and that many quite grave misunderstandings and difficulties could have been avoided if only the one machine had had some previous knowledge of what the other was intending. It was really useless to rely on the PM only for occasional co-ordination: American and British simply must get together and create a joint machine not dissimilar, in essence, to that of the combined Chiefs-of-Staff. Only so could we get our own views, whatever they might be, across and if we did not we should, by the force of events, have to accept whatever the American planners – predominantly military at that stage – might see fit to elaborate. At first my suggestion was firmly turned down and I vigorously protested. It was not surprising, I reflected, that the Americans had misconceived our Italian plans and that our representatives could not argue back. We had now fired a little broadside at a range of three thousand miles and were expecting our negotiators to carry on with that. If it were ineffective it was apparently suggested that only the personal intervention of the Prime Minister could advance matters at all. In other words we got into a jam largely because of failure to exchange views at the planning stage, and then we invoked a *deus ex machina*.

In the middle of August I was however suddenly authorized to go to Washington accompanied by two members of the Chiefs-of-Staff organization. I was also provided with a pretty restrictive 'directive'. But I knew that once in Washington I would be able at least to discuss certain views of my own. So we set off in an ancient bomber to America via Reykjavik and Labrador, and after a week in Washington I joined our delegation to the Conference of Quebec, coming up by the Canadian Pacific Railway from Montreal, my first experience incidentally of the great roomy trans-Atlantic railways. It was indeed a profitable visit, and I also enjoyed myself hugely in the exciting and unrationed surroundings of the American capital. Norman Davis was just as helpful as he had been in March, and I also had talks with Ray Atherton, General Strong, Leo Pasvolsky, Dean Acheson and Adolf Berle. Dean Acheson was at that time engaged on economic work only and was in a state of considerable depression and indecision, partly as a result of the numerous questions that had been advanced by the smaller nations. I urged him not to lose heart and told him that in my personal opinion the smaller allies would not push some of their objections to the extreme limit and that they would be likely to accept the present plans for relief if certain of their objections to the power of the central committees could be met.

It was at this point that I made friends with Jimmy Dunn, then Cordell Hull's favourite official in the State Department and we subsequently saw eye to eye on most outstanding problems. The chief points raised in the talks were the possibility of negotiating some 'four-Power declaration' which would, as I myself had for long maintained, facilitate all kinds of detailed planning by providing it with the necessary political background. But first there should be some Anglo-American talks which would lead up to four-Power discussions. Certainly the Americans, whatever their suspicions of the Russians, would wish by every means to associate them with Anglo-American plans, and would even go so far as to agree to the subsequent discussions taking place in Moscow.

The other great point under discussion was the general nature of a European settlement and here I see that I thought I had at least succeeded in disabusing the Americans of the false impression which they had gained of our action on communicating to them the document entitled 'Principles governing the terms of surrender of the Axis Powers in Europe'. They had thought that this was a manoeuvre designed to put off decisions regarding the 'world council' and to revert to the idea of the establishment of a 'Council of Europe', in advance of any world machinery. Davis was so good as to say that my remarks in this connection by themselves justified my visit to Washington. I suppose that in the talks on this subject I was more or less consciously arguing against the views of my own PM, but I was nevertheless justified in so doing, at any rate in my own estimation, by the knowledge that the Four-Power Plan in its latest form had, after all, not been repudiated by the Cabinet, and that in any case there was no other Cabinet paper which had been approved on the subject of the post-war settlement.

Back in England I was quickly drawn in to further discussions at a high level on the development of the 'United Nations Plan for Organizing Peace'. Conscious of the fact that this plan was most unpopular in the highest circles, it was, I said, my duty, as a good civil servant, to put up an alternative plan which, from various indications which had reached me, might be more in accordance with our policy. Seeing that, as I understood it, no plan should be more than two pages of typescript in length, the thought might be held to be a trifle compressed, but otherwise it seemed to have many virtues. The document, not unnaturally, was entitled 'Early Morning Thoughts'. It was, of course, circulated, as a joke, to a few personal friends only.

The chief recommendations were that the objective of our post-war policy should be the merging, or fusion, of the USA, Great Britain and the British Commonwealth and Empire; the restoration of 'the ancient glories of Europe'; and the construction of 'a really workable *Cordon Sanitaire* extending from the North Cape, southwards and eastwards, to

Mukden'. The great thing would be to preserve indefinitely the combined Chiefs-of-Staff organization in Washington and to run the whole vast 'Free World' in the interests of Anglo-America. The 'ancient glories of Europe' could be preserved by a Council of Europe which could be a sort of dependency of the combined Chiefs-of-Staff: Europe should thus be divided up into exactly equal 'confederations'; basic English should be the language of the whole Anglo-American area; the *Cordon Sanitaire* would be equipped with huge armaments supplied to the 'free' border states concerned; the economy of the area should be managed by the 'Combined Boards' in Washington, and more to this effect. There would, of course, also be a Council of Asia (with basic Pidgin as its language) and a Council of the Americas (employing basic American). If the Russians did not agree to all this they would be boycotted by the combined Chiefs-of-Staff.

I must confess that this exasperated vision of a Churchillian future came rather nearer to the reality of 1948 than the Anglo-American plans of 1943. Bill Bentinck indeed said, only half-jokingly, that it was much the best post-war plan that he had so far seen, and far superior to the Four-Power Plan. Even though an extreme parody, it was certainly nearer to what were understood to be Churchill's views than those of the Foreign Office. In particular it brought out what I myself had always felt to be the paradoxical nature of the Prime Minister's feeling for 'Europe'. But sub-consciously, perhaps, it was the expression of a fear that what did happen might happen. The Cold War, the grim confrontation of the two Super-Powers, the domination of the world by two different ideologies, that was what we wanted, in the Four-Power Plan, to avoid. Nobody can say we did not try.

In August there was a significant development, though we did not altogether realize its importance at the time. Until then the huge, but most efficient Chiefs-of-Staff organization had had a small body called the 'Military Sub-Committee', which was entrusted with such forward military planning as was possible. With this body I had had some contact, chiefly in connection with the Italian armistice terms and it became more and more clear that the Reconstruction Department of the FO should get together with the military and do some real thinking about coming events connected with the eventual collapse of the enemy powers. After a good deal of departmental jostling, settled eventually by that splendid fixer, Edward Bridges,* it was agreed to set up a new sub-committee of the

* Civil servant; secretary to the cabinet, 1938–46. Permanent Secretary to HM Treasury 1945–56.

Chiefs of Staff entitled 'Post-Hostilities Planning Sub-Committee', and, even greater wonder, I was asked to preside. There was indeed a precedent for an FO chairman of a Service body, for since 1940, Bill Bentinck had been chairman of the JIC or Joint Intelligence Sub-Committee, and this, as I have already said, was a great success. But the idea astonished the Americans who were accustomed to their Military's insistence on running every aspect of the war, and who had the greatest difficulty in achieving any unity of view between their COS machine and the State Department. Besides there was much greater inter-Service rivalry in Washington than there was in London. In particular the idea that a civilian should actually preside over a number of distinguished men in uniform never failed to give rise to incredulous American comment, as being almost contrary to nature.

The first task that the new committee had to face was the completion of a suitable armistice for Italy; and here it must be admitted that it rather fell down since the admirable and all-embracing document (produced chiefly by the 'Military Sub-Committee' of the COS with which the Reconstruction Department had up till then been co-operating) designed to provide for the unconditional surrender of an enemy was not, in the event, wholly suitable for imposition on what quickly turned out to be a co-belligerent. Still, it was of considerable use, if only as a sort of curtain-raiser to Germany, and on my return from Quebec it was to this that I had to bend my mind. Of course the papers we produced were not normally my own work, though sometimes I did do some drafting and redrafting. We had an excellent staff recruited from the three Services and divided up into four sections – 'Control', 'Armaments', 'Strategic' and 'Research' – and the committee itself was composed of officers of the rank of Rear-Admiral or the equivalent, all of them highly intelligent, opinionated and self-confident men.* All our papers were, therefore, pretty well prepared and even so they had to run the gauntlet of the FO departments concerned before being finally approved and dished up to the Vice-Chiefs of Staff who normally sanctioned them without difficulty, though there was one great exception which I shall mention later. Indeed, quite a few emerged almost unscathed, as Government policy. Of course some of them had already been cleared with the Americans at our own comparatively lowly 'planning' level. But it soon became evident that something 'cleared' at such a level and in such a way by two powerful bureaucracies was pretty difficult for the powers-that-be to change.

On Germany, for instance, it so happened that the Post-Hostilities

* Rear-Admiral Bellairs, Major-General Grove White and Air Vice-Marshal Longmore.

Planning Sub-Committee, which had only had the vaguest of directives*
was the first to come out with the idea of three more or less equal 'zones'.
The idea was – though I have only my recollection and that of my
Number Two in the Economic and Reconstruction Department, Jack
Ward, on which to depend as I have not been able to consult any of the
PHP papers themselves for the publication of which we shall have to wait
until 1973/4 – that since it was entirely doubtful whether we should ever
reach the Rhine before the Russians, we might as well propose an equal
division of the country (apart from East Prussia) among the three victor
powers. This would also be in accord with our general philosophy,
namely that the great thing was to preserve a Great Power coalition and
avoid the fell possibility of a Third World War. And since the East was
less populated, and indeed rather less industrialized than the West, it
would be right and proper for the Russians to have rather more territory
than the British or the Americans.

This being so it was logical that Berlin, while remaining the capital,
should fall into the Eastern Zone and that the two Western Powers should
have access to it, concerning which at that time it was assumed that there
would be no difficulty. What became the frontier between two rival
power blocs was thus drawn from the Baltic to the Bohemian frontier
with strict regard for parity and indeed for administrative convenience –
as few *Kreise* or *Bezirke* as possible being cut in half. Nor was it, of course,
then imagined that it was likely to endure for more than a shortish period
of direct military rule, the central power being naturally exercised from
Berlin. I also seem to remember that we proposed the occupation of
Austria by the Americans only – a suggestion which was soon rejected by
the Russians who naturally favoured a three-Power occupation for that
country too.

It is rather extraordinary that the proposal for zones in Germany, so far
as I remember, was never seriously challenged by anybody, the only real
change being suggested by the Americans who would have preferred to
have the northern Zone rather than the southern one. (This dispute dragged
on for a long time and was eventually settled by the PM.) It is again an
instance of how proposals made at a pretty 'low' level can, even if unconsciously, affect the course of history. So far as I remember, the project

* (a) To prepare drafts of armistices.
  (b) To submit plans for their enforcement.
  (c) To consider post-war strategy problems and ensure their examination.
  (d) To reply to inquiries on military matters for other departments.
  (e) To advise ministerial committees on reconstruction problems on any military
      questions.

was duly referred first to the Ministerial Committee and after the latter's approval to The European Advisory Commission – which, after a year's campaign on my part, had been established as a result of the Moscow Conference of Foreign Ministers in October 1943 – and accepted without question not only by the Americans but also by the difficult and suspicious Russians. As a matter of fact I believed that, much later still, the PM maintained that he had never approved the project thought I have no doubt a copy went to No. 10 and it is indeed possible that Churchill would not have approved it if he had had time to devote thought to all the implications, though what alternative he could himself have expected to get through the machine at that stage is rather difficult to see. What could have been done would have been to change it after Yalta – but more about that when we come to it.

At this point I might say that, looking back, it was undoubtedly the success of the Moscow Conference of October 1943, when Eden and the devoted Strang really got down to work with the Russians and brought them out of their shell, that led to real progress being made in post-war planning. It is true that this was the right moment for any real development since, for the first time perhaps, the Russians were confident of ultimate victory but still only with the help of their powerful allies. When the victory became to all intents and purposes certain, they were more difficult to deal with. When it was achieved, they were, as we all know, impossible. It was after Stalingrad and before D-Day that they were 'at their best'.

Before leaving the PHP sub-Committee, which became fully alive after Moscow, I find that we put up the first plans for the terms of surrender of Germany, involving the idea of three periods – simple military occupation, a 'middle period' involving a control commission, and the eventual settlement with the Germans taking over the administration. All this involved a vast and complicated argument not only with everybody concerned in Whitehall but also with the Americans, who at one stage, I find I noted, seemed to prefer a kind of 'Super AMGOT' (Allied Military Government in Occupied Territory) for a long period of time. But it was not only on Germany that we laboured. Much thought was given to 'post-war military security', the whole conception of an international police force was eventually rejected, as involving a world state, which the Moscow Conference had explicitly rejected, preferring 'the sovereign independence of states large and small'. More hopefully, a 'Military Staff Committee attached to the world council' was discussed at length and all its implications fully explored.

So far as Germany was concerned we contemplated, of course, a joint occupation followed by a peace treaty after which the country would settle down and all Allied forces be withdrawn. Within this framework, 'dismemberment' was naturally a possibility, and here, as we have seen, opinions were much divided, though I see that I noted that the alleged recent decision of ministers in favour of dismemberment had been received in certain quarters in the Service Departments with a 'whoop of joy'. A little later, trying to re-arrange my own ideas, I find that as it seemed to me (a) 'hot' dismemberment, i.e. dismemberment immediately after the collapse of Germany was probably out, because there would not have been the time to organize or impose it; (b) the long-term argument against it always was that it would increase 'centripetal' tendencies; but (c) the Russians would probably be quite prepared to keep their forces in their zone for a very long period and it was therefore quite possible that an initial division might become permanent in the sense that they would simply not allow their zone to join up with the West; and (d) such permanent division would mean that Western Germany would turn more and more towards the Anglo-Saxon powers and Eastern Germany towards the Soviet Union, this resulting in increasing friction between the three Powers. The balance of advantage no doubt, therefore, lay in maintaining a unified Germany if we could, more especially since the idea of actually bringing the Western Germans into a Western bloc, from the economic, to say nothing of the military, point of view might well be impossible for obvious reasons for a good many years, owing to opposition on the part of those Western European states which had recently been overrun by Germany. Thus the best bet would still seem to be to do our best to get something like the United Nations Commission for Europe going. The Americans, in any case, kept telling us that nothing would induce them to keep any sizeable force in Germany for more than a very short period: and, after all, the Russians had withdrawn to Russia after the defeat of Napoleon. Why should they not do the same thing again?

So it was on the question of the 'control' of Germany (or the Germanies) after the period of occupation that we spent a good deal of our time. What would happen if Germany rearmed or became once more aggressive? Should there be, in default of a 'United Nations force', some arrangement under the UN for the three Great Powers to take action in the shape of a joint re-occupation? Or might it – as rather favoured by the Air Ministry – be possible to keep Germany in order by the threat of air action, in other words, of bombing? Eventually this suggestion was ruled out of court by the thought that public opinion would never allow such a threat to be made. On the whole the consensus was that only genuine three-Power co-operation could ever 'keep Germany down' and that if such co-operation was impossible the chances were that the Reich would inevitably rise again by playing off one of her existing adversaries against the other. And again, in such dread circumstances, there was little hope that any 'world organization' would ever work satisfactorily or result in the preservation of world peace.

It all seemed to point to the necessity, if this were humanly possible, of preserving the war-time alliance and making it the basis of the post-war settlement. And here, of course, we worked in with the general concept of the United Nations plan. It is not perhaps surprising that our paper on 'The Military Aspect of any Post-War Security Organization' went through fifteen drafts and took five months to complete. But eventually it did constitute the British contribution to the enforcement section of the document that was to end up as the Charter of the United Nations, and I suppose that if the UN had ever worked as it was meant to work the world would have been grateful for the indefatigable labours of the PHP Sub-Committee. As things turned out the whole exercise was probably a waste of time.

This was the general mood of official thought at the end of 1943, and it was certainly dominant at the time of the Conference of Tehran. I believe I was invited to form part of the British delegation to that conference in case anything should crop up with regard to zones or to the (still very vague) conception of post-war security; but nothing did, and I therefore spent much time in the house which I had occupied sixteen years previously as a junior secretary. Tehran had not changed much during those years. The great *chenars* dominated the compound; the hideous 1880 Government of India 'Residence' had not been enlarged. The little *jubes*, or rivulets ran down the side of the Lalezar. The bazaar was much the same. The 'Oriental Secretary', more especially after the removal of Reza Shah, was still a power in the land. One disastrous episode. On my arrival at the airport I found myself greeted in rapid Persian by an enthusiastic Dabir-i-Moayyad, my old Persian teacher, in his familiar brown *abba* or ceremonial gown. To my infinite embarrassment I could hardly understand a single word.

I can in no way, therefore, add to the general knowledge of what passed at this celebrated conference. I did witness the ceremony at which Mr Churchill handed over the Sword of Stalingrad to Marshal Stalin, who passed it on to Marshal Voroshilov, who then let it fall out of its scabbard – a bad omen as many of us thought. I do remember thinking that Stalin, who looked rather absurd in his brand-new uniform and gold-braided hat, was nevertheless an impressive figure, and from what I was able to hear of the actual discussions it seemed pretty clear that he was very often able to impose his will. I remember also a Persian lunch party for the Chiefs-of-Staff which, at my instigation, was given by the Oriental Secretary, Alan Trott. The menu was to include such dishes as *fisinjan* (pigeon breasts cooked in pomegranate juice with nuts and rice), *gaz*, or Persian nougat, special kebabs, the whole served with Persian bread, which looks like brown paper, and washed down with various delicious sherbets and, of course, vodka at the beginning and end. The reaction was surprising. The Airman thought it all marvellous and asked for second helpings. The Soldier thought it was interesting, if not entirely acceptable. The Sailor thought it was really rather terrible and did not like it at all. So fortified, I eventually arrived back in London after an appalling air journey in a Dakota from Cairo to Algiers where I remained for a few days surveying the new field of activity of General de Gaulle.

In London I found myself increasingly drawn in to the work of the tripartite European Advisory Commission which had at that time really got going and the labours of which have been well described by Lord Strang. In May 1944 the Post-Hostilities Planning Committee was re-organized and given new terms of reference which, however, did not affect its operations materially. The substantive change was the departure of the three original Service members and their replacement by officers of rather junior rank, but perhaps more in the confidence of their respective machines. This was no doubt in its way a recognition of the increasing importance of the committee which continued its work on the post-war set-up in Germany and the strategical problems likely to be posed as soon as hostilities ceased, notably the extent to which British interests might be directly menaced by the Soviet Union, the likely arms requirements of our minor allies, the future of the Italian and, indeed, of the French Empires, the extent to which Britain ought to be involved in the Levant, and indeed in the occupation of Eastern European states including Greece, the possible new frontiers of Poland and of Italy, and a host of other questions. But as the year wore on I myself became more directly preoccupied with the overriding question of a possible 'world organization', and towards the end of 1944, I seem to remember that I rather faded out of this strictly strategical picture.

As has already been said, my own ideas about 'Europe' began to take shape late in 1942 and early 1943 and had chiefly taken the form of some body, to be constituted as soon as hostilities ceased, of which the kernel would be the three victor Powers, plus France, as soon as this became practical politics, and with which would be associated, in varying degrees, the lesser European allies. The function of this body, which would take its decisions by the unanimous vote of the major participants, would be to cope with the innumerable problems arising at the end of the war, with the general object of facilitating a return to normal conditions in all the countries west of the Curzon Line, thus preparing the way for an eventual withdrawal of the forces of occupation from the whole area. In particular, it would deal with such matters as boundary disputes, the distribution of relief, the repatriation of refugees, the organization of transport and communications, and so on. Its terms of reference should relate entirely to the European continent and should have nothing to do with, for example, the relations of certain of its members with their empires or overseas territories. In a general way it should be subordinate to any world council that might eventually be formed. Unless, I thought, we were to contemplate the signature by the USSR of a separate armistice and the creation of a situation in which Russia would organize a separate system of her own in Eastern Europe, these principles were a pre-requisite for any concerted effort to cope with the chaotic situation which would follow the collapse of the Axis Powers in Europe.

At the Moscow Conference of October 1944, the United Nations Commission for Europe which seemed to make a certain appeal to the Russians, was not adopted, and was in a sense supplanted by the European Advisory Commission to which allusion has already been made. But the function of the EAC was to get inter-allied agreement on measures to be taken to wind up hostilities, and on the machinery to be installed for this purpose and for the immediate control of the defeated powers; it did not regard itself as a body which could direct the affairs of the Continent for a considerable period of time. The problem of what to do about 'Europe' therefore remained and was the subject of much speculation both inside and outside the Government machine. In April 1944, I therefore considered – for my own satisfaction chiefly – the possible formation of a Western 'bloc'. The problem seemed to me to decide how our whole European policy should be fitted into our policy towards the rest of the world – no less a thing than that. Up to date we had had no very positive policy. We favoured, in a general way, 'confederations', in Eastern Europe. In addition the PM had proposed a 'Council of Europe'; but it was not yet very clear what exactly he wanted. The Secretary of State for his part favoured, in principle, a 'United Nations Commission for Europe' (UNCE). This last suggestion had not been followed up. On Germany, we had no settled policy. On the other hand, the whole recent trend of Russian policy had been towards building up what in effect might prove to be a 'sphere of influence' in Eastern Europe.* The Russians might even be aiming at securing a 'special position' in Italy and France as well. So, even if we could not suggest 'a similar system' in Western Europe, it would surely be highly dangerous to do nothing at all. What should consequently be our objectives?

As I then saw it, we should aim at some defensive system both in the East and in the West of Europe. We should also try to avoid any situation in which Germany might be used by the Soviet Union for her own purposes with a consequent tipping to our disadvantage of the Balance of Power. We had originally hoped that this might be achieved by co-operation among the Big Three; by friendly relations between ourselves and the nations of Western Europe (more especially France); and of the creation of confederations in the East which would not be under any special Russian influence. But clearly the Russians would not stand for this. In these circumstances dismemberment had been suggested. But here opinions were divided. There were therefore various *possible* policies.

We could (a) accept what seemed to be the Prime Ministerial thesis and plump for a 'Council of Europe' with its concomitant of a break-up of Germany and the creation of rather artificial European confederations. But if we did this we would be certain to come up against Soviet opposition and would be by no means certain of American support. Or (b) we could base everything on a possible union between Britain and France, as proposed in June 1940. But, apart from its practicability, this now seemed to run counter to the PM's present thinking. Indeed he now seemed to favour a common citizenship between Britain and America rather than between Britain and France. Besides it would be difficult to sell this idea to the Russians. Or (c) we could change our position altogether and work for some Western European association of nations in which we could both participate and take the lead, with the ultimate thought of embodying in it all Germany west of the Elbe. But this would naturally mean abandoning all interest in Eastern Europe. Alternatively (d) we could encourage a customs union between France and the Low Countries. But it did not seem likely that we could ourselves enter into this because it would almost certainly have to end up in a political union and how could we square this with the continued existence of the British Commonwealth? Finally, (e) we could revert to the general idea of a United Nations commission for

* See Note at the end of the chapter.

Europe constructed under the umbrella, as it were, of a world system. This would imply one defensive system in the East and one in the West, the whole coordinated by the Great Powers.

On the whole it looked as if (e) was the best bet even though it might well mean cutting Europe in half and thus to some extent be indistinguishable from (c). It was undeniable, too, that the UNCE might be difficult to work in practice and it would certainly give the Soviet Government a handle for advancing their own interests in Eastern Europe. On the other hand we should hardly be able to prevent them from doing this if they really wanted to. But as against this UNCE would have the advantage that the Russians would hardly have the suspicion that the system was aimed against them, and the states of Western Europe might well believe that it was desirable in the interests of their security against Germany and also (conceivably) against the Soviet Union. It could moreover work whether Germany was officially dismembered or not, though if she were the chances of friction with the USSR would no doubt be greater. The Anglo-Soviet treaty would in any case remain in operation; but the Soviet Union could no more object to some alliance between Western European states than we could object to similar alliances with the Eastern ones. Nor could the USA, though we might legitimately hope for some kind of 'Atlantic' security system involving bases in Iceland, the Azores and French West Africa. But in general we could hardly decide on our European policy until we knew whether the Russians were coming into a world organization or not, and we should certainly do our best to persuade them to do so.

A little later, brooding on the same theme, I recollected that, as it seemed to me then, what should if possible be avoided was a division of Europe into British and Russian spheres of interest (it was then assumed that America would quickly withdraw her armies), both sides trying to enlist the favour of Germany. This was the chief reason for trying to achieve some European organization 'responsible for the security and welfare of Europe as a whole', which would itself come under the world organization. The European organization should, of course, comprise the USA but it was arguable that any tendencies towards American isolation might best be countered by the emergence of the UK, in association with the Dominions and certain other states (I was thinking of Western Europe) as a completely equal partner and on all grounds capable, with the USSR and the USA, of filling the political vacuum created by the at least temporary disappearance of Germany as a Power. But no such defensive organization would be conceivable without France. A weak, disorganized, and still more, of course, a hostile France, would be a disaster of the first order. If France came in, however, the organization should include the Low Countries, Scandinavia (even Sweden perhaps) and, if possible, Portugal and Spain. There might be British fighter bombers in the Low Countries, Dutch long-range bomber squadrons in the UK. Arms and equipment for the whole group should be uniform (no doubt largely British but also American) and produced as far as possible in the area covered by the group. There would in addition be a strategic necessity to push our defence zone as far East on the Continent as possible. Empires should, however, be individually defended. And, finally, the whole set-up should not be an exclusive sphere of interest directed against another bloc. On the contrary, all such defensive organizations should be integrated in the world organization.

I think, in the light of hindsight, that this was not a bad basis for a policy, and I must say that I never departed from it seriously in my own thinking. It makes it fairly clear, in any case, why I opposed so strongly the PM's 'European' counter-thesis, and I find that in May, this continued to fill me with alarm, more especially since by then there had appeared on the scene a paper by Count Coudenhove-Kalergi*, which seemed to be approved in principle by Churchill. The Count's scheme was for a 'European Council, members of which would be elected for terms of four years by the House of Congress meeting as a single association'. At least three of its members must be citizens of states with populations of more than twenty millions. (There was thus no guarantee that Britain could be represented in it.) The whole would constitute the 'United States of Europe'.

It was accordingly by no means certain that the intention was that Britain should form part of the USE, though in the PM's thought the latter would arise naturally out of the 'European Regional Council', to which the UK certainly would belong. If, however, Britain was to join the USE it was pretty clear that the USSR would claim membership too, in which case the proposed new body would extend from Limerick to Vladivostok and the whole of the Count's elaborate plan would go by the board. Indeed, under this conception the USA would no doubt have to be a member too, and 'Europe' would accordingly be virtually indistinguishable from the world organization. The short point, I remember noting, was that both Count Coudenhove-Kalergi's and the PM's plans were completely haywire. If the PM really wanted to achieve and perpetuate some Anglo-American-Soviet alliance, the only way was to work towards a

* Founder of the Paneuropean Movement.

world organization on the basis of the five memoranda which had by that time been prepared by the Department.

The argument persisted, but we soon learnt that the PM had withdrawn his paper in the face of objections by the Dominions to his (originally, I think, Stafford Cripps's) idea of a 'Council of Asia' and a Council of the Americas' (including Canada). He remained, however, wedded to his 'Council of Europe', and even, it was thought, to the 'United States of Europe' as well. In an effort to persuade him to change his mind, anyhow to the extent of accepting the 'United Nations Commission for Europe' as an immediate solution of the European problem, I noted that it was, of course, evident that if, in spite of our efforts, the worst happened and our relations with the USSR deteriorated (which would involve the disappearance of any effective world council or of any European association on which the Soviets were represented) we should at least have some line of defence in Western Europe on which to fall back and should not be confronted either by a Sovietized Europe or by a Europe dominated by Germany. As I saw it, the great dangers in the creation of a 'European state' (without Britain) were (a) the fact that the USSR would regard this as a threat to its interests and (b) there would be grave danger of the 'state' being dominated by Germany in the long run. The result would therefore be that the Russians would break away from the Three-Power Alliance and organize Eastern Europe entirely on their own lines. On the other hand, by pursuing the three mutually consistent policies of 'World Organization', UNCE and Western European Defence, we might be able to achieve our final objective, namely, the maintenance of the existing alliance, the long-term control of Germany, and the restoration of permanently peaceful conditions on the Continent.

The battle continued for a time and Field-Marshal Smuts entered the lists on the side of Lord Layton* and the PM, suggesting the formation of a European state in which neither the UK nor the USSR would participate. But there were signs that the PM was no longer pressing his own solution very strongly. After all, D-Day was fast approaching. Later on he expressed himself in public on lines which in no way clashed with the original FO paper, and I thought that there was perhaps no longer any urgent need to make reference to his plan as a kind of alternative policy in the 'Covering Memorandum' which was to act as an introduction to our five memoranda on the 'world organization'. In the meantime what

* Economist. Head of Joint War Production Staff, 1942–3; Vice-President of Consultative Assembly of Council of Europe, 1949–57. Deputy Leader of Liberal Party (in Lords), 1952–5.

seemed important was that the PHP committee should urgently investigate the idea of Western European Defence: and this I believe they did, though I have no record of the result. When the PHP papers are published this one should make interesting reading.

The 'five memoranda' were, naturally, blessed by ministers – in the first instance by the 'APW Committee' (Armistice and Post-War Committee) and in the final submission to them of the various papers I had nevertheless inserted the paragraph previously left blank on the proposed United Nations Commission for Europe which was drafted for the sole purpose of getting the PM to agree to the paper as a whole. But the PM now seemed to be disinteresting himself from the future of the world. It would have been preferable, had we known this, not to have put in the new paragraph at all; but it might be that it was harmless. The whole point of the UNCE was that it came into the category of measures necessary for winding up the war and *not* into the category of measures necessary to maintain the peace. My own view was that some kind of projection of the European Advisory Commission (which is all that UNCE would be) would be inevitable, and indeed it might, apart from its immediate and practical importance tend to reinforce the Anglo-Soviet alliance as a kind of bridge between Eastern and Western Europe. (It will be observed that in order to get my scheme accepted I had rather changed my ground as regards its basic objective.)

The stage was now set for the all-important talks between the three Great Powers (and China) on the world organization; but before finally getting our 'memoranda' through the Cabinet and its various committees and then sending them to the Americans and the Russians, we had to cope with a virtual revolt on the part of the British Chiefs of Staff. This started on 9 February when they refused to approve a paper, prepared in the PHP Sub-Committee, on the problem of organizing 'security' under any world organization that might be established. In particular they disagreed with the suggestion that there might be a 'Military Staff Committee' consisting of the military representatives of the Great Powers which would be responsible, in the last resort, for enforcing the decisions of the world organization. They regarded this idea as moonshine. It was inconceivable in their view that the Russians would be associated with themselves and the American Chiefs of Staff in the way suggested. China, in any case, was a joke. The only possible solution was to perpetuate the combined COS into the period of the peace – as the PM had more or less suggested. If the 'world council' had occasional need of forces it would meet and the members would be accompanied by their own military advisers. There was hence no need for any standing military organization. In practice any 'incident' which occurred in the Soviet sphere would be dealt with by the Soviets and in the rest of the world it would be dealt with by the combined COS.

I argued before the great men that, however this might be, we as a government had declared that we were in favour of establishing at the earliest practicable date a general international organization for the maintenance of international peace and *security*, and we had also agreed to discuss a security system with the Americans and the Russians. We could hardly fail therefore at least to put up some scheme of a genuinely international character. Unless, of course, we abandoned the 'four-Power thesis' altogether. It was pretty clear, however, that the COS *did* reject the 'Four-Power thesis'. What was to be done? It was then that the brilliant and imaginative Portal declared after the argument had gone on for three-quarters of an hour that the whole question – which might even be more important than the war itself – ought not really to be referred to the harassed chiefs themselves. The sensible thing to do, he said, would be to appoint the COS successors then and there and tell them to go on winning the peace while he and his colleagues went on winning the war! The chiefs were anyhow asked to put their objections in writing and eventually a formula was agreed under which it was made clear that the decisions of the Military Staff Committee would in practice have to be taken with the consent of all those concerned. For it could not be seriously imagined that the Brigade of Guards would be ordered to engage in hostilities by a Russian GOC against the will of the British Government of the UK.

Nor could it be denied that the COS were right to express the doubts and apprehensions that they did. And, as things turned out, it was obvious that we were at once too optimistic and too theoretical in our approach to the 'security' angle of any world organization. Yet the necessity of at least considering some scheme for an international force capable of preserving peace remained, since if there were to be a 'world organization' at all – and all the governments were determined that there should be one – then it should be able to take enforcement decisions, and if it did take such decisions it must, presumably, possess some means of putting them into practical effect. Besides the whole policy of resisting the Russians as far as possible – even, if necessary, with German support – was not at that time one which could conceivably have been adopted by any British Government which wanted to remain in power. Some might believe that it was realistic. Others (such as I myself) would admit that it was an attitude which we might well have to adopt if things went wrong; but practically nobody formally suggested that we should adopt it as the basis for our planning. If we had done so we could not have agreed to take part in any discussions on a possible world organization. Besides, if the Americans had adopted it there would have been some risk of a separate Russo-German peace.

So we proceeded with our own projects for a world organization, and eventually they were all cleared through the necessary governmental committees. Then (on 22 July) we got the American counter-plan, and after a little delay (on 12 August) the Russian. There were, indeed, considerable differences between the three contributions. The American was perhaps more legalistic than the others; the Russian was much shorter and less complicated and, naturally, more 'Great Power' in tendency; but all concurred in the need for having a council of the Great Powers plus some other states, together with an assembly representing all members. The Russians, it is true, wanted the world organization to deal only with 'security': they thought economic and social matters should be conducted entirely separately. It was evident, too, that they favoured a system under which all the major powers would, in effect, have a right of veto on any decisions of the world council. And finally their original demand was that *all* the constituent republics of the Soviet Union should be represented in the assembly.

We thus return to the famous Four-Power Plan which, when we left it, had become the United Nations Plan for Organizing Peace. One of the developments early in 1944 had been the emergence of a powerful and competent 'planning' body in the USA. Pasvolsky appeared to be on the up grade, but there had also been an increase in the influence and importance of Dunn. This planning body was still not linked to the military machine – as ours so happily was – but it was large and impressive and seemingly capable, as indeed was our own, of coping with the individualistic, not to say wayward approach to post-war problems of the great men who respectively presided over the two national administrations. Soon their attitudes became very relevant because it was increasingly evident that, if progress were to be made, it could only be as the result of long technical discussions between those on both sides of the Atlantic who had made a serious study of the very complicated issues presented by any international 'security' organization and who had had at least some experience of the League of Nations. In the Foreign Office, too, it was felt very strongly that great efforts should additionally be made to bring the Russians into such discussions as soon as we possibly could, which was very shortly.

NOTE

Though I have undertaken not to quote from official documents belonging to the 'closed' period, I think I can legitimately reproduce the reflection of mine dated 1 December 1943, which was only written for my own edification and not placed on the file:

It is quite true that the Yugoslav partisans are Communists . . . and the argument usually is that by encouraging the partisans we should in the long run be handing over the Balkans to Russia. I am by no means clear myself that this would necessarily be so. Has there been any real study . . . of the partisan leaders' political background? If there are old 'international brigadiers' among them it is quite possible . . . that they may not altogether welcome the latest manifestations of Russian Communism with its strong national leanings. Is it not therefore conceivable that if Tito eventually emerges as the most powerful partisan in the Balkans he might be able to establish a communist, but not necessarily pro-Russian South-Slav federation?

10

The Great Conferences
(1944-5)

This, then, was the background against which, at the beginning of August 1944, we assembled at Dumbarton Oaks, the Georgetown home of Mr and Mrs Tasker Bliss, specially lent for the occasion. On arrival we found that the American group was to be led by Edward Stettinius, the new Under-Secretary of State. Ed was a successful and very good-looking grey-haired East-Coast businessman, the epitome of enthusiasm, honesty and drive. Unfortunately he was both naïve and inadequately informed. However, he had some first-class brains around him, the most powerful of which was perhaps that of the celebrated Alger Hiss, who was designated as our secretary. But it could hardly be said that Leo Pasvolsky and some of his colleagues were, in their respective ways, anything save experts of the first order either. The Russian delegation was headed by the redoubtable Andrei Gromyko, then, as now, a quarter of a century later, imperturbable, sardonic, scrupulous, humourless and formidably exact. Perhaps not entirely humourless. There is one story which reflects to his credit. Years later, when the first 'flying saucers' appeared over America, Gromyko, when asked what his theory was, replied 'Some people say that these objects do not exist and that their apparent existence is due to the altogether excessive consumption of Scotch Whisky in the United States. But I say this is not so. The objects are real and are the result of the activities of a Soviet discus-throwing champion in Eastern Siberia who is quite unconscious of his strength.' However we never got as far as this with Gromyko in the course of our discussion at Dumbarton Oaks. He was accompanied by the excellent Arkadi Sobolev, a young, bear-like and most pleasant Leningrader then at the beginning of his subsequently brilliant career.

Before settling down to what promised to be a difficult and immensely complicated negotiation, Stettinius had the idea that the three delegations ought to get to know each other better. He therefore suggested that they should all get together at the Waldorf Astoria Hotel in New York and spend an agreeable evening talking together informally and seeing some spectacular New York evening show. This was not a very alluring prospect for the puritan Gromyko, who excused himself, but the rest of us accepted with alacrity. After an excellent dinner we found ourselves in the Radio City Music Hall contemplating the final disciplined paroxysm of those celebrated chorus ladies, the Rockettes, each one selected not only for her extreme beauty and dancing capacity but also for her intelligence and charm.

After the performance Ed consequently led us behind the scenes and we were at once surrounded by these dazzling beauties wearing, I need hardly say, scarcely anything at all. Undismayed, our leader made a graceful little speech in which he said that our meeting with them was an occasion which they would always remember since here, girls, were distinguished men from all over the world who had come to agree on and to set up a world organization on which the whole future of young Americans would henceforward depend. It was a great thing that America should have been chosen as the place for these talks. And now, Alec, he concluded, you say a few words. Our reserved, not to say shy, senior diplomat did his best but his words hardly aroused much enthusiasm.

Ed then urged the acting head of the Soviet delegation, a tough-looking youngish General, to say a piece. The effect was electrical, and the interpreter had difficulty in conveying the sense of the ensuing flood of words. Broadly speaking, we understood that the General for the last three years had had a frightful, but exciting time; fighting his way back from the Volga to the Don, from the Don to the Dnieper, from the Dnieper to the Pripet Marshes, successfully ensnaring and slaughtering the treacherous Nazi invader who would shortly be evicted altogether from the sacred Russian homeland. Sleeping in the woods, wading through the rivers, rallying the partisans, bivouacking constantly in snow and mud, he had, we gathered, hardly had the time to change his uniform since Stalingrad. And now, what had happened to him? He found himself in the middle of a collection of the most beautiful and amiable girls in the world. It seemed like paradise. As an ideal, it represented everything that he had been fighting for. This was indeed true democracy. The ladies appreciated this very much, as indeed did we all. What happened subsequently to the gallant General I do not know. But it is hardly necessary to read *The First Circle* by Solzhenitzyn to be pretty certain of our friend's no doubt horrid fate.

After this the conference got down to work in a businesslike way.

There were to be plenary meetings at which all the delegations would be present, but the real work was to be done by a small 'Steering Committee' consisting of Stettinius (as permanent president) assisted by Dunn and (usually) Pasvolsky, Gromyko and Sobolev plus an interpreter and Cadogan and myself, the secretary being Alger Hiss. Decisions of principle of this body would then be referred to a 'Formulation Committee' which would put them into words and also try to hammer out compromises if necessary. On this I was the British representative, assisted by Webster and on military matters by Capel-Dunn; Dunn and Pasvolsky represented America; and Sobolev plus another member of the Russian delegation the USSR. The lawyers were to form a 'Drafting Committee' which would pull together the whole resulting text. It will be seen that the so-called 'Formulation Committee' was what would normally be thought of as the Drafting Committee. This was the result of Pasvolsky's suspicion of lawyers, partly due, I think, to his belief that they would be more likely to contest his own proposals than civil servants or politicians. Anyway, the great Will Malkin was largely side-tracked and this was unfortunate as his was probably the best brain among all those present and he was an acknowledged expert on the League of Nations too. What is certain is that the major decisions were all taken in the Steering Committee, and the highly important donkey-work was done in the Formulation Committee where the discussions on an expert level were pretty high powered, all those present being confident of their own ability to influence their chiefs.

Looking back, I do think it was rather extraordinary that we got agreement in such a relatively short time on matters of the greatest importance such as the machinery for the peaceful settlement of disputes and for possible enforcement action; the composition and the role of the Security Council and the General Assembly; the creation of an Economic and Social Council; the powers of the Secretary-General; the role of the Military Staff Committee; the principle of regionalism; matters affecting the internal jurisdiction of states; and even the question of human rights and fundamental freedoms. Bit by bit the brackets round disputed passages were removed and eventually only two remained – the crucial voting issue and the demand of the Russians for the representation in the General Assembly of at any rate some of the Soviet Republics. A unique feature of this conference was that it was the only one in which the Russians took part with hardly any apparent *arrières pensées* and with an obviously sincere will to reach agreement.

It is true that the Cabinet at home became a little restive, in spite of the elaborate reports that were telegraphed home. Not unnaturally they had the impression that matters of great moment were being decided without their being in possession of all the arguments and facts. But we could only say that everything was being agreed *ad referendum*, and in any case we had not departed in any very material way from our original instructions. On one occasion I was informed on the telephone by Jack Ward, who had been left in charge of the Department, that there really had been a ministerial protest, but after a long talk at cross-purposes it emerged that this was due to a phrase in one of our reports referring to 'international enforcement action' having been deciphered as 'international avoidance of action'. It only proved the impossibility of conducting such negotiations at long range.

When it was all over it was seen that we had got agreement on all essentials with the one really important exception of exactly how the Security Council should take its decisions on matters affecting peace and security. Even here we had agreed that it should do so by a majority of seven out of eleven including the votes of the permanent members. What was not agreed was whether – as the Russians insisted – a permanent member should be allowed to exercise its vote even when it was itself a party to a dispute. There was also some doubt as to what was implied by the word 'decisions'. The Russians seemed to argue that unanimity among the permanent members (the 'Veto') should apply even to procedural matters, thus making even the discussion of a dispute dependent on the approval of all the Great Powers.

During the later stages of the discussions with the Soviet delegation, as the result of a long talk with Cadogan, I had been authorized to put to Pasvolsky that one possible compromise would be to get the Russians to agree not only to there being no 'Veto', not only in procedural matters, but also on decisions taken under the chapter dealing with pacific settlement, it being however retained in the chapter dealing with enforcement action. And indeed that might not be a great concession on our part since if it really came to the point of considering enforcement action against a permanent member it would be obvious that the whole machinery had broken down and would have to be abandoned. After my return to London I wrote to Dunn and said that I personally was more and more attracted by the idea. Evidently it took root since towards the end of the year it had become the official proposal of President Roosevelt for ending the deadlock and was finally accepted by HMG at the end of January 1945. Meanwhile I had (at the end of November) also been at work on Sobolev during a tête-à-tête lunch with him at the Soviet Embassy and seemed then to get him to admit that the proposed Veto even on discussion was a non-starter always supposing we wanted to have a world organization at all.

Looking back it occurs to me that this talk may have been of a certain importance in helping the Soviet Government to make up its mind to accept the voting compromise. Sobolev had started off by asking what was the general feeling in British governmental circles about it? I said that opinions were divided, ranging between those who believed in the early creation of something not far off a world state, and who thus strongly favoured a completely Veto-less organization, to hard-boiled advocates of a simple Great Power alliance. In any case HMG had not as yet made up their mind and I just did not know which way the decision would go. On Sobolev observing that all the Soviet Government wanted was that all 'decisions' of the Security Council should be taken with the unanimous consent of the permanent members, I said that it all depended on what was meant by 'decisions'. One thing HMG would certainly insist upon – and I thought the Americans too – would be that *discussion* of any issue should in no way be prevented. Sobolev replied that he did not believe his government intended any such thing: *action* against any permanent member was what they feared. If that was the fear, I retorted, it could be dismissed at once. The organization of 'sanctions' against any permanent member was in practice out of the question. For if it ever came to that point a world war would be imminent, Charter or no Charter. I therefore myself greatly hoped that the Soviet Government would not reject the 'compromise' which had been put forward in the latter stages of our talks at Dumbarton Oaks and of which he was aware. Sobolev, though he did not assent, did not dismiss the possibility either.

One of our difficulties was that Churchill had himself from the outset championed the Soviet thesis on voting in all its stark simplicity, and it seemed in January that the Soviet Government was going to be pretty intransigent on the subject unless they had satisfaction on the other major point left outstanding at Dumbarton Oaks, namely the representation in the General Assembly of all, or at any rate some, of the Soviet Constituent Republics. At one stage it looked as if President Roosevelt was preparing to bargain one against the other. The doubts in the Department as to the wisdom of this attitude were great. We thought that we ought to stick out on both points and that the Russians would probably give way on the republics, though we were by no means sure that they would accept the voting compromise.

At any rate it can well be imagined what exciting talks took place that hot August in the splendid ballroom of the Blisses and indeed up and down their garden. One feature of the discussions that drove Stettinius almost frantic was the regular appearance in the *New York Times*, the day after they took place, of a long, detailed and in every respect accurate account of the proceedings of the main committee. Ed had been particularly enjoined by the President, who had a potentially isolationist Congress breathing down his neck, to preserve secrecy at all costs. So the leak was disheartening to say the least. James (Scottie) Reston, the world-famous columnist responsible for the scoop, naturally refused to divulge the source of his information. All he would say was that it was no member of any of the three delegations. Nor was the mystery ever officially solved, though some suspected the Chinese with whom we were going to negotiate next, the Russians having decided not to sit down at the same table with the representatives of Chiang Kai-shek.

The all-important meeting that was to achieve final Allied unity on how to wind up the war and what to do immediately thereafter was now looming on the horizon. Yalta had been selected as the place, partly because Stalin refused to leave Russia – though he had been to Tehran – chiefly because President Roosevelt, largely with the influence of Harry Hopkins, was intent on bending over backwards to meet Russian susceptibilities in the hope that the Soviet Government, convinced of American sincerity, would reciprocate by at least paying some attention to American (Western) views on the right way to organize the world. I myself was keen to go, since I had been largely concerned with the elaboration of the rather complicated UN 'voting formula' that the President had now made his own; but for some time I was told that my Number Two, Jack Ward, would probably be selected; and it was only when he got rather ill that I seemed to have a chance. The attitude of the powers that be, as I observed to the Private Secretary (Nicholas Lawford), seemed to be 'better a sick Jack than a live Jebb'! But eventually I received my marching orders.

At Lyneham Airport the FO contingent was divided up, apparently by hazard, into two parts, some going towards one converted York bomber, some towards another. Our own machine took off for Malta, where the great men had already forgathered, but early next morning we found ourselves in Naples, the pilot having apparently run out of juice. The other one failed to locate Malta, stooged around for some time and eventually was ditched off Lampedusa. All might still have been well had it not struck a submerged reef. As it was, most of the occupants were killed, among the FO victims being the much loved Peter Loxley, my successor as Private Secretary to Cadogan, and Armine Dew. We were not told about the tragedy until we arrived in the Crimea on the following day having flown over the Peloponnese, the Aegean (including Samothrace where, we were told, it was just possible there might be one remaining German fighter), European Turkey and the Black Sea. It depressed us a great deal though we could not help reflecting on our luck in having gone one way rather than the other at Lyneham.

There was, however, no time to brood on the tragedy. After some delay we were bundled into cars and set out on the long journey to Yalta. My own temper was not improved by the non-arrival of my suitcase which had apparently been misrouted to Cairo. It did not look so far on the map, but even when we got to the great villa, Alubka, home in the past of the Vorontzov-Dashkoffs, where the British delegation was to stay, we were informed that the smaller fry were not to be put up there but in a 'sanatorium', a good half-hour further on, over an even more sinuous road. The next morning after various briefing meetings we set off for the Tsar's palace of the Livadia, half an hour away in the direction of the town, where the President and the American delegation had been installed and the conference itself was to assemble.

The Livadia was much bigger than the Alubka, but less interesting – a huge square white pile with nothing much remaining in the rooms and a large ballroom very suitable for the conference. The juniors were not encouraged to be present behind their superiors at the great round table except when their own subjects were under discussion; but I managed to evade this injunction to some small extent, enough anyhow to form an impression of the performances of the principal actors. I had not seen the President since the end of the Dumbarton Oaks Conference and was much distressed by his appearance which was, frankly, terrible. He seemed also to have slowed up to a marked extent and certainly did not display that quick come-back for which he was famous. It was evident, too, that he was chiefly out to get Stalin on his side; and he did not seem by any means averse from teasing Churchill about his Imperial commitments, and notably Hong Kong, the presumed object being to demonstrate that the Americans at any rate were in no sense Imperialists and that, therefore, it might well be possible for them and the Russians to arrive at some agreement even if their British colleagues found it difficult to come along.

Churchill, for his part, took all this very well. He, too, was anxious to come to terms with Stalin if this were in any way possible; but I had the impression that he was beginning to think that this was going to be a much more difficult operation than he had imagined a couple of years previously when he believed he had made a genuine personal break-through. Already the Polish question was becoming acute and it was evident the Russians were not going to accept anything save the Curzon Line as the Eastern frontier of Poland. Seeing that this represented, more or less, the ethnic frontier and that the 1939 frontier had been imposed on the Russians after the Revolution by force of arms, the proposal was hardly something that we could resist even if we had had the power to do so. But the real problem was the clear intention of the Russians to install their own Communist stooges as the Government of Poland and to eliminate, or at any rate reduce to as small a proportion as possible, any participation in the direction of affairs by the legitimate government in exile. In other words if we were unable to guarantee the freedom of the Polish people we were indeed in danger of going back on our word. It was true that we had 'guaranteed' Poland and gone to war in fulfilment of our guarantee. But that hardly meant that we were committed to her pre-war frontiers and there was a reasonable case for her 'moving west' and occupying at least some areas of Hitler's Reich – exactly how much to be determined at a peace conference.

Churchill, ably backed up by Eden, did all, as it seemed to me, that he possibly could for the Polish Government in London, but I never myself had much hope that the pressure would work. I could not in any case help admiring the extraordinary negotiating ability of Stalin, who never said anything much until right at the end of a discussion when he quietly put forward a suggestion that often seemed acceptable. Of the three pro-tagonists, indeed, it was he who had the greatest natural authority; and while recognizing him for the appalling tyrant that he certainly was, one was bound to admit that it was not only his unparalleled ferocity but also his sheer political ability that enabled him for thirty years to be the undisputed Tsar of all the Russias. On Poland he always tried to appear to be sweetly reasonable – 'The Poles' he remarked, 'are a great people, but very quarrelsome!' – thereby trying to give the impression that the rows between his own Polish stooges and the free government in London were only in the nature of a rather irrelevant feud. On paper what we got for the Poles was quite good, and some maintain that Stalin had difficulties with the Politburo when he got back to Moscow. The trouble was that the agreement was hardly signed before it was torn up.

When after a very long introduction by Stettinius, the famous 'voting formula' came up for consideration, the Dictator was in a particularly reasonable mood. After the PM had sought to illustrate the point by a not entirely felicitous reference to its effect, as he saw it, on a demand by the Chinese for the return of Hong Kong, Stalin merely said that he would have to think about it, and proceeded to preach a little homily on laying the foundations of Great-Power unity which would outlast the present generation and continue for at least fifty years. He had also interrupted Winston's speech on Hong Kong by inquiring, prophetically enough, how the PM would apply the formula in the event of a demand by Egypt for the return of the Suez Canal? The next day he merely said that he accepted the formula. Perhaps my work with Sobolev had had some effect on Molotov who must have explained to Stalin that it really was not worth making a fuss about this, more especially if the Russians could obtain some satisfaction regarding the separate representation of the allegedly 'independent' republics of the Soviet Union. Here, in spite of strong British protests, the President decided to give in on the representation in the General Assembly of at any rate the Ukraine and Byelorussia. There was much indignation in the British camp.

My own immediate interest in the conference had now disappeared, but I was soon to be drawn into the negotiation of the famous 'Declaration on Liberated Europe' which had been put forward by the Americans and which, in its earlier form, would have been a document obliging all the Allies to see that, among other things, free elections were held in countries 'liberated' by them and to make it in some way legally incumbent on them to do so. The final version merely said that the three would 'assist' the liberated peoples to do such things and would 'consult together' when necessary. Still it was something. According to Stettinius* the American delegation wanted to put forward the equivalent of my own brain-child, the 'United Nations Commission for Europe'. This would have been much better, but they were unable, I believe, to persuade the President to bring it up, though I myself referred to it in private conversation with some members of the delegation.

It seemed to me at this time that the signature of the Declaration on Liberated Europe, even if it did not result in our inserting pro-Western elements into the governments of the 'liberated' states of Eastern Europe, would at least give us an excellent bargaining counter in the event of its effective repudiation by our allies; and I remember an agitated discussion in the Livadia with Harry Hopkins (in bed), in the presence of Jimmy Burns, in which I attempted to resist any whittling down of the original text by Hopkins. In the event it *was* whittled down, but not, perhaps, irremediably: the signed text, after all, morally committed the Russians

* Edward Stettinius: *Roosevelt and the Russians* (London, 1950).

to the holding of 'free elections' in the countries 'liberated'. There was an inquest on the document when I returned to London, some of the lawyers arguing that if the Russians were committed by the document so were we in Greece for instance; but the general consensus was that, legally, nobody was committed very much. Still, the declaration did have a certain bargaining value, more especially after it was, in effect, torn up by the Russians on their entry into Bucharest and Warsaw. And as I always thought its possible violation by the Russians would give us an excuse for not withdrawing to our zones unless we wanted to.

In that event we should have ensured that about four-fifths of the territory of Hitler's Reich and an even greater proportion of its industry remained with the West. It would thus never have been possible to set up an Eastern German state and the potential power of Western Europe if it were ever formed, would have been enormous. It is indeed arguable that by withdrawing we abandoned the real fruits of the war. On the other hand there would have been no possibility of saving most of Austria from permanent Communist occupation, and the whole resulting situation – which could only have been maintained by the continued presence of large American forces – would have run clean contrary to the whole conception of building up a new world order with the Russians. It would thus have encountered much opposition in the British Parliament and even more in the US Senate. Churchill would, indeed, have favoured it but it was anathema to Roosevelt. If I had not by that time been in San Francisco I should quite possibly have been opposed to it myself.

But the general point which I would here make is that it was not the Yalta agreement that divided Europe and brought the Russians to within a hundred miles of the Rhine. That is a legend. Europe was divided into two parts by the advance of the Russian armies which could certainly not be halted before the final collapse of the Nazis. Nor was it at Yalta that the policy of basing the whole post-war structure on cooperation with the Soviet Union was adopted. As I have tried to show, this policy was formulated and agreed upon years before, and it is difficult to see what other one could have been adopted given the circumstances. The policy *might* have been repudiated between February and May 1945; but here again, as I say, it is doubtful whether this would have been practicable, whatever the foresight of our war-time rulers. In any case the idea that 'Yalta' was a great betrayal and a sell-out to the Soviet Union is an illusion. It was certainly unnecessary for the President to give so much away in the Far East – notably the Kurile Islands and Port Arthur – so as to make sure of Russian intervention against Japan. Even so we must

THE GREAT CONFERENCES (1944 – 5)

recognize that the atomic bomb had not yet been successfully exploded and it was commonly thought that very large American casualties would accompany the invasion of the Japanese mainland. But that had nothing to do with Europe.

I often wonder whether the Russians had really made up their minds at Yalta to break with the West and pursue a completely independent line in Eastern Europe – just intent on organizing their 'glacis' and nothing else. Probably this was so, but it is by no means certain. Not only did they agree to the 'voting formula', but they seemed genuinely to want to try to form some world authority and had no difficulty in accepting an invitation to take part in a negotiation to that end. 25 April was eventually proposed by us (I said that this was indeed the right date as it was my forty-fifth birthday) and that date, together with San Francisco as a place, seemed to appeal to them very much. So that was settled. We had no idea then how much the differences over Poland were, in the interval, to affect our plans. At the moment all was sweetness and light. Before lunch at the Russian villa, Monsieur Scriabin* himself took me on one side and, after expressing the hope that I had not been too uncomfortable (had he heard of my loud complaints on arrival?) congratulated me on the part which I had played in helping to smooth out difficulties connected with the 'voting formula'. You might have thought, without being too ingenuous, that there was just a chance of the world's Great Age beginning anew. Alas, we were soon to be sadly disillusioned.

We had not much more than two months after Yalta to prepare for the great conference at San Francisco, which was allegedly to decide on the future of the world, so I had a pretty active time getting everything ready. It is perhaps not generally known how near we were to postponing, or even to cancelling San Francisco altogether. The row with the Russians over Poland got worse and worse; it was evident that, given the calls on their time consequent on the prospective end of the European war, the most important statesmen could hardly spend more than a week or two at the conference; 'trusteeship', only mentioned at Yalta, could present the United Kingdom with very acute problems that would require much thought; the French had put forward contentious views on 'enforcement'; it was not at all certain that, not having been at Dumbarton Oaks or Yalta, they would agree to become one of the so-called 'sponsoring Powers' or even, more significantly, accept the famous 'voting formula' (although happily they did do this fairly early on); and, in general, it was very doubtful whether there could be agreement

* Molotov's real name. He was a first cousin of the composer.

on so vast and complicated a problem directly involving nearly fifty countries in the few weeks that, at the most, the conference might be expected to last. At the end of March, therefore, I suggested for consideration that we might, perhaps, renounce the idea of actually getting agreement on a new world organization at San Francisco and arrange for, as it were, a more extended Dumbarton Oaks conference, endeavouring to get agreement on certain principles only which would then be referred to the various participating governments for individual consideration, after which a general conference might be held perhaps with better prospects of success.

However all such ideas were, no doubt very properly, rejected and the delegation, apart from its leader, Anthony Eden, and our Ambassador, Halifax (who were to join us after a meeting in Washington) duly set out. It consisted at the ministerial level of Clement Attlee, Lord Cranborne, MPs to serve on committees, and a body of FO officials, headed by Cadogan, and including William Malkin, the Principal Legal Adviser, Neville Butler, the Under-Secretary in charge in the FO, Professor Webster and myself. Two members of the staff of the Washington Embassy (one of them, Paul Gore Booth, a future Permanent Under-Secretary*) were also to be made available. I do not say this in any vaunting spirit, but the mere fact that, apart from the Prof (who was more theoretical than professional in approach) I knew more about the actual details of the various points under discussion than any other member of the delegation save, no doubt, Cadogan, resulted in my being put in various key positions, and notably as deputy to the Foreign Ministers Committee, where most of the more important decisions were actually made in the sense of getting out agreed proposals for submission to ministers. Since I had been at Dumbarton Oaks I was also chosen for the so-called 'Coordination Committee' which again Pasvolsky was determined should do all the work that the ordinary person might have imagined the lawyers would do, notably checking and putting into coherent and logical form the proposals and conclusions of the various committees established to consider each chapter of Dumbarton Oaks, and even referring back conclusions to the committees for elucidation.

Extraordinary though it may appear in retrospect – and in view of the many criticisms of Dumbarton Oaks voiced by the smaller Powers who, however, were clearly not going to push their objections to extreme lengths – there was (apart from Poland) only one major crisis during the

* Head of the UN and Refugee Departments of the Foreign Office 1947–8; Permanent Under-Secretary of State 1968–9; now Lord Gore-Booth.

conference when it looked as if it might possibly break up in confusion. This occurred on 2 June when after some five weeks of agitated debate, Gromyko flatly rejected the thesis that there should be an automatic obligation on the Security Council to discuss and consider *any* dispute duly brought to its attention: in other words an implicit demand by the Russians that they should have the right to veto even the discussion of any subject which seemed to them to be undesirable. This was too much for Senator Vandenberg who had only with difficulty been brought to accept the Yalta 'voting formula'; nor was it, of course, acceptable to any other sponsoring government. But Gromyko insisted that 'automaticity' was a 'retreat from the Crimea', and declared that the Soviet Union would not sign the Charter unless the principle were abandoned. A dismayed delegation telegraphed home various possible ways of ending the conference if the Russians stuck to their guns, the least unpleasant of which seemed to be to approve the Charter provisionally with a reservation about its coming into force until the outstanding point had been cleared up. Meanwhile both the President and the PM appealed to Stalin, the former calling in aid Harry Hopkins himself who was then in Moscow. If Harry never did anything else, he saved the San Francisco Conference by persuading Stalin to overrule his subordinate. The crisis was over.

The work which I myself was called upon to perform seemed important at the time and looking back on the countless papers, memoranda, telegrams and so on that I then composed I suppose that I may have had some influence on the course of events, in the sense that I certainly helped along the process of general agreement. Nor, in spite of the extreme pressure under which we worked, have I heard it said that the Charter, whatever else may be said of it, was ill-drafted or internally inconsistent. As this, however, is not intended to be in any way a history of the conference, but only a description of the development of my own ideas, I might say that, so far as I recall, there were three matters on which I believe I had a certain influence.

The first had relation to what came to be known as 'The Hidden Veto' – a wonderfully journalistic description of an alleged lacuna in the Dumbarton Oaks and Yalta formulae. It had been agreed, as we have seen, that decisions in the 'pacific settlement of disputes' section should be taken by an agreed majority of the Security Council including the concurrent votes of the five permanent members though 'parties to a dispute should abstain from voting', in other words, no veto under this heading by a Great Power of any decision or recommendation. This seemed satisfactory so far as it went and it was regarded as a good sign when the

Soviet Government accepted it at Yalta. But some cunning small-Power lawyers in the commission concerned said 'Ah, but what if a permanent member of the Security Council is really a "party to a dispute" but acts through a third party, for instance supposing Russia backed up Bulgaria in some assault on Greece, and thus prevented the Security Council from declaring Bulgaria an aggressor even though she had evidently performed an act of aggression?'

Reams of paper changed hands on this issue and the lawyers had a field-day. Much indignation was aroused by the seeming solidarity on the point of the 'sponsoring Powers'. But eventually it was accepted that the issue was a false one. If you were going to accept a Great Power veto on any 'enforcement action' it was not worth while providing on paper for a safeguard on what might be improper behaviour by a Great Power in the 'pacific settlement of disputes' section, for the simple reason that if a Great Power (or at any rate a Super-Power) was determined to behave improperly there was no effective means of preventing it from doing so save war. And anyhow the Yalta voting formula did provide that a Great Power party to a dispute could not vote in the 'pacific settlement' section and would therefore put itself in the wrong if it refused to accept any action proposed under this heading.

Another point with which I was largely occupied – and which occupied more of the time of the conference even than the Veto – was domestic jurisdiction. How far, if at all, could a dispute or a situation arising out of a matter of internal interest in any state be said to be a threat to international security? What, in any case, was 'domestic jurisdiction' in international law? What was to prevent the Security Council, if it were so minded, from taking up the cause of any minorities – a matter which had plagued the League of Nations from its inception? The Australians, for instance, otherwise in favour of a strong and powerful world organization were particularly concerned to see that their immigration policy was not in any way prejudiced by action in the Security Council or the General Assembly; the South Africans were vitally concerned for obvious reasons; but most states had some skeleton in their cupboard the key to which they would much prefer to keep in their own hands. What about Ireland, or Algeria, or the Nagas or the Kurds? What, even, about the Negroes in the United States of America? What, above all perhaps, about the 'murdered' Baltic States? Eventually there was a compromise. 'Nothing contained in the present Charter shall authorize the UN to intervene in matters which are essentially within the domestic jurisdiction of any state or shall require the members to submit such matters to settlement; but this principle shall not prejudice the application of enforcement means under Chapter VII.' The reader can imagine the amount of ink that flowed in regard to the word 'essentially' alone, or indeed how 'enforcement action', if otherwise justified, could in fact be prejudiced by a matter governed by domestic jurisdiction. All things considered, it was remarkable that we got agreement on this knotty point at all. It only shows that at San Francisco all – even the Russians – were really determined that there *should* be agreement.

A third direction in which I may have had some influence was in the debate on how far 'security' should rest after the war on alliances and how far on the Security Council itself. In other words, should the necessary 'enforcement action' against any recurrence of aggressive tendencies on the part of the ex-enemies – or anybody else – be taken in accordance with such engagements as the Anglo- (or Franco-) Soviet treaty, the Security Council only being required to ratify such action *ex post facto*, and should any such action have to be approved by the Security Council in advance? On this last point I had long conversations with Sobolev, who seemed at first to be suspicious lest we might find in the Charter a means of avoiding our obligations under our treaty with the Russians, and I eventually seemed to convince him of the correctness of our views – which incidentally I had elaborated in a long memorandum earlier in the month.

The point was really important, for at the back of my mind I always had the fear that if we accepted the 'regional' doctrine – i.e. the basic predominance over the Charter of treaties – which for a time was maintained with vigour by the French – we might end up with a world organization containing no real assurances that the USA would intervene to maintain the peace in any area where it might be threatened. It seemed essential, therefore, if we could, to get the principle admitted that the world organization was the final authority and that no regional enforcement action should be taken except with its approval and this principle was effectively embodied, after long and animated debate, in Article 51 of the Charter, which however did admit that in the event of an 'armed attack' nothing should prevent a member from exercising its 'inherent right of self-defence until the Security Council (had) taken measures necessary to maintain international peace and security'.

My general argument was not however intended to be directed against alliances as such. On the contrary, alliances between the Great Powers, provided they were consistent with the principles and purposes of the world organization, and provided enforcement action was not taken except with the approval of the Security Council, would be most valuable as tending to reinforce the solidarity of the Great Powers and to permit also of certain very salutary regional arrangements. For instance, under any alliance which we might conclude with France it might well be laid down that we should jointly organize with the Low Countries, and possibly also with Norway, defence arrangements directed against Germany. Equally, the Anglo-Soviet and Franco-Soviet pacts might be regarded to some extent as an insurance against the possibility of the world organization's breaking up or failing to function owing, for instance, to a wave of isolationism in the USA. People would say to themselves, 'Well, anyhow, whatever happens Germany cannot really make trouble provided we and the Russians are determined that she should not do so.' The same line of argument might be pursued if by any chance Russia ran out of the world organization or by some action on her part made her existing treaties a dead letter. In that case, I said, 'an alliance between the Western democracies and the US would seem to be an absolute necessity if the Western democracies – and in the long run America herself – are to survive.'

Perhaps all this kind of reasoning may be thought today to have been pretty useless as too hypothetical and theoretical; but it cannot be said that we were not trying to think ahead and construct machinery that had some faint chance of being worked successfully. And short of agreement on a world state, or at the least a world authority based on regions, there was no reason why the Charter should not have worked reasonably well if only there had been the slightest will to work it. I imagine that the reason why this general will did not exist was primarily fear – chiefly fear by the Russians of the US atomic bomb and determination not to be subjected to what their holy books told them must inevitably be 'imperialist domination'. And yet it must be clear that Stalin, by over-reacting, over-played his hand. If he had used the Veto less and simply pretended to cooperate with the West while in fact building up his empire, he might well by the end of 1947, have had pro-Soviet governments in all the Western European democracies which he could then probably have swallowed in less than a decade.

I shall speculate further on this fascinating possibility later on. Now I would only record how the conference finished on time but only as a result of Pasvolsky and his colleagues on the 'Coordination Committee' (housed on the top floor of the Opera House) working themselves silly until almost any hour during the final week; how the Russian text was elaborated with the help of a hastily summoned Isaiah Berlin; how Lord

Halifax got stuck in a crowded lift; how the Prof got much the worst of an argument on the 'Hidden Veto' in a committee battle with the redoubtable Herbert Evatt of Australia; how he failed also to strike the right note in a draft speech by the Secretary of State who, with complete justice, complained that it was 'Ciceronian'; how he nevertheless came triumphantly into his own by drafting (in conjunction with Field-Marshal Smuts who was, ironically enough, particularly concerned with the passage about promoting social progress and better standards of life 'in larger freedom') the fine prelude to the Charter (often now recited); and how I discovered that one of Attlee's favourite works was Sorel's *Réflexions sur la Violence*.

Anyway, the show eventually came to an end. The journalists and columnists were on the whole rather disappointed. They had expected the dawning of a new day, and all they observed was the birth of something that bore a suspicious resemblance to the League of Nations. If Dean Acheson was (as he says) 'present at the Creation' these observers would probably have said of me that I was, at Dumbarton Oaks and San Francisco, 'Present at the Conception and the Abortion'! Not that the infant was in fact still-born, since, after all, it has survived for over a quarter of a century. Nor did I feel that way myself as I left that lovely town. I really believed, indeed, that, though things were unlikely to work out as we had planned, the chances were that we should be able to avoid a major war in my own time at any rate, by, among other things, using the United Nations. And so we have, as a matter of fact, though nobody could say that the 'Balance of Terror', which has preserved the peace, had anything much to do with the United Nations.

Right at the end of the conference it was clear that I should have to remain on for a day or two in order, as it were, to take over the torch from the Conference Secretary, no less a person than Alger Hiss. For it had been agreed that the Executive Committee of the Preparatory Commission of eleven members who were to prepare the way for the first meeting of the General Assembly in London would assemble there in a couple of months' time and that I myself would probably be designated as its 'Executive Secretary'. This was lucky. The aeroplane in which I would otherwise have returned and which contained, among others, Will Malkin, Denis Capel-Dunn and my own lady Private Secretary, Miss Collard, disappeared in the Atlantic and wreckage was never found. Air travel was indeed a bit risky in 1945. I myself, I seem to remember, came back from Baltimore in a flying boat which took ages and ages but was at any rate large and comfortable. It was not long after I touched down that I was told to go out and join the extraordinary Conference of Potsdam, appropriately known by the code name 'Terminal'.

I suppose my presence in Potsdam had been required in case anything to do with the UN came up, which it did not, though I had some useful talks with the Americans and indeed with the Russians. The garden suburb where we were housed had in no way suffered as a result of the war; nor had the Cäcilienhof, the huge and ugly palace of the Crown Prince, where the conference itself took place. Round a table in the vast, dark hall were all the familiar figures save one – Roosevelt. The war was over and even the Russians were relaxed. But on the roads round about, grim processions of refugees with little carts, and sometimes a horse, wandered hopelessly up and down, often pushed out of the way by tough-looking Russian and often Tartar troops, and every few hundred yards a buxom young Amazon directed the traffic with conscious pride.

I had only been in Potsdam for a day or two when the great switch-over took place. To the astonishment of Stalin, and indeed to the surprise of the British delegation, it was announced that Attlee and Bevin* would shortly arrive to continue the negotiations. We now know that it was as near as anything that Hugh Dalton took over the Foreign Office in July 1945. In the Labour Party it had been assumed that he would. Bevin, for his part, actually wanted to go to the Treasury and the new Prime Minister had informed Dalton of what was in store for him and even of what clothes he would need at Potsdam. Then Attlee saw the King who, again as we now know, expressed a preference for Bevin. And no doubt other influences were brought to bear. Eden, for instance, says in his book *The Reckoning*, that Dalton's appointment would have been 'very bad',† and no doubt there were many others at the centre of power who disliked Dalton, suspecting also that he would be too pro-Russian and anti-American, and, indeed, too 'Leftish' in a general way. Was there anything in these apprehensions? I doubt it. Dalton might not, it is true, have been as effective as Bevin, if only for the reason that he might have been less rugged and less capable of imposing his policy on his colleagues and indeed on the House of Commons. But he certainly was not pro-Soviet, and he was undoubtedly madly pro-Pole and pro-Czech. Moreover he would certainly never have quarrelled with America. Was it not he who, at the Treasury, was the most influential in getting the House of Commons to

---

* Trade Unionist and Labour MP; Minister of Labour during the War; became Foreign Secretary in 1945. Died in 1951.
† Anthony Eden, *op. cit.*, p. 551.

accept the great American loan? Besides, the main lines of our policy after the war were largely dictated by circumstance. No British Government could have accepted the Russian pretensions in Germany and Europe. It is true that Dalton might have been less adroit than Bevin in handling 'Marshall Aid', and subsequently in preparing the way for what was to become NATO; but as against this he would probably have been more 'European' than Bevin and might well also have done better in the Middle East.

So far as I personally was concerned the arrival of Dalton at the Foreign Office might have been supposed to be an advantage. I should no doubt have had to stay on dealing with the UN until after the end of the first part of the first Assembly in February 1946 and after that he would probably have wanted me to become his head Private Secretary, in which post I could no doubt, had I wanted to exert it, have had almost as much influence as Lord Harvey, though it would have been in many ways a terrible bore. Alternatively, I could have played much the same role as I did under Bevin and then succeeded Sargent as PUS in 1949 in place of Strang, who might have replaced Cadogan at the UN. But in that event after two years, having no doubt become quite unpopular, I should have found myself, at the age of fifty-one, with a new boss in the shape of Anthony Eden and goodness knows what would have happened to me then. Besides I would have missed all the interest and excitement of New York during and after the Korean War. It only shows how little these kind of considerations matter. Anyhow, it never occurred to me at the time that people regarded me as a 'Daltonian'. In French, *daltonien* means colour-blind and it is true that, in politics, I have sometimes found it rather difficult to distinguish between red and blue. Nor, as a matter of fact, did I ever, to my knowledge, covet any particular post or do anything to obtain it. The only exception was when Kirkpatrick retired in 1956 as PUS and I made it known that I would like to succeed him.

Attlee, who had been at Potsdam from the beginning as a sort of observer, was just as much surprised as anybody else by the result of the election. When he came back as PM he moved straight in to the great villa vacated two days previously by Churchill, and seemed, at first, a little at a loss. He must have looked down the list of the British delegation in search of a familiar face, for Sigi Waley and I found ourselves at dinner alone that night with our new ruler. The outstanding quality of Clem was not so much his modesty – it was, I think, Churchill who made the rather cruel remark that 'he had a great deal to be modest about' – as his simplicity and good sense. He was a living exception to Lord Acton's assertion that all power corrupts. It is true that, on the reverse of the medal, he did not seem to have any very impressive ideas about things in general, or perhaps I should say that I did not myself hear him express many. He was more of a listener than an exponent. In principle he was, we understood, a 'world government' man; but then so were many people – in principle. When it came down to what exactly we ought to do next he was almost invariably sensible – a sort of British Truman! At dinner we talked mostly about the conference and the Russians, of whose system of government he was, I need hardly say, highly critical. In fact, I do not believe he shared the conviction of many of his colleagues – including, I rather think, Bevin, in the early stages of the administration – that things would be easier owing to the possibility of 'Left talking to Left'. But I did not meet Uncle Ernie himself until the Potsdam Conference was over. My presence in London was urgently required and I flew back before it ended.

Birth of the United Nations
(1945-6)

Labouring away on the United Nations, I had not altogether lost touch with the great foreign political problems which if possible should be faced before it was set up. Thus in January 1945 I recollect that I was pressing hard for an Anglo-French treaty to supplement the Franco-Soviet treaty which had just been signed in Moscow by General de Gaulle. The suggestion that the existing Anglo-Soviet treaty should be made tripartite, put forward in all innocence by the Foreign Office and which Stalin would no doubt have accepted, was summarily dismissed by the General for the reason, as we now know, that he wanted first to impose an acceptance of his own German, and no doubt also of his Levant policy before consenting to any treaty engagement with ourselves. But what I was always after myself was the creation of some sort of regional defence arrangement with all our Western European allies, and it did not seem to me that such an arrangement would be in any way inconsistent with the Dumbarton Oaks proposals. After all, the whole theory of the original Four-Power Plan had been to create a world organization which would rest on the firm intention of the victor Powers to prevent any further resurgence of aggressive tendencies on the part of our enemies; and any regional arrangements to this end were surely to be welcomed, provided that they were (as ultimately they were) authorized by the Charter, and not inconsistent with the free choice of all the independent states concerned, however small or militarily insignificant.

All such ideas had, however, to be abandoned, so far as Western Europe was concerned, or at least postponed, when it became clear, as it shortly did, that the French Government was going to demand the occupation, by France alone of all the Rhineland, to say nothing of a special regime for the Ruhr as well, the intention being, if possible, to arrange for a separate Rhenish state, and indeed for that age-long objective of French policy, a Rhine frontier. It may be thought by some that we would have been well advised to agree to this, but if we had we should have certainly come up against formidable American opposition, nor should we have had Russian approval either. De Gaulle himself had just tried to obtain it and had failed. We therefore had to wait until after the General retired from the scene for the first time in January 1946 before signing with France the Treaty of Dunkirk in March of that year, and until March 1948 before creating 'Western union'. And when that took place the whole situation had changed profoundly. It was no longer a question of defence against possible German aggression, but against the gradual political expansion westwards of the Soviet Union.

Shortly after VE Day a more powerful intelligence than mine had been concentrating on long-term policy. I was still in San Francisco when Sargent advanced his own preliminary ideas on our correct post-war objectives; but I was relieved to find on my return that his conclusions were not very dissimilar to my own, save that, in the immediate future, we were to 'take the offensive' in challenging Communist penetration in as many of the Eastern countries of Europe as possible and (very properly) counteract any attempt of the USSR to communize and obtain political control over Germany, Italy, Greece or Turkey. With all this in mind, and in relation to my new job of getting the UN going, I see that at the end of July I was much concerned with the problem of 'bases', on which much ink had been spilt during the preceding three years, i.e. the general idea that world security might be ensured by some joint manifestation of the power of the UN all over the world, and by 'UN' was naturally meant in the first instance the three Great Powers responsible for the collapse of the 'Fascist' totalitarian empires. Urging then, that this question of 'bases' should be referred to the Military Staff Committee as soon as possible, I referred to the broad conception of Clement Attlee, which I believed he had advanced (I rather think in Potsdam) before he actually became PM. This was (a) that we were not in a position to resist a Russian claim physically to dominate the Straits and an attempt (by the Soviet Union) to place herself in a strategic position to enforce her right to have 'free access to the oceans'; (b) that if the Russians attained these objectives they could only have a selective importance in the light of modern war conditions now that air power transcended all frontiers and menaced all home lands; and (c) that in view of our economic position we might not ourselves be able to continue to be solely responsible for the defence of the Suez Canal and Singapore.

Criticizing this attitude I said that there was an antidote to every conceivable offensive weapon. Air power might be soon out of date and replaced by rockets. But even rockets might eventually be dealt with by new defensive weapons. If this were so, then land and sea bases might continue to be very important for a long period of time. The Deputy Prime Minister had referred to 'power politics' but what exactly did he mean by this phrase? Short of the constitution of a world state, international politics could only be an expression of power, and Marshal Stalin had said this in so many words at Potsdam. Whether you agreed with him or not – and personally I did – the fact was that the Charter of the UN was based on the physical power of the major states. It would thus only work if they agreed to cooperate, which meant that they must, if possible, come to some broad agreement regarding mutual respect for their various interests. An effort to achieve such a harmonization was at the moment proceeding. It would clearly involve bargaining, and this could only take place on a basis of power. A state with insufficient force could only make a bad bargain. But each state must at least say what it wanted and this entailed making it clear that in the last resort there were certain interests which it could not abandon except under compulsion. And compulsion might mean war.

What were the presumptive Russian political objectives? These clearly included not only the control of the Straits, but also, if possible, the political control of Turkey and Greece, i.e. the formation of governments in those countries broadly equivalent to those already formed in Roumania, Bulgaria and Yugoslavia. It was true that the Russians might be pursuing these objectives by what might be called a 'defensive-offensive'. For instance their recent attack on our Greek policy was perhaps due to a desire to keep their end up in other Balkan countries. If we made it clear that we did not in practice intend to interfere (in spite of the famous deal between Churchill and Stalin) in the three northern Balkan countries they might well revert to their previous attitude towards our policy in Greece which had been manifested by Stalin at Yalta. It was in any case significant that the hostile Potsdam line had been adopted on the day following the presentation of our own paper on Yugoslavia. The truth was that the *objectives* of the Russians remained constant: whether they pursued them actively or not depended entirely on their estimate of the opposition that such action was likely to arouse. And this in its turn depended on whether they thought that it would be likely to involve a real breach with Britain and America.

So the real question was, did we *want* to oppose the creation by the Russians of a sort of Scapa-Flow in the Sea of Marmora and an EAM (Communist) government in Greece? If we did, we should first of all have to obtain the support of the Americans. Failing that we should have to try to embark on a kind of fighting retreat, allowing the Russians to have only a partial success. And I proceeded to outline what this might be, bearing in mind that we should presumably continue to maintain a British presence in Cyprus, Palestine and Aden, which, after all, were still effectively British possessions. I cannot recall what happened to this rather stark *exposé* of the realities. If it ever got to the new PM I doubt whether he would have agreed. But I have no doubt at all that it would have made an appeal to Bevin, in whose sole hands, and to the pained surprise of some of his colleagues, it quickly became apparent that Attlee had left the control of our foreign policy.

Next, in the middle of October 1945, I had a long discussion with Sargent on the relationship between the Council of Ministers and the proceedings in Church House. The recent break-up of the Council of Ministers without any agreed conclusions was not, I suggested, necessarily disastrous since they would no doubt come together again shortly. But it had an obvious bearing on the future world organization since, if the Russians were being so difficult about a three-Power control of Germany, how could a five-Power system work in the Security Council? It also gave rise to an even more important speculation, namely, if it were impossible to reach agreement on first-class issues in talks between Foreign Ministers, what hope was there of solving disputes at all, without recourse to war, in the UN?

After noting that the question of the control of ex-enemy states was removed from the scope of the UN under Article 53 of the Charter, I said that the real danger to the infant world organization was the apparent likelihood that no progress would now be made towards the formation and successful functioning of the 'Military Staff Committee'. At the moment all the evidence in Church House was that the Russians were playing down arguments in favour of establishing this committee and seemed less keen on the whole idea of collective enforcement action. Why was this? Presumably for two reasons. The first was that since San Francisco the Americans had exploded and employed the Atomic Bomb. The second was the difficulties encountered over the whole European settlement and the future of Germany. The first, however, need not necessarily have a bad effect on the relationship of the Soviet Government to the West especially as it was probable that they were quite capable in a few years' time of making it (the Bomb) themselves. Nor would they in any case contemplate any struggle with the West so long as the West remained united and until such time as their own bad internal situation was relieved. In any case they were well aware that the West was, and probably would continue to be for many years, ahead of them in scientific techniques and that even if they were able to manufacture an atomic bomb they might not be able to deliver it to its destination except by aero-planes which by that time would be out of date as a means of offensive warfare. So, while the American Government might have increased their irritation, it did not seem to be the main reason for their intransigent attitude.

The real reason, as it seemed to me, lay in the German problem, the solution of which might either bring us together or drive us apart. Many FO memoranda during the last two years had pointed out that the Great Powers must either work out a common policy for Germany as a whole, or, whether they liked it or not, reconcile themselves to the formation of two possibly opposing blocs in Europe. It was always recognized that the first would be very difficult, but that it should at least be attempted, if only because the dangers of the second solution were so manifest. We had indeed already attempted it by creating the Control Commission and we were now toying with the virtual reconstruction of the *Reichsbahn*. But in practice the absorption of the eastern industrial districts of Germany in Soviet-controlled Poland, the complete spoilation of the remaining eastern German provinces, and the open advocacy by the French of dis-memberment in the West had all tended in the opposite direction. This raised the vital question of the future of the Ruhr. It was easy to talk about its 'internationalization' but, apart from the fact that no line could really be drawn round it, either the products of the Ruhr would be available for exchange against products of East Germany and Central Europe, or they would not. If they were, it would imply something like the first pro-posed solution for the German problem, namely international control. To argue otherwise would be to admit that the Soviets would be granted a large say in the control of the dominating industrial factor in Western Europe without any *quid pro quo*.

All this tended to suggest that there should be a strong Anglo-French *entente* which would form the basis of an industrial and military Western European system. But there would be an unpleasant corollary. For the Soviets would not willingly play a part in the establishment of the world organization unless they were allowed to develop an analogous system in Eastern Europe. What would be fatal to the prospects of the world organization would be if the West opposed such a solution and endeav-oured, by stirring up trouble, to pursue the policy of what might be called the '*Cordon Sanitaire*'. The pursuit of the 'optimum solution' might go on for a little while longer, but I did not think it would really work, given the necessity of a complete reversal of existing Russian policy in Germany and the difficulty in arranging for complete great Power harmony in the face of quarrels outside Germany that were also likely to arise.

So my conclusion was that we should have a new policy, differing rather from that recommended by Sargent, involving:

> The abandonment of any attempt to reconstitute the Reich in favour of a scheme to organize Germany west of the Elbe as an entity under the permanent control of the UK, France and (perhaps) of the USA;
>
> implicit recognition of the 'special position' of the USSR in all European districts (save Greece) east of the Anglo-American-Russian boundary in Germany and Austria, with the partial exception of Poland and Yugoslavia;
>
> the conclusion of peace treaties with the existing governments of Roumania and Bulgaria (I appear to have forgotten Hungary!);
>
> a 'hands off' attitude towards Russia in regard to Western Europe (including Sweden), Italy, Greece, Turkey (except possibly for a modification of the Straits Convention by general consent), the Mediterranean generally and Iran;
>
> the conclusion of an Anglo-French alliance and of military agreements with the other Western European states based on this; and
>
> American credits for the USSR and assistance to the UK.

At the end of 1945 it was, I repeat, generally accepted that the Americans would not retain their forces in Europe for more than a year or so after the Armistice. Otherwise I was, in fact, recommending a policy which was only adopted some three years later under the compulsion of fear generated by the first *Coup de Prague*. Looking back, and as the reader will be well aware, my judgment was quite often at fault. But at least on 'Europe' I think that, in the light of hindsight, it was probably reasonable.

It will be seen what my state of mind was when I was about to enter a quite unknown field – that of a virtually international official whose job was presumably to think in terms of the world community and not in those of any individual country. It was not quite that, because after all I was still paid by HMG and only seconded for the job.

But in any case at the beginning of August 1945, I found myself preparing for the first session of the General Assembly of the United Nations, fixed for 10 January 1946. I had not actually been nominated for this job at San Francisco; but since Alger Hiss had refused to serve, it had been agreed that it would be best for the Executive Secretary to be a national of the country where the Preparatory Commission was to meet. This being so, I was a fairly obvious candidate. The first thing was to get a building for the 'Executive Committee' of the Preparatory Commission which had been established at the latter's first meeting in San Francisco. It consisted of the representatives of fourteen states, all remarkably distinguished men.* Its duty was to draft and submit to the full commission a report on all the host of matters requiring decision before the General Assembly itself could meet. In addition the committee – or rather its Executive Secretary – would have to recruit at least the nucleus of a Secretariat without which neither the Commission nor the General Assembly would be able to operate. The committee duly met on 16 August and produced its report on 27 October.

Everybody agreed that the first General Assembly would have to be an impressive occasion and that it should take place in the centre of London. For its preparation Church House – where the Lords had sat for a while after the destruction by bombing of the House of Commons – was the obvious place and we got hold of it without difficulty. But the choice for the meeting-place of the Assembly lay between the eight-hundred-year-old Westminster Hall and the Central Hall, Westminster, an early twentieth-century erection on the other side of Parliament Square. The romantics among us (including myself) were much in favour of using Westminster Hall – the scene of many of the greatest events in our long parliamentary history; but eventually we were defeated by practical considerations – heating, ventilation and acoustics being among the most persuasive. So Central Hall it was to be. But first we had a tremendous task to perform in the Executive Committee. This included agreement on

* Paul Hasluck (Australia), later Governor-General
  de Freitas Valle (Brazil), later Ambassador to Canada
  Lester Pearson (Canada), later Foreign Minister and Prime Minister and President of the UN Assembly
  Don Manuel Bianchi (Chile), Ambassador in London
  Wellington Koo (China), Ambassador in London
  Jan Masaryk (Czechoslovakia), later Foreign Minister (murdered in 1948)
  René Massigli (France), Ambassador in London, formerly Foreign Minister of de Gaulle and later Secretary-General of the Quai d'Orsay
  Philip Noel-Baker (United Kingdom), Minister of State
  Nasrullah Entezam (Iran), later Foreign Minister and President
  Luis Padilla Nervo (Mexico), later President of the UN Assembly
  J. H. Van Royen (Holland), later Ambassador in London
  Andrei Gromyko (USSR), Ambassador in London, later Foreign Minister
  Edward Stettinius (USA), previously Secretary of State, replaced by
     Adlai Stevenson, later Governor of Illinois and US Representative to the UN
  Ljubo Leontich (Yugoslavia), Ambassador in London.

the agenda – always of the greatest interest to the Russians; on the establishment of the various committees of the Assembly; on the all-important
rules of procedure (for the Assembly itself, and for the committees);
on the exact role of the Secretariat; on the modalities of Assembly voting
generally; on the functions and operation of the Military Staff Committee;
on the winding up of the still existing League of Nations; and indeed on
the site of the organization itself.

You can picture the bustle and the confusion. First of all there was the
staff. I well remember my first recruit, a splendid British parachutist
called Brian Urquhart. He walked into my office in uniform explaining
that he had had to leave the Army owing to his parachute failing to open
and his hitting the ground at a hundred miles an hour: but though he
seemed to have temporarily broken many bones, his head was undoubtedly
unaffected and I engaged him as my PA there and then, nor did I ever
regret it. Today Brian is one of the chief pillars of the UN Secretariat.
Then there was Jean de Noüe, also in uniform, this time French. He became the *Chef du Protocole*, more difficult perhaps in the United Nations
than in national service. Jean resigned a few years ago and his beautiful
wife, Belle, subsequently died, mourned by a host of friends. Next there
was Martin Hill who is still in the Secretariat. And Victor Hoo, the
nominee of Chiang Kai-shek, an able and popular official. And Ben
Cohen, from Uruguay, who was put in charge of information and remained in charge till 1954. Finally there was the American nominee,
Andrew Cordier, a tower of strength from Yale, later Acting President of
Columbia University, New York. He quickly became the expert on
Assembly procedure – the equivalent of the Clerk of the House of
Commons – and remained such, always sitting on the left of the President
of the Assembly until he rejoined Academe in 1962. Other prominent
members of the Secretariat were Henry Hope, a one-armed war hero
who went back to business, and Duckworth Barker who ran most of the
press side under Ben Cohen.

I continued, however, to be concerned about the Russian contribution
to the Secretariat, and constantly urged Sobolev and Gromyko to supply
a contingent of about half a dozen from the Soviet Foreign Service or
from the Narkomindel. Nothing happened for weeks and then suddenly
the door opened and there appeared A. A. Roschin, the only Russian
recruit to the Secretariat so far, and a very agreeable and able official,
followed by a band of nice-looking young men, all apparently in their
twenties, clad in identical blue suits and white shirts. I asked them to sit
down and tell me their names. Most sounded vaguely familiar, like

Timoshenko, or aristocratic, like Vorontzov (these were not the actual names, but they represent the impression created). I formed the view that they were all connected in some way with the top Soviet aides, or 'ruling class'. I asked them what their specialities were. None seemed to have any. So I divided them up arbitrarily among the various sections where they made no impact at all, staying for the most part with members of the Soviet Embassy and not advancing any particular views while in the Secretariat. Only one was reported as behaving in what we in the West would call a normal way, going out occasionally in the evening by himself, chatting up the girls, and even expressing an individual opinion now and then. After a fortnight or so all mysteriously disappeared and were no more seen. It may well be that the more human and talkative one is still at Karaganda, if indeed he is not in a lunatic asylum. These refinements of the Soviet system were not then so well appreciated as they are today.

While all this was going on I was sitting in my new office when I got a message saying that the Secretary of State wanted me to come over and tell him how things were going on the UN front. Though I had just seen Bevin at Potsdam, I had never talked to him before, and had therefore no idea how we should get on. The initial reception was a little formidable. In fact he said nothing for a few moments after I had sat down and simply looked me over in my chair. Finally he observed, 'Must be kinda queer for a chap like you to see a chap like me sitting in a chair like this?' Slightly nonplussed, I thought it better not to take up the challenge. So I just shrugged my shoulders and smiled. Bevin was rather nettled. 'Ain't never 'appened before in 'istory' he remarked, scowling ferociously. I thought I couldn't let that one go by. 'Secretary of State', I said on the spur of the moment, 'I am sorry that the first time I open my mouth in your presence is to contradict you. But you're wrong. It has.' 'What do you mean, young man?' 'Well,' I said, 'it was a long time ago – rather over four hundred years I think. But there was then a butcher's boy in Ipswich whose origins, I suspect, were just as humble as your own, and he became the Foreign Secretary of one of our greatest kings. And for that matter, a Cardinal too. His name was Tom Wolsey. And incidentally, now I come to think of it, he was not unlike you physically.' 'Well', said the Secretary of State, visibly impressed, 'I must say, I never thought of that.'

Possibly my comparison was not absolutely correct, though after all there was something in it. A career being more open to talent in the early sixteenth than in the early twentieth century, Wolsey was able to become the 'Babe BA'. Poor Uncle Ernie, perhaps equally intelligent, never had a chance to do that. What is certain is that, from that moment onward, I could do little wrong so far as Bevin was concerned. The great man – for such he was – never minded his subordinates speaking up. More particularly he never minded me. 'And what does Mr Minority think?', he often subsequently used to say at conferences. As for myself, I thought he was splendid. What I chiefly appreciated, I think, on reflection, was his natural quickness and cleverness. He usually got the essential point with no difficulty at all. And his long experience in dealing with men had made him very, very shrewd. Nor did he have the slightest suspicion of a chip on the shoulder, as he might well have done, being the illegitimate son of a housemaid in Dulverton. Everybody was, in fact, treated alike, that is, unless they were considered to be enemies when he could be absolutely ruthless. For this reason alone he was for most people a very lovable man.

Of course he had terrible faults. He was rather vindictive; he was very vain; he was often prejudiced – against Jews, Catholics and the lower middle class for example. But he was immensely loyal and he expected loyalty from others. There is no doubt that he believed that he would himself have been a better prime minister than 'Clem'; but he refused absolutely to intrigue against Attlee who had, after all, been democratically elected Leader of the Labour Party. And, of course, he defended his own staff through thick and thin. He was also patriotic in the best sense of the word, that is to say that, without in any way being contemptuous of foreigners, he was proud to be English and always keen to establish and fortify the place of our country in the world. For all these reasons he can, I feel, be ranked next to Churchill as the natural British leader that the war produced.

His prejudices were, however, real enough. I remember, for instance – in 1947 I rather think – that he took me with him to a Trades Union Congress in Southport. Together with Florence, his wife, and a detective we got into a first-class compartment. The train was rather full and people often went by in the corridor, including from time to time a Catholic priest in a soutane. Whenever this happened Mr and Mrs Bevin became uneasy and Mr Bevin muttered 'black crows'. I understood that he believed that Catholic priests brought bad luck and nothing that I could say had any effect. The prejudice was quite irrational. Once when I had got to know him better he even confided to me his views on class distinctions. Again, these were as emotional as they were surprising. 'You know, Gladwyn,' he observed in a meditative way, 'I don't *mind* the upper class. As a matter of fact I even rather like the upper class.' (I think that by 'upper class' he meant anybody who had been to a 'good public school', not only Dukes or Earls.) 'They may be an abuse but they are often, as like as not, intelligent and amusing. Of course I love the lower class. It's my class and it's the back-bone of this country. But, Gladwyn, what I frankly can't abide is the *middle* class. For I find them self-righteous and narrow-minded.' I said I thought this was a horrifying generalization. Surely he must admit that there were admirable people in all classes, and horrible people too, for that matter. But here again it was no good arguing. I think the reason for this prejudice was that he was a little jealous of people whose origins had perhaps not been much more noble than his own but who had somehow or other managed to become better educated in a conventional way. This no doubt accounted for the special aversion which he had for Herbert Morrison.* But there was another reason.

He had unfortunately never much use for intellectuals as such, or what he himself conceived to be intellectuals, and that irrespective of the class from which they were derived. In particular, he was never greatly enamoured of Labour intellectuals, such as Cripps, or Laski, or Crossman, or even the saintly and well-disposed Phil Noel-Baker, who served him loyally and with great efficiency in the Foreign Office as Minister of State, and who, incidentally, had been largely responsible for the successful operation of the 'Executive Committee'. (With Dalton relations were a bit easier, perhaps because Dalton was not as intellectual as all that.) After all, he had not himself had the time to read very much or absorb a great deal of theory. It could even be said of him, as *mutatis mutandis*, Ben Jonson said of Shakespeare, that he had 'small Lenin and less Marx'. He knew the broad lines of the Marxist doctrine of course. He had heard of Proudhon; he was not unaware of Kautsky. But what he had got was a very good notion of the actual condition of the working class in Britain and how it could best be improved. To this extent he was, and remained, a Trades Unionist. What could have happened if he had gone to the Treasury, as previously arranged, is anybody's guess. I must say I doubt whether he would have been any more successful there than Winston Churchill.

By the end of August the Executive Committee was shaking down and beginning to make progress. Adlai Stevenson, then virtually unknown outside America, had taken Ed Stettinius's place as the US delegate and was a tower of strength. He and his wife Ellen took a house next door to

* Labour MP; Home Secretary and Minister of Home Security in war time Cabinet. Deputy Prime Minister in postwar Labour Government; Foreign Secretary for seven months in 1951.

where we were then living in Mount Street so I used to see a good deal of him and, as so often, fell into the habit of talking things over in the frankest possible way with my American colleague. When the French speak about the 'Anglo-Saxon bloc' and the 'special relationship' between Britain and America they are usually unaware of the often great differences of outlook which in fact separate our two peoples; but they are right to this extent, that when an Englishman and an American are working together on a common project it is usually much more easy for them to understand each other than for an Englishman and, for instance, a Frenchman, in a similar position. It is not only the language, which naturally is a great help, it is the process of thought and of reasoning which often creates a bond between, shall we say, an English graduate and an American from one of the great East Coast universities. Such a bond can be formed between an educated Frenchman and an educated Englishman; but it is much more difficult and a real effort has to be made on both sides. Anyway, Adlai remained a life-long friend and a great servant of the United Nations.

It was not until the latter part of November that we had a real tussle with the Russians who by that time were certainly showing less enthusiasm for the organization than previously, if indeed enthusiasm was ever the right word. This concerned chiefly the question of appointments to the various posts in the Preparatory Commission and its committees and eventually in the General Assembly. In particular they made a determined effort to get the presidency for one of their own tame Poles. They also insisted on the Vice-Presidents including representatives of the five permanent members of the Security Council. They were no doubt right to try to keep their end up, but their suspicions of the motives of the Western Powers, and notably of America, seemed to increase day by day.

I myself came under the fire one day of Gromyko, for I had had the audacity to circulate a paper suggesting that the *rapporteurs* of the various Assembly committees might conceivably be drawn from the members of the new Secretariat; in fact that there might be established a sort of corps of professional *rapporteurs* who could perhaps be relied upon to give a more objective account of the labours of a committee and to submit recommendations representing the general will than nationals of any particular country. With a fearful frown, the Soviet representative announced that he had a 'serious criticism' to make of the Executive Secretary, on hearing which I said, with a perhaps rather undaunted smile, 'I tremble!' There was much laughter, and Grom's tone altered considerably. But I need hardly say that my intelligent proposal was rejected and never again saw the light of day.

The Russians at an early stage made it quite clear that all they really cared about was the Security Council, and more especially the influence which they themselves might be expected to have in its operation. At one point they suggested that the Security Council should have a completely separate Secretariat, that is to say one whose members were not interchangeable with other members, and when this was thought to be undesirable demanded that at least the head of the section should be a Soviet citizen. This was agreed to in the initial stages, but subsequently they accepted an excellent Yugoslav, called Protitch, who continued on in that position for many years.

We struggled on, but towards the end of November I became rather concerned by the increasing tendency in Britain to suggest that the voting formula in the Security Council adopted in San Francisco was all wrong and that efforts should be made to discover a more reasonable one before the UN actually came into operation. This disturbed me a good deal. Writing (very personally) to Alec Cadogan from Church House, I said that it appeared that both the Government and the Opposition were committed to the view that:

(a) important and urgent world problems of a political nature should as soon as possible be confided to the World organization for settlement;

(b) it would be highly desirable at an early stage to abolish what was invariably referred to as 'the Veto'; and

(c) it would be also desirable, at an early stage, to take some preliminary steps towards the constitution of a world state.

The first view, but not the second or the third, appeared to be shared by President Truman.

However, on (a) the Charter implicitly stated (I said) that the conclusion of peace settlements and the carrying out of their terms was not the business of the world organization but rather of 'the governments having responsibility for such action'. This provision could only be altered with the consent of all these governments. Therefore the UN would *not* be able to assume the task it was now apparently desired to confide to it.

On (b), the literal interpretation of Eden's and Craborne's statements was that the unanimity rule in the Security Council should be entirely abolished. If so, six small states and one Great Power could overrule four Great Powers on any given matter – e.g. policy in regard to the Atomic

Bomb. If this was not so, then the suggestion presumably was that Article 27(3) of the Charter should be revised, so as to omit the phrase 'in decisions under Chapter VI and under paragraph 3 of Article 52', in other words that we should revert to our original proposal which was, rather tardily, accepted by the Americans, namely that in all circumstances 'parties to a dispute' should refrain from voting. Logically, and in equity, there was everything to be said for such a proposal. But in the first place it would necessitate rather long and cumbrous action under Article 108 *in which action all the Great Powers would have to concur*. And in the second place I strongly suspected that if it ever came to the point, opposition in the US Senate would be found to be almost as great as opposition by the Soviet Government. But even if such opposition could be overcome there was no guarantee that the government concerned would abide by their signature. All that would probably be accomplished by such an initiative would be the placing of a large spanner in the works of the world organization which might well result in its failing to function.

The moral seemed to be: however illogical or unethical the Charter, every effort should be made to put it into operation *as it was* as soon as possible. But this would imply that it would be unwise to refer too much in public to the necessity for a revision of the Charter; that direct discussion on treaty settlements between 'the governments having responsibility for such action' should be acknowledged to be one of the bases on which the UN must rest; and that, above all, one unpleasant truth should be emphasized – Atom Bomb or no Atom Bomb, no international system would work in existing conditions, unless harmony on great issues prevailed among at any rate the three really Great Powers.

My impression always was that in the Foreign Office much of the criticism of the San Francisco settlement came from Eric Beckett, who had succeeded Will Malkin as Legal Adviser. Eric was a man of great brilliance, but, as I always thought, of too theoretical a cast of mind. He had not been himself at Dumbarton Oaks or San Francisco. If he had been he might have had a more realistic impression of what we were up against and of what the world was actually like. Of course he was right, in a sense, in always insisting on the inherent weakness of the San Francisco system and of the obvious ways in which action by the UN in the political sphere could be frustrated unless the Super-Powers were in basic agreement. Indeed he may even have been said to have been prophetic in his warnings about the *impasse* which we would probably reach unless – which was after all highly unlikely – the Charter could be substantially revised and all concerned abide strictly by a new Charter.

But if the reader has followed the account of our struggles to create a meaningful world organization up to this point he will, perhaps, agree that it was better to get what we could get than to get nothing, which was the only apparent alternative. And, after all, the UN has now lasted for over a quarter of a century and, in spite of largely betraying the high, too high, hopes that were placed in it in 1945, does play a useful part in situations in which the Great Powers feel the need to come closer together and yet somehow lack the means. So perhaps my own appreciation at the time was the only sensible one. Certainly, looking back, I do not regret having expressed myself as I did.

The Preparatory Commission of all Members of the organization met for the second time in Church House on 24 November in order to discuss and approve the report of its Executive Committee. It had been preceded by a mock rehearsal in which I got the entire Secretariat to impersonate the delegates and see how our draft rules of procedure would work in practice. I myself was 'elected' President and dealt with various 'points of order'. Martin Hill represented 'Antarctica' and made a moving speech about the misfortunes and ambitions of the Penguins. Somebody else – a Patagonian I think – replied suitably. The available space, which was restricted, had to be used to the best possible advantage: facilities for the press had to be appraised; the restaurant inspected; the communications system tested; all the 'nuts and bolts', in fact, had to be shown to be in working order. And they were. When the Preparatory Commission itself assembled everything went entirely according to plan. A dignified and eminent lawyer from Columbia, Señor Zuleta Angel was, as previously arranged, elected President, and imposed himself very well. The machine began to function effectively. Some of the recommendations of the Executive Committee were suitably amended.

Then came the great day when all the leaders assembled for the first General Assembly. Central Hall, Westminster had been transformed by the Ministry of Works and every delegate had a beautiful light-blue chair, rather similar to those used at our coronations. There was just enough room for the five delegates per member which we had thought to be right, plus the five advisers behind them. On the rostrum were the President, flanked by the Executive Secretary, acting as Secretary-General, and, on the left, the 'Clerk', Andy Cordier. Suitable speeches were made to celebrate the beginning of a new age, the inaugural one of the Prime Minister being excellent; but most people could not help remembering what had happened to the League of Nations and there was less 'mystical' faith in the Parliament of Man in the British press than there had been in

1919. In America it was different. The United States was for the first time playing a leading – in practice, the leading – role on the world stage and they were determined to make a success of the undertaking. Typical of this serious determination was the fact that they successfully frowned on their British colleagues' tendency to refer to the new world organization as 'UNO', which sounded rather flippant, and insisted on 'UN'.

Paul-Henri Spaak of Belgium was elected President – rather against the will of the Russians who greatly preferred Trygve Lie, of Norway. He was an entirely brilliant president and one who could make an appropriate and convincing speech on almost any political subject at a moment's notice. After being 'President of the World' he became successively 'President of Europe' in 1949, and Secretary-General of NATO in 1957, ending up by succeeding me as President of the Atlantic Treaty Association in 1966. And he was perfectly consistent in his attitude in all these posts, always insisting that Western Europe should by one means or another unite, thus forming the Eastern 'pillar' of the Atlantic Alliance which in its turn should operate under the general aegis of the UN. Indeed I believe his first love has always been for 'Europe' – with Britain, if possible, without her if necessary.

After the early election of the President there was a fairly long delay before the election of the Secretary-General. This caused no surprise as there was no consensus of opinion about the right candidate. At one time 'official circles' in London seemed to favour Ed Stettinius who had some support, I believe, in the USA. Personally, as I told Alec Cadogan, I did not think that he would be very good and suggested that, if any candidate from a large power was to be considered at all we might advance the name of Richard Law,* who had worked so hard on UN problems when in the Foreign Office and whose heart would certainly be in the job. But Whitehall then seemed rather to favour Lester Pearson, who was admirable in every way, if only the Russians would look at a 'Western' candidate, which they probably would not (it will be remembered that under the Charter all permanent members of the Security Council have a veto in the election of a Secretary-General). Should the West likewise veto any Communist candidate I had the impression that the Russians might not oppose Jan Masaryk. But by that time it was clear that they would not veto Trygve Lie, a Norwegian socialist and he was in fact duly elected on 29 January, when I left my elevated perch and retired behind the British delegation, Spaak paying me a nice tribute and alleging that I was 'la perle des Secrétaires-Généraux provisoires'!

* Now Lord Coleraine.

It was during these few days that I was first conscious of becoming, as it were, a figure in my own right, and I did not like it much. More especially I was the subject of popular interest when the (no doubt quite erroneous) whisper went around that Bevin was tipping me as a possible Secretary-General. Journalists were always asking me to make 'statements' or give interviews, which I resolutely refused to do, preferring to regard myself as a temporary official only and being still most suspicious of the press. Nevertheless photographs of me appeared and I was sometimes represented as a sort of 'mystery' man, who was organizing everything behind the scenes. One scribe, after describing more or less what I was up to, exclaimed, 'This afternoon I saw Mr Jebb running from Church House to the Central Hall with a *very* strong expression on his face!' Furious, I should think rather than 'strong'. It may have been the day after I had been woken up by the telephone ringing at 3 a.m. and the representative of a paper in the Middle West asking me to make a 'statement' on progress. This after I had been working flat out for nearly six months with much too little sleep.

Meanwhile we had also elected the six non-permanent members of the Security Council which was thus enabled to function. Both Australia and Canada were candidates for the 'Commonwealth' seat, neither agreeing to stand down in favour of the other. I explained very clearly the system of voting, and indeed explained it twice. Every member would receive a blank sheet of paper and would write on it the names of the six member-countries of his choice. That and nothing else. When the votes were counted it was observed that one enthusiastic Latin American supporter of Canada had only written down that name along with five others but had signed the form with the name of his own country, followed by an exclamation mark. Since equal votes had been cast for Canada and Australia (which in ordinary circumstances would have meant a run off) this particular vote for Canada had to be declared invalid and Australia became a member of the Security Council for two years. *Quantula sapientia mundus regitur*!

The constitution of the Security Council had one rather dramatic result. No sooner had it been formed (17 January) than Persia hauled the Soviet Union before it in protest against the latter's failure to carry out its undertakings to withdraw its troops from Iran by the end of the war. It was rather as if a rabbit had bitten a stoat. I remember breaking this news to one of my Russian colleagues on the Secretariat, explaining that we, as good international civil servants, would have to see that the Persian complaint was handled with impartiality, efficiency and dispatch. Seldom have I seen a human being more visibly agitated. He muttered something and disappeared. Nor do I recall his being much help thereafter. A big horse-shoe table was hastily rigged up in the room where the Preparatory Commission had recently met. The rules of procedure had not been adopted (I seem to recall that they never were officially), but the draft rules were applied and a President was duly elected. Then the Russians had to defend their indefensible case – a stooge local government had, I think, already been installed in Tabriz, and the situation was altogether rather grim.

The horrible Vyshynsky nevertheless deployed all his great forensic talents, so successful in the past in getting his best friends condemned to death at bogus 'trials' in the Soviet Union. Disturbed by all this, Ernest Bevin delivered himself of slightly mantic utterances. Leaving my seat by the President and edging along the back of the table I asked Alec Cadogan who was sitting behind the Secretary of State whether he was, indeed, as seemed possible, threatening to use his veto? 'I haven't the slightest idea', said Alec: 'You had better ask him!' But I felt that it was hardly up to the Executive Secretary to do any such thing either by passing up a note or by whispering in his ear. So the formidable heavyweight at the table continued to brood and to exhibit displeasure which undoubtedly had a considerable effect. The question was adjourned but was taken up again shortly in New York and eventually the Russians gave in and withdrew their troops. If people ask what success the UN has ever had in the foreign political field at least Azerbaijan in 1946 can be chalked up to its credit.

Part of the credit undoubtedly must go to the late Trygve Lie with whom I was naturally in close contact during the time when he was taking over the Secretariat and before he moved it to New York on 15 March. From the first he took a strong line on the Persian issue and I am sure he communicated his views very directly to the Soviet Government, indicating that if they refused to withdraw their troops he simply could not answer for the consequences, by which, I imagine, he meant that if they insisted on breaking their pledged word they risked a major confrontation with the Western powers, backed up by the full weight of international public opinion. Incidentally, Lie was largely instrumental in getting the Russians to evacuate the Danish Island of Bornholm in the Baltic where they had no business to be, but which they hung on to, perhaps under the erroneous impression that if they went the British or Americans would at once take their place and proceed to fortify it.

But there was another event in that month which 'shook the Chancelleries', as they used to say in the nineteenth century, during these critical weeks. In a speech at Fulton, Missouri on 4 March, made in the presence of President Truman, Winston Churchill directly criticized the Soviet Government and gave public expression for the first time to the presence of an 'Iron Curtain'. Looking back on the Fulton speech it is rather difficult, in the light of hindsight, to see why it created such consternation. There were then many, however, in Britain – more particularly perhaps in Labour Party circles – who maintained that it was a terrible shock for the Soviet Government, causing them to become convinced of the hostility of the 'Anglo-Saxons' and of the latters' desire above all to re-create the famous *cordon sanitaire* round the workers' paradise in order to separate the USSR from the outside world and eventually encompass its downfall. This was also the line put out by high Soviet officials, one of whom told me in confidence that he had been with Stalin and Molotov when the news was received in Moscow and that its effect had been precisely as described above.

I was myself at the time not unresponsive to this line in spite of my considerable suspicion of Russian motives and believed that Fulton was probably a mistake as likely to make the Soviet Government even more uncooperative than it otherwise would be. Certainly this was the Secretary-General's view. He told me that though he largely shared the sentiments expressed in it, the speech had, he thought, played into the hand of the anti-Western elements in Moscow and into that of the 'seven thousand Russian Generals', many of whom were now without employment. I believe he tried to convince Bevin of the correctness of this view and to get him to 'repudiate' Churchill in some way; but the Secretary of State did nothing of the kind. He had already made his own views known in a speech in the House of Commons on 21 February, in which he said that, according to some, we were 'drifting into war with Russia'. But he himself 'could not conceive of any circumstances in which Britain and the Soviet Union would go to war'. When he had 'discussed the Western bloc with (Vyshynsky)' – or rather not the Western bloc but the 'Western arrangements of friendly neighbours', Vyshynsky's answer to him was 'I believe you'. But he was certainly not going to repudiate Churchill for, though he would not then admit it publicly, he knew that what the latter had said at Fulton was true.

Was Lie nevertheless justified in believing that Fulton had at least put the clock back, if indeed it had not been actually responsible for the triumph of the anti-Western 'hard-liners' in Moscow? I doubt it. From Yalta onwards, that is to say well over a year before Fulton, and in exact proportion to the amount of territory that they 'liberated' the line of the

Soviet Government had got harder and harder. There was Poland, Roumania, Turkey, Persia. There was their behaviour in Germany where from the first they set their face against any real inter-allied co-operation in the administration of the country as a whole and concentrated above all else on the total exploitation and strict communization of their Eastern zone. Most significant of all, perhaps, was their manifest and increasing reluctance to get down to the organization of the Military Staff Committee on which, as I have already shown, the peace-keeping activities of the UN, if they were to have any real meaning, so largely depended. We had suggested that even previously to its actual constitution the designated members of this committee might at any rate assemble in London and at least talk things over among themselves. The Americans did send over a high-powered team and the French were, I seem to remember, quite prepared to play, but the Russians showed no enthusiasm, and indeed on 4 January 1946, Molotov himself announced that it would be 'premature' to do anything of the kind.

We ourselves were, however, taking the Military Staff Committee extremely seriously as, from what I heard, were the Chiefs of Staff. Lord Alanbrooke, I was told, was only concerned lest the total numbers of forces put at the disposal of the Staff Committee would be so large as to make the British contribution appear insignificant; which seemed to show that he at any rate was taking the committee seriously. And I also heard that the War Office, not unnaturally, wanted a rough estimate of what forces were considered necessary to overpower any particular country! Lord Tedder's attitude, again very sensibly, seemed to be that, before taking any definite decision as to the 'ear-marking' of forces, we ought to be told who was likely to be the potential aggressor. All this demonstrated the deep waters into which we were likely to get when we came to negotiate the famous 'special agreements' prescribed by the Charter. But there was at least every desire on our part to have intelligent discussion as between high serving officers on all these matters. Enormous papers were prepared; Jack Ward was largly responsible for getting the Security Council to take a preliminary decision to set up the committee before the UN left for New York; but as is known nothing came of all this activity owing to Russian obstruction, and eventually the committee became a simple formality, the members, who got increasingly less high ranking, simply agreeing to meet every so often to agree on the agenda, which was the date of the next meeting, and then disperse. It is, as I say, arguable that the thing could never have worked properly in a world dominated by independent Great Powers and even more independent Super-Powers.

What is certain is that it was Russian suspicions, well before Fulton, which were chiefly responsible for its failure to function at all. It was thus in some ways a sadder and wiser man who in March 1946 resumed his duties as Counsellor in the Foreign Office.

12

Under-Secretary
(1946-8)

It was, on the whole, with relief that I returned to the fold all the more so since there seemed to be a prospect of working under Bevin on the coming peace treaties with Italy and the minor European ex-enemies. And indeed I was shortly made an Under-Secretary with this responsibility, becoming deputy to the Secretary of State in the negotiations which were to start up with a meeting in Paris of the Council of Foreign Ministers on 25 April. By far the most important of the treaties, from our point of view, was that with Italy, and its negotiation presented several difficulties. First and foremost, the future of the Italian colonies, followed by the disputed frontier with Yugoslavia; that with Austria; reparations; and the disposal of the Italian Fleet. There were, I need hardly say, also a host of minor problems, including the French claim to two villages and a power-station on the frontier of the west of Turin called Tenda and Briga (usually referred to by the Secretary as 'Brenda and Tiger'), put forward, partially we thought, for presitge reasons with which we were by no means unsympathetic after what France had had to undergo at the hands of Mussolini.

By early April I see that I was in the thick of purely diplomatic fencing, and enjoying it very much. Was Jimmy Byrnes being over-impetuous in suggesting the fixing of a definite date for the conference (12 May)? No doubt we were right to agree to 25 April as the date for a meeting of the Council of Foreign Ministers in Paris. But surely we did not want to be brow-beaten by the Russians (whose line was that they would not come to a conference unless the Foreign Ministers had agreed on all substantial points beforehand) into making concessions which we might otherwise not feel disposed to make? Would it perhaps in these areas be preferable for the French to summon a conference of only those states which were prepared to attend? Or might there be no conference at all, each power signing a separate treaty with the ex-enemies? One evident disadvantage here would be the blow to Great Power cooperation in the UN, always supposing that we still attached major importance to this. Alternatively, what about a sort of a second 'Potsdam', this time with France? Eventually the date of 25 April held good for the Council of Foreign Ministers, which lasted till 15 May.

I shall never forget Sammy Hood's and my arrival for the first time since the war in Paris during that cold late spring of 1946. The lovely town had then been liberated for over one and a half years and seemed outwardly much the same, but there were acute shortages and we had been told that it was the right thing, for us at any rate, to live on the official rations in order to set an example. This conception, however, was foreign to the staff of the Hotel George v, and we quickly understood that it would be regarded as abnormal, not to say unfortunate, if we insisted on only ordering small quantities of rather basic nourishment. The first night I, rather nervously, ordered some champagne for my little team, a drink to which we had become unaccustomed after three years of fearful red wine from Algeria, only suitable for consumption with blue whale steak.

When the Secretary of State came out things cheered up quite a bit. It was his favourite relaxation to assemble his devoted staff in his suite after dinner and once in a while lead them in old-fashioned (but perfectly decorous) choruses, the rather raucous din resulting occasionally in mild protests by the management. Edmund Hall Patch, of the Treasury, a great favourite of Bevin's, was prominent on these occasions. And somewhat to our surprise, we discovered that William Strang had a fine tenor voice. The great point of these jollifications, Ernie Bevin said, was to show that the Foreign Office officials were human – though as a matter of fact he need never have had any great fears about that. Unquestionably no other head of delegation could have so proceeded. The idea of the Soviet delegation, under the leadership of Molotov, bellowing out *Stenka Razin* in the recesses of the Russian Embassy defies the imagination. I suppose Jimmy Byrnes conceivably might have done something similar, though hardly Georges Bidault* and certainly not Lord Castereagh. What is clear is that, even if the sing-song did not reveal the essential humanity of the Foreign Office *tchinovniks*, it undoubtedly revealed that of the Secretary of State.

Duff Cooper was then our Ambassador in Paris. He was a great personality and a very lovable man. He and his wife Diana held what can only be called a court in the great house in the Rue du Faubourg S. Honoré

* French Prime Minister 1946 and 1949–50.

and all Paris could be found at their parties, more particularly since their distinction between *résistants* and *collabos* often seemed to be a little blurred. Duff was greatly respected in France, both because he was a genuine Francophile and because he was a shrewd politician and an *homme de lettres* as well – something that the French greatly appreciate and which they find more often in their own statesmen than in ours. His book on Talleyrand was a small masterpiece and he had a great knowledge of French history too. As for Diana, her beauty and intelligence were then as legendary as they are today, so everybody agreed that we could hardly be better represented.

Duff used to come to the delegation meetings in the George v, but did not seem to take much interest in the *minutiae* of our negotiations. Quite rightly, since there was not much in them (except possibly in regard to the Italian colonies) which were likely to affect our relations with France, his main concern. He was brooding chiefly, I think, so far as high policy went, on the possibility of a much closer association between our two countries, preferably in the framework of some 'Western union', and I do not believe that he had ever accepted the 'Four Power' conception, that is to say the necessity, as we still saw it, of trying to cooperate with the Russians and achieve some kind of European and German settlement which they would be disposed to take.

It was much to the credit of Ernest Bevin that he agreed to the Coopers staying on at the Embassy until 1947. Duff's was, after all, a political appointment, and he must have been under fairly strong pressure to appoint a career diplomat, or even an outstanding member of his own party. But apart from the fact that both the Ambassador and the Ambassadress were great favourites of his, I am sure that he recognized the desirability of retaining Duff (who had served as our representative in Algiers before the liberation of France) until the immediate internal difficulties of the country had been overcome and it had settled down into what looked like being a fairly stable regime bearing, incidentally, a marked resemblance to that of the Third Republic.

We did not get agreement on all outstanding points – and notably on the Italian colonies – before the Council of Foreign Ministers broke up on 15 May, but it was nevertheless agreed that the full peace conference should open on 29 July. The Palais du Luxembourg, which normally houses the French Senate (the future of which had still not been constitutionally determined), was put at our disposal and we all assembled in its red velvet Second Empire splendour, the United States being represented by Jimmy Byrnes (who had taken over from Stettinius earlier in the year), the French by Georges Bidault and the Russians by Molotov. The real work was to be done either in meetings of the deputies of the four 'sponsoring' powers or in committees of the whole conference; and this time, as the Council of Foreign Ministers had shown, we were not destined to have acute conflicts with the Russians, though in some subjects they were difficult enough.

I do not however propose to dwell at any length on this conference since, as it seems to me, it was not of the first importance, nor in any case did it affect my own outlook on things very much. I worked away, competently enough I imagine, at the various outstanding difficulties, assisted by my new private secretary, Shirley Morgan,* daughter of the writer, Charles Morgan, who was a personal friend of ours. Shirley tells me that she knew I had the reputation of intimidating my secretaries, but that she had early on decided not to be intimidated. So when the buzzer went she did not, to the amazement of her colleagues, instantly fly to take down, but if, for instance, she was eating an ice-cream actually finished it before complying! Of course I had not any idea that I was intimidating her or anybody else, and anyhow I always greatly preferred people who stood up to me, and never could abide having dealings with nervous assistants.

Some people thought that the mere fact that the 'Peace Conference' was meeting in Paris at all meant that in some way it would be comparable to Versailles, the consequences of which did shake the world and are still with us. This shows the damage caused by historical parallels. It is true that in some ways Paris might be thought to have been even more significant than Versailles, since, after all, the Russians were present as well as the Americans; but there was no question of settling the fate of Europe in the Luxembourg Palace in 1946 to say nothing of that of the world. The first had already been settled – though we did not then admit it – at Potsdam: the second at San Francisco. What remained was really a squabble about a port and a few hundred square miles of land between the Italians, more or less backed up by the Western Powers, and the Yugoslavs, at that time more or less backed up by the Russians, none of the powers concerned, however, being in the least disposed to push things to the point of war. That and the vexatious but not in itself first-class issue of the future of the Italian colonies. All the rest was tidied up quite satisfactorily, though it must be admitted that one quite large issue – the complete freedom of navigation on the Danube – was pushed on one side by the Russians for obvious reasons.

Not all Western observers noticed this essential difference. Harold

* Later the Marchioness of Anglesey.

Nicolson, for instance, who had played a major role behind the scenes of Versailles and was now looking down (from the Press Gallery) on his young companion of the Tehran Legation sitting in a red velvet chair, did not think that the one conference at all measured up to the other, and noted that the standard of representation seemed less impressive than in the great days of Clemenceau, Lloyd George, Balfour and President Wilson. So it was, no doubt; and no doubt, too, as he also noted, the craft and practice of diplomacy had suffered in the interval owing to the progress of the 'mass media' and the insistence by the public of a full knowledge of everything that was going on. But, within their limits, good and constructive work was done in the various committees in spite of the national passions, which were often unrestrained.

I remember once coming back to my own committee and finding, somewhat to my alarm, the young Fred Warner, who had only just joined the Service, in full spate on something which did not appear to have much connection with the Foreign Office brief. I remember also that in the Political Committee, after furious and lengthy debate on Trieste, in which the Yugoslavs had been particularly intransigent, it was decided to limit speeches to five minutes before taking a vote. The Yugoslav representative was Moshe Piyade, a veteran partisan intellectual of great brilliance and enthusiasm. After speaking for about ten minutes he was quite properly called to order by the South African chairman, but I suggested that in view of his great sincerity he should be allowed to finish his speech as soon as he could. Piyade then proceeded for another five minutes to gabble off the remainder (in French) at such speed that not a single word was intelligible, finally throwing his script to an interpreter and sinking exhausted into his chair. In the end after six more years of struggle the Yugoslavs lost out on Trieste, and nobody in Yugoslavia now pays any attention to the fact.

The same, I suppose, may be said of the Italian colonies. Nobody now in Italy regrets their loss. The Italian political situation may be difficult; but, broadly speaking, the economic (as opposed to the political) development of the country since the war has been a great success story. Anyone recalling the declaration of Mussolini in the thirties that a 'colonial outlet' was essential to an overcrowded Italy which otherwise would sink into some kind of depression, including, presumably, severe unemployment and a lowered standard of living, must admit that the Duce was talking arrant nonsense. The real reason, as we now see it, for the 'colonial outlet' uproar was to maintain himself and his regime in power. The reason why the disposal of the Italian Empire by the victorious allies took so long was not because of any solicitude for Italy: though probably by depriving her of her colonies they were, unconsciously, doing her a favour. The difficulty lay in reaching a solution in which all of them might see some advantage, or at any rate one in which no one of them might be thought to be put at some great disadvantage.

The objective then, as indeed now, of the Russians was, if possible, to obtain a physical foothold in the Eastern Mediterranean, and perhaps even in the horn of Africa; of the French to have no solution which was likely to prejudice their own position on 'the southern shore' (when we came down initially in favour of some kind of independence for Libya, René Massigli told us it was 'a bombshell for the French'); of the British to maintain their military link with Cyrenaica, where incidentally they had assured Sheikh Idris el Senussi that he would never again come under Italian rule; of the Americans to create some kind of 'trusteeship' that might be a model for all other dependent territories. Countless meetings were held to try to reconcile these divergent and indeed irreconcilable objectives. In one (of the four Foreign Ministers) Bevin dozed off for about half an hour – or appeared to do so – and left me to do the talking. But at the end of the meeting he emerged from what seemed to be a trance and firmly told his colleagues that he agreed with every word that I had said! Usually, however, he was very much on the ball and fully capable of coping with the combination of Molotov and Vyshynsky. Mr Byrnes, for his part, was invariably flanked by two senatorial heavy-weights in the shape of Messrs Connally (Democrat) and Vandenberg (Republican) who never said anything and maintained a rather disapproving silence throughout which must have been rather discouraging, not to say embarrassing for their leader. Bidault was extremely agile, but even he, with the aid of the most skilled diplomatists in the world, could not find a suitable compromise.

So the negotiation could not be concluded in Paris and was adjourned to New York where the three ministers were going for the second part of the first session of the United Nations. And even then it was not settled. For though the Treaty of Peace with Italy was finally signed on 10 February 1947, it contained a 'Joint Declaration' by the Four Powers to the effect that they would 'jointly determine' within one year the fate of the colonies (which Italy formally renounced), such 'final disposal' being made 'in the light of the wishes and welfare of the inhabitants and the interests of peace and security'; that if they were unable to agree within one year the matter would be referred to the General Assembly of the United Nations; and that in the interval the deputies would continue to study the question and would send out a commission to supply them with the necessary data. Needless to say they did not agree on the correct solution within a year and the question was therefore referred to the General Assembly which, as might be supposed, decided in favour of complete independence.

I myself was from the start strongly opposed to this solution, urging that Libya which consisted of three small centres of population separated by hundreds of miles of sand, the whole with not more than one million inhabitants, could not possibly be a state 'willing and able to carry out its obligations under the Charter', to use the language of that document, and to admit that it could be such a state would be to open the floodgates and create an Assembly of tiny and often irresponsible nations represented, as often as not, in the UN itself by clever New York lawyers. This is what happened. Soon, no doubt, Monaco and San Marino will be casting votes equal to that of the Soviet Union. I am all for the smaller states which frequently play a most useful role in an organization at present dominated by two Super-states; but there are limits.

It had been arranged that I should combine my job as deputy to the Secretary of State for the peace treaties with that of UN Adviser, so it was with a double function that I left with my boss for the second Session of the General Assembly in New York on 23 October. New York was still to some extent a gay and carefree city in 1946. The enormous Waldorf Astoria Hotel where we then had our rooms and offices seemed very luxurious after the austerity of war-time London. Ernie himself was in fine form, but beyond a powerful speech or two did not intervene much in UN affairs which he left to Phil Noel-Baker, Hartley Shawcross* and Hector McNeil, and indeed, so far as the Security Council was concerned, to Cadogan. Nor could the Secretary of State have done better. Phil's passionate attachment to and knowledge of the UN added weight to the British cause, just as it had done in the twenties and thirties at Geneva; Hartley had one of the best legal brains of his generation and his advocacy was quite invaluable; Hector was a first-rate and convincing speaker, and was extremely popular with all Americans as well. Taken all in all, I should say that our delegation that year was probably the strongest we have ever had. Besides, we felt on the top of the wave. The war was over; a better world was at least beginning to emerge; the Labour Government was going to undertake all the great reforms that had for so long been needed in England; everything was possible and all was new.

* Chief British prosecutor at Nuremberg war crimes trials. Labour MP 1945–58; Attorney General 1945–51; principal delegate for United Kingdom to the UN 1945–9.

Very soon, however, the discouragement which I had experienced earlier in the year returned in a more acute form. As veto followed veto and the Russians became more and more obstructive, not only on such matters as the Military Staff Committee, but on the control of atomic energy, disarmament, human rights, or indeed on any subject you could think of save only (to some extent) the peace treaties, I got more and more indignant. Finally, on 30 October, Molotov made what I thought was an altogether deplorable speech expressing his general point of view and I made some unofficial comments severely criticizing almost every point he had made and ending up by predicting that the whole Russian policy now seemed to be working up to some kind of showdown with the Western Powers, no doubt over Germany. It was in fact only little over a year later that the Soviet Government took the plunge and organized the famous blockade of West Berlin. More particularly I attacked Molotov's thesis of the 'two tendencies', one peaceful and democratic, the other warlike and Fascist, which, as he saw it were now struggling for supremacy in world affairs.

It is only fair to note that Sobolev, to whom, at lunch, I advanced a number of these criticisms, not unnaturally defended his chief very vigorously. He protested, for instance, that the USSR had been deeply offended at our not consulting them in advance as regards the terms of the Trusteeship agreements. This, he said, was treating the Soviet Union as a Power of no importance, simply because owing to her defeat she had not been represented at the 1919 Conference of Paris. On Iran he also alleged that the Soviet Government were deeply wounded by the question being left on the agenda of the Security Council; and as for twisting the Persians' tails, what about us and the eviction of Reza Shah during the war? Anyhow the Russians had behaved irreproachably about Persia during the last six months (which was true). On the 'two tendencies' Molotov did not, of course, mean that the Soviet Government could not cooperate fully with governments differing from its own in composition and outlook: the Comintern had been dissolved and it must be clear that the Communist parties in Europe did not now follow any central directive. As for the Veto, this was dictated by a profound mistrust of the campaign now waged against it which, the Soviet Government believed, was being encouraged by the UK and the USA. Perhaps the Australians were not just our agents (though Herbert Evatt had twice 'provoked' Gromyko into using the Veto), but Dr Belt of Cuba (the Cuban Ambassador in the USA) was certainly a stooge of the Americans. Sobolev in fact simply refused to believe that the latter were not hell-bent on revising the Charter.

Could I in any case imagine that the Soviet Government was in a position to wage an aggressive war? But why, I retorted, should they then accuse the Western Powers, who, unlike the Russians had demobilized, of wanting to do any such thing? And why give the impression that the Russian intention was to set up 'stooge' governments in Turkey and Persia? Sobolev denied all this. He agreed that the great hope was some-how or other to get the UN to work, though this would be difficult enough, he thought, in New York, which he detested.

How far, I wonder, was the Russian reaction or over-reaction based on fear, and how far on a genuine intention to undermine the position of what they undoubtedly regarded as an adversary? Maybe there had after Yalta been some kind of decision to keep the West at arm's length and do everything possible to disrupt the close association between Britain and the United States. But I believe that the chief motive was simple fear that the Soviet regime might be endangered if there was any close contact with the West. There was no doubt whatever that a great number of Soviet officials and even soldiers who had had dealings with the West during the war were infected by 'dangerous thoughts', notably as regards individual freedom of thought and expression which were totally at variance with the Soviet system. The Soviet Government had therefore not only to limit the number of contacts that could be made with Westerners, but had also to build up a picture of external 'aggressors' whose one object was to destroy the Socialist motherland. All this had to be done over and above the natural desire to secure the age-long objectives of Russian policy, namely warm-water ports, a 'glacis' in Europe and a consolidation of their Asian Empire. In other words, genuine cooperation on the part of the Soviet Government with the other governments concerned in the positive organization of a world peace system was impossible: the most that might be expected was a tacit mutual undertaking not to interfere in certain specified areas.

Even if this theory is only approximately true it must follow that the favourite suggestion of the Soviet Government and their apologists, namely that the prospects of intelligent cooperation with the Russians were all ruined by Churchill's Fulton speech* in March 1946, is, as I have already noted, a fantasy. What Soviet Russia wanted, as Churchill said, was not war, but the fruits of war, and the indefinite expansion of their power and doctrines. If you substitute 'the Western system of free enter-prise' for 'Christian civilization' (said by Churchill to be the chief object of Soviet attack), these simple truths could not be seriously disputed. The

* See also Chapter 11, p. 185.

fact that they had been uttered by Churchill could not therefore by itself involve any change in an existing situation. If there had ever been any chance of the Soviet Government's adopting an attitude which might have made genuine cooperation with the West possible it was before San Francisco. After Potsdam, failing a revolution in Moscow, the Cold War was inevitable. The only question was the intensity with which it was waged: whether indeed there was a prospect of its developing into a real war – which I consistently doubted – or whether it would merely result in continuing 'tension'. Some people thought that the latter was a terrible prospect and that we ought to go to great lengths to end it; but we have now lived with it quite successfully for over a quarter of a century.

It was not only with the Communists that we were preoccupied in New York during that autumn. The problem of Franco Spain presented itself at once, and for the Labour Party, then as now, but more especially then, the very name 'Franco' acted as a red rag to a bull. The Caudillo has now, I believe, suppressed the Fascist Falange altogether and is actively preparing the ground for a monarchy; but some still regard his regime as practically indistinguishable from that of Stalin or indeed of that of 'Papa Doc' in Haiti. In 1946, however, the Falange still had considerable influence and memories of the Civil War, which had only ended in 1939, were still painfully vivid. The delegation also included some pretty 'hot-gospellers' on the subject of Spain, the chief of which was perhaps Barbara Castle. But the policy of the Foreign Office under Bevin was distinctly moderate. Refusing to be stampeded into measures which he believed would be quite counter-productive, such as military action or economic sanctions, or even the withdrawal of diplomatic representation, the Secretary of State, ably backed up by Hartley Shawcross, though he argued against debarring Franco Spain from various international organizations, ended up by voting for it in the General Assembly as a concession to the deep anti-Franco and anti-Fascist feeling which he recognized was widely shared in the United Nations generally, and which indeed he shared himself. But he was far too realistic a man to think, as some of his colleagues thought, that Franco could be brought down by gestures or resolutions. To bring him down force would be required: and to that he was firmly opposed.

At the beginning of 1947 it was obvious not only that the whole idea of Great Power cooperation was in grave danger of collapse, but that Britain herself was in some danger of collapsing; and I find that as early as February I noted that unless we could so organize our production and our export trade as to be able to stand on our own feet – even with a slightly lower standard of living – we should, after the American loan ran out, either have to live on the charity of America, and therefore cease to have any real foreign policy of our own, or not count for very much in the councils of the Great Powers owing to the inevitably drastic curtailment of our armaments and our overseas commitments. One means, I reflected, whereby we might to some extent alleviate our economic plight, and also our political position, would be some form of economic union with the Western European countries and, if possible some special economic relationship with the Western German zones as well. If Russian policy should continue to be totally uncompromising we might, before the American loan ran out, be able to establish a centralized Germany and go in firmly for a Western bloc – provided, I added, that we could overcome the French Communists (who then looked as if they really might soon be seizing power).

Strangely enough I also see that about this time (February) I was still taking the view that we ought not to despair of eventually getting agreement with the USSR on the long-term control of Germany which might well, in default of such agreement, become once again a menace owing to both sides competing for her favours; but in spite of reverting to this possibility several times during the year I finally had to agree that there was in fact no way round the basic dilemma: unless you were prepared to accept terms which could well result in Germany's being united on Communist lines, or alternatively unless you were prepared to evict the Russians from their zone by force of arms, there was only one solution – continued division of Germany. The formula that by 'German Unification' we meant 'reunification of the three existing German zones in peace and freedom', i.e. *de facto* acceptance of existing frontiers, no employment of force and free elections, was all very well; the only difficulty was that the Russians would never admit free elections. Why we ever thought they might and went on about it for so many years is a mystery to me. Presumably in order not to discourage the Western Germans. Yet, for as long as the West held together, the danger that the latter would succumb to Soviet blandishments was (and is) very slight.

In May there was nevertheless much talk about bases and our whole position in the Middle East. The military naturally took the view that we should, in principle, have enough forces in that area to counter any possible aggressive move by the Soviet Union. I did not dispute this but noted that in any Anglo-American/Soviet war – which obviously we should do everything to prevent – success would depend on the immediate use by the West of the Atomic Weapon. If we failed to use this (we must remember that this was in early 1947 before Russia or, indeed, Britain had developed the Bomb) there was every reason to suppose that the continent would be overrun and possibly the Middle East as well, thus opening the way for the control by Russia of the whole land-mass or 'World Island' and the rendering untenable of the position of Great Britain – and indeed ultimately of the USA. It was largely because of this possibility that I constantly came back to Cyrenaica in my thinking. A secure air base for us there seemed to me to be essential if we were contemplating any defence of the Middle East at all.

The great event of 1947 was, however, the startling initiative of the President of the USA known as the 'Truman Declaration' made on 12 March in an address to Congress. As is known, this had been precipitated by a formal note communicated to the State Department on 24 February, to the effect that the British Government could no longer afford to provide any kind of assistance to Greece and Turkey and that such assistance would therefore have to stop by the end of the financial year, i.e. in five weeks' time exactly. I do not think that this was really meant to force the Americans' hand; it was simply an acknowledgement of an important fact – that Britain had no more money left in the till. Certainly the tremendous reaction of the Americans was not expected and the declaration therefore came as a surprise. What was unfortunate was that it also came as the Council of Foreign Ministers in Moscow was starting and the Russians must certainly have interpreted it as a premeditated move on the part of the West to torpedo that conference, which was not the case.

I lost no time in subjecting the declaration to a long analysis; for this purpose dividing it up into several 'parts'. The following is a short summary: *Part I*, I thought, was simply an introduction drawing attention to the fact that the international situation was grave and that the security of America was endangered. *Part II* dealt with the specific reasons why outside assistance to the governments of Greece and Turkey was essential. For Greece, such aid was indeed 'imperative' if Greece was to survive as a free nation. This included substantial military assistance. For Turkey only financial assistance was necessary.

In *Part III*, however, we came to the broad political implications of the suggested action. The foreign policy of America, it was laid down, must 'work towards the creation of conditions in which we and the other nations will be able to work out a way of life free from coercion'. In spite of setting up the UN, the USA would not achieve this end unless 'we are willing to help free peoples to maintain their free institutions and their national integrity against movements that seek to impose on them their regime'. If such regimes were imposed by 'direct or indirect aggression' not only international peace, but also the security of the USA would be endangered. But it actually had happened in Poland, Roumania and Bulgaria and a number of other countries. Every nation therefore had to choose between two alternative ways of life: *either* 'majority rule, free institutions, representative governments, free elections, individual liberty, freedom of speech and freedom from political oppression', *or* 'minority rule forcibly imposed and relying on terror and oppression, a controlled press and radio, faked elections and suppression of personal freedom'. The US should therefore support all peoples resisting alternative number two, primarily by means of economic and financial aid. The *status quo* was not sacred but the US would not allow changes occurring in violation of the Charter by such methods as coercion or political infiltration.

Part IV reverted to Greece and Turkey and argued that if Greece should fall under the control of a small minority the effect on Turkey might be disastrous, as indeed it would be in the Middle East as a whole and in other countries as well. *Part V* made it clear what exactly Congress was expected to provide in the way of funds (four hundred million dollars) and *Part VI* was, effectively, a peroration.

The inferences which I drew from this declaration were as follows. It appeared on the face of it to be a hurriedly assembled amalgam of various drafts. Parts I, II and V seemed to bear the imprint of the State Department. Parts III, IV and VI – the 'political' content – might well have been composed by some political figure, or at any rate someone with a knowledge of the workings of Congress. Even if it had not been for the presumed 'political insertion' the statement would have been imperfect and controversial enough. For it was not far removed from a conditional guarantee by America not only of the independence but also of the territorial integrity of Greece and Turkey – something that was not even embodied in the UN Charter. But Parts III and IV went much further even than that. They contained a pledge to help *all free peoples* in their struggle against totalitarianism. Such help might even be military (cf. reference to US security). So it might well be inferred that the USA was going henceforward to assist any anti-Communist government or movement even in Eastern Europe, and even (for the reference was to 'peoples') in the Soviet Union itself.

My conclusions therefore were:

(1) If the Soviet Government continued to encourage Communist movements outside the Soviet Union there must be an enduring struggle between them and the US Government.

(2) The proposed American support for all non-totalitarian governments or movements undoubtedly applied to the Soviet 'sphere of influence' in Eastern Europe and elsewhere.

(3) It was not clear what would happen if any government 'went Communist' by legal means; but it was obvious that the US Government now regarded its own 'way of life' as quite incompatible with the 'way of life' of the other Super Power thus making it difficult to see how the two governments could possibly cooperate in the UN.

(4) (a) If this were so, however, how was it that America had agreed to Communist governments being admitted as founder members of the UN?

(b) How could the US be expected to act impartially in the UN in any dispute between a Communist and a non-Communist country?

I did not put these questions in a sense critical of President Truman's action which was, so far as Greece and Turkey were concerned, obviously necessary and greatly to be welcomed. But the mere posing of the various questions did bring out the fact that the UN could not work if any powerful nation used it as a stalking horse for the propagation of its own way of life. Thus a Communist could only feel that President Truman was using the UN as a means of imposing, all over the world, a way of life which, in Commonwealth eyes led to unemployment, slumps and the exploitation of the working class. It followed that two huge *Weltanschauungen* were in direct conflict and the whole basis of the UN had been shown to be fallacious. This did not mean that conditions of 'armed neutrality' might not exist for a considerable time. It would probably also be in the Soviet interest to carry on as if nothing had happened, and this in spite of the fact that the US had now to all intents and purposes declared the USSR to be unfit to be a member. All we could do, in any case, was to see that the UN carried on somehow, in the hope of better times and of the creation of circumstances in which it might once again become a living reality. In a way my analysis was a sort of funeral oration.

But the situation was really not as bad as I thought, either from the point of view of the UN itself or from that of the Cold War which in a sense had begun at Potsdam. I had, indeed, taken the declaration too seriously. A great deal of the political rhetoric had probably been inserted for the sole purpose of getting Congress to foot the bill for the admittedly essential help for Greece and Turkey. It was actually a red letter day for us when the US did shoulder that particular burden. As the year went on I came to regard the declaration much more objectively. On 17 June I noted that it had already been much modified. On 14 July I had reached the conclusion that the original Truman Declaration, welcome though it was in essence, was a badly thought out and impetuous gesture. The Marshall approach was far more constructive. As we know, the latter was originally designed to put enormous funds, in the shape of 'aid', at the disposal of governments which, in the Truman Declaration, had been publicly branded as the enemies of society.

The declaration was, in fact, overtaken by the Harvard speech of General Marshall and everything that flowed from it. That speech was made after the long Moscow Conference of the ministers had ended in failure and in circumstances which might well have produced a more strident note. The Russians had been clamping down their iron rule in Poland, Hungary, Roumania and Bulgaria with a series of murders and arrests of all those who had ever betrayed any sympathy towards the Western nations. Conscription had had to be introduced in the USA. Taxes were going up. An immense disillusionment was gaining America. And yet the Marshall utterance was not only less alarmist and categorical than the Truman Declaration, it was also in advance of the latter in that it (a) treated Europe as a whole; (b) prescribed a coherent economic plan and (c) contemplated a definite period of years during which it might be expected to operate. What might have happened if it had been made on 12 March rather than on 5 June is a most interesting speculation. It is just possible that it might have changed the course of history. As it was it was left to Molotov to change the course of history by turning down the spectacular offer of American aid to the Eastern as well as to the Western European states. Seldom can a gesture have been fraught with more consequence than that, even though, given the bitter ideological background, it was perhaps only to be expected. Seldom too can statesmen have been more pleased by a gesture than Bevin and Bidault.

If the great achievement of a statesman is to do something right at the right time then it must also be admitted that 7 June was the Secretary of State's supreme moment. For on that day he warmly welcomed General Marshall's initiative and said he was 'exploring actively and urgently' how best to meet it. Then he went to see Bidault and proposed that the European states concerned should all get together and collectively work out the use to which the dollars should be put, in other words, get out a joint programme, agreed to by a number, if not of all, of the European countries concerned. The French are often apt to underestimate the part which the British played, under Bevin's lead, partly because the resulting Organization for European Economic Cooperation, which duly emerged in the following year (under the permanent chairmanship of Oliver Franks*) was definitely non-supra-national; partly because many of them like to think that it was almost entirely the work of Jean Monnet assisted by Robert Marjolin.† It is perfectly true that had the British Government at that time been ready to inaugurate a system embodying the conception of an independent commission, qualified majority voting in a Council of Ministers, and so on, 'Europe' might have at least been started in 1948. But to imagine that such things were possible in that year is to ignore any reality. Even the great Congress of the Hague which Churchill and Sandys organized in May (and which I will touch on later) did not go as far as that. The average British voter, for his part, would certainly at that time have regarded any such plan as 'chaining him to a corpse'! What happened was that for ten years, from 1948 to 1958, the British did run 'Europe' in their own way but, after Suez did not observe the writing on the wall which they could and should have read betimes.

I did not myself have anything to do with the great European Relief Programme, as it was called at the time. Marshall Aid was certainly the most imaginative and creative policy ever conducted by the USA. Without it there was no doubt whatever that Western Europe would have consisted of countries which, by the force of things, would have had increasingly directed economies and thus have become increasingly subservient to the Soviet Union. Thus France might have become a larger Poland, and even if Western Germany had been specially favoured, her dramatic economic recovery would have been impossible and she might have become more and more tempted by siren-voices from the other side of the Iron Curtain. In Italy, the Communists would almost certainly have taken over. And even in the UK the situation would have been extremely grim. In the long run, and even if this was not her real intention, there is no doubt that the Soviet Union would by the very force of things have assumed the hegemony of Europe.

While these great events were taking place, I was, as I say, still pretty heavily occupied with the UN and indeed with certain loose ends connected with the peace treaties (only signed in February 1947), more particularly the Italian colonies. Nor was I caught up in Palestine, though

* Ambassador to the United States 1948–52.

† French economist; Secretary General of Organization for European Economic Cooperation 1948–55; Vice-President of Commission of European Economic Community 1958–67.

when the Secretary of State took the crucial decision to remove the British garrison I remember that I approved though not, perhaps, for the same reasons as he did. Bevin had, as is known, announced soon after taking over the FO that he would 'stake his reputation' on solving the problem of Palestine, and his failing to do so embittered him very much. I am afraid therefore that his decision to withdraw the army by a date only a short way ahead and to fling the whole problem into the UN was inspired at least to some extent by pique. There is little doubt, too, that he thought it might teach the Jews, who had been spending a good deal of time murdering British soldiers, a lesson. But, of course, it did not. I myself believed that we should come out if only because it seemed to me that Palestine was just about the last place in the Middle East in which to have a 'base' and was anxious, if possible, to get our troops into Cyrenaica.

Towards the end of the year things began moving pretty fast. President Truman had, as it were, thrown down the gauntlet before the Russians with his declaration and now the new Secretary of State, General Marshall, under the guidance of Dean Acheson, was already working towards the constitution of something like an organized Western defensive association. Some time previously Churchill had warned the Russians against provoking that 'powerful bird', the American eagle, with a sharp stick. Now at last the bird was reacting, and reacting very vigorously indeed. So, for that matter, was Ernest Bevin. More and more, after the failure of the final Council of Foreign Ministers in November, his mind was turning away from the pretence that we could only proceed by Four-Power agreement when the Russians would never agree and towards the formation of something – as yet he was not positive what – which would call a halt to what he instinctively – and rightly – felt was a powerful attempt by an outside power to impose itself on our small sub-continent and to suppress all freedom in so doing.

About this time (end of 1947) I had some long discussions with Hector McNeil on our relations with the Super-powers. In the Office itself, I remember telling him, there was a certain division of opinion between those – the majority – who held that the Russians were entirely, or almost entirely, to blame for our difficulties and those who, while agreeing that the Russians were mostly to blame, tended to criticize the American tendency to assume that whenever the Russians were in a minority they were also in the wrong. I was in this last group, being apprehensive of their simple approach. Many Americans seemed to believe indeed that in international, just as in national affairs, there was no alternative to anything but majority rule. They did not see that whereas inside a nation a majority was a real thing, in international affairs a majority of nations might well be a minority. And I naturally developed at length my own well-known theses about the Veto. But I always ended up on the note that these motes in the American eye ought not to deter us from concentrating on the beams in the eyes of the Russians. Until the latter became slightly more reasonable in their general approach it would be wrong for us to try to correct what we might think were blind spots in the American outlook. The Minister of State, who was on the Right of his party and very pro-American, undoubtedly agreed.

I suppose Hector was, in some ways, the young Scottish analogue of Uncle Ernie. Anyhow, they got on extremely well. Certainly the one was as earthy as the other, and Hector had much of the native intelligence and shrewdness of his boss. But he had a good university training (at Glasgow) and could express himself on paper extremely well, though his handwriting was without exception the most indecipherable that I have ever struck. He was also naturally kind and human. The only trouble about Hector was that he was almost too kind and human, and when he lost his job with the fall of the Labour Government in 1951, he seemed to lose interest in politics as well, dying of a heart attack in 1952. If the Labour Government of 1945, instead of working itself to death by the time of the 1950 election, had preserved real vitality, Hector might even have become Foreign Secretary in succession to Bevin.

Some say that Hector, who had made the great mistake of appointing Guy Burgess his Assistant Private Secretary in 1947, was shattered when the latter, after his disastrous year in Washington, absconded to Russia in May 1951. I can well believe it. Nobody was more anti-Communist than he was, and the thought that he had, quite unwittingly, put Burgess into a position where he could undoubtedly observe most of what was going on in the innermost councils of the Office must have been particularly galling, all the more so since, as I recall, he had given the Assistant Private Secretary the job of analysing Soviet propaganda lines with a view to their refutation. But it is also true that Burgess wrote Left-wing pamphlets for McNeil which occasionally gave partial approval to well-known Soviet theses. The essential mistake was to give Burgess any responsibility at all, for he was a totally irresponsible character. I remember subsequently wondering with Isaiah Berlin what work the unfortunate Russians could suitably confide to Burgess in Moscow, more especially since it was believed that they regarded homosexuality as a criminal offence. We decided that he would either be shot (a possibility which incidentally is solemnly discussed in Tom Driberg's rather oleaginous biography) or, more probably, die of boredom. The second suggestion turned out to be correct.

Poor Hector! I do believe he might with rather more luck, and perhaps a little more cunning, have been a good Foreign Secretary. Incidentally it was he who first suggested that I myself was not perhaps in the right job. I remember drafting some eloquent speech for him to make in New York at a committee of the Assembly and his saying, 'Why are you here preparing this wonderful stuff for me? You ought to be dishing it out yourself!' I recall replying that politics were not for me, and then wondering whether, perhaps, one day I might take it up. But I was really very happy just giving advice, more especially since it usually seemed to be accepted! I remember, too, how after we had negotiated the statute of the Council of Europe and the new body was about to be established, there was talk about my being Secretary-General, and I made clear to Hector that I would at least consider the job if it were offered me, which seemed quite unlikely. He became quite indignant and asked me whether I really thought that 'Europe' was more important than the 'North Atlantic' which, as the reader will see in a moment, I had also been organizing, or trying to organize, before reverting to 'Europe'. It was my job, Hector suggested, to get on with that, and, one day, I might even have some hand in running it. Anyway, the idea of an 'Atlantic community' was the thing, and that of forming 'Europe' was subsidiary. In 1948, this was a proposition which I did not really dispute, and indeed there were then few people in Whitehall who would have asserted the contrary. But even then I felt obscurely that we were perhaps not paying as much attention as we should to the place of 'Europe' in the general scheme of things.

The November Council of Foreign Ministers was a disaster as had been the one in March and Bevin, his last hope of working a Four-Power system, or even as acting as a sort of bridge between East and West frustrated, was sometimes rather gloomy. But this never lasted for long and I feel I must end this chapter with a little story which illustrates this. Just after the end of the conference I was lunching with Hector McNeil in the Strangers' Dining-Room of the House of Commons when, to our surprise, we saw Uncle Ernie come in and sit down alone, seemingly in a black mood. Nevertheless we thought we might try to cheer him up and asked whether we could join him. Rather reluctantly he agreed. By way of jollying him along I observed that, though the conference might have been a failure I expected he had had some nice things to eat and drink? 'No', he replied gloomily: and then, after a pause, 'You see, I was at the

Embassy.' I said that with rationing still continuing in Britain the Embassy could hardly be expected to be flowing with champagne and caviar, and he willingly agreed. But then, with one of his malicious twinkles, he said, 'Do you know Brindle?' Now Brindle was the Petersons' elderly Scottie to which they were, not unnaturally, devoted. 'Yes,' I said, 'I do: but how does Brindle come into it?' 'Well', said the Secretary of State, 'it was like this. Towards the end of our little meal, they gave me, with the cheese, what I took to be dog biscuits, so, I said, by way of a joke like, and quite unsuspecting, 'Lady Peterson, these look to me like dog biscuits?' 'As a matter of fact they are, Secretary of State' she said, 'but we like them.' Well, after a bit of a pause, I said, 'Lady Peterson, I 'ope I'm not depriving Brindle of his dinner?' And do you know what she replied? 'That's quite all right, Secretary of State, Brindle won't eat 'em.'

13

Political Deputy
(1948-50)

If 1947 was the year in which the whole projected post-war settlement collapsed, 1948 was the year in which an alternative settlement was constructed. It was to last, roughly, for ten years. In Western Europe it was the period of Anglo-American predominance, chiefly exercised in the Organization for European Economic Cooperation (OEEC). For me the year was a memorable one because during it I was, if only in an advisory capacity, better placed to influence events than before, or, no doubt, subsequently.

As I have already said, from the end of 1947 Bevin, though originally he had been very careful not to do anything which could in the slightest degree provoke our Russian ally, was definitely turning towards some defensive system in Western Europe. Unable, as we have seen, during the first reign of de Gaulle (1944-6), to obtain a bilateral treaty with France for mutual protection against the possible re-emergence of an aggressive Germany, he had finally succeeded in signing one at Dunkirk in March of that year. He attached much importance to this and it was the occasion of considerable rejoicing. The French at that time were well disposed towards us and we to them, though some of their aims, such as the Rhine frontier, seemed to us to be unfortunate and we were not very happy about their determination to hang on to Indo-China. If the British Government, as was their intention, were going to give India independence, was it not swimming against the tide to try in effect to maintain another European empire in that part of the world even if this was not the professed French intention? The same applied, as far as we were concerned, to the Dutch in Indonesia. The great thing was, as we saw it, to try to establish a new and, if possible, an intimate relationship with old dependencies which, in our weakened state, it was impossible to hold down by force, even if that was desirable.

But by the end of 1947 it was plain that, whatever the long-term dangers inherent in a reunified Germany, the whole world balance of power was changing. Eastern Germany was being rapidly absorbed into the Communist bloc and for that reason alone it was obvious that Western Germany would have to be in close association with the Western bloc, unless indeed the West was to allow her to gravitate towards the East also. After the total failure of the six-week Conference of Foreign Ministers in Moscow in May and the ensuing one in November, the Secretary of State had been brooding on these great issues. Early in January he had privately expressed his belief to us that we should, with the backing of America and the Dominions, seek to form some Western system comprising, so far as possible, all democratic Western European states and, as soon as this became practicable, Spain and Germany also. I do not think that at that stage he was thinking in military terms only, but rather of some sort of friendly association of democratic peoples determined to resist the expansive tendencies of totalitarianism.

He gave public expression to this idea in a more general way in his great speech of 22 January 1948, with which no doubt I had a good deal to do, though he was not the man to accept any particular draft. As often as not I would put up some eloquent piece for him to utter and he would gaze at it and say 'Very good, very good: the only trouble is, it isn't *me*'! The message of the 22 January speech in any case was simple, and ran as follows. The Potsdam agreement was perfectly right in principle. Germany should not be dismembered and a new German state should be 'evolved on a new basis' with continuing four-Power control. But this possibility had been ruled out by Soviet conduct – very little debate and constant hurling of insults. Then there was the rejection by the Soviet Union of Marshall Aid, and he had 'good grounds' for saying that 'rather than risk the generosity of the USA, particularly Eastern Europe, and Europe itself joining in a great cooperative movement', the Soviet Union was prepared to risk 'the creation of any possible organism (Bevin was always attached to 'organism' as opposed to 'organ' or 'organization') in the West'. His further opinion, he went on to say, was 'that they thought they could wreck or even intimidate Western Europe by political upsets, economic chaos and revolutionary methods'. On the final day Molotov had said that acceptance (of Marshall Aid by France and Britain) would be 'bad for both of us, but particularly France'. And indeed there had followed the great political strikes in France and a tremendous anti-Western campaign led by Vyshynsky in the United Nations.

This really was the crux. Did you, or did you not believe this version of events? Personally I did. You may say, if you like, that it was really fear of being dominated by America which had resulted in this impossible attitude on the part of the Soviet Government. But nothing could have been more tactful and more helpful, and less indicative of any desire to 'dominate' than the Marshall approach. No, if fear there was, it was a fear that the unholy Communist regime in Russia, not Russia herself, would be in danger if Marshall Aid was accepted that resulted in Molotov's virtual declaration of Cold War on the West in July 1947. And this was something that the Western democracies, unless they wanted to be dominated in their turn could in no way avoid. They had not won a war against one totalitarian system in order to be dominated by another. At the end of the war there was, or was thought to be, at least some chance that the leopard might change its spots. But as 1946 went on they became more and more visible, and they certainly have not changed today. Ask Dubcek or Solzhenitzyn. At the end of 1947, however, we had fewer witnesses to the spots than we subsequently had, or now have. So the fact had to be publicly demonstrated.

After the demonstration, Bevin propounded the answer: it was 'Western union'. We had not proposed this before because we had wanted a union of all Europe. But Stalin himself had not objected to some defensive treaties being signed in the West, and he had certainly not objected to Dunkirk. Therefore 'the free nations of Western Europe must now draw closer together' and 'the time [was] ripe for the consolidation of Western Europe', this consisting of treaties with the Low Countries which, together with our treaty with France, would, in association eventually with other states, form 'an important nucleus'. We were indeed thinking of Western Europe as a unit. But a unit with many links with Africa and South-East Asia and also, of course, with the whole Commonwealth. And the association would not simply stop there. For the USA and Latin America were clearly as much a part of our Western civilization as were the members of the British Commonwealth, and all their resources would be needed. Germany, for her part, 'must not come before her recent victims' and must be prevented from again becoming aggressive; but subject to that we should welcome her return as a democratic nation, and this would enable us 'to pursue the course which will seek to re-unite Europe'. If all this resulted nevertheless in the division of Europe it would be 'by the act and will of the Soviet Government'.

It will be observed that Bevin did not at this stage actually propose a multilateral treaty, still less a multilateral defensive pact. He only hinted, very inferentially, at the military aspect by his reference to the Treaty of Dunkirk. Nor did he positively suggest any wider grouping which might at that stage have disturbed the Senate of the United States, though he did say that the 'resources' of America would be needed. Neither did he contemplate the actual association of Western Germany with the group, though he entirely left the way open for this later. Finally, while repudiating dismemberment, he did not actually propose the reunification of Germany, only (one day) the 'reunification of Europe'. Altogether, it was a very clever speech. The Secretary of State knew perfectly well what he was after, but he had to achieve his end by stages, gaining as many allies as he could in the process. The speech had a great echo all over Europe. Bevin did not have exactly the magic of Churchill. But he was at that moment in control of British foreign policy and Churchill was not.

This then was the background against which, early in February 1947, I formulated my views in a note called 'The Threat to Western Civilization' of which the following is the gist. This threat, I said, impelled us to examine the extent to which the Soviet Government appeared to be achieving their aims and the steps that we should now take in order to frustrate them. Only one conclusion could be drawn from recent events. Not only was the Soviet Government not prepared to cooperate in any real sense with any non-Communist or non-Communist-controlled government, but it was actively preparing to extend its hold over the remaining part of continental Europe and subsequently, perhaps, over the Middle East, and no doubt the bulk of the Far East as well. In other words, physical control of the Eurasian land-mass and eventual control of the whole world island was what the Politburo was aiming at. No less a thing than that. The immensity of the aim should not betray us into believing in its impracticability. Unless positive and vigorous steps were shortly taken by those other states in a position to take them, it might well be that within the next few months – or even weeks – the Soviet Union would gain political and strategic advantages which would set in motion the great machine of 'world revolution', leading either to the establishment of a world dictatorship or (more probably) to the collapse of organized society over immense stretches of the globe.

All our evidence pointed to the probable staging by the Soviet Government of some political show-down during the next few months or weeks. We could not be sure where exactly this show-down would take place or even that it would not occur in several places at once. All we knew for certain was that its object would be the frustration by one means or another of Economic Recovery Program (ERP) and the consequent development of a situation in which the Communist cause would triumph in many countries as a result of a process of economic decay. (At this point, the reader may remember, Marshall Aid had not yet been approved by the American Senate.) But there was no reason to suppose that the Soviet Government would welcome a world war, which would undoubtedly result from its overstepping the mark. No issue would therefore be forced until the moment was ripe and victory almost certain. So if democratic countries could present a really united front and the economic means were made available by America, the danger of war was not imminent. Indeed the only danger of war arose from the possible non-fulfilment of these two conditions. If they were fulfilled Communism would be forced back on to the defensive and we might, for many years, look forward to a period of peace. The second condition depended on the USA; the first on ourselves, i.e. the UK, which must give an example of resolution to the Continent and to our friends all over the world. Irresolution would have terrible results even if ERP were forthcoming. The following were the main issues.

The fundamental contradiction inherent in European politics since the formation of the Third International lay between an imposed solution of social and economic differences, which could only mean dictatorship, and voluntary, reasoned, and human solutions summed up in all that we meant by 'democracy'. The fact that the Eastern dictatorship called itself a 'Dictatorship of the Proletariat'; the fact that it had stolen much of the phraseology of advanced Western thought; could deceive nobody any longer except those who wanted to be deceived. It was impossible to maintain that the self-appointed rulers in the Kremlin represented the workers in the same way that HM's present Government represented the workers of the UK. And this, with all their faults, applied to all governments of Western Europe save Iberia.

If, therefore, the workers of Western Europe were so exhausted by the recent war, or so distrustful of their own power to achieve a fairer share of the benefits of industrialization, or even to preserve their accustomed freedoms, there was no doubt that they would have peace indeed – but, in the long run, the peace of the grave. Nor should anybody think that if free societies were blotted out in Western Europe we could continue to exist on our own in our island. If we were not thought to be worth defending by America, the stresses and strains could overthrow our parliamentary government and replace it by a police state. These, then, were my recommendations:

1. Instead of trying to go on with bilateral treaties we should aim urgently at a multilateral economic, cultural and defence pact with

France and Benelux which could be left open for accession by other Western European democracies.

2. This done, there should be consultations between the UK, France, Italy and Benelux, and any other desired states, with the USA in order to see how the latter could best back up such a multilateral pact, and arrange for further expansion.

3. Since Italy was at present the weakest link in the proposed chain, a special effort should be made to bring her into the system.

4. So far as we could, we should also do our best to bring the real facts of the situation, as we saw them, home to the Americans.

The immediate positive step should be, I thought, a meeting of officials in Brussels followed by a conference there of the Foreign Ministers of the states concerned. These – in parts rather too highly coloured – sentiments were, broadly speaking, those of the Cabinet, and after urgent consultations with the French (Jean Chauvel then being my opposite number) the officials did meet in Brussels on 7 March, I was there associated, as the British representative, with my old friend George Rendel, Ambassador to Belgium, our instructions being to get agreement on a draft which had already been submitted (on 19 February) for consideration to the governments of Benelux. There followed a meeting of ministers which resulted in the Treaty of Brussels being initialled on 13 March and actually signed on 17 March. When you think of the issues involved and the complexities of legal drafting this must surely have been a record in multilateral international negotiation!

But perhaps it was not surprising. On 25 February, indeed, the Russians under the eye of their Ambassador Zorin, had simply turned out the legitimate democratic government of President Benes and replaced it by their own Communist stooges. It was the famous *Coup de Prague*. The effect of this was electrical. If the Russians could do this to one European democracy nearly three years after the end of the war, what was to prevent them doing it in other European countries, and notably in Western Europe? Certainly nothing much in the way of armed strength. At that time, in the words of General Lemnitzer, all the Russians really needed in order to get to Brest was some good pairs of boots. And in France and Italy they would no doubt be enthusiastically welcomed by the very strong local communist parties. The few British and French divisions in Germany could not be expected to make more than a token resistance, and the Americans had withdrawn the great bulk of their strength. Incidentally Yugoslavia was still in the Communist camp, the revolt of Tito only occurring later in the year. What the French call a *grande peur* seized the Western world. It may not have been altogether reasonable, but it was at least understandable. If the world was really, as Molotov had said, divided into 'two tendencies', the great bulk of people were now determined that one of them at any rate should not be allowed to win.

Before the coup two things had rather worried Bevin so far as I remember. The first was whether the treaty should follow the example of Dunkirk and be firmly based on the principle of resistance to possible *German* aggression, or whether it should invoke the famous Article 51 of the Charter of the United Nations, i.e. the article which authorizes the 'inherent right of self-defence' in the event of an 'armed attack' against a member. The French favoured the former solution principally with an eye to relations with the USSR. In the event they had satisfaction. The treaty referred both to Article 51 of the Charter and to the need to guard against the danger of an aggressive Germany.

More importantly, I recall, the Secretary of State was convinced that we ought in any case to sign and ratify the defensive pact without waiting for any positive assurances of American support. He believed, indeed, that such support would eventually be forthcoming; but nobody could be sure which way Congress would jump. Probably it would agree to the provision of adequate arms, but whether it would agree to any contractual obligations to assist the Brussels Treaty Powers in the event of their being the victims of aggression was by no means certain. Whether it would actually join some 'Atlantic' union was less certain still. In a way it was a gamble. Everybody knew that the 'Western union' powers could put up only a token resistance in the event of a real Russian attack and that the only real 'deterrent' was the nuclear weapon of which the Americans still had the monopoly. But whether the Americans would go so far as to use it unless they had the assurance that the Europeans were willing and able at least to begin to defend themselves conventionally was an open question. What seemed certain was that the more the Europeans showed willing, the more the Americans were likely to do.

After Brussels it was thus evident that the next step was to get in touch with the Americans. As a matter of fact it had been decided in February (before the events in Prague) that I should be the right person to act as a sort of dove sent out from the Ark, and I was duly dispatched, but only got as far as New York when I was recalled, since the moment was deemed unpropitious. However no sooner was the treaty signed than I arrived in Washington with instructions to find out how the land lay and, generally speaking, to put the case, in very informal and non-committal talks, for the early formation of something like an Atlantic alliance. The first meeting took place (on Bevin's initiative) on 22 March and was followed by five more, and the 'consensus' which eventually emerged did, I think, bear a strong resemblance to the North Atlantic Treaty, formal negotiations for which began in Washington on 4 July. The American side was led by Lew Douglas, assisted, among others, by Jack Hickerson, Ted Achilles and the then Colonel Gruenther. Mike Pearson led for Canada. After the end of the talks successful efforts were made by the Americans to sell the whole idea to Senator Vandenberg, whose famous resolution was presented to the Senate on 11 June and passed by sixty-four votes to two, thirty-two Senators abstaining.

I have some vivid recollections of this encounter which took place in the recesses of the Pentagon, great trouble having been taken to maintain secrecy, in this case with fairly good results, though I believe that the celebrated Joe Alsop must have had some wind of what was taking place since he published only a fortnight after the end of our talks a piece to the effect that the American Administration was considering joining an Atlantic pact! But at least Scottie Reston did not, as in the case of Dumbarton Oaks, publish a complete record of the proceedings day by day in the *New York Times* (see Chapter 10). The reason for the secrecy, I suppose, was (a) that the US administration were still very much in two minds about the way in which they would propose to follow up the Brussels initiative; (b) that they had a difficult task ahead in persuading a potentially isolationist Congress of the desirability of any forward move that they might propose and (c) that the French had not been seeing eye to eye of late with the 'Anglo-Saxons', more especially as regards Germany, and that it might therefore be better at least to get some sort of understanding with the British on general policy before tackling them.

Until they are published it would not however be proper for me to disclose any details of what was then said. Nor indeed could I since, unlike so many of my colleagues, I kept no diary, nor have I any papers bearing on the subject at all. All I do know is that Al Gruenther has always said – and said in public – that he was deeply impressed by my own opening remarks which, presumably, were devoted to an *exposé* of the advantages of moving towards some 'Atlantic' conception of defence embodying a treaty in which America would join with the Brussels Treaty powers – then known as the 'nucleus' – in guaranteeing Western Europe against external attack. What was a fact was that, on the British side, it was I who conducted the negotiations, the Ambassador, Lord Inverchapel (who was about to leave), being only associated with it *pro forma*, the chief Embassy adviser, who took the minutes with Robin Cecil and helped with the telegrams, being the Russian spy, Maclean.★ However 'secret' the negotiations, there can be little doubt, therefore, that the Soviet Government had had a pretty full record of what happened from the very moment when they took place.

What everybody must know is that there were at that time varying conceptions, both on the British and on the American side, as to how we had best all proceed in facing an obvious threat, and this apart from the likelihood of the one solution or the other finding favour with Congress. For instance, it might well have been possible – as Al Gruenther says he himself believed until the Pentagon talks began – for the USA to have merely provided in vast and standardized quantities the tanks, aeroplanes, guns and so on needed to create, no doubt under 'Western Union', a veritable European Army with which the Germans might gradually have been associated, the Americans retaining, perhaps, only a token force of their own. If this European Army were attacked by the Russians it might have been possible to have an assurance by the President of the USA that he would not exclude the use of American nuclear power to protect American troops. It could be argued that this would not only effectively have held the position in Western Europe without any of the subsequent huge NATO apparatus, but also forced the European nations to make a reality out of Western union – probably by closer political union.

It might likewise be argued that, even if there was a contractual liability on the part of the USA to defend the Western Union countries if attacked, such a guarantee should only extend to those countries – the 'nucleus' – and should not necessarily cover the 'flanks', i.e. Scandinavia and Italy, which could perhaps either be neutralized, as in the case of Scandinavia (which might become a sort of super-Sweden), or form part of some Mediterranean grouping along, eventually, with Greece and Turkey. The difficulty here was that there could be no real guarantee that the flank – more especially the northern flank – might not be turned by the Russians unless it were under an American guarantee; while as for a Mediterranean grouping the point was to know when to stop. If Turkey was to be guaranteed why not Persia, or for that matter Afghanistan or Pakistan or even India – which brought you right up against the problem of China. And could Turkey really be said to be an 'Atlantic' country? In any case it was long before the arming of the Western Germans was seriously thought of as practical politics. It was at that time violently

★ Robin Cecil maintains that I used to tear up his painstaking records of the proceedings and re-dictate the whole thing myself. But I feel he must be exaggerating.

resisted by the French and not at all popular in Britain or the Low Countries either.

There remained a great argument against the whole idea – and it was shared on both sides of the Atlantic: the proposed treaty would 'unduly provoke the Soviet Government'. This I never believed. I could not imagine, I remember declaring to a high-ranking member of the State Department, that Russian intentions would be changed in any way by the simple conclusion of some Atlantic defence system. On the contrary, the conclusion of such a treaty would be the one thing needed to prevent the USSR from embarking on any ill-considered scheme of expansion. What *might* be dangerous, I thought, was what I regret to say I once called the 'ill-considered and emotional hullabaloo' at the Hague Conference (which we will come to in a moment) for some 'United States of Europe', that was to say some union of Europe which would include the Soviet satellite states. For this could only be interpreted as indicating a desire on the part of the West to establish a vast concentration of European power – possibly with Berlin as its capital and with a re-unified Reich of over eighty million inhabitants as its principal member. This really would alarm the Soviet Government: and if they thought that that was what we were after, there would indeed be no possibility of compromise. Whereas the Soviet Union might, and probably eventually would, accept the close association of European states west of the Iron Curtain, and even conceivably come to regard them as a valuable element in the Balance of Power, they would never agree to a Continental bloc extending from Lisbon to the Polish frontier, for the constitution of such a bloc would at once pose the question of the Eastern frontier of Poland and the whole status of the Baltic States – to say nothing, I might well have added, of its likely effect on the Ukraine.

During this 'post-Brussels' period, and before the opening of the official 'Atlantic' negotiations in July, there had indeed been one considerable event – the Congress of Europe at The Hague. This had been heralded by a statement by the Provisional Committee of the United Europe movement in January which declared that 'United Europe' would have the 'status of a regional council under the UN Charter' and would 'seek the friendship of the USA and the USSR'. It would be 'premature' to define the precise constitutional relationship between the nations of a unified Europe. In any case it was recognized that the UK had 'special obligations' towards the Commonwealth; but Britain was a part of Europe and 'must be prepared to make her full contribution to European unity'.

At this moment I said I had never been able to find out what exactly

Churchill was aiming at. If it were a sort of 'Western union' on the general lines of the Secretary of State's thought, well and good. If it were however a 'United Europe' on the lines of the 'Pan Europe' scheme of Count Coudenhove-Kalergi it was quite another thing. Even at that late hour we did not, I imagined, wish movements in the direction of European unity to have as their chief characteristic an anti-Bolshevik crusade. If we could in the near future get a five-power treaty much of the wind might be taken out of the sails of the Hague Conference. If we did not, then it would be better if no governmental representatives took part in a meeting which would be advocating ideas which were not at that moment even partially realizable.

The confusion in my own mind was certainly not cleared up by Churchill's opening speech on 7 May. 'We cannot aim at anything less' he proudly declared, 'than the Union of Europe as a whole'. If this meant anything, it meant that the intention was that Russia – and hence the entire Soviet Union, because the two could in no wise be separated – should be a member of the Council of Europe. But then we heard, 'Thus I see the vast Soviet Union forming one of these great groups. The Council of Europe, including Great Britain joined with her Empire and Common-wealth, would be another. Thirdly, the Western Hemisphere with all its great spheres of interest and influence has already become effective, and with it we in Britain and the Commonwealth are also linked by Canada and other sacred ties.' If this meant anything it meant that Russia would not be inside, but outside the Council of Europe. If this were to be the operative phrase, however, it was clear that we should have to get Russia back within her own boundaries before we could form the Council. And the mere suggestion that we should attempt to do this would frighten the Russians like nothing else.

It was, in fact, the old Winstonian conception which I had attacked so savagely during the war; and it certainly seemed to me to have become no less dangerous with the passage of time. All the more so since Churchill was himself clearly not a 'European' at all. If he had had his way, Britain would have been 'associated' with a Europe that would extend from Lisbon to Brest Litowsk (and hence almost certainly, in the absence of a war with the Soviet Union, have been dominated by the immense power of a reunified Germany), but would never have formed part of it herself. Why the European federalists should have apparently thought at one time that he was thinking of British membership of a federal Europe I have never understood. He always made it quite clear that Britain, if he had anything to do with it, would stand aloof. In this respect he hardly differed from

Bevin whose attitude was so displeasing to British 'Europeans' at that time. Bevin was never against a federal Western Europe without the UK – though he no doubt thought that it would never happen. As for me, though I then believed that the idea that Western Europe should be united on a federal basis was asking too much of human nature, I never thought that if by chance this happened it would be a good thing for us. We had remained 'aloof' once or twice before, and it did not seem to me that it was an experience to be repeated.

Nevertheless the congress was held and, in spite of my doubts, it did produce a document which had a great effect on thought in all political circles: what is more, it produced a coherent European movement, dedicated to the furtherance of the 'supra-national' idea which has had ever since a profound effect on European politics. Perhaps if I had attended I would myself have been then and there converted to the 'supra-national' thesis; but I was not there, and in any case I was the servant of a Government which was united in thinking that, whatever might happen on the Continent, the UK could not contemplate entering anything which would limit its own entire freedom of action. 'Unity', as we said then, was one thing: 'union' was another. While, therefore, we might well favour a commission to guarantee Human Rights, as proposed by the congress, we could not accept a 'European assembly' if by this was meant one which would have any plenary powers. An advisory assembly, on the other hand, might well do useful work. If Britain was to join, that was the condition. But I do see that in July, when thinking about Jean Monnet's view that ERP (soon to be OEEC) would probably collapse after four years unless it were tightened up so as to become more or less equivalent to a federation, I reflected that, if we did postulate some economic collapse, the arguments in favour of a federation were greatly strengthened. For a political federation would presumably connote a common currency, free movement of capital within the group, and unrestricted movement of persons.

If all that happened it was obvious that the economic situation of Western Europe could only be improved, and it was arguable too, that it could only be improved by the complete absorption of Western Germany in such a federation. However, the political obstacles in the way at that time – and indeed for any period during which the (economic) situation was not completely out of hand – seemed to me to be so great as to be almost insuperable. For in order to arrive at the desired state of affairs, local interests in various places would have to be ruthlessly suppressed and the standard of living in some of the proposed partners of the federation lowered in favour of the less favoured countries. Thus it seemed to me that federation, if it ever came about, could only be achieved either by the imminence of some complete collapse, or as the aftermath of a new war. I daresay there was a lot of truth in this stark, and in the event largely unjustified, judgment then, and I have since formed the view that it is quite possible – and highly desirable – to create, not a 'federation' in the old sense of the term, but a new type of community in which, as confidence increases, more and more decisions will be taken by 'supra-national' means with the willing consent of all the members. It also remains true that the time must be ripe.

Looking back, however, I feel that the whole urge towards European unity in 1948 sadly miscarried. The great producer of union is, admittedly, fear and this existed early in the year when, as we have seen, the *Coup de Prague* was largely responsible for prompt agreement on the first effort to form a European nucleus, namely 'Western Union'. In June, fear was applied again in the shape of the Berlin Blockade which was not called off until May 1949; and all through that period Western Europe lived, or thought it lived, under the threat of war. The fear this time resulted in the conclusion of the Atlantic Alliance, and that was as it should be. But what should have accompanied this great reaction of the Western world was an increasing advance towards real European unity also. In other words somebody in authority should have then advanced the theory of the 'two poles' in the Western world and made it an actual condition of the consent of America to entering any definite alliance. It is true that American pressure to this end was often exerted by officials and politicians but it was not, I think, formulated as a definite doctrine during 1948. If it had, it might perhaps have been best to concentrate above all on enlarging and strengthening the Brussels Treaty Organization (for instance, by arranging for a parliamentary body and an international Secretariat with considerable powers) and not to have invented the Council of Europe at all. For the latter was a compromise between the non-federal theses of the British Government and the rather vague longings of the European federalists which would probably not have been entirely satisfied even if the British had taken another view. Many governments, indeed, were by no means then wholly susceptible to federal ideas when it came to the point.

Thus schemes not unlike the subsequent Pleven Plan (for a European defence community), greatly modified it is true, might well have come up to an enlarged Western union during 1949 which would have made the rearming of the Germans and their eventual incorporation in the modified Brussels system much more easy of accomplishment. Also, since the organization would have been largely military, neutrals might only have been allotted some kind of associate status. Equally, the social and cultural work, subsequently taken over by the Council of Europe, would have given the Brussels organization a great deal to do even if progress was slow in other directions. Moreover, the Brussels group would increasingly have spoken with a single voice in OEEC, thus slowly hammering out an economic policy for Europe independent of Marshall Aid. And, finally, there would only have been one European assembly – in Paris no doubt – instead of several potentially rival and overlapping ones as at the present time. It would have been for that assembly to have gone on badgering the governments to adopt a more 'supra-national' attitude and policy. And so, little by little, Western Europe would have been formed and not divided, as it is today, into two. By the middle fifties it should have consisted of nine states – the present seven of WEU plus Norway and Denmark – in association with Sweden, Switzerland, Ireland, and no doubt also, for other reasons, Greece and Turkey. And the nine would by that time most certainly have worked out a system for taking decisions in all spheres, military, political, economic and cultural. Above all our little peninsula would not have been lamentably divided in all these spheres, save, to some extent, the cultural.

Just think for a moment what the consequences might have been. No Suez expedition – for could such an aberration have taken place if there had been even the slightest progress in the direction of harmonizing the foreign and defence policies of all the nine 'nucleus' states? No de Gaulle – because nationalism would, with the progress in real European cooperation, have been at a heavy discount. No European Economic Community also, it is true. But instead a much less complicated but still partly 'supranational' body which could have resulted in a Customs Union and gone happily on from there. No French 'mutiny' in NATO either. It might not have been Jean Monnet's paradise, but it would certainly have been infinitely better than a creaking Community of Six, a powerless WEU, a rather purposeless EFTA and no political entity of any kind. Why did it all go rather wrong?

It is customary to blame the blindness of the Labour leadership. If they had only seen the light and had indirectly participated in the Hague Congress, accepting its conclusions and shedding the last vestiges of their nationalism on the way and plunged ahead towards some federation, all would have been well. There might then have been early elections to a Constituent Assembly; a new constitution would have been devised by some modern Abbé Siéyès; Germany could very soon have joined this democratic group; and the United States of Europe would have been born. This seems to me to be a dream. *Natura nihil facit saltu.* Revolutions only succeed as the result of some disaster or when the ground has been prepared for them many years in advance. Whatever the attitude of the British Government at that time – and in view of public opinion it would only have been possible to change it very gradually – it would not have been possible to set up a definite union in Western Europe with British, Scandinavian, still less 'neutral' participation in 1948, even if it had been possible to do so among the Six, which is in itself open to question.

But where I believe we British were perhaps at fault was in not going a little further within Western Union itself towards meeting the federalists' demands. After all Attlee himself had said on 5 May that 'in advancing towards Western union we are prepared, with other powers, to pool some degree of authority' though it is true that he immediately added that he was 'disturbed' to hear suggestions that we might 'get closer to Europe than to the Commonwealth'. If we had gone in this direction it would not indeed have been necessary, as the result of public opinion on the Continent and of pressure by the USA to agree at the end of September to negotiate for the formation of something, the 'Council of Europe', which in the nature of things could only be a sort of rival to Western Union, in the sense of an alternative means of arriving at the same goal. For in doing so we pleased nobody. As a result of our insistence during those negotiations on the strict acceptance of the non-supra-national principle in the Council of Europe we reduced it to political impotence. At the same time we agreed that all the constructive side of the Brussels Treaty machine – social, cultural, even to some extent economic questions – should be removed from it and vested in the Council, which was also forbidden by its Statute to occupy itself with defence; that was reserved for 'Western Union'.

When NATO came into operation in 1950, the remaining military side of Brussels was effectively transferred to the 'Atlantic' body, and the hopeful European 'nucleus' of 1948 was thus reduced to a sort of vermiform appendix. This was revitalized to some extent in 1954 when, after the collapse of the European Defence Community, a rearmed Germany joined it and it became the Western European Union, complete with a parliamentary assembly. But by that time the Six were already thinking of constructing their own Europe on supra-national lines if they could, and the way was thus prepared for the emergence of the three European 'communities'. After Suez they succeeded in doing so without us with the result that is known. 'Europe' was divided.

It is true that one of the difficulties about resisting the demand for the construction of a 'Council of Europe' with British participation, and concentrating on a development of the Brussels Treaty Organization lay in the fact (a) that, contrary to our original desire, the Treaty of Brussels was based on the need to provide security against possible German aggression, thus making it impossible, without revision, to associate the Western Germans with it and (b) that it did not provide for any Parliamentary Assembly or indeed for any genuinely international Secretariat. But it would at least have been possible for HMG, had they so desired, to suggest that the talks on 'Europe' generally should be based on the possibility of such a revision. Moreover, it was at that time impossible for the Western Germans to join the proposed Council of Europe either, since no West German government had as yet emerged. This alternative course was not, however, suggested by anybody, and I certainly blame myself for not having thought of it. For it might have changed the course of history.

I well remember in any case the circumstances in which this error, as it now seems to me, took place. Once HMG had agreed to negotiate it was a question of with whom and how. After much toing and froing it was agreed that talks – they could hardly be called negotiations – should take place in Paris between five selected British, five French, three Dutch, three Belgian and two Luxembourg delegates. The British team were Dr Dalton (who had recently resigned as Chancellor of the Exchequer), Sir E. Bridges, Lord Inverchapel, Professor Wade and T.H. Gill. The French were Edouard Herriot, François de Menthon, Guy Mollet, Paul Reynaud and Charles Corbin (the French Ambassador in London at the beginning of the war) – a formidable team! I was the Secretary-General. It was a collection of 'Europeans' – more especially on the French side. But the British for their part could hardly be said to have been federalists.

Long discussions took place in the Quai d'Orsay. In front of me was Guy Mollet, pro-British, even more pro-federalist, and I shall not easily forget his face when one day I came back, after a visit to the Foreign Office, with the news that we could not accept some suggestion of a quasi-federalist nature – I forget what, but probably something to do with the powers of the proposed consultative assembly. Bevin, indeed, remained quite adamant on such points, though I think that Dalton and Bridges would have been prepared to be a little more accommodating. Our original proposal had been that there should simply be what we called a 'consultative council' and no parliamentary body at all; but eventually the idea of a consultative parliamentary assembly as well as a ministerial council emerged, on the strict understanding that the assembly should indeed be purely consultative and that there should be no question of its being directly elected.

So the Council of Europe was, rather unhappily, conceived. There followed formal negotiations which ended on 5 May 1949 when the statute was signed in London. Strasbourg was selected as the seat on a suggestion of Bevin's, and it is quite true, as has so often been alleged in the press, that it was I who suggested the place to him. This was not, as the story goes, simply because I had been happy there as a student, but because it seemed to me that a French town on the borders of the German world might be symbolic of the reconciliation between the French and the Germans which, since Winston Churchill's splendid Zurich speech in 1946, had been so generally desired and which has now so happily come about. It cannot be said that the Council has been a failure. It has done immensely good work, largely below the surface as it were, which will surely bear fruit. But it has not been, nor can it ever be that European entity on which so many hopes have been and still are set. One day its political functions will be merged in the structure that should have come out of Brussels and may still come out of the EEC and WEU. *Qui vivra verra.*

All this time I had also been much concerned with the United Nations. As Under-Secretary in charge of UN affairs I was also the chief adviser to the delegation at the 1947 and 1948 Assemblies. Those were the days when we had quite an influence in the Assembly and when a speech by a British Foreign Secretary was still listened to with great attention. The Commonwealth, too, was definitely an entity in those days, in the sense that efforts were made to reach a Commonwealth point of view. Nor had we abandoned hope of an occasionally useful development in the UN. Much time was taken up during the year in a consideration of whether the Berlin Blockade issue should be taken up in the Security Council or in the Assembly. I myself was against this, if only for the reason that it had to be shown whether the blockade really was a 'threat to international peace and security'. In the event, no action was taken.

In January 1948, I see that I was fairly objective as regards the world organization. The United Nations would, I thought, continue to function badly during the year, but the Slav bloc were unlikely to leave and we for our part should certainly do our best to maintain the organization in the hope of better times. The 'best hope of making it function properly' lay in successfully organizing Western Europe so as to eliminate Communism there and if possible to construct a 'Middle Power' consisting of Western Europe plus the bulk of Africa which, while remaining friendly with the USA would no longer be economically dependent on that country and hence capable of pursuing an independent foreign policy. Attempts to revise the Charter would meet with no success. Nor would negotiations for disarmament. The continuing US monopoly of the nuclear bomb, while a safeguard against war, would result in increasing East/West tension and increased efforts by the Soviet Union to consolidate her Eastern bloc. On the other hand, the organization of collective security based on Article 51 – i.e. 'outside the Charter' – could and should be considered, and I then outlined various proposals, one of which was not at all unlike the coming Atlantic Pact, though no countries were then specified.

As 1949 progressed and merged into 1950, the great European debate became more and more intense in Strasbourg, but in Whitehall we stuck to our definition of 'union' and 'unity'. We also did our best, with more success, to organize the military and political side of the Brussels Treaty Organization. I was the British representative on the 'Permanent Commission' of that organization (which consisted, apart from myself, of the Ambassadors of the five other countries in London) and much good work was done preparing the military and political machine that was soon to be taken over by NATO. But it was on Strasbourg that eyes were fastened; and since the more devoted parliamentary 'Europeans' had never really accepted the limitations placed on the role of the Assembly under the statute, great, and partially successful efforts were made to circumvent it, though they never led to any break-through. The Secretariat too had teething troubles, partly due to the fact that it, too, originally conceived itself as part of a supra-national organization when in fact it was nationalism which was uppermost in the Council of Ministers and the Assembly was really powerless to act.

All this resulted in a certain impatience on the part of many intelligent American officials. They told me very frankly from time to time of their forebodings, and how they thought that we would be well advised, while maintaining our realistic theses to a large extent, to go rather further towards an acceptance of the 'European idea'. For instance, why not accept some sort of qualified majority voting in certain defined spheres in the OEEC? Or let the Strasbourg assembly have very limited powers in certain fields also? The UK, if it went as far as this, would have a position of real leadership. As it was (and this I knew from other sources) there was a growing hostility to the UK in many European circles, and notably in the Economic Committee of the Council of Europe, where the tendency was to suggest that the Continent must now organize itself quite independently of Britain. I defended myself at that time as best I could and remember asking one very high official whether the USA would be likely to accept 'qualified majority voting' in any organization to which it belonged, getting the rather surprising answer that it very well might – on the natural assumption that decisions taken by such means were not necessarily binding!

Others told me that what they thought was necessary was somebody who could play, in the European field generally, the same 'galvanizing' role that Oliver Franks had played in the early days of OEEC. They also thought that there ought to be some middle course between 'union' and 'unity'. For instance, why could not the UK be a member of the proposed European Payments Union? Others again urged complete freedom of trade and movement, which prompted me to ask whether the United States would agree to lift their quotas on immigrants. But I must say I felt rather awkwardly on the defensive in all these exchanges as we progressed into 1950. And there were distinct indications, too, that the French Government, and notably Robert Schuman, were not, to put it mildly, entirely in favour of our rather 'aloof' and governmental attitude towards the Council of Europe. So I daresay I was neither as surprised nor as horrified as some when, without telling us (but telling Dean Acheson!) he came out on 9 May with his famous coal and steel project, devised, as we know, by Jean Monnet. Indeed I remember saying that, in my view, we ought at least to negotiate about this and not turn it down out of hand.

I should mention at this point that towards the end of 1948 I presided over a body known as the 'Russia Committee'. This grew up quite naturally in order to coordinate policy in the light of that new phenomenon, the Cold War. One of its functions was to make appreciations of what we believed the Soviet Government was up to and how far we ought to disregard, or alternatively pay attention, to their frequent dire threats. The idea was that all the political Under-Secretaries – and notably Frank Roberts who had more to do with our Russian policy than anybody else – should meet every so often and discuss what I suppose would now be called 'position papers', usually put up by a member of the 'E. and R. Department', or indeed by myself. Great efforts, usually successful, were made to arrive at a common 'official' view, and I believe the experiment was an undoubted success. Later this body was taken over by the Permanent Under-Secretary himself and became, in effect, a planning machine. But the advantage, if advantage it were, was that there was no planning section as such: all the Under-Secretaries were in on the papers from the start and there was then no clash between 'theoreticians' and working officials usually wrestling with important immediate problems. Bevin himself welcomed the new committee and took much interest in it but I believe that when Eden returned to the Office in 1951 it rather faded out. All Secretaries of State have their own ways of running things and there is no doubt that Eden's knowledge of the techniques of diplomacy was superior to Bevin's, so may be he found a 'planning' body, still more so a section, to be a hindrance rather than a help. 'Planning' in general is a debatable aspect of foreign policy since theory is not only difficult to formulate but often impossible to apply. Much depends on personalities and the essential thing, if possible, is to have a highly knowledgeable and practical Permanent Under-Secretary working with an imaginative minister. In such ideal circumstances there is probably no need of 'planning' as such. But I repeat I believe that the Russia Committee did fulfil a useful function. Certainly it conditioned our whole policy for 'containing' Soviet expansion during a very critical time.

14

Public Figure
(1950-1)

On Sunday, 25 June 1950, I was busying myself in the garden and thinking vaguely about my new post which I would be taking up in a few weeks' time. This was that of British Permanent Representative on the Security Council of the United Nations in New York. Some of my friends thought this would be a backwater, but it meant promotion to 'Grade One' though I was barely 50, and I myself thought it would be likely to be interesting, if unexciting. I was in many ways sorry to leave the Office and more particularly Uncle Ernie. 'Whatever you may say about Gladwyn,' that extraordinary figure had just been reported as saying 'he ain't never dull!'

Alec Cadogan had left New York and Terence Shone was in command. All was quiet. There had that morning been reports of some border incident in Korea, but I had not taken it too much to heart. Then the wireless told me that the Security Council was meeting and next day, Monday 26 June, I heard that they had decided that there had been a 'breach of the peace'. What had seemed to me originally to be a minor border incident was becoming more serious. That evening the telephone rang. The Resident Clerk said that I was wanted in London urgently and would I bring enough clothes for at any rate a week or two. I arranged to take the Tuesday morning train, and on the way thought a bit about Southern Korea, on which I must say up till then I had not focused very intently. I seemed to recall that the Americans had fairly recently said something to the effect that it was not included in their 'defensive perimeter'. If so, the probability surely was that somehow or other the invasion of South Korea – if it were an invasion – would result in the collapse of the rather unpopular and seemingly not very democratic Syngman Rhee and the formation of a new government that would make a new deal with the North, thus unifying the country. Or at any rate that the affair would be patched up without the Americans deploying any armed forces, to the general disadvantage, no doubt, of democracies everywhere, and of the UN in particular.

With these rather gloomy reflections in mind I walked into my old room in the Office where Bob Dixon was now installed as deputy Under-Secretary of State. 'I suppose', I said, as I sat down, 'that the Americans will somehow arrange for this business in Korea to be settled out of court?' 'My dear fellow,' replied Bob, 'they are going in with everything they've got! It's terribly serious.' I was staggered, but I must say relieved. For if the American reaction had been other than what it was, it was obvious that not only would Molotov's 'tendency' have gained a major victory, but the United Nations would have become a quite unconsidered backwater. Instead of heading for a dull lagoon, indeed, I was now heading towards a very stormy sea. What did the Foreign Office want me to do? Get into the first available aeroplane, said Bob, and stay in New York until you can suitably take a week off to come back and clear up your affairs. So on the evening of Wednesday 27 June, I arrived in New York. By then the Security Council had passed the critical second resolution whereby members of the United Nations were asked to 'repel an armed attack and restore peace in the area'. As a matter of fact the USA had begun moving troops just before the resolution was passed. Both resolutions had, of course, only been possible because the Soviet Representative, Yakov Alexandrovich Malik, was absent owing to the Soviet boycott of the Council and was consequently not able to exercise his veto.

There was, therefore, not a great deal for me to do immediately. There was considerable excitement, but to the journalists at the airport I merely said that we were one hundred per cent on the side of the Americans in this crisis and would help them all we could. Nobody, however, noticed the new arrival much and I was able to take stock of the position without making any major pronouncement. And, indeed, short of what I had said on arrival, there was at that moment not much to add. The Americans had been given the go ahead: it was for them to make the running. In the Security Council there had been one abstention on the first resolution – Yugoslavia – and two more on the second – Egypt and India. But that there had been an 'act of aggression' under the Charter no one, save, presumably, the Russians, could possibly doubt. For the time being all who supported the United Nations in any way could only hold their breath.

It was my first independent post, but it was not much like a large Embassy. The difference between being British representative in New York and the chief adviser to the delegation to the Assembly (which I had been for the last four years) was not all that great and the problems were in any case much the same. Besides we had by that time made many good friends in New York not only among the delegates but in New York society as well. In particular Nin Ryan,* that Egeria of all discerning British statesmen, was a tower of strength and you could always meet whoever you most wanted to meet at her parties. To mention other friends would be like quoting most of the Social Register! What we did find was that New York Society was most agreeable and intelligent and took a great interest in the United Nations. I am told it is different now, but then you could walk about the streets after dark in complete safety. From our offices on the sixty-first floor of the Empire State Building we looked down on what was still, by and large, a happy town.

The presidency of the Security Council rotated monthly. The Indians had it in June, the Norwegians in July and the Soviet representative, if he were to return, would have it in August when he would be followed by myself. Nobody knew whether Mr Malik, still skulking in his tent on Long Island, would come back to preside or not. But on 20 July he announced his intention of doing so. Evidently he would query everything that the Council had done so far and, so far as he could, prevent it, by exercising his veto, from functioning further. His position as President would give him additional opportunity for mischief and in any case for much propaganda. Everybody expected trouble, but few imagined what was actually going to happen. Before going into that perhaps I should briefly refer to the background.

By the end of July the South Korean Army had been totally defeated. The remains of it, together with the two American divisions that had been hastily flung in to help them, was virtually confined to the small perimeter of Pusan in the south-east corner of the peninsula. The Americans were by now wholly committed to the war and the alternatives before them were either to evacuate and allow the North Korean Communists to claim a victory, not only over them, but also over the United Nations, or to maintain their toe-hold and gradually expand it if they could. The only comforting feature, in so far as it was one, was that the Russians had not shown any sign of entering the war themselves, either by reinforcing the North Koreans, or by making any threatening gesture. Nor, at that stage, had the Chinese. It looked therefore as if the Russians (though they must almost certainly have winked at, even if they had not actually provoked the aggression) had not expected the instant reaction of the Americans for which, as we know, Dean Acheson was largely responsible,

* Mrs John Barry Ryan, daughter of Otto Kahn, the banker.

and were therefore in considerable embarrassment as regards their next move. Few thought that they would risk a war with the Americans if they could possibly help it.

But in the United States it was different. That country was now actually at war, even if it had not been officially declared. American soldiers were being killed, and some had already been captured. Intense emotion had thus been engendered. The events of the last few years, the Cold War generally, had persuaded most that it was the Russian Communists who were the real enemy and Gallup polls showed that the majority of the American people were convinced that they would be before long at war with the USSR. There was also a genuine fear of the effect of a South Korean success on the American position in Japan. Altogether the atmosphere was dangerous and quite explosive.

It seemed to me then – and indeed it was an idea that had been forming for some time – that one of the chief advantages of the Security Council might be that of a lightning-conductor. The General Assembly was, of course, supposed to fulfil this function and so it did to a certain extent. But there emotion tended to be focused on passionate 'causes' such as anti-colonialism, or human rights, or refugees, or 'aid', or even disarmament, all of which were important – no doubt in the long run much more important than anything dealt with in the Security Council – but could not be treated in a political way. But it was in the Security Council – in so far as disputes were not removed from its jurisdiction altogether – that you had the clash of real national interests: a place where those 'cold-hearted monsters', the nation-states, could at least indulge in parleys before coming to blows and, in doing so, abide by certain elementary rules. Nationalist emotions, which might reach explosion point if the dispute were confined to bilateral negotiations through official channels, might therefore be to some extent defused by arguing out the controversy in public – preferably by experts acting under instructions and not by politicians who could hardly help being primarily conscious of the effect that their interventions were likely to have on their reputation at home.

The possibility of thus operating successfully was increased – and not decreased as the traditionalists would have it – by the invention of television which, in 1950, was just getting to the point of 'national hook-ups', i.e. the point at which events could be seen all over America at the same moment (far ahead of anything comparable in the UK, still chiefly dependent on radio and not on TV at all). Thus if 'our side' were conscious that their representative had made a valid point in a debate with 'the other side' it would be much encouraged and its collective mind might tend to think less of current difficulties and reverses. The tension, in other words, might to some extent tend to run into the ground. Besides, if the 'other side' made any reasonably valid point, this might also cause a drop in 'tension'. It was not that a 'solution' of the difficulty was likely to be found by this kind of proceeding. That would no doubt have to be worked out by others, perhaps far from Lake Success. It was the show itself which was the thing.

The new President was quite well suited to this kind of forensic battle. He was (and is) a large, well-mannered bureaucrat with a pleasant voice and an easy smile. While hardly ever deviating from the party line, however absurd, he never indulged in crude abuse, like the odious Vyshynsky, nor did he ever lose his temper – or indeed his head. He was therefore a formidable opponent. He could no doubt have been more formidable if he had had a better case, or even had he been able to seize on gaps in his opponents' arguments and exploit them in a legal way, as Vyshynsky did. But that is not his line. He was in fact – and no doubt largely because of his iron-clad instructions – a little wooden, and thus inflexible, but he did his best and you could not help respecting him. And I am also sure that, high up in the Soviet hierarchy as he was, he had little doubt about the innate superiority of the Soviet system over the 'anarchic' capitalism of America.

My American colleague was a very different type. Warren Austin was an elderly Senator from Vermont, one of the more remote and conservative states of the Union. There he had agricultural interests – more especially his apples were famous – and he gave the general impression of being a highly successful gentleman-farmer. He was also shrewd and sensible. But nobody could say that he was particularly brilliant in controversy. What he did have was a considerable capacity for indignation, and what he conceived to be the sheer obstruction of his Soviet colleague often drove him wild. His great advantage was his obvious honesty and sincerity, and you could be absolutely sure that he would keep to his side of a bargain. Nor was he jealous or scheming at all. That said, it was pretty clear that he was a little old-fashioned both in his oratory and his outlook, and probably therefore not entirely suitable to represent the USA in what was to develop into a sort of triangular diplomatic boxing match.

I say triangular because Jean Chauvel, the French representative, though greatly superior to myself, and no doubt to the Senator, in ability and in diplomatic experience, suffered from the considerable disadvantages of (a) talking French; (b) not being in any way an orator; and (c) being, I

PUBLIC FIGURE (1950 – 1)

think, a little contemptuous of this way of doing business anyhow.
Behind the scenes he was indeed a power: full of good sense and always at
hand with the right formula during any crisis. But it would certainly never
have occurred to him to concentrate on making an impression on the
American public. For the rest, both the representatives of India and Egypt
were chiefly intent in seeking compromise solutions whereby the war
could be ended by some 'package deal' involving the replacement of the
Nationalist by a Communist Chinese: neither of which attitudes, even if
they were sensible (which they then were not) could be said to be exactly
popular. And though Tingfu-Tsiang, the delegate of Chiang Kai-shek,
was able and likeable, and thus made a direct appeal to many Americans,
it was obvious that his country could not in the circumstances have much
effect on the course of events.

So when on 1 August Yakov Alexandrovitch took over the presidency
the performers were all lined up and the television producers had instructions to turn their machines constantly, on the look-out for (highly
profitable) squalls. So far as I was concerned, however, I did not, in spite
of my theories, conceive of myself as a very suitable public jouster,
still less as a popular defender of democracy and the Western World.
I was, I thought, a pretty efficient bureaucrat and organizer, who,
had practically never made a public speech and was, in his own estimation, incapable of making one. But this, I remember thinking, is
not of course a parliamentary occasion. There will be no need to make a
sort of House of Commons speech. The text, carefully prepared beforehand in accordance with the wise instructions of the Foreign Office, will
be, in effect, read out. And if it takes, as seems probable, half an hour or
more, there will follow at least an hour during which it will be translated
both into French and into Russian. If therefore Mr Malik should say anything very devastating, there will be all the time in the world to think up
some come-back behind the scenes with intelligent advisers before reading that out too. There might even be time to ring up the Foreign Office
and ask them if they approved it! (The only difficulty here was that with a
five hour time-difference there was usually nobody in the Office at the
crucial moment to whom any appeal could be made.)

One advantage I did have. I was never nervous, nor did bright lights
worry me in the least. Besides, I never got worked up. Nor did I mind
very much what other people – even what the press – thought of my
efforts. I just fired them off and the audience could take them or leave
them so far as I was concerned. I did get annoyed if I was definitely mis-
reported: indeed I was sometimes (perhaps because of my accent) re-

ported as having said the exact opposite of what I did say: but criticism did not distress me much. Sometimes indeed it was very useful. I think what I am trying to say was that, if possible, absence of vanity as well as of self-consciousness is a definite asset in any television game. But I never analysed it all like this at the time. I just weighed in and read out my prepared statement, hoping for the best.

It thus remains a largely unexplained mystery why, after about a fortnight of the Russian presidency, I became a sort of popular hero, outshining most of the film-stars and receiving thousands of letters a week from all over the USA. It was indeed credibly reported that my 'Hooper rating' – at that time the method employed for determining the popularity of a 'television personality' – was Number Three in America, immediately below Bob Hope and just in front of the wrestlers, Indeed. quite a number of taxi-drivers actually told me that when I came on they switched off the wrestlers. Quite a few urged me to 'run for President'. People came up to me in the streets. In restaurants all heads – other, I hope, than my own – were turned. I did not find this a very pleasant experience. Watching the proceedings of the Security Council became in fact, for America in August 1950, the equivalent of *The Forsyte Saga* or *Coronation Street*. There was a caricature in the *New Yorker*, which I now have framed at home, of a plump citizen in the Bronx sitting glued to his box and his wife, opening the door, is saying 'Point of Order, Sir Gladwyn, dinner's ready.' You might really have thought that the utterances of a rather junior British diplomat were of some world-shattering importance in themselves. How did this frankly extraordinary situation ever come about? Let us glance at what actually happened in the Security Council.

It will be recalled that the Security Council under Indian presidency, passed the crucial resolutions before I arrived at the end of June. It did little in July under the pacific presidency of Arne Sunde, the Norwegian save pass another one, presented by Chauvel and myself, which set up a unified UN Command; asked the USA to nominate a Commander-in-Chief; and authorized the use of the UN flag. On the last day of the month it passed another organizing relief for South Korea and was considering yet another forbidding members of the UN from aiding North Korea. All thus had been pretty quiet and without publicity. Then, on 1 August, Malik took over and the fun began. The new President started off by refusing to recognize the representative of what he called 'the Kuomingtang Group', that is to say, Nationalist China. This naturally resulted in a row. Who was Malik to say that Tingfu-Tsiang did not exist juridically when he was, after all, regarded by a majority of members as representing China? After a long debate it was decided by a 8–3 vote that the President should be overruled. The President then announced that, because Tsiang had voted, the vote was only 7 3. Further row. Things were certainly hotting up. Then the President produced an agenda in which the item which had figured in it up till now was replaced by a wholly tendentious phrase removing blame for the aggression from North Korea. He 'ruled' that this agenda should be adopted. Even more excitement. Who was he to 'rule'?

Moves were naturally made to reverse the ruling. A vast set speech followed, accusing the Americans of almost every crime, and saying that all that the Council should concentrate on henceforward was a 'peaceful settlement'. By this time everybody's blood was up. It became clear that one of Malik's chief tricks was to produce a draft agenda to which nobody had agreed, and then in the debate on whether it should be adopted or not, make hour-long speeches going into the substance of the new item which he had prepared for discussion. Since all speeches had to be translated twice consecutively that usually meant that we were forced to adjourn before any vote could be taken even on the agenda. Malik seemed to be coming pretty close to making the Security Council appear ridiculous.

The next day I made my first attack on the President and on 3 August Malik produced his famous 'evidence' of US aggression (including photographs of Foster Dulles in a trench), and argued at immense length that the war in Korea was not an instance of aggression but a civil war. The Senator, by that time almost choking with rage, replied in a speech which the President described as 'hysterical'. It was not that, though it was certainly violent. I followed him in a rather more acidulous vein. The next three meetings were sheer frustration, Malik producing every possible red-herring. My first long speech on 11 August had at least this success, that it provoked a come-back. 'As regards the efforts of the UK representative' the President said, 'to play the part of the theorist and commentator on the world-wide historical liberating philosophic Marxist doctrine, these can be disregarded, first because his comments are devoid of philosophic knowledge and secondly because he attempts to defend the theory of the inevitability of perpetual domination by Anglo-American imperialism over the peoples of Asia and the Far East, a theory which is outmoded and has long since been discarded and rejected by all freedom-loving peoples. Let us consign the theory to the British Museum. It neither does nor can find widespread acceptance.'

Three more meetings produced an excellent analysis by Chauvel, further mountainous speeches by Malik and, finally, my own intervention of 22 August which once again drew a long refutation on the following day, the President declaring that I was the 'typical representative of bourgeois diplomacy' who 'resorted to well-known tricks' and was following in the footsteps of such characters as Bevin, McNeil and Shawcross. 'You are wasting your time, Sir Gladwyn,' he gravely announced. That was really the end of the jousting. But on 29 August I did support Malik on one thing, namely the desirability of the Security Council's inviting representatives of the Chinese People's Republic. This was to come up later in a big way.

I have re-read my various utterances in the debate during the first half of that fateful August. Though dated, they have, I think, stood the test of time fairly well. So far as television is concerned, it is not, of course, what one says that matters so much as the impression one creates. But the text may still be of some interest, so I give extracts in an Appendix. On the substance I think there can be no doubt whatever that my case was a good one. Nor could there be much doubt in the mind of the audience that I myself believed in it – it was not just play-acting or special pleading. The general theme of the purity of Western as opposed to the impurity of Soviet motives has, it is true, become dimmed in recent years, partly owing to the row over apartheid and partly, owing to Vietnam. But then we were, as it were, in the morning of the world so far as the United Nations was concerned – and how could the arch suppressors of liberty legitimately criticize our intentions? If ever there was an issue which could be considered in terms of black and white it was produced by the unprovoked attack of North Korea on South Korea – 'naked aggression' as Clem Attlee was subsequently to call it.

Let no one think, however, that I claim any great credit for this August performance. It was not as if I was an actor with a difficult part, when indeed I might have been praised for succeeding. On the contrary, I was simply reading out my prepared scripts. Nor was it as if what I said had any significant effect on the course of the war in Korea, or even on Anglo-American relations, though what effect it did have was no doubt good. It did perhaps encourage the American public more particularly my cracks at certain absurdities in the Soviet position. Certainly I think it helped them to believe in the essential rightness of their cause. But possibly the chief profit lay in the fact that the propaganda which I put out largely neutralized the carefully thought-out Soviet propaganda. This was borne out by the pains to which Malik went to refute my allegations.

Probably, he was nervous about the effect that these might have in the 'third world' and among the neutrals.

Naturally, too, when I assumed the presidency on 1 September there was a gasp of relief from the American public. The immediate admission to the Council tables of the South Koreans, who had for so long been excluded owing to the machinations of a stage villain, was dramatic. I was, in the popular imagination, the good liberator, the young man who had defied the bad dictator. Whatever I said or did I could hardly fail to be acclaimed. Even the *Chicago Tribune*, not noticeably pro-British in tendency, came to the conclusion that, for a Limey, I had not done too badly. They even published on page 1 two photographs of the brutal Communist who had been defying democracy and the young Englishman who had been defending it. Unfortunately the pictures were mixed up. Not that it mattered much because Yakov Alexandrovitch, as I have already said, was in 1950 a very good-looking and quite likeable fellow.

This did not stop him from protesting long and loudly against my 'ruling' as he called it on the admission of the South Koreans. The protest only did him harm and he could not in any case eject the South Koreans. Then he attempted, as usual, to revise the agenda. I 'ruled' that even if he did revise it this would not prejudice the presence of the South Korean representative. The advantage of 'ruling' was that, unless successfully challenged, the ruling stood. The Egyptians objected to this. But I successfully maintained that it was the only possible way to make progress. There followed another half-hour of pure propaganda. I said that if Malik assumed the right immediately to 'controvert' everything that anybody said on any subject we might be sitting for ever. He said that he could now say what he wanted to say in one sentence. I said that I should like nothing better than to hear a speech of one sentence by the Soviet Representative. Finally, whether as a result of exhaustion or of my frequent 'rulings' we were allowed to hear the representative of South Korea who had been excluded from our debates for over a month. Then of course it was time to adjourn.

The next meeting or two was pretty rowdy, but I did finally succeed in getting all the pending resolutions put to the vote, often using the 'ruling' as a device to shorten discussion. So we proceeded to vote down, very slowly, various other resolutions (during the course of our debate Austin suddenly produced from under the table some Russian-made machine guns and to the sensation of the mass audience handed them round the table for inspection!) and finally came at the end of the month to an absurdly worded one called 'Complaint of invasion of Taiwan (Formosa)', which represented an accusation by Peking that the Americans, owing to their support of Chiang Kai-shek, had actually 'invaded' that island. In the course of this debate the Russians demanded that the Peking Government should at least be invited to send representatives to plead their cause, and the Ecuadorian had another resolution down in much the same sense. We (the British) were all in favour of an invitation going out to Peking, partly because we had recognized the Communist government and felt that it ought to be treated with at least some consideration, and partly because we sincerely believed on general grounds that even an adversary ought to be heard, on the legal principle of *audi et alteram partem*. But of course Tsiang was bitterly opposed and so was the USA in principle. Having discovered, however, that I had just the bare majority of seven votes, I resolved to force the thing through. After frightful obstruction we eventually got around to putting the Ecuadorian resolution to the vote when, to my horror, Bebler, of Yugoslavia, abstained instead of voting for, so the whole manoeuvre failed. Consternation in our camp. Agitated behind-the-scenes conference with Bebler.

As a result of this, Bebler said that he had made a mistake and should have voted for. Further confusion, but we eventually agreed to meet again the next day – effectively the last day of my presidency. He then introduced the Ecuadorian resolution as his own and it was adopted by seven votes for, two against, and two abstentions. Tsiang then, as expected, protested that it had not been adopted since he had exercised his veto. He quoted the statement of the four sponsoring Powers at the San Francisco Conference which did in fact say that in the event of a division of opinion on whether a vote was procedural or not the point would have to be decided by a non-procedural vote. In spite of this I immediately 'ruled' that the vote we had just taken *was* procedural, which it obviously was, and therefore not subject to the Veto at all. Eventually my 'ruling' stood, 0-0-0, that is, nobody in favour, nobody against and nobody abstaining! I had effectively smashed the great bogey known to the jurists as the 'Hidden Veto' (see p. 159) and created a very considerable precedent for the future.

The whole scenario had been very carefully worked out with my brilliant legal adviser, James Fawcett, a Fellow of All Souls, and now Number Two in Chatham House. When exactly I should 'rule' and how; whether or not I should refer to the four-Power statement; how I should cope with Tsiang's come-back; all these things had been considered before the legal coup was attempted. Afterwards it was criticized. Tsiang, for instance, called it 'a clever but unusual manoeuvre'. He also said the point should be referred to the International Court of Justice. But the great thing about it was that it worked. The popular press said that the Council had been 'Jebb-propelled' – considered by most to be a compliment, I think. There remained the question of its possible effect on US public opinion, then, by a majority, strongly in favour of Chiang Kai-shek. Here Ernie Gross was most helpful. He at once made a speech in which he made it clear that although his delegation, which had abstained, was strongly opposed to that part of the resolution which invited the Peking Government to send a representative to plead its cause any time after 1 December (the General Assembly being expected to deal with Korea before then) he nevertheless certainly agreed with my action in laying down that the vote was procedural.

As soon as Gross had finished I therefore said, for the benefit, I need hardly say, of the vast audience, 'I should like to associate myself fully and immediately with what the representative of the USA has so admirably said. The spectacle of a Great Power willingly subscribing to a ruling of the President on a matter concerning the Veto, even though by so doing it is in its own belief going against its own immediate interests, is at once heartening and inspiring. Perhaps it may even prove to be what in Latin is called *auspicium melioris aevi*.* However, I had the impression that my 'Hooper Rating' was perhaps not quite so high. As I was not seeking any 'Oscar', this was not a matter of great concern; and indeed when in four months' time, for reasons which will soon become apparent, I was no longer any rival to the all-in wrestlers I was delighted. I always remembered what an Italian friend had told me in Rome when I congratulated him on rapid advancement at a very early age – '*Il Campidoglio è vicino alla rupe Tarpeia*'!†

For the time being, however, I remained fairly popular and one pleasing feature was the appearance, a little later, in my office of a delegation from the New York Society for General Semantics who presented me with a 'Citation' for my 'outstanding contributions to the cause of Peace in the Security Council of the United Nations; for plain speaking, for unmasking the propaganda technique of "upside-down language" and for the most important application of semantic criticism in the field of international relations', signed by Mr Allen Walker Reed (President) and Mr Max Sherover (for the Director). I was rather touched by this tribute and have also had it framed. In other academic circles I am afraid that I made less appeal. Syracuse, indeed, gave me an honorary degree, but I never really

* 'The prospect of a better age.'
† 'The Capitol is next door to the Tarpeian Rock.'

penetrated academe, possibly through not having made any effort. Oxford is an exception, though I think they may have honoured me *par esprit de solidarité* more than anything else. Or it may even have been my intense devotion to the home of lost causes. To return to my theme, at the end of September interest shifted from the Security Council to the General Assembly. A powerful delegation headed by Bevin was already heading for the scene of slaughter.

This vast publicity may possibly have had what is something called a 'mixed reception' in London where, after all, my actual appearances were not observed, and even what I said was as like as not too late to make the morning press, references in the evening press being mostly restricted to the gossip columns. I had no reason to suppose that Uncle Ernie was worried; but sometimes I had the impression that William Strang was like a hen whose job it was to see that no serious harm was occasioned by a chick that had taken to the political water like the proverbial duckling. Diplomats ought not, I have no doubt he thought, to do the work of politicians. They ought rather to negotiate in secret and dish up the correct formulae to their 'masters' who can then take the credit in Parliament or elsewhere. Perhaps it could not be helped in the circumstances, but in principle our representative in New York ought to have what I believe is now called a 'low profile'. I fully understood this attitude – and indeed approved of it. The only trouble was that when I was given a chance I could only express myself in what I suppose might be called 'political' language. It was my nature and I could not help it.

Harold Nicolson – who was, of course, violently opposed to 'open diplomacy' of any kind – had a piece in a Sunday paper at the end of August in which he spoke of 'the frenzied publicity which surrounds Lake Success' and said that it had imposed upon me 'the odious prominence of a film or baseball star'. 'Sir Gladwyn', he was so kind as to add, 'has never aspired to be a crooner or an auctioneer. He is a highly trained diplomatist whose sole desire is to conduct public business privately and to secure by confidential negotiation dependable results.' I was gratified also to read that he considered me to be 'the fortunate possessor of great powers of physical endurance, a sense of humour, an incisive intelligence and a remarkable combination of tolerance and scorn. He is also extremely courageous. These qualities have enabled him to endure with sardonic patience the pantomime of Lake Success.' 'The circus atmosphere encompassing these momentous deliberations', Harold continued, 'must be galling to a man of his patrician temper. He cares deeply about the Charter of the United Nations. It must be with despair that he is forced to watch the paragraphs which he drafted at Dumbarton Oaks and San Francisco being hurled, spanner by spanner, into the machine.'

I thought this, to say the least, rather highly coloured, so I wrote to my old friend and one time mentor saying that as a matter of fact the only thing that did disconcert me a little was the number of unknown people who came up insisting on shaking hands and hitting me on the back. To this I received renewed sympathy together with a PS which ran: 'I was talking to William Strang yesterday who said that it was bad luck on someone who had done such really serious and important work to become front page news. I said I thought you would not mind so much as all that. "I am not so sure", said William. Anyhow, the Foreign Office regard your handling of the Lake Success debates with delighted awe.' Harold had by this time got it right. I did not 'mind so much as all that'. But on the other hand I never had the slightest illusions.

But I must say the Foreign Office, if a little nervous, was very appreciative of my efforts while Uncle Ernie, which was the great thing, seemed to like them quite a lot. There was never any whisper, at any rate, that he might be thinking of replacing me by some prominent politician. Even so you might have thought that I was hogging too much of the limelight, though in practice there was little that I could do about that. But no. When he came over for the General Assembly at the end of September he observed as I came into the room, 'Well, 'ere comes the Great Man. Do you know what one of my dear political friends said to me just before I came out? "I suppose you're off", he said, "to bask in the reflected glory of Sir Gladwyn Jebb"! *Basking*! Well, who knows, it might do me some good (throwing himself on a sofa). Come over 'ere and apply the treatment.' Poor man. He certainly was not well. 'It's the old ticker', he used to inform us. Within a few months it had ceased to function.

With the Secretary of State there came out that year, as I have said, a powerful team which included Hartley Shawcross, Hector McNeil, now the Minister of State, and Kenneth Younger* who had been steadily making a name for himself in the United Nations. Much time was taken up in debating and approving – on American initiative – a resolution called 'Uniting for Peace' which was an attempt to circumvent the Veto in the Security Council by authorizing the Assembly to take certain enforcement action if action in the Security Council were blocked by the vote of any one Power. We were on the whole against this since we thought it dangerous to put real power into the hands of a body which might, by a

---

* Labour MP 1945–59; Director of the Royal Institute of International Affairs 1959.

two-thirds majority, vote for action disapproved of by a permanent member. In effect, the one occasion on which this resolution was successfully applied was over Suez. But the Americans were enthusiastic and we had to go along. The eventual draft did not authorize the Assembly to do much more than it would have been able to do anyway.

The immediate excitement as regards Korea had now died down and the Secretary of State had returned to London. But it flared up with the entry of the Chinese into the war at the end of November. About two months previously, McArthur after the staggering success of his landing at Inchon had re-occupied Seoul, destroyed the North Korean Army and was in force on the thirty-eighth parallel. On 3 October Chou-en-Lai had told the Indian Ambassador that if the United Nations forces crossed the Parallel China would enter the war. In ignorance of, or disregarding this warning, Kenneth Younger was instrumental in getting the General Assembly to pass on 7 October a rather ambiguous resolution in favour of elections supervised by the United Nations and maintaining UN forces in the country for as long as was required to install a 'unified, independent and democratic government'. The only trouble was that the Americans were simply not prepared to enforce such a policy against resolute opposition. In spite of this – and indeed in spite of the resolution – General McArthur, on 9 October, called upon the North Koreans to surrender and, failing that, announced that he would take such military action as might be necessary to enforce 'the decisions of the United Nations'. A week later he was on the 'waist' of Korea. Beyond that, up to the frontier on the Yalu River, his instructions were to employ only South Korean troops. These instructions he disregarded.

I was myself very apprehensive at our action in crossing the parallel to any considerable extent. Our object, as it seemed to me, should be to defeat the aggression and restore the situation as it existed before 25 June. I confided my doubts to Ernest Gross, the Number Two in the US delegation until the Republicans came into power at the end of 1952. Ernie was not only a first-class lawyer but he had very real political sense as well. He was a member of the inner ring of American advisers on foreign affairs which was perhaps the chief glory of the Truman administration. Phil Jessup, George Kennan, Chip Bohlen, with all these stars I had a good deal to do after the war, but, by the force of things, I had with none of them quite the same relationship as I had with Gross. All through the dramatic summer and autumn of 1950 we saw each other most days and after a time we got to a stage when we could discuss each other's difficulties absolutely frankly in the sure knowledge that neither of us would be given away. I thus got to know very well the things that were really worrying the Administration, and he also had a pretty shrewd idea of the preoccupations of the Labour Government in London.

Thus in New York there was formed the best possible basis for Anglo-American cooperation – absolute personal confidence between the men on the job. And soon we were to need it. I shall never forget the night when Ernie came round to see me at Essex House with the terrible news of the rout of the eighth Army by the Chinese and the impending threat to the Tenth Army on the north-western flank. It was obvious that there could be a danger that British public opinion might attack McArthur and the American policy of the non-recognition of China and that the Americans might tell the British that it was all partly their fault for not having sent enough troops. It was clear, too, that if it were the occasion of a major reverse there might be a certain amount of defeatism in both countries. We had a long talk about all these grave possibilities and how to confront the resulting situation in the Security Council. And no doubt we both signalled back much the same advice.

The disaster was in any case to have an immediate reaction in London. Alarmed by an unguarded reply by the President at a news conference on 30 November, which was interpreted as meaning that he might authorize the use of the nuclear weapon in Korea, the Prime Minister accompanied by the Chiefs of Staff, flew over to confer with the President, stopping off for one night in New York on the way to confer with the delegation.

There was not much advice that we could give him except to emphasize the necessity of standing firm and once again holding the adversary in Korea. But already there were rumours that the Americans would shortly press for the condemnation of the Chinese as 'aggressors'. To this I was myself opposed. The Chinese had, after all, not backed up the North Koreans at the beginning of the latter's undoubted aggression: all they had done, after due warning, was to intervene in order to save the North Koreans from total defeat involving the occupation of the entire country by the forces of the USA. And, after all, we had recognized Peking and wanted, if possible, to bring that government into the 'polite society' of the United Nations. We were also, not unnaturally, concerned lest American preoccupation in Asia should lessen their will to organize the defence of Europe.

A full account of Attlee's encounter with President Truman is given by Dean Acheson in his book.* It emerges from this that the Prime Minister –

* Dean Acheson: *Present at the Creation*, (New York, 1970), pp. 478–85.

'Abler' he says, than suggested by Churchill's description of him as 'a sheep in sheep's clothing' but still 'profoundly depressing' – was prevented from taking foolish initiatives aimed at the recognition of China by the Americans in return for China's agreement to a cease-fire and, above all, checked in his pernicious attempt to get the Americans to say that they would not use the nuclear weapon except after previous consultation with ourselves. Able and often right as he was the Dean always seemed to me to be a little too contemptuous of those who differed from him, and indeed of those who endeavoured, usually vainly, to get in his way. It never seemed to me, indeed, that the original British policy of recognizing the *de facto* government of China was anything save sensible, and if the Americans had followed our example at the end of 1949 it is possible that subsequent history might have been very different.

It is true that the status of Formosa might have led Peking not to 'recognize the recognition' – as has, after all, been partially the case with us, since we have never got further than a Chargé d'Affaires. Once Chiang Kai-shek was installed on Formosa (still, technically, Japanese territory) it would have been quite impossible for the Americans to have allowed the Communists to turn him out. Nor would the Communists have been in a position to turn him out for many years. Formosa would therefore almost certainly have remained a separate state, and for such time as she was separate the Peking regime might have refused to become a member of the United Nations even if invited to do so. But Sino-American relations would almost certainly have been less acidulous.

We for our part were, however, rather less conscious of the difficulties in the way of better relations between the Americans and the Chinese than we might have been. It was only a year since the Communist victory in China, and nobody quite knew how they were going to behave. So no doubt we had some excuses. I remember feeling pretty strongly that we ought to treat the new regime with the utmost care. When the delegation from Peking had duly arrived in New York late in November just before the arrival of the Prime Minister) and General Wu had made his distressingly uncompromising speech – in Manchu, before the Security Council and when I approached, a little late, I thought it was a baby screaming – I had had him and his colleagues to lunch with us, together with a well-known sinologue, and we had at least had an interesting talk, though nothing came of it. What is so attractive about the Chinese is their extreme intelligence; and in spite of the 'Cultural Revolution' I have little doubt that their innate individualism will eventually result in something less monstrous than the present 'Big Brother is Watching You' regime. But though we had the impression that what we said was at least understood and that there was certainly more than one tendency in the Peking camp, nothing, as I say, came of this party, and our guests left for the Soviet country club where they were staying.

A little while after the Chinese had returned to China, however, we gave a cocktail party at Wave Hill – I have forgotten the precise occasion. Malik, who had been their host, was invited and came, for some reason, alone. After it was over it was found that his car had stalled and could not be got to work. I offered him a lift to the UN in mine. He accepted. On the way he expanded at length on the tendency of the Chinese to regard *all* foreigners as devils, not only those who 'come by sea' but also those who 'come by land' as well. In any case the Chinese represented *all* foreign devils as having white skins and the Russians for their part could do absolutely nothing about that. What my colleague was surely trying to tell me – and remember this was fifteen years before the great communist schism – was that it should not be assumed that the Russian and the Communist Chinese Governments would necessarily always be allied, and might even, in certain circumstances, come to blows. The Russians, in other words, might not always, and even for very long, regard the West as their only, and their implacable enemy. In any case, when making their plans, the West should allow for this possibility.

Until the Korean situation was once again more or less stabilized militarily in the spring we continued to be much occupied with China, and in January, when the politicians had had to return home, I was myself left in charge of the important proceedings in the first committee of the General Assembly. The result can be studied by those who care to follow these things in Command Paper 8159 called 'UN Resolutions on Chinese Intervention in Korea', published by HMG in March 1951, which also gives the texts of my various speeches. As this was really the last of my individual political interventions on any large scale, perhaps I might finish this chapter by a brief description of the issue and the result.

On 13 January 1951, the Political Committee finally approved by 50–7–1 (the USA voting for) the famous 'Five Principles' to which allusion has already been made.* These were (1) a cease-fire; (2) advantage to be taken of a cease-fire to consider further steps for the restoration of peace; (3) in order to prevent the carrying out of the original General Assembly resolution that Korea should be a 'unified, independent democratic sovereign state with a free constitution and a government

* See p. 242.

based on free popular elections', all non-Korean armed forces to be withdrawn, by appropriate stages; (4) interim arrangements to be made for the purpose and (5) as soon as a cease-fire was in existence the General Assembly should set up a body, to include representatives of the UK, USA, USSR and the People's Government of China, to achieve a settlement of Far Eastern problems *including among others those of Formosa and of the representation of China in the UN* (my italics). It will be seen that this was a highly important and potentially very constructive proposal. It had the enthusiastic support of HMG and the very lukewarm support of America. However on 17 January it was turned down, almost flatly, by the People's Government. In particular Chou-en-Lai stated that Peking, though in favour of a 'peaceful settlement' involving the withdrawal of all foreign troops from Korea, would also contemplate a simultaneous withdrawal of US forces from Taiwan and (in effect) their own presence in the UN. Even more uncompromisingly a cease-fire should only take place after negotiations on such matters at a seven-Power conference (China, USSR, UK, USA, France, India and Egypt) to be held in China. Immediately on receipt of this document, the USA tabled a resolution finding, among other things, that the People's Government by aiding the aggressors and themselves engaging in hostilities, were themselves 'engaged in aggression in Korea'. It also proposed the constitution of a committee to consider urgently 'additional measures to be employed to meet this aggression'.

I had made one 'holding' speech before this resolution was actually tabled denouncing the attitude of Peking generally – 'representatives from nations selected by the People's Government itself would have to make a long pilgrimage to Canossa'; instead of making every effort to see that aggression does not pay . . . 'in future the United Nations should devote itself to the problem of how best to reward aggression' etc.; but ended up with a reference to a recent communiqué of the Commonwealth Prime Ministers and saying that I could hardly believe that Peking could ignore totally this olive branch extended by the democratic populations of 550 million people. On 25 January, having obtained instructions, I fired off another of about one and a half hours which was also in the nature of a 'holding' operation, the Indians being in the process of trying to get some 'clarification' of Peking's attitude and Lester Pearson being on the point of suggesting a seven-Power conference at Lake Success or in New Delhi which would not, however, begin to operate until a cease-fire had actually been achieved, and some twelve Arab and American countries making a similar but less qualified suggestion.

My speech was therefore really directed not towards any further effort to avoid the denunciation of Peking as aggressors – which they clearly were in a technical sense – but to oppose a suggestion that there should be any serious effort to penalize them for their aggression – which one could at least understand, even if one could not excuse. We should, above all, as I saw it, ensure that the sacrifices of our troops in Korea were not in vain. 'It would be a poor return for these sacrifices if we involved ourselves in a course which led to still further sacrifices, without having any clear conception of the objectives at which we are aiming and without the assurance that all possible means of peaceful negotiation have been tested in order to limit these sacrifices and to enable the bloodshed to come to an end.' There were three ways in which the Korean question might be solved:

(a) a UN solution by force of arms, that is to say the occupation of Korea by UN forces; or

(b) a non-UN solution, that is to say the withdrawal, enforced or otherwise, of UN forces and the institution in Korea of a Communist regime; or

(c) an agreed solution, that is to say a solution which pays at least some regard to the views of the greatest interested country, namely China.

The first solution might be beyond our power; the second would, we hoped, be beyond the power of the other side; the third solution must therefore be the one at which we were presumably aiming, and it must be in harmony with the principles and purposes of our organization.

Feverish efforts were now made by me to avoid a situation in which I should have to abstain on, or even vote against, the US resolution, and on 30 January they were successful – though only just I think. A statement that Peking had 'rejected all UN proposals' was changed into 'had not accepted all UN proposals', and (more important) the committee to consider 'additional means' was authorized to defer its report if a 'Good Offices Committee' of two persons reported satisfactory progress in its efforts. I must say I was relieved when the telegram came authorizing me to support the US resolution with these amendments and I very quickly did so. But in the Assembly debate two days later I made our position absolutely clear by saying 'My Government quite frankly has the gravest doubts whether any punitive measures can be discovered which are not dangerous, double-edged, or merely useless, nor any which will materially assist our brave troops now fighting in Korea.' The crisis was over, and the danger of an extension of the war had largely disappeared.

People have often asked me what my real reactions were to becoming, for a time at least, the idol of America and having often to take decisions of great importance at very short notice without being too confident of sanction from on high. I think that I was, on the whole, stimulated rather than intoxicated by these strange circumstances. I enjoyed the fact that my actions seemed to meet with general approval, but I never even remotely imagined that my success was likely to be repeated in any other forum, least of all in my native land. I consistently thought of myself as an administrator rather than a politician or a demagogue and believed that I had to some extent demonstrated this ability by forming, and for a time running, the UN Secretariat. As it happened no further opportunity was granted me of again taking over some great machine. Perhaps the authorities concerned were frightened that I might in some strange way unduly dominate whatever I happened to touch. Perhaps I should have; but I never dreamt of doing anything of the kind. I had no dreams of glory nor, whatever people may have thought, any sense of publicity. I tended, therefore, as I have said, to live very much in the present, and I am sure that this is the happiest way of life. Is it so small a thing to have endured the sun, to have lived light in the spring, to have loved, to have thought, to have done, to have advanced true friends (e.g. Ernie Gross) and beat down baffling foes (Jakov Malik)? I think not; and perhaps I have been destined for purposes other than mere administration. All I can say with absolute truth is that 1950 was a most enjoyable year for me. In fact I have never had a year that I enjoyed more than 1950.

15

Less Public Figure
(1951-4)

After February 1951, I did not again, I think, play any very important political part in the UN. I still made speeches in the Security Council on matters such as Kashmir, and the row with Persia over Abadan: I still advised the Government and indeed, when it came out, the delegation; but I was less of a 'public figure' than I had been, and this was very right and proper. After all, I had always been a public figure rather *malgré moi*. For instance, when in mid-April I found myself undertaking a lecture tour in California I tried my best to avoid publicity. The row over General McArthur's behaviour was coming to a head and the nation was seriously divided, the Republicans, by and large, tending to favour the extension of the war recommended by McArthur – bombing of the Yalu River bridges, bombing of the Manchurian factories and war with 'Communist China', 'the unleashing of Chiang Kai-shek', the occupation by UN forces of the whole of Korea, in fact the whole programme of the 'no alternative to victory' school of thought. One thing I was determined not to do, and that was to get involved in this internal battle. There could, of course, be no real doubt which side had the sympathies of my government, and consequently of myself: but any rash word from me might have had serious consequences. Though it was hardly an exact parallel, I was always mindful of the sad fate of Lord Sackville, our Ambassador who wrote an indiscreet letter to the supporter of one side during an American election.

I therefore composed technical lectures on the interpretation of the Charter and the juridical position of the UN generally; and though I did not shirk questions I indicated that they had all better be about the UN as such and not about current political issues. It was, in fact, the beginning of the theme that tended to dominate what might be called my 'second period' in the United Nations, namely an effort to formulate the correct philosophy which could henceforward justify the existence of the World

Organization. My first effort to this effect went down in San Francisco reasonably well, because there I could, after all, concentrate on the famous conference of 1945 and recall what had been said then and how things had turned out since. But in Los Angeles I had not this advantage and in any case the tension between the General and the President seemed to be getting worse. I therefore gave what I think must have been my dullest lecture, and very properly got a comeback of which the following is an extract:

As an Englishwoman who cares passionately about the success of the UN I am going to speak plainly. I listened to your extremely boring speech of last night with very mixed feelings. I have been proud of your achievements in the Security Council but last night I felt really disgusted with Eton and Magdalen for letting loose on the world one of their finest products without giving him a single lesson in elocution or in how to affect a *rapport* with the audience. My American friend remarked when it was over 'Well that's the best speech I have ever heard in a "foreign language"' meaning that he had not been able to understand your enunciation. A woman behind me remarked, 'The English drop their voices half-way through every sentence and you never hear the end.' Many people gave up attempting to follow or hear and went to sleep. They were also deeply disappointed at the content of the speech. They did not want to hear about the constitution of the UN, but about the burning issues of the moment, such as were referred to in the questions. Everybody said you came to life over the questions and answered them magnificently though with a somewhat superior manner.

I wish I had retained the name of this excellent correspondent; but it has unfortunately got lost. She was dead right. But I repeat that I really was out to bore this particular audience.

Having liberated my lead balloon, I went to dine with Douglas Fairbanks and his charming wife, Marilou. At their agreeable house were assembled the cream of Californian society. There was the local Senator, a prominent Congressman, Miss Ethel Barrymore (the doyenne of the American stage), the American equivalent of our Astronomer Royal, the President of the University of California, our own Consul-General, Bob Hadow (with whom I was staying) and many others. Dinner was served formally in the English manner at one long table. There was a distinguished butler and several footmen. The ladies eventually left and the gentlemen gathered round our host to enjoy a glass of excellent port. We were just lighting up our cigars when there was a sort of scuffling at the door and in burst the butler, evidently deeply moved. He advanced towards Doug and in a hushed voice said 'Sir, Sir, the President has fired the General!' Pandemonium broke loose. Doug sent for radios. We rose to our feet and joined the ladies. Everybody talked at once and some listened to the commentators commentating from all over America. Eventually three groups emerged. That round the Senator was strongly pro-General. Miss Barrymore was the centre of the pro-Truman faction. And Doug, as became a host on such an occasion, was doing his best to form a fairly neutral group, with which I need hardly say I hastened to associate myself. Actually I was delighted and it pushed my admiration of Truman to even greater heights. More effective, I had always thought, than Roosevelt, and a much nicer man too for that matter. All his major decisions, after a short initial period, were right. But I had to be careful. It had already been reported in the press (and denied, though it was true) that I had referred to McArthur in private conversation as 'the mad satrap'.

Perhaps the disappearance of Uncle Ernie early in 1951, first from politics and then from life, was also a turning point for me. For over four years I had had a man at the top who seemed to understand me and in whom I had great confidence. The patient reader will no doubt have noticed the affection that I felt for him. If he had retained his full vigour it is quite possible that the Tories would not have won the 1951 election and my own subsequent career might have been very different. Not that I did not get on with Herbert Morrison, Bevin's successor for a few months. He stayed at Wave Hill for a day or two and we were on perfectly friendly terms. But it was evident that he knew practically nothing about foreign affairs and that his whole outlook was parochial. It seemed to me extraordinary that Attlee had not nominated either Hartley Shaw-cross or Hector McNeil. Both would have been good in the job. Perhaps Hector would have been the better of the two, if only for the fact that lawyers for some reason have often been poor Foreign Secretaries – look at Simon, or even Reading. But there is little doubt that Hartley – who was presumably the senior – would have been excellent in many ways. Perhaps it didn't much matter since neither would have had the job long enough to make any kind of name. The Labour Government had, it is true, a new and forceful Chancellor in Hugh Gaitskell, my old stable companion. He came out to New York in September on his way to Washington in order to discuss our financial situation with the Americans. There was no doubt that the shock of the Korean War had induced us to rearm beyond the limits of what was tolerable in time of peace. This in itself was an ancillary reason for the eventual defeat of the Government. Nor was it a necessary one, unless you really thought that the danger of war in Europe was actually imminent. Myself, I never did. Just as I had thought in 1948 at the time of the *Coup de Prague* that there would be no war provided only that the West put itself in a position to make at least some resistance, so I thought in 1951, that the Soviet Government would not risk a war against the West if the US was present in reasonable force in Germany, because once there, if they were seriously attacked, there was always the possibility of the use against Russia of the Atom Bomb.

In spite of Hugh the Labour administration, with its tiny majority, had almost lost the will to govern. It was therefore a good thing to have new brooms in Whitehall, more especially perhaps in the Foreign Service. Here the great post-war decisions had by now all been taken. There were not many options left open for the newcomers. NATO obviously had to be built up; so did OEEC. The Americans had to be assisted to the limit of our power in Korea; we could not abandon our own effort to defeat the Chinese Communist insurgents in Malaya; India and Pakistan had to be allowed to go their separate ways; CENTO and SEATO were in the offing – all the main lines of policy had been firmly established. It even looked at that particular moment, as if the French would be able to hang on to Vietnam. 'Europe' might indeed have been the scene of some new departure, but very early on it was seen that the Tory Government's European policy was identical with that of its predecessor. So even here no change was the rule. The achievements of Anthony Eden, which were notable, were yet to come. At the moment there was not much doing in the United Nations.

The sixth session of the General Assembly, which met just after the British General Election, at the end of 1951, was held in Paris (to give time for the new UN building in New York to be got ready) and we took a small house in the Square du Bois de Boulogne, just off the Avenue Foch. Paris was then still recovering from the occupation; and since I did not have a vast amount to do, we saw a lot of our French friends and went to many plays – particularly the Comédie Française. Since this book is about myself perhaps I should say that Racine is my favourite classical French playwright and *Phèdre* and *Bérénice* my favourite works – though I also have a weakness for Corneille. One of our social triumphs was to effect a conjunction between Nancy Mitford and Field-Marshal Montgomery. Monty had started the ball rolling by saying to me one morning out of the blue: 'Read a novel the other day. Hardly ever do. By a woman, too. You wouldn't know it, I expect. It's called *The Pursuit of Love*, by Nancy Mitford.' 'Monty', I said, 'Nancy is one of our oldest and dearest friends: You must meet her!' 'Well, haven't much time. But if you like. Short lunch.' Nancy, suitably approached, had said 'But, darling, he's

divine. So *Roman* and *Shakespearian*. Of course I should be charmed.'
So there they were next to each other at our narrow table and, needless
to say, both being of great intelligence, they got on like a house on fire.
Afterwards, when I was Ambassador, we usually had, at the end of each
summer season, a jolly lunch *à quatre* under the big *marronier* in the Embassy garden (now dead). And, always, it was the greatest fun.

The Assembly in Paris ground on, and at one moment I found myself
presiding, the UK having, in accordance with custom, been elected as
one of the Vice-Presidents and no other senior member of the delegation
being available. It proved to be a stormy session. In particular the Yugoslav
delegate was particularly obstreperous, always rising on bogus points of
order. Eventually I got bored with this and decided to risk *la manière forte*.
Upon Bebler rising for about the sixth time on a point of order, I said
firmly: 'No point of order arises: I call on the honourable representative
of Guatemala.' It worked. The great thing in chairing any difficult
assembly or large meeting is to choose the right second for striking the
'come on now, let's chuck it and get down to business' note. Nothing is
more painful than a nervous or hesitant Chairman: but equally a bullying
type may provoke a riot. The collective animal in front of you has to be
handled, in other words, like a horse which is inclined to bolt.

One of the newcomers to the Foreign Office was Selwyn Lloyd who
had been appointed Minister of State. Nobody then imagined that four
years later he would be Foreign Secretary, but he was from the first
popular in the Office and a great worker. We sometimes thought him
rather too hesitant, not to say diffident, in manner, but I think that this was
really due to an inherent (and too great) modesty. If he had been more
confident in his own good judgment he would certainly have played a
more considerable role. It is even possible that in that event we might
have avoided the Suez disaster – of which more later. What is a fact, I
feel, is that Dean Acheson rather misconceived his character and was much
too hard on him in his book.* Selwyn may have sometimes been too eager
to reach a compromise, but he was never the kind of weak schemer that
Dean suggested.

Back in New York at the end of 1951, we faced a rather bleak United
Nations. Real political interest had now shifted from Korea, where the
war was bogged down, to Europe and the still incipient NATO. I was
out of all this and only heard at second-hand what was going on. Our
immediate interest lay in the take-over of the American Administration
by the Republicans – out of office for twenty years. We did not look

* Dean Acheson: Op cit. pp. 583, 656 and 701-5.

forward to this with any great enthusiasm. Many Republicans, and notably Senator Taft, had vigorously opposed all the more constructive efforts of the Truman Administration. Many seemed to be 'China Firsters', associated with the famous China Lobby and seemingly intent on war with Peking and the 'unleashing of Chiang Kai-shek'. Those who were pro-NATO often appeared to be more pro-German than pro-British. Most responded to the anti-Communist crusade, then in full flood. Altogether not a very pleasant prospect. As for President Eisenhower himself, nobody could imagine that he had any deep knowledge of foreign policy. And his habit of spending much time practising chip-shots on the White House lawn, though endearing, did not exactly inspire confidence abroad. In private talks with him, as one of our more celebrated statesmen once remarked, it was 'rather like negotiating directly with George III'. Still, Eisenhower was in some ways an impressive figure. He did have an idea of the importance of Europe; and there was no doubt that his experiences in the war had left him a true friend of the United Kingdom.

The foreign policy of the USA under the new regime would, however, we understood, be left almost entirely to John Foster Dulles. This famous character had many qualifications for the job. He had attended the Peace Conference in 1919; he was a prominent member of the Foreign Affairs Association and a very well-known lawyer; and he had even been associated in several projects with the Truman Administration. When I had myself only been in New York for a few weeks, John Foster had had me out to Oyster Bay to lunch with his brother Alan, the Head of the CIA and we had then, and subsequently, long and agreeable talks about things in general. I might therefore be said to know him reasonably well. While acknowledging, however, all his qualities, I never felt really cosy with John Foster. There was perhaps too much of the missionary in him for me and too much also of the clever lawyer. (I think that, on the whole, my theory that brilliant lawyers are not usually good Foreign Secretaries is of universal application!). Still he was intelligent and very hard-working and I have no doubt that the comparatively level course of American diplomacy during the next four years was largely due to him. He knew also that in supping with the Soviet Government one had to use a very long spoon. His main defect was, I feel, a constant desire to rationalize his foreign policy and reduce it to a phrase. 'Agonizing reappraisal', 'roll back', 'massive retaliation' were all concepts incapable of realization and on the whole they diminished the credibility of the American approach.

With Cabot Lodge, who was to be my colleague in the United Nations, things were different. Cabot was a Bostonian aristocrat with an intimate knowledge of Europe and, more particularly, of France. He was indeed one of the very few American politicians (or English for that matter) who could rise to his feet and make an extempore speech in excellent French. In no way an intellectual, Cabot was a first-class operator in the Security Council where he sometimes gave the impression of being, as it were, a power in his own right. Generally speaking, the State Department seemed to have a less tight hold on their representatives than under the Democratic administration when Dean Acheson with his brilliant team tended to dominate the show. Perhaps this was inevitable seeing that the Democrats during their long period of office had been able to create a corps of really admirable experts which, under the American 'spoils' system could hardly, even with the greatest goodwill, be fully operated by the incoming Republicans.

Unfortunately, there was the reverse of goodwill. The extreme Republicans had got it into their heads that the American defeat in China – for when the Communists took over in 1949 such it was – had been something for which the State Department was uniquely responsible: and from there it was a short step to suggest that the reason for the failure was that 'Communists' had infiltrated the department and practically taken over the foreign policy of the USA. 'Treason' was in the air. When therefore Alger Hiss was convicted of perjury in January 1950 a wave of hysteria hit the nation and the witch hunt began. The infamous Senator Joe McCarthy gradually took over and the principle of 'guilt by association' seemed to be well on the way to depriving the nation of the services of many of its best-qualified servants. For a foreigner, and a diplomat, it was a depressing period. You longed to be able to intervene in the controversy, which you obviously could not do, though in private conversation you could more or less say what you thought. Still most of my pals from 1942 onwards had been temporary or permanent members of the US Foreign Service whom I knew to be the most loyal and devoted men, and it was dreadful to see them mostly under direct attack or deep suspicion.

As a matter of fact I did once get a word in. On some television programme – I forget which – I was, as usual, being rather harried by Republican news-hawks. This time they concentrated on the Dean of Canterbury who had, I must say, been making even more of a fool of himself than usual in his eulogies of the most important totalitarian slave-labour system. First of all I had, of course, to explain that Dr Hewlett Johnson* was *not* the Archbishop of Canterbury, and that even

* Dean of Canterbury 1931–63. Champion of the communist states and the cause of Marxism in England and was dubbed 'the Red Dean'.

if he had been the Government could not control his political utterances if he chose to make them. But, said my interlocutor, here is a respected Anglican divine, a member of the Establishment, actually preaching Communism which is admittedly the arch-enemy of all the Western democracies. Why don't you *do* something about it in England? I'll tell you why, I said severely. The simple answer to your question is that *England* is still a free country! The newsman was a good chap as a matter of fact. He said afterwards over a drink, 'Sir Gladwyn, I felt as if I had been pole-axed!'

One man was a great comfort to us in this dark period – Ed Murrow. This great American was, of course, the chief 'newscaster' of the Columbia Broadcasting Service, the famous CBS which, in spite of the generally liberal views of the people who ran it, was after all a commercial undertaking that could hardly go beyond a certain point in coming out against the national hysteria. We used to go out to Quaker Hill where Ed and his splendid wife, Janet, had a sort of luxurious log cabin and they often used to come to us. Ed was a deeply sensitive and conscientious man who had been brought up in the far-western state of Washington. He was the 'Red Indian' type of American, tall and thin with a lean and lined face, rather slow of speech, who radiated a sort of benevolence towards the world. Anyway, it was he who on his television programme, and taking a considerable risk, first dared, in March 1952, to bell the McCarthy cat in a critical broadcast. From that moment the Senator began to lose his grip and the fundamental good sense of the American people began to reassert itself. By the end of 1953 the witch hunt was abandoned.

In the spring of 1953, the Security Council, becalmed because of the continued absence of an armistice in Korea, with which it, as a body, had nothing to do, was deadlocked on another front. The Secretary-General, Trygve Lie, had only been elected for five years in 1946, but the Russians, displeased at his attitude during the Korean War, had declined to re-appoint him in February 1951, and any successor would, under the rules, be subject to their veto. The Americans, equally displeased with the Russians, for their part insisted on the renomination of Mr Lie, and at that stage said they would blackball any alternative candidate favoured by the Russians. At intervals this question was considered, though perhaps not very seriously since, so far as we were concerned, we were quite happy to carry on with Mr Lie who could scarcely be deposed for the simple reason that the Russians objected to him. Still, the position was both irregular and rather unsatisfactory, and the UK delegation at any rate thought that it should, in principle, be ended, provided only there was a candidate who enjoyed our complete confidence and could suitably take over from Lie.

However the only people who seemed for some time to appeal to the Russians were certainly not such as to command our confidence, still less that of the Americans, and the deadlock continued. Then one day in March 1953 at a private meeting of the Council to consider the matter, it was evident that the Russians were making an effort to suggest candidates who might be acceptable to the West and even to consider certain persons whose names had been bandied about but who were certainly not ideal from our own standpoint. At that moment it occurred to me that, since a Scandinavian had, in principle, a better chance than most of being acceptable to all, we might think of Dag Hammarskjöld, whom I had just met with Stafford Cripps, and whose record, I knew, was impeccable. I did not have any authority to put him forward myself, but I suggested him to my French colleague, Henri Hoppenot, who had no hesitation in doing so. At the next meeting Malik, to everyone's immense surprise, said that the Soviet Government could agree on Hammarskjöld, and so the major road block was removed. He was eventually elected on 7 April.

I must say that when I suggested his name I had no real knowledge of this extraordinary and brilliant character. But when I did get to know him I had no reason to regret my initiative. Dag was an intellectual if ever there was one. His passions were of the mind, and in the Middle Ages he would probably have been the head of a monastic order explaining the mysteries of some new religious philosophy with all the subtlety of an Abelard, though certainly not in the distracting presence of any Heloise. Women, indeed, did not come into his life very much, unless they were of the order of Mrs Pandit or, indeed, Eleanor Roosevelt. He was therefore perforce a rather solitary figure. But he was a leader; and there is no doubt that he regarded the United Nations as a mission. Indeed I sometimes thought that he almost regarded himself as a Lay Pope. If he did, he should have realized that the Secretariat was not exactly the equivalent of a Papal Chancery. Even less was the General Assembly a College of Cardinals. He could not, in fact, have anything like the apparatus that is at the disposal of the Holy Father. Nor was there any generally acceptable philosophy which could illuminate his path. The Charter does not really indicate the things that states should do in order to achieve grace. It lays down rather what they should not do in order to avert disaster.

It was fascinating in any case to compare the performance of this Swedish aristocrat with that of the Norwegian trades unionist, his predecessor. Trygve Lie was by no means an intellectual. The people he liked associating with were for the most part American tycoons. He had indeed courage and common sense; but he was not very articulate and sometimes a little elephantine in his approach. Still, he was a good Secretary-General, in the sense that he was genuinely impartial and something of a father-figure. But it could not be said of him that he knew much about the niceties of diplomacy. One evening when we were entertaining both him and the President of the General Assembly, Mike Pearson, to dinner, he perceived from the plan that he was on his hostess's left and the President on the right. Darting into the dining room before he joined the receiving line, he reversed the order so that Mike, advancing to his predestined place was confronted with a card labelled 'The Secretary-General'! I must admit that this showed that Mr Lie had considerable aplomb, though according to his own *Chef du Protocole* (whom we had duly consulted) he was not, this time, justified in his action.

Hammarskjöld, on the other hand, was quite at home in any society, but more especially European. He also had a more complicated approach to any problem than anybody I have ever met. His English was nearly perfect but as often as not I could not really understand what he was driving at, and I suppose I am reasonably quick on the uptake. This was a great advantage. The majority of the problems he confronted were quite insoluble, anyhow in the short run, so it was probably a good thing to try to get the parties together on the basis of some complicated formula that none of them properly understood. Bemused by the Secretary-General's eloquence they often felt that they had agreed, or were about to agree to some solution which they could at once have turned down if it had been suggested by anybody else. But this may have been for quite another reason. For Hammarskjöld had more charm than most, and a strong desire to please. When he died in the air crash at N'dola I made a tribute on the radio which came from the heart. He was a man you could hardly help being fond of and many felt almost protective towards him – the lone, but gay scholar with the cares of the world on his shoulders, walking about with a copy of the works of the poet Rainer Maria Rilke in his pocket and producing a rather complicated solution on any given political problem at the drop of a hat.

In 1953, the Commonwealth was still in existence. Indeed, it even counted for something in my day. Periodically we used to have meetings, actually under my own chairmanship, to discuss problems of general interest and try to hammer out a common view. Korea, had naturally been an occasion for presenting a more or less united front. Khrishna Menon, it is true, was not normally very Commonwealth minded; but even he was occasionally persuaded that the Commonwealth might be to some extent a body of 'like-minded' states which were not the satellites of the one Super-Power or the other. The Americans found Khrishna terribly difficult, but I got on with him all right. It was best, in spite of his grim fakir-like appearance, not to think of him as an Indian at all. And indeed he was a completely *New Statesman*, London School of Economics type, who could not, I believe, talk any Indian language. Ahmad Bokhari, of Pakistan, was for his part very pro-Commonwealth. This brilliant man, who became a great friend of mine, was most effective in the UN. We had our rows of course – we all did – but I repeat that even as late as 1953 there was something remaining of the 'happy-family' feeling that is supposed to animate all Commonwealth members. It must be admitted, however, that there were then only seven members, none of whom were 'emergent' Africans.

It was natural therefore that we should jointly celebrate the Coronation. All agreed to hold a reception in Wave Hill – very well suited for that kind of thing with its great terrace overlooking the Hudson River and its long, sloping lawns. We agreed on expense sharing; on the assembly line; on the flagpoles with all the seven flags; on a band; on the composition of the list of invitees – on everything save one thing, and that threatened to torpedo the whole affair. It was the matter of the Anthem. Clearly the band would have to play 'God Save The Queen'. Nobody objected to that. But the South Africans insisted that if 'God Save The Queen' was to be played, then the band would have to play also 'Die Stem van Suid Afrika', the Union's own national anthem. That was understandable, but if the proposal were accepted then naturally all the other anthems would have to be played as well. The Australians thought they would have to plump for 'Waltzing Matilda', the Canadians for 'O Canada'. The Pakistanis said that their own had recently been changed and they hadn't got the score, as it seemed it was a very long semi-orchestrated piece. In any case if all the seven anthems were played one after the other it was thought that people would have to stand to attention for nearly half an hour. The situation was clearly impossible.

In desperation, and all because I thought it might amuse him, I directly approached Churchill, then in charge of the Foreign Office, asking him whether, with his great authority, he could not do something to persuade the South Africans to change their attitude – perhaps just for this one occasion? He telegraphed back that he would try: and no doubt he did, for the South African representative finally said that seeing that the ceremony was to be in a British house he would agree to having only

'God Save The Queen' provided everyone else did. What would have happened if he had not agreed I cannot say. But at this distance of time I think I can record that in his telegram the former prisoner-of-war had said, 'I will not have this Boer hymn!' I am afraid it was about the last time that the South African Government was persuaded to do something by the UK Government against its will.

I continued my speech-making and lecturing activities in the United States and Canada, usually propounding what the United Nations could and what it could not do. The death of Stalin in March and the Korean Armistice in July lightened the general atmosphere. NATO was organizing itself successfully and the threatened Soviet riposte had been limited to the Warsaw Pact. It almost looked as if we had weathered the postwar storm and were approaching calmer waters. In Louisville, Kentucky, I caused some local indignation by quoting from John Gunther's *Inside America** on the reactionary nature of the Louisville and Nashville Railway, but only by way of emphasizing that we in Europe relied implicitly on John for our information and that, if he was wrong, perhaps they could let me know why? My host, Barry Bingham, the son of an American Ambassador to the Court of St James's was in any case in the vanguard of progress in Kentucky and his wife, Mary, was on the board of Radcliffe College, in Cambridge, which has produced many of the most intelligent and civilized women in the United States. In their great house on the outskirts of Louisville we listened to some Negro singers who seemed perfectly happy and at ease when we all had drinks after the performance. It was before race became a sort of festering sore and the liberals really did think then that it only needed time to absorb the blacks fully into the American society. How long ago all that seems now! And yet it was only about twenty years. We could then drive through Harlem without locking the car doors and even wander about Central Park in the evening.

In Atlanta, Georgia, which we found to be a go-ahead progressive town and not the rather sleepy backwater that we had expected, we found an extremely dynamic mayor who obviously had everything under complete control. At the end of the dinner when there was the customary tinkle of the Chairman on the wine-glass, he said to me, 'Mr Ambassador, when I hear that noise I now have what I believe is called a "conditioned reflex": I rise to my feet and I speak. All I want is an aide, to whom I turn and say, "How long?" Five minutes, ten minutes, half an hour, an hour, even two hours, it's all the same to me. I just *speak*.' And so he did – ten

* John Gunther: *Inside America*, (London 1947).

minutes. Perfect in form; entertaining; no very positive statement one way or the other. It seemed to me that this was really the summit of the politicians' art. It convinced me, not that I wanted convincing, that politics was an art which I myself could never master. And it certainly is an art, even if a rather minor one.

In 1945 I had had some very rudimentary ideas about how to cope with the nuclear problem. In the late forties, while still in the Office, I had had further thoughts, which I developed at much greater length in New York during 1951 and 1952. It was not my specific field, but after all if you were concerned with the UN you could hardly be unconcerned with a problem on the solution – or non-solution – of which the whole new world organization might depend. At this time the official Anglo-American view was still simple enough. The USA no longer had a monopoly of nuclear power, but its lead over the USSR was still very great and might, for all one knew, continue. The Baruch plan, for the control of nuclear energy by internationalization, even if it ever had been workable, which was doubtful, had died as long ago as 1947; and short of some kind of nuclear arms limitation involving an almost impossible system of inspection, no real progress appeared to be practical politics. Perhaps this situation was tolerable in the forties, but early in 1950 there was already talk of the 'Super', or Hydrogen Bomb the appearance of which on the scene would clearly change the whole situation. Foreseeing this development, my view early in 1951 was that the best thing might well be to seek a convention banning the use of the nuclear weapon altogether in war.

A little later, while maintaining this proposal, I had reached the conclusion that, whatever the theory might be, in practice the arrival of the Super Bomb would result in both the Super-Powers doing everything to prevent war from breaking out as between themselves. Control over its production seemed most unlikely, but as a Third World War was even more unlikely that perhaps did not matter so much. Europe was in a particularly vulnerable position since (this was before the arrival of rockets and missiles) the Russian nuclear bombs could be exploded over that part of the world much more easily than they could over North America, so from our point of view we had every reason for supporting a 'ban the bomb' policy. And even if we thought a nuclear war most improbable we should, perhaps, in view of our exposed position not only get an assurance from the Americans that they would not deploy nuclear weapons against Russia from British bases except with our consent, but also make some precautionary shelter measures. But the logic of the situation, as I saw it, pointed increasingly to the necessity of the two

THE MEMOIRS OF LORD GLADWYN

Super-Powers coming together on some European settlement which they could both live with. And this we should foster to the limit of our power.

In 1953 I reverted to these thoughts and to the arguments that had always been deployed against them, namely (a) that if we agreed to any ban we should be debarring ourselves from using the only weapon in which we still had a superiority, and (b) that we should be at a great disadvantage if we had to wage a war with conventional arms only. But within a few years would (a) still be true, and as for (b) would that not be a position in which we should be anyhow? I tended therefore to support the initiative of Khrishna Menon, who was then agitating in favour of a ban-the-bomb-in-war convention in UN circles. With Menon I did not normally agree, but on this point I thought there was a good deal to be said for his general attitude.

The doctrine of the preponderance of power was, however, still orthodox in the Western world and naturally I accepted it as such in all public utterances. But I continued to think in my 'for intérieur', as the French say, that it would one day have to be abandoned; and at the beginning of 1954 I again criticized it in a long private letter to Ivone Kirkpatrick as essentially 'negative', the broad argument being as follows. If we (the West) did not want to force a settlement in Europe then we should one day have to contemplate a political settlement, and with this the 'preponderance' doctrine was not really compatible. Maybe we should have to rely on 'tactical' nuclears for the defence of Europe, but would this be of much avail if the Russians had them too? The distinctions between nuclear and conventional weapons seemed in any case to be becoming increasingly blurred.

My conclusion was that the Russians would avoid a war at almost any cost until and unless they had 'neutralized' Germany, Turkey and Japan: that failing such conditions, they would seek to avoid charges of 'aggression', but would fight if forced to do so to protect their existing position; that, logically, and from a strictly military point of view, the West should nevertheless present some 'ultimatum' to the USSR demanding their evacuation of Eastern Europe; that in practice the West could and would do no such thing; that stalemate in Europe could therefore have to persist until such time as it was quite clear that a deal would have to be reached on a basis of nuclear parity; and that when that point was reached it would be obvious that the nuclear weapon did not confer on the West any particular military advantage. Looking back, it occurs to me that what I was really groping after was what actually happened some fifteen years later, namely the Treaty on Non-Proliferation and the kind of limitation which lies at the back of the Soviet-American discussions known as SALT. But I only give the bare bones of the mountainous correspondence in which my ideas were embedded to give the reader an impression of how my own thought developed and with what I occupied much of my time.

Before leaving the American scene, I ought also to explain very briefly, for, after all, it was my *raison d'être*, the general theory about the role of the United Nations that I developed during the second part of my stay. For the first year or so all was clear; we were fighting unprovoked aggression along with the Americans, and that was that. It was the 'glad, confident morning' of the UN. But when in the late spring of 1951, after the sacking of McArthur, the military line became stabilized once more north of Seoul and the only outstanding question was how to negotiate an armistice (which took another two years), the whole future of the world organization inevitably came under review and I made a series of speeches all over America in which, with the approval of the Department naturally, I increasingly sought to disseminate the idea that it was chiefly the avoidance of hostilities on which the UN ought to concentrate, and not so much on how to resist aggression by military means if unfortunately aggression should occur, this task being left to regional bodies, such as NATO, which (in the continued absence of the Military Staff Committee – see pp. 143–4, 170) alone had the physical means of carrying military measures into effect.

In so doing I frequently had recourse to the simple principle on which the UN had had, perforce, to be constructed, namely that of a minimum of harmony between the five – or at any rate the two – major powers. Since it was just not possible to impose the will of a majority of nations, however democratic, on one of the two Super-Powers, however despotic, without recourse to force, which would mean another world war, it was necessary to accept the Veto as a condition of any world organization. If it were abused in the event of a flagrant aggression it might, and indeed it would, be necessary for the majority, and notably for the USA, to go to the assistance of the victim; but in practice this would mean either America's taking military action all by herself, or by enlisting the aid of those friendly powers who were in a position to assist her. And such powers could in practice only mean NATO. The USA, who would have to take the lead because without her nobody could or would come out into the open against a Power backed by the Soviet Union, could also, with the resolution 'Uniting for Peace' (see p. 241) invoke the moral, and to some slight extent the material backing of any members of the General Assembly who were so disposed. But in the circumstances contemplated the UN itself would have been disrupted. All states, including one Super-Power, supporting the 'aggressor' would have automatically left. And many others, feeling 'neutral' might well also have withdrawn. All that really remained would be the name and the flag which would in effect become the property of one group inside the world organization. And the core of this group would be NATO. It could hardly be anything else.

But all that did not mean that the UN did not have an important political role to play, in the political field, where, even then, it was to some extent side-tracked. It could, after all, summon the disputants; propose solutions, encourage mediation; even send out peace observers and, occasionally, peace missions of specially recruited troops with the object, so far as possible, of holding the fort and separating the contestants. It had had a real success in Palestine, where it had been of the greatest use in ending hostilities, and it had also largely kept the peace in Kashmir. There was no reason why, provided the Super-Powers were not violently engaged one way or the other, it could not have similar, limited successes in the future. And in any case was it not a fact that it was in the UN building that the first contact had been made (actually, I believe, between Dr Jessup and Mr Malik in the washroom) which eventually resulted in the Russians calling off the Berlin blockade in 1949?

What I thought misconceived (and to prevent this was the real purpose of my many interventions) was the suggestion that the UN would be far better off without the Russians, their allies, or indeed without the neutrals. Then it could organize itself, so it was often suggested, without any let or hindrance against 'Communist Aggression'. In some ways this resembled the Herbert Hoover thesis of a basic Anglo-German-American-Japanese alliance run from the United States, in other words a sort of Fortress America with certain peripheral allies. In answer to this I said, and repeated many times, that NATO after all existed, to say nothing of other regional groupings too, all of which were directed against 'Communist Aggression'. What was the point, this being so, in disrupting the world organization? To do so would only result in a rival world organization – in Tashkent or somewhere – and would in any case tend to drive the Russians and the Chinese together like nothing else.

The Foreign Office, though they agreed in principle with this rather stark thesis – and of course it was nothing like as stark as I have perforce had to represent it in this briefest of outlines – were nervous of its effect on the American public which had, from San Francisco onwards, been well oversold on the United Nations. Might I not be in some danger of actually encouraging that isolationism which it was my principal object to discredit? A very long correspondence ensued, but on the whole my thesis was thought to be less dangerous than the alternative one of encouraging false hopes and I was allowed to proceed. This I did increasingly and all over the country. In Britain, so far as my voice was heard, which was not much, the line was approved, and I got a very appreciative letter from Judd, the secretary of the United Nations Association.

Not so in the United States, where it encountered substantial criticism, both in the press and among the *cognoscenti*. Jack Hickerson of the State Department weighed in with a long reasoned piece, and so did the great Ham Armstrong, with an even longer one. I had also a very long discussion with Ernie Gross and that high priest of UN orthodoxy, Leo Pasvolsky. The main line of criticism was always the same. I was wrong to suggest – not that I had suggested in so many words – that it was not the 'primary purpose' of the UN to resist and counter 'aggression', by force if need be. The reaction to the Korean aggression had been the UN's finest hour. Why should it not, if necessary, rise to the occasion again if necessary? Yet even at the finest moment – that is to say immediately after the UN had gone into action in Korea – a number of states had concentrated chiefly on ways and means of ending the conflict peacefully, and notably by taking into consideration the views of a neighbouring Communist Great Power. The UN, Ham thought, had seldom been seen to less advantage than when a group of members within it 'seemed ready to take the line of mediator between victim and aggressor in Korea'.

Naturally I saw what the American experts meant and appreciated the importance which they attached to the general notion of the UN's standing for a simple principle of general application, namely collective resistance to aggression. But just as in my thinking about the nuclear weapon I had arrived at the conclusion that 'Western' theses could not be acceptable for ever, so, in the wider political field it appeared to me that we should one day have to come to some political settlement with the forces of the East. And it was in helping on such a *rapprochement* that, as I saw it, the real future of the UN lay. Of course the West must not, if possible, decline in strength as compared with the East. Of course it must maintain its democratic and libertarian ideas. Of course it should be ready to resist successfully if attacked. But one day it might be that, confronted by a dynamic but by no means dangerous West, the forces of the East would become less fearsome and thus, possibly, less totalitarian. It was in expectation of this day that the UN should be maintained as a whole and not be allowed to break up.

I do not think I convinced my critics, but they were apparently to some extent impressed by my views. Anyway, Ham suggested that I might formally record them in an article in *Foreign Affairs*. I said I would have to consult the Foreign Office who were at first reluctant to agree. It was then against convention that a serving member of the Foreign Service should express contentious and personal views in print on major political issues with which he was concerned. Strang felt, at first sight, that this should be the privilege of ministers. But eventually it was agreed that it might be to the general advantage that someone who still had a considerable personal following in the USA should be authorized to put forward a thesis which was, broadly speaking, acceptable to the Government and with which they therefore presumably hoped that the Americans would agree. And so the article did appear in the April 1953 issue. Nobody re-reading it now would think it particularly heterodox!

In December 1953, Eden, who was staying with us at Wave Hill, the lovely, early nineteenth-century house on the banks of the Hudson in Riverdale which we had taken after leaving Cadogan's house in Oyster Bay, did me the great honour of offering me the Paris Embassy. Although the prospect of living for several years in Paris was delightful, I would have preferred to be Permanent Under-Secretary of State in the Foreign Office and said so, to no avail. It really did seem to me, however, that I was better qualified to be a Foreign Office official than à *mondain* diplomat. Such qualifications as I possessed lay, I thought, more in the realm of administration and of the formulation of policy. Nor was it my strong point to be terribly nice to people, to think up little schemes on how to get round difficult points, to flatter the great, and so on. However, I did my best to act the part. And in doing so I was much assisted by my wife who is a natural hostess and who for her part much preferred being Ambassadress in Paris to being the mere wife of the Permanent Under-Secretary in London.

Still, one is a poor judge of one's own case and it may well have been that Eden's judgment was correct and that I was better suited to Paris. And as I say, the prospect of living in that beautiful house, which we knew so well, and of seeing our French friends whom we loved so much, was in itself most alluring. I did try a little later, on the quite mistaken assumption that this would be either possible or desirable, to get myself appointed our representative to NATO as well (NATO then being situated in Paris). Some members of the NATO Council were at that time, I understood, also Ambassadors to France and it occurred to me that there might be certain advantages in this example being followed by us. Suitable (diplomatic) ministers might, I thought, do most of the work on both sides of the house and the Ambassador could *planer au-dessus*. There were then, as a matter of fact, no less than three British Ambassadors in Paris – to France, to NATO and to OEEC. What I ignored in making this suggestion was that there might well be – as they say in the City – a 'conflict of interests' between the work of the British Ambassador to France and the British Representative to NATO, the latter having, perhaps, to take a strong line which might, in principle, not be in accordance with the desires or indeed with the instructions of the former. So the suggestion was, very properly, turned down, and I certainly found on arrival that there was quite enough for me to do as Ambassador to France anyhow. That there might well be a 'conflict of interests' in such a double job was, I believe, conclusively demonstrated some eight years later when my poor colleague, Bob Dixon, one of our foremost diplomats, led our official delegation to Brussels for the first negotiations on the entry of Britain into the EEC. Not only did the additional work shorten his life, but owing to the difficulties encountered with the French in Brussels, he was often much embarrassed in his capacity as Ambassador.

So we left New York in March and I made a final, and I fear rather dull speech to the Pilgrims. It did at any rate show that we were sorry to leave, which in many ways was true. But, politically, the UN was getting less exciting and, on the whole, more difficult. The great days when we and the Americans largely ran the show were over. The era of the 'under-developed' countries was about to begin. Racial superiority, great-power domination, neo-colonialism, etc. were becoming greater public enemies than dictatorship or aggression. In fact the latter were becoming almost fashionable. I doubted whether I was the right man to cope success-fully with the now popular issues. For this the United Nations had to await Lord Caradon. It was time for me to retreat once more into the less-exposed world of diplomacy. So we sailed down the Hudson River without too many regrets.

16

Ambassador
(1954-8)

At the Connaught Hotel, where we stayed for a week or two before 'proceeding' (Ambassadors always 'proceed') to Paris, I did my best to read
myself in, and of course I was constantly in and out of the Foreign Office.
The atmosphere there was a little tricky. Ever since Robert Schuman's
startling and unheralded initiative in 1950 there had been a vague feeling
in Whitehall that the French were not 'playing the game'; that they were
inclined to take an individual and at the same time rather unpredictable
line; and that in any case, owing to constant changes of government, the
Fourth Republic was a weak sister who must be kept on the straight and
narrow path of Western solidarity by a firm, purposeful and self-confident
Britain. Had we not, after all, virtually founded OEEC and was it not
working very well? Had we not also been one of the chief inspirers of
NATO, and was not NATO still the only real hope of maintaining collective resistance to Soviet expansion? Was it not also now self-evident
from a military point of view that NATO could not function properly, if
indeed at all, unless the democratic Western Germans were enabled to
contribute towards the general defensive effort? If the French had (as we
thought) rather unjustified fears about the rearmament of these good
democrats, then by all means let them get together with the Germans in
the construction of a 'European' army in which both the German and the
French contribution would be merged, thus disposing of any specifically
German threat. But naturally, as the Conservatives had demonstrated as
soon as they came into power in 1951, we for our part did not want to take
any part in such a merging. With our Commonwealth and our 'special
relationship' with America we were in a different position from France.
Very understandably, it was the old Churchillian policy of the 'three overlapping circles'. To doubt this then was to run the risk of being thought
peculiar and even heretical.

The official head of the Foreign Service at that time was Ivone Kirk-

patrick, with whom I had served in Rome way back in the early thirties
and who was a personal friend of long standing. Ivone was an intelligent,
combative, sardonic, courageous, but in some ways rather limited Irish-
man who would, I always thought, have made, like so many of his compatriots, an excellent general. In diplomacy, on the other hand, he had a
tendency to score points and to demonstrate to his foreign interlocutors
the extreme weakness of their case. And not only foreigners. For he was a
very brave and forthright man, entirely capable of speaking his mind to his
own superiors. Unfortunately, though he had long experience of Germany, having been there in the late thirties, and having indeed accompanied (indignantly) Mr Chamberlain on his various pilgrimages to the
Nazi Canossa, ending up with a spell as our High Commissioner in
Bonn and Head of the German Section of the Foreign Office, he had never
served in France, and it never seemed to me that, to say the least, he fully
understood the workings of the Gallic mind. In any case long conversations with him did not disclose what he believed should be the general
objective of our policy towards the French. Nor, I need hardly say, did I
receive any written instructions on this point. The Prime Minister, with
whom I had an interview, was, I thought, hardly at his best. What I understood him to say was that I must be very careful not to underestimate the
strength of the great French Army. My main function, I gathered, was to
go out and, so far as possible, prevent the French from being so tiresome.
Detailed instructions on how to do this would be sent to me from time to
time. The great thing at the moment was to get our neighbours to accept
the European Defence Community and not hold up the rearmament of
the Western Germans any further. Thus armed, I set out from Victoria
at the end of April with Cynthia and Stella on the Golden Arrow. It was
the lunch hour and few beyond the family saw us off.

Not so the other end. At the Gare du Nord were a number of smiling
and familiar faces headed by my old friend Maurice Schumann, then
Minister of State in the Government of Joseph Laniel. Many old friends
of *tout Paris*, most of the Embassy, half the Quai d'Orsay. It was a splendid
welcome. There was instant conversation. The great thing about the
French is their intelligence and their *savoir vivre*. We 'proceeded' to the
Embassy in the vast Rolls, driven by the doyen of Parisian chauffeurs,
René Picot. Rue Lafayette, Place de la Madeleine, Boulevard Hauss-
mann, Rue La Boëtie, Rue de Miromesnil, Rue du Faubourg S. Honoré:
how many times was I to re-make this *trajet* during the next seven
years! And then the huge *porte cochère*, the lovely house *entre cour et jardin*, the
assembled staff, many already familiar. We felt we had indeed come home.

But the capital was unquiet. The Bidault-Schuman regime, based on the Mouvement Républican Populaire, which had dominated French politics since the departure of General de Gaulle in January 1946 was approaching its end. It was not the internal situation which was responsible for this: internally, the reforms of the Fourth Republic had worked well. It was the sub-conscious need of national decisions on Germany, but above all on Indo-China that produced a real malaise. In particular, the situation in Northern Annam was critical. The French army, rashly advanced towards the Laotian frontier, was already encircled by the revolutionary forces of General Giap, sustained by material coming down the long jungle track from China. A real defeat was in the offing. And further south the government of Bao Dai was wobbling. Indeed the situation, as the French military frankly admitted, was, in their graphic language, *complètement pourrie*! In spite of vast American aid it was becoming more and more clear that the French could not hang on to their Far Eastern Empire for very long. A cartoon in the *Figaro* called 'Dernier Réduit' depicted prominent MRP members of the Government, including Maurice Schumann, Pleven and Bidault in a dug-out using up their last cartridge. On 17 May Dien Bien Phu fell and many French officers and men were made prisoner. This was felt by a good many Frenchmen, more particularly among the *bien pensants* and the *gratin* to be a national humiliation. Some would not even go to any festivity. But to the majority it was a sure sign that the war must now stop. The Laniel Government, which had been so much associated with the prosecution of the war, lost its majority and fell on 12 June; the long reign of the MRP at the Quai d'Orsay was over; and on to the stage with a huge majority stepped the man who declared that he would not only achieve a satisfactory settlement in Indo-China, but also settle other outstanding issues – Pierre Mendès-France.

The new President of the Council and Foreign Minister had an impeccable political record. But he had always been a loner – never a real member of the *République des Camarades*. Like all strong and independent-minded politicians, therefore, he was unpopular in the Chamber. And he got his majority owing to the general opinion among what Trollope would have called the 'Tadpoles and Tapers' in the Palais Bourbon that, since someone had to take the responsibility for winding up the *sale guerre*, it had better be an individualist who could be easily sacrificed when he had done this unpleasant, but necessary job. Anyhow there he was, declaring that he would end the Indo-China war within thirty-two days or resign. And, as everybody knows, thanks largely to the admirable diplomacy of Anthony Eden, he did.

I was in no way concerned with that particular deal, save for maintaining constantly that success would be necessary if we were ever to achieve a satisfactory solution of the European problem posed by the acceptance, still more by the rejection of the proposed European Defence Community project. At one moment it looked as if the Americans would come into Indo-China to back up the French, but when that proved to be an illusion the Bidault policy (vigorously pursued since the beginning of the Geneva Conference on 26 April) collapsed, and the way was prepared for the 'scapegoat'. And when, as we have seen, Mendès was successful, all kinds of attacks were made upon him by his enemies who thought he could always be pushed back into his place by a flood of ugly rumours. However from the start, I myself took Mendès to be a difficult but entirely honest man who was determined, if he could, to make a success of his mission. And that included Europe.

I had only been in Paris a fortnight when I tentatively advanced my own judgment on the future of the EDC. This was that, contrary to the opinion of my predecessor, it was on balance unlikely to go through. I should in any case be agreeably surprised if it did. For since Oliver Harvey had submitted his last estimate, Marshal Juin, ex-President Auriol and Edgar Faure had all come out against it. So had 59 out of 105 Socialist Deputies. The Gaullists and Communists were as hostile as ever. Quite likely the project would never come to the vote. If it ever did, it was extremely doubtful whether there would be a majority. It therefore seemed to me high time that we considered some *solution de rechange*.

A few weeks later I developed, at much greater length, the reason for this hunch. As the fear of general war receded, so the popularity of the European Defence Community had declined. To many Frenchmen, indeed, it was now not far short of being equated with the *Neuordnung* of the Nazis. It might still be saved by a successful outcome of the Indo-China negotiations, but only if the Americans came in to that conflict themselves, which was unlikely. Surely, therefore, it was reasonable to assume the failure of EDC and to work out another solution permitting German rearmament by common consent. The only way of getting early and general agreement, as I saw it, was for us to join with France and Germany on a footing of equality in some organization less rigid and potentially federalistic than the EDC, but necessarily narrower and with more authority than NATO. Such a plan had already been devised in some detail by Senator Maroger. It seemed to me to be the epitome of good sense and I urged our acceptance of it in a general way. It was not for me to say whether such a solution was practical politics in the UK: all I did know was that it was the one sure way to avoid a major crisis in France and the possible lapse of that country into neutralism with all the consequences of such a development on the general defence of Western Europe.

A month later (in mid-June) I said that it looked as if by mid-July the EDC would be dead. A 'NATO solution' – i.e. simple admission of Germany to NATO and her rearmament within that framework – seemed unlikely, in that the French would not accept it. Short of anarchy there thus remained only a 'European solution'. But this necessarily implied a measure of supra-nationalism. I thought that we ought at any rate to prepare for the discussion of such a solution at a conference to be summoned in London. The French were, no doubt, in a rather psychotic state of mind. What was certain was that it was no good trying to cure this by a treatment of shocks. A few days later Mendès took over the Government. This, I thought, was a portent. For it represented in all probability an unconscious popular desire to be rid of Indo-China and to achieve a 'new deal' in Europe other than the European Defence Community.

I did not, in any case, believe the ugly rumours that were spread abroad about Mendès by his enemies. The idea that he was going to 'do a deal with Molotov' (Indo-China against the EDC) in particular seemed to me to be inherently absurd. There was no reason to suppose that the new *Président du Conseil* was a neutralist. He was – and had been for long – if you liked to put it that way, a 'defeatist' as regards Indo-China. But there was no reason to suppose that he was anti-NATO. He did not happen himself to believe in the practicability of the EDC and still less in the likelihood of its being approved by the French Assembly. That was really all. In any case I liked Mendès and much appreciated his desire to get the country out of a rut. The real question was how we could best help him. One of his major failings (as a member of his own staff had told me) was 'his appalling habit of thinking aloud in the presence of foreign Ambassadors'! Pierre Brisson★ had also told me, and I believed him, that the chief weakness of the new *Président du Conseil* was that he had too great a belief in reason, and not sufficient perception of the *méchanceté des hommes*! When I told this to André de Staercke† he said 'Yes, I do think he is a man who wants to be loved. *Mais il faut l'aimer tout le temps et très fort*'!

However it was not the personality of the new Prime Minister that worried me so much as the policy which we should pursue on the assumption that the EDC was rejected by the French Parliament. In the considerations advanced in mid-June I had urged that the 'minimum of

★ Editor-in-chief of *Le Figaro*.
† Belgian representative to NATO.

supra-national content' in any alternative should include some guarantee
that we for our part would not withdraw or reduce our forces in Germany
except with the consent of our European allies. This was a theme to which
I reverted again and again and in one presentation after another, more
especially after the EDC had been duly rejected at the end of August
following Mendès's refusal to accept various compromises put up by
Spaak and others and on his unsatisfactory interview with Churchill and
Eden at Chartwell in the middle of the month. I know that in this period
Mendès became unpopular with our rulers because they suspected him
of professing to do his best to get EDC accepted while secretly trying to
work for its rejection. But I think that he was, rather objectively, certain
that without almost impossible concessions on our part the scheme was
doomed whatever he might think about it himself.

Eden, as is known, spent some time travelling round Europe after the
rejection trying to pick up the bits, eventually succeeding in this delicate
operation during the London Conference at the end of September
when he unexpectedly announced that Her Majesty's Government were
in fact prepared to act as I had for so long suggested and he had for so
long violently resisted. Without this undertaking it is quite safe to say that
a very dangerous situation would have arisen, possibly involving the
neutrality of France. Mendès was, I think, also grateful to me for the
support which I had evidently given him: and indeed I had had frequently
to appear in the guise of devil's advocate or prisoners' friend as a result.
But looking back I have no doubt at all that I was right in maintaining the
motives of the Prime Minister should in no way be suspected. It is also
noteworthy that only twenty-five days before the Secretary of State's
historic declaration on the maintenance of our armed forces in Germany
I had received instructions from the Foreign Office to go and formally
protest to him for having once again reverted to this totally unacceptable,
and, indeed, 'shop-soiled' idea – which, since it was my own, I had certainly not discouraged. It only shows, and I do not say this in any self-
congratulatory way, how policies which seem to be, and no doubt are,
quite unacceptable can become entirely orthodox in a very short period
of time. Naturally, too, in consistently urging it I never suggested that it
was necessarily the best line to take in the general interests of the country:
that was for the Government to say. Only that it was certainly the best
line to take from the point of view of our relations with France and, indeed,
as I thought, in relation to Europe. Nor was my original formula eventually accepted as such. It was, no doubt quite rightly, hedged about by
provisos to the effect that if we felt we could no longer afford to keep the

four divisions and the existing air force in Germany we had a right to appeal to our colleagues, and that troops could be withdrawn temporarily to meet some sudden overseas emergency. But it nevertheless remained true that without the formula, the conference would have failed. And if it had failed we would certainly, as I maintained, have faced the probable break up of NATO and quite possibly the gradual Sovietization of Europe. When he heard Eden making this historic declaration, the French Ambassador wept.

The impression that the London Conference was a close-run thing was confirmed by the unexpected rejection of the London agreements by the French Chamber on Christmas Eve. This was largely due, it is true, to the MRP and their friends, many of whom wanted to register a vote against the man whom they regarded as the murderer of the project on which they had set such store. But there is no doubt that there would have been many more Deputies who would have voted against 'Western European Union' if it had contained no guarantees at all. In such an event we could not have restored the situation (as we did, at any rate to some extent) by issuing a pretty stiff press communiqué to the effect that it was not a question *whether* the Western Germans should be armed but *how*, together with a reminder that our own engagement to maintain our troops in Germany depended naturally on ratification of the London agreements. For in such circumstances the French Deputies would have felt no guilt over the rejection and the way would have been opened for a pretty vigorous anti-British parliamentary campaign. I myself had wanted, wrongly as I now think, to go rather further than the FO, but eventually I came to the conclusion that their formula was just about right. Mendès grumbled a bit about it afterwards but I don't think that even he really objected. I suspect that he was probably relieved.

As things went, I well remember that first Christmas in the Embassy with intermediaries rushing to and fro and the Prime Minister frequently on the scrambler demanding the latest news. Doug Dillon was my American opposite number and at the end of 1954 there was still enough recollection of the 'special relationship' of war-time days to result in pretty intimate consultation with my US colleague. My relations with him, though very friendly, were however never as close as they had been with Ernie Gross. Doug was nevertheless a convinced European, and we were both in agreement as to the desirability of backing up Mendès in so far as it lay in our power to do so. All through that last crisis Mendès's behaviour had in fact been impeccable. He had referred constantly and at length in the course of the debate to the absolute necessity of ratifying the agreements. The disaster on Christmas Eve was not his fault. The reversal of that vote a few days later was largely due to his exertions. He emerged from the battle outwardly strengthened, but inwardly scarred. And his enemies were closing in for the kill.

He was then opposed by all the 'Europeans' and the Communists which was a formidable combination. But he had alienated the sympathies of all the 'neutralists' too, who had placed great hopes in him at the time of the liquidation of the French 'presence' in Indo-China. Indeed *Le Monde*, the leader of the neutralists of all parties at that time, had observed, with some justification, that the initial rejection by the Assembly of the Paris agreements on 24 December was the 'real voice of France'. Perhaps it was the great political power of this 'real voice' which admittedly made him wobble towards the end of his term, when he suggested that perhaps we had better have a Four-Power conference before the final ratification by the Senate of the Treaties of Paris. Mendès's one consistent support lay with the Radicals and the more intelligent Gaullists, including some of the Independents who nevertheless suspected his potentially revolutionary economic ideas. Obviously, therefore, after solving the joint problem of the '*sale guerre*' and German rearmament the scapegoat was doomed. But he was generally respected. At the end of October one of his most prominent neutralist critics, Claude Bourdet, had described his position quite admirably as follows:

Confiant en son seul jugement et entouré par des collaborateurs enthousiastes qui l'isolent soigneusement de toute contradiction; aimé par le pays qui lui est reconnaissant de son courage et de son succès, mais sans contact réel avec le pays, sinon par monologues; sans parti, sinon un assemblage de côteries qui le haïssent tout en utilisant déjà son nom; sans amis, si ce n'est des rivaux ou des auditeurs, l'homme d'Etat le plus sérieux et le plus solitaire de la Quatrième République poursuit imperturbablement son chemin.*

Curiously enough he often irritated quite a number of people who were well disposed to him politically, by his rather informal manner. I remember in the late summer going down to see him in the keeper's cottage at Marly whither he had fled for a day or two to get away from it all and think. After having delivered some message I took my leave and he

* 'Entirely sure of himself and surrounded by enthusiastic assistants who carefully shield him from any opposition; loved by the country which appreciates his courage and success; but without any real contact with the country, unless monologues imply contact; without a party, unless it be a collection of small groups that loathe him while making use of his name; without friends, unless rivals or audiences can be so reckoned, the most serious and the most lonely statesman of the Fourth Republic proceeds undaunted on his way.'

accompanied me to the gate, where we were at once photographed by journalists. Unfortunately whereas I had got on a fine new summer suit, Mendès was dressed in a pullover and looked as if he had just come in from doing a bit of gardening. The resulting picture appeared in papers all over France and was used by Mendès's enemies as proof that he was not treating the British Ambassador correctly! It was monstrous, but he sometimes laid himself open to this kind of misrepresentation. Perhaps he was simply not cunning enough.

Nevertheless if he had been a tougher scapegoat he might have succeeded in imposing himself and reforming the *système* like the great big extrovert goat of 1958. But he would have had to have had a revolutionary situation from which to profit, and that situation had not yet arisen. It was only at the end of 1954 that a cloud the size of a man's hand appeared over the Aurès mountains in Algeria, and even then it was not appreciated that the whole of that province would soon be in a state of revolt. Indeed at the beginning of 1955 there was a firm resolve to keep the tricolour flying in the whole of the Maghreb, or at any rate in Algeria.

Mendès was followed by Edgar Faure who was succeeded in January 1956 by Guy Mollet. The Faure regime was remarkable for the first 'Summit' meeting with the Russians, at Geneva between 16 and 23 July 1955. This was followed by a Foreign Ministers' conference in October. The so-called science of 'Summitry' was now being pursued with zeal and intelligence by the Foreign Office under the high direction of that convinced Summiteer, Harold Macmillan, whose favourite subject it was. The general idea was that by careful preparation it might be possible to get the four countries concerned at least to take the first step towards solving the German problem and thus ending the Cold War. All kinds of plans had been devised for this purpose. Perhaps the first to be vigorously pushed was that of Paul Van Zeeland in 1950–1, for a mutual withdrawal of forces. Then there were the plans associated with the names of Anthony Eden and (later) of Adam Rapacki, the Polish Foreign Minister. All along disarmament had been debated in parallel, as it were, and in every conceivable forum. And always in the background there was the nearly insoluble problem of Berlin.

At the Foreign Ministers' meeting in October at Geneva, Macmillan, always romantically minded, had suggested that I might loan the magnificent Embassy plate, or some of it, for a banquet which he proposed to give Molotov at the Hotel Beau Rivage. Reluctantly I agreed to part temporarily with these wonderful objects, provided they were suitably insured. But the gesture failed to impress. At the table I was placed next to Molotov and at a suitable moment asked him whether he admired the table with its silver plates, the room lit up by the candles in their priceless candelabra, and the great salvers arranged along the wall. The minister, however, did not display any admiration. 'In *Moscow*' was all I could get him to say, 'In Moscow, we have *electric* light.'

I had always been doubtful about the desirability of 'Summitry'. In particular I had always doubted the wisdom of our coming out very strongly, as we always did at that time, in favour of the reunification of Germany, insisting that unless this were accomplished an impossible situation would arise, 'tension' would inevitably increase and in the long run there would even be a danger of war. Myself, I always saw things in a less apocalyptic way. However morally justified reunification might be, however much one might sympathize with a divided German nation, it seemed to me that in practice reunification could only come about either by the liberalization of the DDR or by the Sovietization of the Federal Republic. I was quite certain that the first, given the reaction of the Russians to anything of the kind, was impossible; it was equally clear that the second was undesirable. Better relations between the two parts of Germany was naturally another thing. But 'reunification' seemed to me to be highly dangerous as a slogan, and to describe it as 'the cardinal aim of our foreign policy' nothing less than folly. Incidentally a good many people, I said, even in the Federal Republic, thought that the present frontiers had come to stay and I should not at all be surprised if these included Chancellor Adenauer. Whatever we might say for propaganda purposes, surely the real justification for the rearmament of Western Germany was to defend the existing *status quo* and, by achieving a *Gleichberechtigung*, to attempt to graft Western Germany on to the body politic of the Atlantic Community.

The real impetus to 'Summitry' had been occasioned by the death of Stalin in March 1953, and for a time it almost looked as if Malenkov would set the Soviet Union on a new line that really might result in a general settlement. But the arrival of the joint leadership of Bulganin and Khrushchev coincided with a considerably tougher policy and I see that I suggested to William Hayter in a private letter that this might not in itself be a bad thing. The more intelligent policy of Malenkov (conceivably inspired by Burgess and Maclean) might, I thought, have been much more dangerous. Aneurin Bevan, Marshal Tito and Hubert Beuve-Méry* had made much headway with the line that all we had to do was to talk nicely to Malenkov in order to obtain the withdrawal of all Soviet

* For many years Editor of '*Le Monde*'.

troops from Germany; and had it not been for his fall we should probably have never had the WEU ratified by the French Senate. Anyway nothing much happened at the famous 1955 'Summit', or indeed at the subsequent meeting of French Ministers. In particular as regards Berlin, and Germany generally, the Russians were quite unyielding. My American colleague, Doug Dillon, was always persuaded that they did not want to reach agreement and personally I agreed with him. During this year, therefore, I had, in accordance with my habit, been brooding – chiefly for my own satisfaction – on the whole question of East/West relations, and in March I composed one of my first efforts to investigate the problem of 'tension'.

Tension, which might be defined as fear of war or of revolutionary change, was, according to Khrushchev, entirely the fault of the Americans, who should go home and no longer maintain any bases on foreign soil. If they did so the Russians might be prepared to go back to Russia leaving behind, however, strong local forces in the satellite countries. Germany would have to leave NATO as part of the deal and would thus become neutralized. But it would be almost inevitable that in such circumstances, the Soviet Union being so much nearer than America, she would fall under Soviet influence. Thus tension might be eliminated, but only because the USSR would control the Continent.

In fact, tension could only be abolished, or sensibly reduced if the Soviet Union ceased to be a Communist dictatorship and adopted some form of democratic regime – and this went for Communist China as well. As this was most unlikely, it would undoubtedly continue and would only be increased, not diminished, by any unilateral concessions on the part of the West. Indeed it might even be said that some measure of tension was necessary if the West was to maintain its unity of purpose and incidentally preserve its own free regimes. No doubt in spite of such general principles *some* bargaining with the East would be necessary and here I discussed such possibilities as the demilitarization, in the event of German reunification based on free elections, of East Germany and even of Poland west of the Vistula. But really all such schemes were only practicable in the context of some general arms limitation agreement – again highly desirable, but scarcely likely. Western Germany would have to remain a member of NATO and WEU, for 'neutralization' would destroy the whole basis of Western defence and open the way for eventual Russian domination. So the depressing, though inevitable, conclusion seemed to be that a limited deal with the USSR was most unlikely and that in any case the division of Germany would continue. The real danger for the West, I thought, was no longer a formal Soviet offensive and the opening up of a Third World War; it was that in Germany for nationalistic, France for economic and Italy for demographic, reasons, fellow-travelling or philo-Soviet governments might during the next ten years emerge and, so to speak, take NATO in the rear.

The conclusion was that we should do everything we could to foster the unity of Western Europe both economically and politically. If the West should, in the hope of seizing that will-o'-the-wisp, the *Détente*, rashly agree to anything tending towards the neutralization of Germany, the Soviet Union would be well on their way to getting what it wanted. And in order to resist this pressure it might well be necessary for the United Kingdom, in spite of the obvious reasons against it, to come closer than hitherto to the continent of Europe. I do not think that, some seventeen years later, I would be inclined to alter this judgment very materially.

It will not surprise the reader to hear that, holding these opinions, I took a rather dim view of the invitation to Messrs Bulganin and Khrushchev to visit the UK in April 1956. What exactly was this visit designed to achieve? No doubt there was much to recommend it from the local political point of view but if – as seemed likely – the Foreign Secretaries were still deadlocked on Germany in the spring of the year, the Soviet visit could only have one of three results. It could soften up the Soviet leaders and persuade them of the error of their ways. This was highly improbable. It could help to ratify the *status quo*. But though this might be sensible what would the result be on our relations with the West German Government? It could result in our toying with Soviet ideas about the right way to begin to reunify Germany. This could be extremely dangerous. I failed to see, therefore, how the visit could strengthen Macmillan's hands in the game of foreign policy. The visit indeed could only do good if the Foreign Ministers had got some kind of agreement on what should be done before it took place and this had been ratified by the heads of governments.

We should also consider the effect in France. If there was a Soviet 'Royal Tour' in Britain there would certainly also be one across the Channel, where after all there was a strong Communist Party and where the neutralists were much more influential than they were with us. Some people tended to think that the Fourth Republic was not immensely stable and that a Front Populaire Government, if things went wrong, was by no means out of the question. If this tendency prevailed France might well leave NATO and fix up some special relationship with the Soviet Union. Here I was off the rails. When the Russians came to France they were greeted even more enthusiastically by the Right-wing nationalists than by the Communists. And it did not occur to me in 1955 that what I imagined would be the policy of the Front Populaire would to a large extent be pursued by the Gaullists.

Apart from brooding about Russia, 1955 was largely devoted, so far as I was concerned, to reporting on, and discussing the steadily worsening position in North Africa, and more especially in Algeria. In the spring I had arranged an official visit so as to find out for myself, if I could, what was happening. We went to Tunisia first and there I was much encouraged by the intelligence of French policy and by the way those concerned were obviously preparing for the day when Tunisia would become independent within, it was to be hoped, some kind of French community that would enable her to maintain special ties with the old metropolis. The Resident General, Boyer Latour, a rather old-fashioned but most sensible French General, had us to stay and talked to me entirely frankly about his problems. I was much impressed. We also travelled round the country. At Jerba, on the island of the Lotus Eaters, we saw some of the two-thousand-year-old Jewish colony dance in the synagogue the same little dance that David danced before the Ark of the Covenant. In the great Mosque of Kairouan my daughter, Vanessa, slipped easily between the two adjacent columns thereby, it would seem, demonstrating her virtue, while another lady of the party got hopelessly stuck. And at Hammamet, the ancient Carthage, we meditated on the decay of empires over an excellent lunch, returning to take leave of General Boyer Latour with real regret.

A different welcome awaited us in Algiers where I arrived with a high fever, having left my wife behind with flu in Tunis. The new Resident, Jacques Soustelle,* was unable to have us to stay and until my affliction was cleared up I could not call on him before the dinner party at which I was to deliver a speech. This had been agreed with the Foreign Office and the only real point was the final conclusion in which I urged, I hope tactfully, the advantages of *une solution libérale*. But before that I had said that I knew that Algeria differed from colonial territories 'not only because it contained many hundreds of thousands of French colonists whose home it was, but also because there were thousands of Muslim inhabitants of Algeria who were French in the full sense of the term'. The Resident, reading the text, sent his *Chef de Cabinet* to me to urge that it should be changed so as to read '. . . a million French colonists whose home it was

---

* Governor General of Algeria 1955–6; then leader of the '*Algerie Française*' faction inside the French government.

but also nine million Muslim inhabitants of Algeria who were French in the full sense of the term.' I pointed out that this was really asking too much. I gladly accepted the first amendment (though I believe that the real *pieds noirs* were considerably under a million); but to assert that there was no difference between an illiterate non-francophone peasant living in a miserable douar in the Kabylie and an inhabitant of, say, the Ile de France was beyond me. If Soustelle insisted, the only solution was to leave the passage out. He did insist and it was omitted. At the official dinner he was, to say the least, hardly gracious. Only one Algerian – what might perhaps be called an 'old trusty' – was at the party. It was evident that the last thing the Resident contemplated was a *solution libérale*.

Had he but known, he might have been more forthcoming. I was, in fact, a strong advocate of the maintenance of a powerful French presence in Algeria and frequently drew attention to the possible dangers of any complete military withdrawal, more especially one involving any dis- credit to the French Army. The possibility of an extension of the Russian power in the Mediterranean was very present in my mind even before 1955, since it seemed to me then, as it seems to me now, that the real danger is that NATO may be turned from the south. But the absolute intransigence of the Algerian *colons* was, as I saw it, likely to produce a real crisis, which I feared would be only too likely to come about; and I therefore watched with apprehension the progress of what became more and more a civil war, and the increasingly nationalist policies of the local authorities under Soustelle and later under his even tougher successor, the Socialist Robert Lacoste.

In Paris, successive governments did their best in increasingly difficult circumstances. The Americans were, not unnaturally, nervous about the whole issue and perhaps showed this too much. An outline law (the *loi Cadre*) was discussed under Edgar Faure – who made great progress as regards the independence of Morocco – and continued under his successors, Guy Mollet and Bourgès Maunoury, finally being passed under Felix Gaillard in November 1957. But the real trouble was that there was for long no parliamentary majority in favour of any definite policy, whether of the Right or of the Left and that there was consequently no evident national will which a French Government of the day could legitimately express. The war therefore went on and there were constant suspicions in the press that it was being secretly fostered by *les anglo-saxons*, and even, I regret to say, by *l'intelligence service*! The excellent and very pro-British Mollet was quite unlikely to be influenced by such baseless rumours, though I had my work cut out in persuading other politicians that our attitude towards French policy as regards Algeria was above reproach. But in speeches I always did my best to express my sympathy with France in her difficulties and behind the scenes I was always urging that some practical gesture might be made to demonstrate our goodwill, such as the supply of helicopters. I even expressed the view (privately) that if 'national-ism' triumphed in Algeria its forces, backed by the Soviet Union, might 'sweep across the whole of Africa north of the Equator'! If this happened no one could answer for the continuance of any government favourably disposed to ourselves in France itself. The thing to avoid, if we could, was a power vacuum in North Africa. It followed that the continuance of a French military presence there should actually be an objective of our foreign policy.

From July 1956 onwards till the end of the year, the whole scene was, however, overshadowed by the Suez crisis. From the mill near Grasse I had rented for the summer, where I had just heard from Pat Hancock that Hoyer Miller was to have the Office and that I was to stay on as Am-bassador to France, I rushed back to Paris. There were agitated conferences and I was among those who favoured, in principle, some kind of direct action to bring the Canal back under the control of the Company, always provided that we and the French had enough forces available. For it seemed to me that unless we did so we should lose every position that we held in the Middle East – on which point at least I was not far out. I have no doubt now that I was wrong in so advocating in the heat of the moment. And as the crisis wore on; as the attitude of the Americans and others was revealed; and as we became involved in what was in effect a process of negotiation, I personally became gradually persuaded that force was out. Not that my advice was requested. For it was fairly soon apparent that something was happening completely outside the diplo-matic machine of which I had no inkling. Indeed Bourgès Maunoury had quite frankly told me this. When Eden and Selwyn Lloyd came over to Paris on 16 October and had a meeting of several hours from which all officials were excluded, this became even more obvious. My increasingly vigorous protests against being kept completely in the dark about the Government's intentions were, however, ignored save, at the very last moment, for a vague hint of what was impending.

One thing had, however, been apparent to me as Ambassador to France from the start: a successful common policy in regard to Nasser's seizure of the Suez canal was essential if Franco-British relations were not to go from bad to worse. It was also obvious that, rightly or wrongly, the French regarded such success as essential if they were to get the better of the

Algerian rebellion. Were such hopes entirely vain? And, if so, were Franco-British relations bound to deteriorate? The answer is probably, Yes. But it is interesting that a number of intelligent and well-informed Frenchmen, such as General Ely, the head of the French Chiefs of Staff, seem to have thought that a forcing operation at Suez could be brought to a successful military conclusion and so informed their political chiefs who, not unnaturally perhaps, were well disposed toward the idea for general political reasons.

The whole eventual plan, secretly concerted with the Israelis, was based on the assumption that the Americans would not intervene against us in the UN or elsewhere and that any Soviet opposition could be disregarded. Events proved that the first part of this basic assumption was not valid. But even had it been valid, how could we have avoided the consequences of 'success', such as condemnation in the UN, the break-up of the Commonwealth and the sheer impossibility of occupying Egypt for very long?

Looking back, I do not see how such consequences could have been avoided. The question therefore is, would they have been counterbalanced by the prospective gains? These gains would presumably have been (1) the freeing of the Suez Canal from Egyptian control (even if blocked it could have been quickly unblocked) and the re-establishment of the Suez Canal Company; (2) the demonstration that *pacta sunt servanda* and that France and Britain in the last resort could by themselves prevent the emergence of anti-Western governments in the Middle East generally (but this assumption would have to depend on whether we could succeed in establishing a stooge government in Cairo capable of carrying on after the withdrawal of our troops); (3) the withdrawal of the Israeli Army to Israel; (4) the denial of Egypt to the Algerian revolutionaries as a supply base for arms and for training facilities (a real advantage, from the point of view of the French, but scarcely a reason for thinking that the revolution would necessarily collapse); (5) (and most importantly no doubt) the establishment of the *Entente* as a force in the world and as the base for the future construction of Western Europe.

Apart from (5) it would seem that the disadvantages outweighed the advantages. But (5) does provide food for thought. Apart from anything else, it seems hardly likely that negotiations for the establishment of what emerged as the EEC (then in progress) would have continued without us. Nor could we for our part have easily avoided agreeing to enter something much more like an economic union than we had previously contemplated. For we should, after all, have been exposed to extreme economic pressures

283

and in the same boat as the French – a boat which would necessarily have loosened its ties with America. Nor need it have been a Gaullist boat; because, with a little luck, the French might have freed themselves of the Algerian albatross without the aid of the General. Besides at that time the French had not formally decided to embark on their own programme of nuclear armaments. It was to be over a year before that button was finally pushed by Félix Gaillard. It is possible therefore to imagine that France might have somehow been associated with Britain in nuclear matters, within the framework of some European political community. In other words, that what could have been accomplished in the forties, and what may still be accomplished in the seventies might have been accomplished in the fifties.

But, on the whole, a dispassionate observer must surely conclude, in the light of hindsight, that the Suez venture, on any rational calculation, did not make very much sense. The chances of obtaining any worthwhile result were demonstrably less than those of humiliation, an end to the *Entente*, and our likely political exclusion from the continent of Europe. Eden's motives seem almost entirely to have been the result of his determination that a 'dictator' should not once again get away with it, and a resolve that 'aggression' should never be allowed to pay. He did not apparently see that by his very action he was casting himself in the eyes of a vast majority of informed opinion all over the world in the role of an 'aggressor'. Nor did he appear to notice that there was after all a considerable moral, and indeed legal, difference between Nasser's eviction of the Suez Canal Company and (for instance) Mussolini's assault on Ethiopia or Hitler's invasion of Poland. It only shows the unfortunate effect that can be exercised on minds of rulers by historical parallels.

In saying all this I do not ignore the clear fact that, if we had not intervened with the French and had agreed to some solution which would have legalized Nasser's coup, we could hardly have avoided a crisis in Algeria, possibly involving the end of the Fourth Republic to say nothing of the gradual liquidation of our positions 'East of Suez'. But if we had been wise we should then have done our level best to prevent a collapse of the regime by joining wholeheartedly with the leaders of the Fourth Republic in the construction of a valid and democratic 'Europe'. In that event there would probably have been no Fifth Republic, no French break with NATO, and no unviable 'Common Agricultural Policy' either for that matter, but rather one commonly agreed between our partners and us. As a general observation it may be said that Suez only showed to what an extent our politicians, and indeed the great bulk of our people, were then living in the shadow of our Imperial past with small conception of the real problems that awaited solution. Compared with all this, the 'moral' aspect which distressed so many people so much, though important, is rather secondary. A blunder, as Talleyrand said, is worse than a crime; and it is difficult to avoid the conclusion that, as things went, Suez was a blunder.

Though they were much too polite to say so, it was evident that the French ministers, who had left the military lead to us, were much shaken by our inability to resist American pressure to call the whole venture off. Shortly before this occurred and the French paras were racing down the road to Port Said, I was in the Matignon attempting to give some message to Monsieur Mollet who seemed to have been talking for a long time on the telephone to the Prime Minister. In the waiting-room I ran into no less a person than Chancellor Adenauer. '*Sind Sie zufrieden?*' he asked me rather grimly; to which I could only reply '*Bis zu einem gewissen Punkte, Herr Bundeskanzler*'! But though this was obviously coincidental, it did occur to me that his presence was significant. From now on it must be obvious that the French would turn more and more towards the Western Germans. The days of the *Entente* based on British leadership were over. The negotiations for a Common Market without us would now proceed in earnest. And in less than eighteen months the whole *système*, inefficient in some ways but certainly on the whole pro-British, was duly thrown into the dustbin by the providential man.

Even in these circumstances some recourse to an authoritarian regime could have been averted. It could, indeed, I repeat, have been averted by a real change of heart on our part as regards 'Europe', and by an offer to accept at least the principle of a common tariff together with a willingness to increase the supra-national content of the WEU. I shall in the next chapter describe how I tried to get things moving in this direction. But it was too much to expect any British government to advance far in this direction as early as 1956. There remained one hope – the visit of The Queen. This had been agreed to before Suez as part of a plan for being as nice to the French as possible, and it was subsequently arranged for late March 1957. Immense preparations were made by the French in concert with myself and the visit was indeed a spectacular success. 'The promenade *sur la Seine*' through an illuminated Paris was dreamlike. The subsequent enormous reception and supper at the Embassy was, I think, worthy of similar occasions in that great house during the previous 140 years. In the Louvre after dinner, the Queen having confessed that she had never seen the Mona Lisa, President Coty gave a signal and in a few minutes two attendents staggered in with the masterpiece which they exhibited to Her Majesty on bended knee. At Versailles the magnificent theatre of Louis le Grand, newly decorated, was re-inaugurated with *Les Indes Galantes*. Outside the Opéra the multitude extended as far as the eye could see. There was indescribable enthusiasm on the way home at Lille, *'deux fois libérée par les armées britanniques'*. And yet when it was all over, where were we? Algeria was grinding on; the Treaty of Rome had just been signed by the Six but not by us; in the Commonwealth the 'wind of change' was nevertheless about to blow. Just before the visit *Le Monde* had a dramatic headline, *'Paris attend la Reine: et l'Europe l'Angleterre?'*. The answer to your rhetorical question, dear Monsieur Beuve-Méry, was, obviously, No. Even a subsequent visit by the vastly popular Queen Mother could do little to stem the tide.

Meanwhile in Algeria things continued to go from bad to worse and got pretty desperate towards the end of 1957 and the beginning of 1958 when the American and British Governments decided to offer the French Government their 'good offices' in solving the Tunisian dispute. How we ever got ourselves into this situation I cannot exactly remember. The 'good officers' themselves, Messrs Beeley* and Murphy,† had many qualifications and it is no reflection on them when I say that this whole project was misconceived. Nationalist feeling was steadily mounting in France and the whole North African issue had to be settled by the French themselves – foreigners really could not do it for them. Towards the end of this rather regrettable experiment I privately noted that the sooner we could get away from the extreme publicity which inevitably surrounded the activities of special envoys rushing from one capital to another, the photos, caricatures and general atmosphere of crisis that such activities inevitably produced, the better it would be for our relations with France and the sooner we should have a government which faced the realities of the Algerian situation. Within a month of so expressing myself we did!

Perhaps I should add that towards the end of 1957, and more particularly during my absence on a tour of the French African colonies the situation became particularly inflamed as a result of our sale of arms to the newly independent Tunisian Government. On arriving back I had to undergo a barrage of criticism by prominent politicians, many of whom were great friends of ours. As a result I composed for my own edification what I called 'A Fairy Story'. It read as follows:

* Diplomat. Later Ambassador to Cairo.
† American diplomat, employed on many high missions during the War.

AMBASSADOR (1954 – 8)

FAIRY STORY

Marianne and John Bull went hand in hand to overthrow a very horrible ogre who was vexing both of them, but particularly Marianne. Just as they were getting the better of the nasty fellow, in steps that beastly Uncle Sam and tells them to stop, as they are breaking the rules. Marianne, being a woman, finds it almost impossible to forgive Uncle Sam for this action, which really lets down the whole family. But she puts a good face on it in the knowledge that her great friend John, the best if not the only friend she has had for a long time, is going to stand by her and protect her during the very unpleasant period that is bound to follow the unsuccessful attempt to do in the ogre. What is her surprise when, after a very short time, John goes off and actually appears to be apologizing to Uncle Sam. Anyhow he makes various apparently profitable arrangements with the Uncle behind her back and without even telling her he is going to.

However, all this could have been borne, perhaps, had it not been for a perfidious act which proved that Bull had been actually betraying his old friend all along. In Marianne's back-yard was a rather uppish little boy, who had recently been making things difficult for her in every way. Consider her rage, therefore, when coming into the yard, she saw Bull in the act of handing over a catapult and some quite lethal bullets to the little beast, and that even before Uncle Sam came along to do likewise. His muttered excuse that he had got the boy, a certain Habib, to say that the catapult would never leave his hands, still less be used against Marianne herself, carried no conviction whatever. What does it matter to a woman what the excuses are? The hurt comes from the intention, not the deed. Why, if her great friend doesn't want her she will find someone else who does. There is, for instance, that rather sinister and powerful fellow over the way with a bad reputation, it is true, but possibly stronger than Uncle Sam. Can Marianne really do such a foolish thing? The trouble is, she may!

17

European Convert
(1957-60)

It will have been seen how, from the moment when I arrived in Paris and could once again focus the European scene, I began to press for some British political commitment to 'Europe', that is to say, for at least a start to be made on means for ensuring that Western Europe spoke increasingly with one voice on foreign policy and defence. But it was not long before I also came to the conclusion that, economically, the system embodied in the OEEC was hardly likely to endure either, given the evident determination of the 'Europeans', federalist and other, to recover from the blow to their hopes occasioned by the rejection by France of the European Defence Community in August 1954, and to establish, if they could, some kind of closely-knit European economic and social unit which would enable them to arrive, by other means, at their ultimate objective of European unity. Before Suez these efforts were not very intensive and the negotiators contemplated a body which should, if possible, include Great Britain; after Suez, and as anti-American, and anti-British feelings developed, they tended more and more to think in terms of a 'Continental' system which Britain might, if she wished, join subsequently.

I cannot say that at this stage I was a convinced 'European', at least in the sense of a believer in a sort of federation, usually referred to as the United States of Europe. In 1955 I tended to think that something could still be made of the Commonwealth and that our system of trading, based on imports of free food and Imperial preferences, could hardly be abandoned, this alone debarring us from joining a quite unlikely European Customs Union. Ever since 1947-8 I had, indeed, felt that something might bring all the small and medium nations of Western Europe closer together; but what with the success of NATO and the good economic recovery under the Tories, to say nothing of the success of GATT (General Agreement on Trade and Tariffs), there was not then, as I saw it, an impelling need to consider any economic integration of the

Continent. In other words, I was not particularly heterodox in my views: I just felt uneasy about the way things were developing.

It was Suez which started me off on a different train of thought. Looking back, that misfortune seems more and more to have been a historical milestone. Though desperate efforts were later made by Harold Macmillan to repair the damage, the old 'special relationship' with America was no more: we had been unceremoniously deterred by our 'special ally' from doing something which we were determined to do. This had never happened before in our history – except possibly under Charles II. The humiliation was total, and it needed no special intelligence to suspect that major changes in our foreign policy, and indeed in our whole attitude, would soon be inevitable unless we were to start off on a period of slow decline.

But even before Suez I had become alarmed by the possibility that the Six would in some way combine to our detriment. The Messina Conference had taken place in May–June 1955 with British participation and had been followed up by the Spaak Committee in Brussels from which however our representative was withdrawn at the beginning of November. In the light of hindsight this was the real parting of the ways; but at that particular moment it was by no means apparent that the Six would get agreement on anything like a Customs Union, still less on an Economic Union. As we have seen, the 'Europeans' had burnt their fingers badly in August 1954 and all talk of 'supra-nationalism' was now banned. Besides, much more importance – even among 'Europeans' – was at that point attached to the development of Euratom. Our own marked preference was in favour of developing further European unity within the OEEC – naturally on a non supra-national basis, and preferably on that of some Free Trade Area, the one being really synonymous with the other.

But I repeat that for my own part I was beginning to be nervous about the end result of this particular philosophy. In February 1956 I strongly urged that we should at least contemplate an association with Euratom, and at the end of that month I was in fact instructed to make a *démarche* betraying a certain amount of official interest in the idea. At that time the French did not seem to be at all unsympathetic to progress in this direction – even the Quai d'Orsay. But the effort came to nothing, largely, I suspect, owing to fears on our part that close association with Euratom might diminish in some way our technical reserves and thus detract from our own effort in a field in which we felt, rightly or wrongly, that we had a very marked advantage.

The intensive phase of the discussions for the formation of the Common

Market had moreover started early in 1956 with the Uri* Committee which resulted in the famous Spaak Report. Now all the main features of what was to be the EEC had appeared and after we had been invited to take part in a discussion of them by the six ministers assembled in Venice in May – and had refused – the real negotiations started and continued almost without remission until the signature of the Treaty of Rome in March 1957. As already noted they had been greatly stimulated by the Suez crisis. Suspecting where they were about to lead, I uttered (in December 1956) my first real cry of alarm. Unless, I said, we were prepared to put forward new and even revolutionary schemes it seemed to me that there was every chance of our being excluded from the Continent. It was just no good pegging away with the Free Trade Area conception inside OEEC. If we wanted to avoid the worst, even the whole conception of OEEC should be called in question. Perhaps it could in some way be combined with WEU. In any case there was no longer any case for maintaining a distinction between the political and the economic organizations. What I feared was that, confronted with the evident need of coming closer to Europe we should miss the golden opportunity by flapping about in a 'larger whole' and relying on now rather outworn conceptions as an excuse for not taking the plunge which we ought to take.

These ideas were subsequently more precisely formulated. There was one preliminary question, I argued, which really must now be faced and answered. Did we want to 'come nearer to Europe', or did we prefer to preserve our total integrity in 'some Atlantic framework'? On the second assumption, our existing policy was no doubt justified; but on the first assumption we should have to take urgent action, and notably by insinuating ourselves as soon as possible into the Brussels negotiations. Even if our sole objective was to achieve a European Free Trade Association – an idea which was gradually being developed as our own answer to the Common Market – we simply must avoid a situation in which the Customs Union Treaty, before being cleared with us, was signed and ratified by the Six who would thereafter only be able to make certain minor alterations by way of protocols. It must have been evident that a project so vital to us should, if possible, be negotiated à sept, and not within the larger 'Atlantic' framework of OEEC. WEU, in fact, or its equivalent, should be, as it were, the nucleus of Europe, and if this were to become a reality it would have gradually to adopt the principle of weighted majority voting in the Council of Ministers.

* Pierre Uri was one of the brilliant young associates of Jean Monnet.

By accepting and recommending this principle we should go a long way towards convincing the Continental 'Europeans' that we were persuaded of the necessity of establishing a genuine community in Western Europe; and it might then be possible to bring the Brussels negotiations to a satisfactory conclusion in the establishment of a Common Market with our participation on some special lines that would, to a considerable extent, protect our own Commonwealth and agricultural interests. This having been done, we could embark on a major scheme of reform of the complicated tangle of European institutions, involving the dissolution of the Council of Europe as then constituted and the setting-up of one European body with one parliamentary assembly consisting of an 'inner core' of the Seven, 'economic members' and 'observers'. In this way we would regain the initiative, make a real start in the direction of 'Europe', and at the same time protect our vital interests.

The suggestion was greeted with astonishment, not unmingled with alarm. From the OEEC point of view it was represented that only in that body could we negotiate a Free Trade Area, if only for the fact that only there were gathered all the states concerned. The Foreign Office took the line (and stuck to it) that we were not yet faced with my *question préalable* and that my proposal for weighted voting in a council of ministers was too revolutionary to have any chance of acceptance. I retorted that whether we liked it or not my question did in fact now pose itself and that we should consider our own likely political future. Unless, I thought, we could hold out the prospect of some European Community to both Germany and France it might well be that the former would buy unity with neutrality and the latter retire into neutrality through despair.

My pleadings were vain, and no doubt in the circumstances it was inevitable that they should be. We had not then as a nation got anywhere near the conviction that we should join forces with our neighbours on the Continent, and our trade with the Commonwealth still represented some forty-three per cent of our total exchanges. It was therefore out of the question that we should actually join a European Customs Union. It could not be too clearly stated, I was duly informed, that free trade in foodstuffs was quite crucial for the United Kingdom. The exclusion of foodstuffs from Free Trade Area arrangements was therefore a necessary condition of UK participation. We did not however object to the negotiations for the establishment of a Common Market among the Six. We even welcomed them. But we could not join them in this enterprise for the reasons given. Further, we were absolutely wedded to the unanimity rule prevailing in the OEEC which was thus the only possible place in which negotiations for a Free Trade Area could be conducted.

All this was towards the end of January 1957 and things were working up to the production of what Selwyn Lloyd called his own 'Grand Design' for a simplification of the multifarious European institutions. Given the principles from which we could not then depart, this was an intelligent and indeed useful scheme. It contemplated, it is true, a slightly strengthened (though not a supra-national) WEU which would, however, work under the 'high political direction' of NATO. In the economic field, OEEC would be the 'main instrument' of economic policy, though there might also be 'some consolidation' of other economic organs, such as the emerging Common Market. Even if extended to include other states, such organs should, however, all function 'within the framework' of the OEEC. They would naturally apply also to the suggested Industrial Free Trade Association. To give the necessary parliamentary colour to the whole streamlined system, there would be only one 'General Assembly of Parliamentarians', all the other assemblies – those of the Council of Europe, WEU, the European Coal and Steel Community, for instance, being abolished. This would be divided up into committees, and those countries such as Sweden, which might not wish to take part in decisions on foreign policy or defence, would not sit on committees dealing with such subjects. There might well also be US and Canadian participation. Even Eastern European countries might join eventually. This Super-Assembly of some eighteen nations would have its own secretariat which preferably would meet in Paris. It would be a forum for the general discussion of ideas and would have no power whatever over the executives.

It never seemed to me that this scheme would have any success. No real progress in the direction of European integration was likely until both the Common Market and the Free Trade Association came into effect – if they ever did. But on the most likely hypothesis the probable composition of the Free Trade Association was the WEU states plus Norway and Denmark. Sweden, Switzerland and Austria might join also, but this then seemed unlikely. In this inner group would in any case be Euratom and the European Coal and Steel Community, and it would consequently represent a powerful nucleus within which it should be quite possible to develop further most of the existing European organizations if we wanted to do so. But did we? That was the question. As I saw it, the 'Grand Design' showed that we had no such intention. All we really wanted to do was to get rid of various redundancies and secure a profitable outlet for British industrial products. That was why we laid such emphasis on OEEC. But the OEEC itself could never organize European unity. There the pace of the (very large) convoy was the pace of its slowest member.

What we presumably objected to – though we never said this openly – was the possible constitution of a 'Third Force' on our doorstep, and if this should prove to be a sort of neutralist bloc pursuing a 'Yugoslav' policy our apprehensions were certainly justified. They would be even more justified if we thought there was any chance in the long run of ourselves becoming a sort of German satellite. But we must consider that the potential Third Force – more especially if we were associated with it – was quite unlikely to be an actual federation. It would rather be a closely knit group of like-minded Western European powers who would agree to follow a common line – which might in some respects and in the last resort be determined by a majority vote in the Council of Ministers – on political, economic and military matters. But there was probably no more likelihood of such an entity being less closely linked with the USA than the UK itself was already linked with America.

However, it must be recognized that over the years this new body would become less and less dependent on American assistance. It would therefore be *possible* for it to develop into a Third Force if it so desired, in the sense of pursuing a policy not altogether approved of by the United States. In all probability nobody in Western Europe would wish to set up a Third Force that would break all its ties with and set itself up as a rival to America. But an alliance was one thing, dependence was another. Besides we could not altogether ignore the possibility (this was written in 1957) that ballistic missiles stationed in the countries of the Western European Union might one day serve to preserve the neutrality of Western Europe in the event of a conflict between the two Super-Powers. We did not presumably want to be 'Airstrip One', or perhaps 'Missile Base A', and if the Common Market collapsed and France and Germany reinsured with the Soviet Union, we might be.

Anyhow, whatever might be thought of these possibilities, the plain fact was that, once the Common Market came into existence, a potential Third Force would come into existence too. The only serious question there would be, should we come in or should we stay out? And if we did come in how much of the Sterling Area would come in with us? As for the proposed 'Super Assembly', the trouble was that, since it would have no powers of any kind, the parliamentarians could only meet in it for a few weeks as it were in a holiday mood, and it was very doubtful whether such a jamboree could serve any useful purpose whatever. Should we then, I inquired, try to torpedo the Common Market? But unless we had the support of the Americans in such an effort (and the contrary was the case) it would fail, in which case we should ultimately be forced into an association with the Common Market on terms less advantageous than those which were probably already available, notably as regards our agricultural interests. The fact was that the outcome of the Common Market negotiations was unfortunately likely to confront us, sooner or later, with a painful choice between doing damage either to 'Europe' or to the Commonwealth. We could not, in other words, have it both ways.

The Office became a little indignant. Who had given me the idea that we had any intention of trying to sabotage the Common Market? On the contrary, we welcomed it, if indeed it could be formed. The thing now was to press ahead with our great new idea of a Free Trade Area of which the Common Market countries, ourselves and all other suitable European countries would be members. As Whitehall saw it, there was no natural incompatibility between the Common Market and the Free Trade Area. All anomalies connected with the free entry into the latter, via the UK of, e.g. foodstuffs, could be got round by an intelligent system of certificates of origin. Besides the Germans seemed to be very much in favour of such a generalized Free Trade Area and even the French had told us that they would not necessarily disagree.

At the end of April I nevertheless made a final effort to get my own point of view across as against that of the 'Grand Design' which by then had been published and had found very little support on the Continent. The time had come, I thought, to define our whole attitude towards closer integration in Western Europe. There was no doubt that we should shortly be confronted with a choice between 'coming in' to Europe, to some degree, and 'staying out' altogether. The balance of advantage, as I believed, lay with the former. The departmental view was that we should not necessarily be faced with the choice. We should therefore pursue a 'third course' designed to prevent the emergence of a 'Third Force' and try to induce Western Europe to broaden its political and economic base so as to make it rather more Atlantic and rather less European in conception. This was essentially the idea behind the 'Grand Design'.

Since I greatly doubted the success of such a policy, I ventured once again to urge a consideration of the risks inherent in 'unduly thwarting' the European movement. I suggested that by advocating, in the political field, some limited system of weighted voting in a European council of ministers, and by trying, in the economic field, to combine the stick and the carrot in an effort to persuade the French to accept the general principle of a Free Trade Area before the ratification of the Common Market (by which I meant warning the Six of the dangers of going ahead without us, and at the same time offering certain concessions on agriculture) we should have a better chance of steering events into a channel which would not endanger our interests.

The signature of the Treaty of Rome, I proceeded to argue, had resulted in our approaching a parting of the ways. The Common Market had a much greater political than economic significance. We however tended to regard it as chiefly, if not entirely, an economic proposition. It might yet fail – i.e. not be ratified – and our own attitude could still contribute to success or failure. But if it should fail, we must consider the consequences. In my opinion they would be grave. Not necessarily from our own point of view, at any rate to start with. The 'stay-putters' might at first seem to be justified. We might carry on in the OEEC and appear to preserve the leadership of Europe. It would, however, be across the Channel that the situation would probably be disturbing. In France a second failure of the European Idea – for that is what it would amount to – could well result in isolationism and xenophobia, and even in some regime which would be prepared to do a separate deal with the Soviet Union. NATO would in any case be directly threatened. And where would Germany be then?

Could there, however, be in such circumstances a sort of 'Hanseatic League' – i.e. a Free Trade Association without France? No doubt this was possible and it might be combined with a sort of northern NATO. But would we really for our part like to form part of a European body in which Germany would be all too likely to emerge in the course of time as the dominant partner? It did not seem to me that this solution was at all desirable. And what would happen to Italy in the event of a collapse of the European Idea was anybody's guess.

We should therefore contemplate the success of the Common Market. We had even said we wanted it to succeed – and that whether it were combined with a Free Trade Area or not. But if we were in favour of it in principle, then we must be in favour of political integration too, for, if successful, the European Economic Community would surely end up one day in a European political community. What would then happen? Well, we should probably be witnessing the birth of a potential 'Third Force'. We would dislike this, first because of its possible adverse effect on our position, and also perhaps because we instinctively felt that if there ever was any question of setting up a 'Third Force' it should be us. We therefore tended to think – or to pretend to think – that it just could not emerge. But it might: and if it did we only had to look at the figures to recognize the enormous power that would be available.

Supposing that it did eventually emerge, what would be the possibilities that would confront us? We might, of course, just stand out, relying on the Commonwealth and on our supposed 'special relations' with the USA. But it seemed to me that we should have difficulty in maintaining such a position with an enormous and powerful neighbour on our doorstep who might even be able to undercut us in world markets, undermine our own 'special relations' with America while increasing our dependence on that country, and even themselves establish with the United States relations more 'special' than our own. The 'Third Force' might or might not become an atomic power; but a non-nuclear Europe could be a Third Force, and even a nuclear Britain could never be that.

There would thus inevitably be strong forces pulling us towards 'Europe' and it was because of the difficulty of resisting them that we were trying to organize a Free Trade Association. But even if we were successful in this enterprise (and I then assumed that we should be) should we really be able to avoid the 'choice'? After all, Free Trade Association or no Free Trade Association, we should be under increasing pressure to join the European Coal and Steel Community, or Euratom, and the WEU might even become a nuclear entity too. Thus our relationship with Western Europe was likely to become increasingly intimate unless it was impeded by some outburst of British nationalism. There was indeed little doubt that when and if the first and critical economic step was taken in the direction of a real association between the United Kingdom and 'Europe' the issue of 'sovereignty' would be raised at home.

Since it would, however, obviously be both bad for Europe and bad for us to stand out altogether, it would seem to follow that British popular suspicions should not be aroused, as they would undoubtedly be if it were a question of asking us to enter the equivalent of a federal union. The question how far any proposal for greater unity would be likely to go in this direction ought therefore to be discussed frankly with the 'European' leaders. At the moment they were highly suspicious of the 'Grand Design' which for them meant 'drowning Europe in a greater whole'; and our idea that the proposed parliament or assembly should, like that of the Council of Europe, be merely 'consultative' was particularly suspect. In general, they believed that our basic intention was to get the benefits of unity without incurring any of the obligations. What should therefore be done?

As it seemed to me, the possibilities of negotiating a sort of half-way house were still not inconsiderable. In particular, as I had for so long suggested, a proposal by us to transform the WEU into something slightly more supra-national – for instance weighted voting in certain clearly defined spheres – might have a profound effect on the 'Europeans' who were determined to advance by one means or another towards the goal of political unity. After all, such a system could be hedged round with 'safeguards', at any rate in the initial stages, and it would have the advantage of being capable of enlargement as confidence developed. If we went as far as this it was even possible that the 'Grand Design' might be accepted and that the Europeans would agree, in the early stages, to accept a merely consultative assembly, or at any rate an assembly with very restricted powers. For, after all, they would have achieved a perfectly genuine 'nucleus', which could be used for further advances and would in any case not have run the risk of dividing Western Europe into two.

Coupled with this essential offer, we should also make certain concessions to the French over the proposed Free Trade Association, notably as regards agriculture. It was not for me to make specific suggestions as to how this could be done, but I was sure that where there was a will there was a way and that even at this late hour such plans could be discussed, provided only we now insisted on re-entering the crucial Brussels negotiations with new, even if revolutionary, proposals. The basic idea would be to get the negotiations back on to a more political footing, thus preventing the emergence of a potential Third Force, nominally economic, but actually political, from which we should be temporarily, and perhaps even permanently, excluded.

There was, indeed, another policy – that of trying to wreck the EEC. It had been officially repudiated, but it certainly was possible, provided only that the Americans came along. But it was terribly dangerous and quite unlikely to succeed since, apart from anything else, the Americans seemed to be very keen on the success of the Brussels negotiations. And if that policy were discarded it was unfortunately always possible that whatever political suggestions we now made would fall on deaf ears, the French, who were by this time not at all well disposed, simply sitting back and refusing to talk, merely awaiting the successful conclusion of the negotiations in which they had already managed to get very substantial advantages for France.

This seemed to me to be the likely attitude of their chief expert negotiator, Olivier Wormser. If so, the sad result would be that we should, in the course of time, have to come in on something like the French terms which were, of course, the adaptation of the Free Trade Association to the requirements of the French and not *vice versa*. Only very great pressure applied before the end of July would have any chance of achieving what we wanted, namely the inclusion of the Common Market in the greater whole of the Free Trade Association. And even if this was brought off and the Common Market subsequently collapsed – as the 'Europeans' maintained it would – the effect on France would almost certainly be disastrous. My general conclusion was that we should decide on the basic question of 'Europe', that was Europe *à Six*. Did we really want it? Were we prepared to associate ourselves with it? If not, the only sensible thing would be at once to consult with the Americans and try to enlist their support for reasons that we might give. If yes, then we should above all concentrate on how best to lead Europe from within. But that would appear to necessitate a considerable development of our existing way of thinking.

It was all no use. I was indeed summoned back in May and had talks at the official and ministerial level. Nor did I fail to appreciate the official point of view. What I had been suggesting was no doubt beyond the bounds of political possibility. All I had perhaps done was to prepare the way for some later change in our policy, and to influence, in some small degree, the thinking of certain key figures in the official machine. It is in any case known what actually happened. French and German ratification of the Treaty of Rome was accomplished in July – surprisingly easily in the former case – and all the ratifications were in before the end of the year. The treaty therefore came into effect on 1 January 1958 and was to be fully operative a year later – that is if the French did not invoke certain 'safeguard' clauses. To all intents and purposes the battle was over. Her Majesty's Government were left wondering what to do next on the stricken field.

Before this, however, I recollect that I was still urging (at the end of July 1957) that we should at least make definite political proposals, involving among other things some kind of weighted majority voting. (Incidentally Marjolin had told me in May that he believed the French would be prepared to pay a high economic price for this kind of political gesture.) At this stage I still did not believe that we could actually join the Common Market as a full member for obvious reasons connected with Commonwealth trade and our 'Imperial' connections. But in a private letter I see that I said that we should insist, as it were, on breaking into their (the Six's) fortified camp (which we should never have allowed them to form) so as to have a full say in the direction of the economy of Western

Europe. To achieve this our only hope now lay in making some pretty tempting offer in more than one field. Otherwise we were more than likely to have the *Neuordnung* (the German European system imposed during the war) all over again. Preferably such an effort should be made in separate secret talks with the French and there was some reason to think that they might not be unresponsive.

The same thought was repeated at the beginning of December. I had been told by the Office in October that the feeling there was that we should partially sink our identity in Europe, and the real problem was not so much one of content as of timing and method. But if we were to ensure that, to use very approximate terms, neither a Nationalist nor a Communist solution was arrived at in France during the coming year, we should, I thought, be well advised to embark on our partial identity-sinking programme at a faster rate than appeared to be our intention. Of course it was *possible* that nothing of the kind would happen; but to guard against an obvious danger it was surely desirable to have some general and well thought-out plan. The Common Market was about to be established and our existing policies had to be adapted to it.

I therefore suggested that we should give full weight to French feeling if there were another conflict of interests in North Africa or the Middle East; go further (perhaps over agriculture) than in our own immediate economic interests we should be prepared to go towards meeting French *desiderata* on a Free Trade Association; not always plead our Commonwealth obligations; support a loan for France; agree to finance our troops in Germany by ourselves – at any rate partially; join Euratom; induce America to give the green light to a French nuclear defence programme; accept an invitation to use the Colomb-Béchard range; encourage tripartite meetings and proceed on the assumption that France was a great power, even if we doubted this; and in talking to the Americans, not agree with their apparent view that the French were leaky, hopeless and past praying for, but rather encourage them to do everything to preserve French parliamentary institutions by behaving towards the French as if they were watertight, confident, and even 'Anglo-Saxon'! France could still remain a good member of the Western Alliance but our own attitude would count for much. In spite of the existing feeling, there was still a certain uneasiness about breaking with us and the following passage which, I said, lost much in translation probably reflected a widespread mood:

Ce à quoi il doit conduire (that is to say a coming ministerial meeting) c'est à une prise de conscience sincère, à travers toutes les querelles de ménage, d'une communauté d'intérêts trop évidents pour être niés. Et pour que cette communauté vive, pour que l'on appelle les conseils de l'Angleterre, et qu'on admette éventuellement ses reproches, Monsieur Macmillan n'a qu'un mot à dire, qu'un pas à faire. Il suffirait qu'une adhésion sans arrière-pensée à l'idée européenne vînt prouver au monde que le Royaume Uni abandonne ses vaines nostalgies, ses efforts touchants, mais inutiles pour rattraper dans leur course les deux Super-Grands et reconnait enfin où sont désormais sa chance et son destin.*

I did not think, I said, that the journalist author of this love-letter really believed that the UK could altogether abandon her system of Imperial preferences, desert the Commonwealth, join the Common Market and entirely 'sink her identity' in Europe. But of the 'three choices' Europe should not always come last. In any case if we did not succeed in fostering the European Idea in Europe, I feared there was no counter-magic to take its place. All that would happen would be that the inexorable pull of the Kremlin would play havoc in the Western world. It would not then be our hydrogen bomb or our special relationship with the USA that would prevent the Soviet satellite empire from extending to Calais.

A little later (January 1958) I was on the same warpath, but approaching the objective from a different angle. The Anglo-American Conference in Washington in November 1957, convened with the obvious, and indeed successful, intention of patching things up with the Americans, had given rise to intense suspicions in France that we were trying to get back to our 'special relationship' under which all NATO decisions would be first concerted by the Anglo-Saxons, the remaining members, including the French, having merely thereafter to toe the line – and indeed the suspicion did not seem to me to be altogether unjustified. But the fact surely was that any kind of 'Anglo-American directorate', flattering though it might be to our self-esteem, would be an insecure basis for our foreign policy unless it could be fitted into a rather larger framework. In the first place, history seemed to show that in international politics relatively small importance attached to personal relationships. Individuals disappeared; it was only institutions that had any value. In the second place, if we were to base ourselves *solely* on a sort of Anglo-American merger – and if this really took place it could, owing to the enormous discrepancy in econo-

* 'Transcending all family quarrels, what it should produce is the genuine recognition of a coincidence of interests too evident to be denied. And if he wants such a coincidence to develop; if he wants Britain to be called in to council when her reproaches would at least be heard, Mr Macmillan has only one word to say, one step to take. For an acceptance without reservation of the European Idea would indeed prove to the world that the United Kingdom, forsaking at once her profitless dreams of past glory and her touching but useless efforts to catch up with the Super-Powers, had at last recognized where lay henceforth her hope and her destiny.'

mic strength, only mean that we should be absorbed by the USA as a sort of forty-ninth state – then I believed there was a danger that we might only succeed in encouraging Third Force neutralism on the Continent. If on the other hand, without abandoning our line to the White House, we succeeded in associating ourselves more nearly with Western Europe as an equal among equals, then we should have more power to influence events when it came, as it surely would come, to real negotiations with the Russians. We should also ask ourselves what might happen if either Germany or France went neutralist in a big way – and for very different reasons both developments were quite possible. And we should realize that in either event the UK might eventually find herself cut off from a Continent under the not so very remote control of the Soviet Union.

It was not by physical means that either we or the USA could prevent such developments. It was certainly not an Anglo-American directorate that could avert the danger. Nor was it a forty-ninth state that could stand out against the menace if it ever took shape or form. Not bombardment, but rather internal sapping and mining might then induce us, too, over the years, to compound with the adversary. In the long run the only hope of forestalling such dire events would be the formation of a real Western European association of which the UK would form part. And if this were ever to come about, it would have to rest on something more like the Common Market than on our original conception of a Free Trade Association. I therefore ventured in all conversations to renew my constant plea for some fundamental reassessment of our attitude towards our European neighbours.

No such reassessment was made, and we proceeded with what I believed was our doomed concept of a general European Free Trade Area destined in some way to 'embrace' the European Economic Community. All through 1958 this idea was pushed indefatigably by Maudling with the result described in the next chapter. One of the reasons for expecting failure was (as I noted) that the Americans were still clearly backing up the Common Market. But the real reason was that the Continentals, and more especially the French, were thinking in terms of politics and institutions. They wished – even General de Gaulle wished – to create some kind of entity. We seemed to wish only a development of trade. The two conceptions were dissimilar. General de Gaulle had at least got this point into his head when he came into power at the end of May. Perhaps we might have done rather better if we had never invented the term Free Trade Area (with its unpleasant historical connotations for France) but simply referred to it as a plan for a 'Common Market' which indeed it was, leaving the Continentals to get on with their 'Community' or Customs Union.

I continued, however, to make suggestions as to how we might conceivably make concessions to the French point of view as regards a Free Trade Area and to speculate on the likely attitude of the General, who might well make a decision in regard to it on political rather than on economic grounds after the French elections in November. All this availed nothing, and we arrived, in December, at the parting of the ways. From then onwards discussion was chiefly on how to proceed and whether to negotiate seriously a Free Trade Association among the 'outer seven'. In this period of doubt I expressed myself towards the end of May 1959 more or less as follows.

The Common Market had now come into full operation and the general FTA had failed. At least the possible isolation of France and the collapse of the European Idea had been averted; but the nature of the future association of the UK with the Six remained to be settled. I had been told back in October 1957 that we for our part recognized that when and if the Customs Union began to take shape, the UK would have to come to terms with it, and that these terms would most likely involve a much closer union of the UK with Europe than existed at that time. We should also, as previously noted, have partially to 'sink our identity' in Europe. All this was qualified, of course. Our ties with the Commonwealth and to some extent our Imperial preferences would no doubt have to continue. But it was in the spring of 1959 becoming likely that, far from 'partially sinking our identity in Europe' we might be gradually excluded from the Continent, even if we were successful in forming some limited FTA. Since such a development would result in a considerable loss of power and prestige, and no doubt also in some reduction of our standard of living in relation to that of our neighbours, we ought to 'make a final effort' to come to terms with the Six, whose Common Market would not now crash, but almost certainly continue.

I then dwelt on the danger of using negotiations with the other Six as anything more than a bargaining lever. I had been given to understand some time previously that in default of a FTA they might be gradually forced into the EEC on the Six's terms. Did this judgment still hold good or should it now be modified? But as I saw it the negotiations for the FTA had failed not so much because of difficulties regarding agriculture, or overseas territories, or the harmonization of social legislation as by the insistences of the French on the acceptance by the UK of the coordination of external trade policies and the harmonization of tariffs. It was therefore in this direction that progress would have to be made if negotiations were ever resumed. As a general rule, and especially when dealing with Continentals, it was better to accept the principle and subject it to derogations rather than turn down the principle from the start. Besides we must remember (I said a little later) that the reason why the Common Market came into existence when it did was because of our own blunt refusal to accept the invitation of the Six to negotiate with them. If we had done so we might well, without sacrificing our own principles materially, have fixed up the nature of the economic association that might have been established between the 'periphery' and 'the centre'.

It had unfortunately now (summer 1959) to be admitted, however, that our long-term bargaining cards were not terribly strong. Over the years our hand, I feared, was likely to get weaker rather than stronger. The sooner, therefore, we came to terms the better. It was absolutely no good thinking that EFTA would in some way dissolve the Common Market. All that was water under the bridge. Our only proper policy should be directed towards membership of the Common Market of ourselves and our EFTA colleagues on 'rather special terms'. Otherwise the conditions for our joining were likely to become more and more unfavourable. It was a question of the Sibylline books. De Gaulle, I thought, at the end of July, in spite of the failure of the famous 'memorandum' (of which more in the next chapter) was not likely to get *tripartisme* – i.e. a sort of inner circle of UK, US, France – so he would no doubt seek a strong Paris-Bonn axis; possibly with *tripartisme* in view if he could ever bring this off with France in the lead. But he might be made more cooperative by nuclear concessions.

My thoughts had admittedly been influenced by long talks (in May) with Wormser of the Quai, perhaps, as I have said, the most intelligent, if not always the most helpful, exponent of the French politico-economic point of view. Somewhat to my surprise, Wormser alleged that the FTA was 'in the long run' desirable, and that de Gaulle, if he wished, could push it through Parliament over the dead bodies of the Patronat. In the meantime negotiations for an EFTA might not be a bad thing, provided always they were not designed to force the hands of the French. Maudling, he thought, was being rather too 'categorical'. He imagined in any case that we had no intention of joining the EEC? If not he did not quite see what helpful step could at present be taken. Clearly the French were sitting pretty, having achieved a position which suited them very well.

Rather despondent, but feeling that some further effort should still be made other than simply rallying the 'outer seven', I returned, in October, to the political aspect and in my anxiety to achieve something in this direction actually recommended that as part of some new deal the EFTA negotiations should not be proceeded with. Here I was clearly wrong, since EFTA was happily achieved and has proved a great success, at any rate from the point of view of increasing trade between the partners. But the very fact that for the last ten years or so Britain has been seeking, if possible, to merge it with the EEC in itself demonstrates that it was not the final answer. At any rate in October 1959 I advanced the idea of a kind of marriage between the EEC and WEU. The idea would be to have a political Secretariat, located in Paris, and joint meetings of the EEC and WEU ministers. OEEC would be replaced by some more 'Atlantic' body; EFTA would not be proceeded with and we (and such of the other seven as wished it) would become 'associates' of the Common Market. There was a good deal of sense in all these suggestions but they were before their time and nothing came of them. The possibility of 'associate membership' of the EEC for the UK came up again, it may be remembered, in 1964, after the first Gaullist veto, and was firmly rejected by the FO. But in the circumstances of 1959 it might have been acceptable as a substitute for EFTA and as a guarantee of eventual full membership. In any event the basic notion of the amalgamation of WEU and the EEC is basically sound and is a notion which has always commanded support among those who really do want a start to be made with a European political community.

So we went on with EFTA, the Stockholm convention establishing it being signed towards the end of the year. But we still believed that *au fond* it was a make-shift and that eventually there could only be one Western European system. We therefore sought means of interesting the French in 'bridge-building' schemes and in proposals that at least the ministers of the Six should give some greater importance to WEU – all to no good. The French position – no doubt laid down by the General himself – was that there was really no need to worry. We could carry on with our Commonwealth and our special relationship with America and there was no reason to suppose that there would be any serious reduction in exchanges, even in Europe, as a result of the slow development of the EEC. This complacency was, it is true, not shared by all those in the French Government. Antoine Pinay, the veteran Independent, who had been de Gaulle's first Minister of Finance, was particularly disturbed by the incipient division of Europe, as was, to some extent, a much younger French politician, Valéry Giscard d'Estaing.

In the New Year I nevertheless inquired whether there was any likelihood that the newly formed 'outer seven' would ever willingly accept a common tariff, and was told that, so far at any rate as we were concerned, this was a non-starter, if only for the reason that (always supposing that foodstuffs were excluded) acceptance of a common industrial tariff would prejudice imports from the Commonwealth, and notably from Canada. Things seemed to be getting into a complete *impasse* and it seemed likely that the decision of the EEC to 'accelerate' its programme of tariff reductions would increase the rate at which we seemed to be steaming into the middle of the Atlantic.

It was at this point that reports appeared in the press to the effect that Harold Macmillan had given vigorous expression to his own apprehensions. The plans of the Six to 'accelerate' would involve the UK (he was alleged to have said) in a foreign exchange loss of a hundred to two hundred million pounds. Britain might even in such circumstances have to resort to dollar discrimination. Moreover the UK's historic role had been to crush the attempts of leaders such as Napoleon to integrate Europe. Should France and Germany go along a road leading to a unified Western Europe, Britain, in the long run, had no other choice but to lead another peripheral alliance against them. He added that in the time of Napoleon Britain had even allied itself with Russia. If the fourth volume of General de Gaulle's memoirs is to be believed, the Prime Minister had already voiced rather similar sentiments to General de Gaulle himself; but at the time I merely said that whatever denials were issued it was not likely that they would be believed by the French!

The Embassy – for its part – would continue with its line that we did not object to the Common Market and so on and so on. But I had to confess that to some extent I did personally share the alleged apprehensions of the Prime Minister. If, as I had so often said, the Common Market really got going there were in fact only two alternatives for us: *either* to stand the racket of the gradual establishment of a powerful entity in Western Europe which might admittedly result, in spite of the economic benefits of EFTA, in our having to withdraw our troops from Germany owing to economic and financial stress, *or* to join the Common Market, though gradually, and not, so to speak in so many words.

What could be done now was not evident, but perhaps we might pursue the line of a gradual harmonization of European tariffs. We had, it was true, now got the 'neutral Seven' round our necks (the reader will perceive that I was still barking up the wrong tree so far as EFTA was concerned) but even so, and given the will, it might be possible for some of the Seven more or less to join up with the Six and for the remainder to have perfectly satisfactory arrangements with them (here I was only some twelve years before the time). But I repeated my personal belief that only by forming a greater Western Europe could we continue to wield any substantial influence on world events. A policy of trying to separate the Six would not work if only because, if it were attempted, we should isolate ourselves from the Americans. But even if it were successful it would be worse because in that event we should have on our doorstep a much more menacing political bloc than was on the horizon at the moment. Curiously enough *The Economist* came out a week later with an article expressing much the same sentiments, and indeed entirely in harmony with the gospel that I had been preaching for about six years. I could only hope, I noted a little bitterly, that *The Economist* would have more success than I had had.

A little later, I said that I believed we rather tended to exaggerate the horror of our one day joining the Common Market. For instance, if we ever did so, we should be no more committed to the prospect of an actual federation than was the government of General de Gaulle, that celebrated Nationalist. But it was clear that in mid-summer of 1960, and more especially after the collapse of the 'Summit', little progress would be made with the development of the 'European Idea'. I discussed all this with great frankness with the General at the end of June and was, I must confess, misled by his protestations that he had never contemplated excluding Britain from Europe, and that 'one day' she must of course come in to his 'imposing confederation', into concluding that an actual application to join the Common Market would not be rejected by him as such, though he clearly thought that this was most unlikely for some time – which was no doubt right. Nor was I alone in clearly, in the light of hindsight, misreading the General's mind. Others in high positions who had access to him had reported that if the British really were to make an application the answer could not, in principle, be No.

However when coming to the erroneous conclusion that the General himself probably would *not* say No, I dwelt at length on the very considerable opposition in France to the entry of the UK into the Common Market. This consisted of the federalists who suspected – more especially if we were admitted by the General – that we should be a formidable and perhaps insuperable obstacle to their hopes of ultimately forming a federal state. For their part, the Patronat, having accepted the Common Market, still maintained an uncompromising opposition not only to anything of the nature of a FTA but also to any reduction of the Common External Tariff. Even more importantly, there was the rather arrogant self-confidence of a dynamic new generation of Frenchmen who were taking over from a generation which remembered and was moulded by defeat in war. These men were much encouraged by the upsurge in trade which had occurred since the signature of the Treaty of Rome; and though this *redressement* might be largely psychological, there was no doubt that France was now much more confident and combative than she had been. Nor could we doubt that echos of the celebrated debate in the Chateau de la Muette in December 1958 still resounded in the ears of certain highly placed French officials. All this added up to a remarkably solid opposition to any attempt to form a wider European trade area, at any rate for a number of years.

The ideas of our entry could, indeed, as it seemed to me, only be proceeded with before then if we took a decision on political grounds to work for a genuinely united Europe on the lines apparently favoured by de Gaulle, and were prepared to accept the Treaty of Rome more or less as it stood, with the notable exception of the entry of free food into the UK which, I believed (wrongly, of course) should be negotiable given Continental goodwill and, more particularly, the support of the General. At any rate it seemed to me that we ought as soon as possible to make the attempt to enter. If we failed in this attempt I did not think the situation would be any worse than if we went on as we were and found ourselves in a position where we could only knock on the door and have it opened to us under really humiliating conditions.

Shortly before I left Paris, I submitted my final views on what might be called the great debate which we had been having over the previous six years. What we seemed, from our official pronouncements, to be saying was that we would be prepared for negotiations between the Six and the Seven for the constitution of a European Customs Union with political institutions of which we should be a full member, provided we could obtain in advance unofficial assurances from the Six that consideration would be given in such negotiations to the special problems that would be created by:

(a) the free entry into the UK of certain Commonwealth goods (chiefly foodstuffs) and the effect on the Commonwealth of our adopting a common European agricultural policy.
(b) the need for protecting our own agriculturalists, and
(c) the needs of our EFTA partners.

Nor would we be contemplating any other institutions than those of the Treaty of Rome. If we made our position quite clear on these lines there would be much rejoicing among the five: but the stumbling block would still be France, and especially those French officials who believed that the longer we waited the weaker our bargaining position was likely to be.

There remained the possibility of a direct approach to the General, preferably verbal. If his reply were negative we should be no worse off and at least know where we were. An approach, if made, would however have to be based on deep historical *and political* arguments and presented in a way which might appeal to his vanity, his fears and his emotions. It was not impossible that he would then give the green light for negotiations, provided always he was sure of our basic political intentions. It was an unheeded swan-song, and rightly unheeded, I have little doubt. But I suppose it is just possible that had the move been made something rather unexpected might have come out of it. Before arriving at a conclusion the reader is referred to my book *Europe after de Gaulle*★ and to what is noted in Chapter 19.

★ Lord Gladwyn: *Europe after de Gaulle* (New York 1970).

18

Working with the General
(1958-60)

It is not true that during the first four years of my term in Paris, I entirely failed to discern the likelihood, or at any rate the increasing possibility, that General de Gaulle might return to power, perhaps as the result of some military revolt in Algiers. The development of my thought was as follows. In April 1956 I said that possibly the North African situation might result in a Popular Front government in Paris, but it might equally be that it might give the French just that shock which they needed in order to pull themselves together. This might result in a government of National Union, or even in a fundamental reform of the constitution. A little later (in December 1956), I said that it was not then probable, but quite possible, that de Gaulle might return to power during the coming year as a result of an economic crisis, or events in Algeria and the Middle East, or both. I therefore saw the great man in the Hotel La Perouse at the end of January 1957, and found him, after seventeen years, much less combative and acidulous, more mellow – even affable. It did not seem to me that he was actively seeking power, though no doubt he would not refuse it if it were offered to him on a plate. His whole attitude was rather detached and philosophical. Indeed he actually described himself to me as 'above and outside politics'. At that moment therefore I judged that his return to power, though possible, was most unlikely. If so, we might consider ourselves fortunate, for his views on foreign policy were dangerous, even if some were interesting.

Both America and Russia, according to him, were likely as time went on to move towards isolationism and to withdraw within their own borders, becoming more and more nationalistic in the process. Thus 'Europe' had a chance of recovering some of her ancient prestige. But Western Europe could never form a political entity. There could be some economic rationalization and standardization; there might be greater political and diplomatic liaison between European nations; even 'common policies' might one day be worked out; but further than that 'integration' could not go. Europe as a 'thing in itself' was an illusion and Jean Monnet was the champion 'illusionist'. Nationalism was the thing. It followed that the existing division of Germany was artificial and could not last. As he saw it, Germany ought to be neutralized up to the Oder-Neisse line on the model of Austria. Some German forces might be retained, but they would have to be limited by general agreement with guarantees against infractions. Perhaps it might be said that this would be dangerous – indeed I had said so – but some risks must be taken, and anyway there was always the Atom Bomb in the background as the ultimate deterrent. If that had prevented Russia up till now from walking over the Iron Curtain why should it not prevent her from invading a neutralized and unified Germany? In the meantime, however, there was no particular reason why we should worry about continued division.

On Algeria he seemed to me to be very sensible. Some hint of 'co-existence' between the Arab and the French communities would naturally have to be negotiated, though what exactly he would do if he came into power he simply could not say except that the evacuation of the old French population from the province was 'unthinkable'! We could take one thing for granted: no solution was possible under the present regime. All he could say was that eventually there would be some kind of solution whereby the whole of North Africa was associated with France in some new and hitherto unsuspected relationship. So passing by the Middle East, which would always be *assommant* (a pain in the neck), and observing that at Suez we ought to have gone straight ahead in spite of all opposition, we got on to France.

In 1940, the General said, he really had had the impression that France might 'die'. Not in a physical sense, of course: there would always no doubt be French hairdressers and cooks, but as a nation she had been saved by the Resistance. He himself, however, had not been able to re-establish France as a Great Power. The reason was that the French were no longer in a mood for *grandeur*, and he could not swim against the tide. But, as he believed, the present regime would one day collapse and there would be a 'new spirit'. Indeed there had to some extent been such a new spirit since Suez, and that was very good. But it could not manifest itself under the present regime and that could only be replaced by 'something stronger' as the result of a crisis. Nor was this something out of the question. After all, there had been thirteen changes of regime in France since the revolution of 1789! By this time the General was in good spirits, but his general approach to politics seemed to be philosophical.

At this time I had also been reporting that one of the most important effects of the Suez crisis had been to strengthen the conviction of the French 'Europeans' that the only way in which the European democracies could preserve some shreds of independence was by uniting more closely. All this had greatly increased the 'European impulse', not only as regards such matters as the Saar, but also in the negotiations for the EEC. My conclusion was that Suez had produced a sort of national *redressement*. It had also demonstrated that neither France nor the UK were any longer 'Great Powers'. Most Frenchmen had concluded that if our two countries' stock was not to decline further they would have to contemplate a closer association with their European neighbours. It seemed to me that both the French Right and the French communists might prevent such a development, but that if they did there would inevitably be some *crise de confiance*. That was why the conception of a Western Europe in which France could play a real and a leading part was so important for all of us. The signals, in any case, were now all set red for danger.

It is true that during this period and until at any rate the end of 1957, the Embassy as a whole tended to think that though de Gaulle was certainly not to be excluded in the short run, the famous Front Populaire was the most likely ultimate successor to the Fourth Republic, and we certainly overestimated this possibility. There could well be, we thought, some *coup d'état*, executed by a rebellious general; but such a move would probably be followed by strikes, the country would become difficult to govern, and a Left-wing government, with Communist support, would no doubt take over. But whatever our speculation about the precise nature of the regime that might follow the Fourth Republic, I had come to the conclusion early in 1957 that some sort of revival of French national-ism was almost certainly on the way, and the row about 'arms for Tunisia' that broke out late in that year seemed to me to be proof of the prediction. Fuel was certainly added to the flame by Macmillan's conference with the Americans in the autumn (see p. 300), during which all fences were hastily mended and the principle of 'joint Anglo-American planning' and a 'pooling of Anglo-American resources', advocated by us, was largely accepted, practically no mention being made of France. It was calculated to promote a wave of anti-Anglo-Saxon and nationalistic feeling in France and to promote the vague impression that this was the kind of future for the Western world which the Anglo-Saxons and notably the British had in mind.

Anyhow, at the end of the year, in discussing all conceivable possibili-ties, I see that the one marked 'Bonapartist', i.e. Left-wing and plebiscitary under de Gaulle's nominal leadership though quite possible, was regarded as 'not very likely'; but a little later, in summing up the general prospects I repeated what I had said at the end of 1956, namely that the signals were still set red for danger. Yet, save for the application of some economic brakes, France was still on the same track. It would, I thought, take real statesmanship, on the part not only of France but of her allies as well, and possibly the emergence of some dominating figure, if she was to be diverted to a safer one. All this time the name 'de Gaulle' was usually mentioned as a possible outcome and indeed early in 1958, I was personally warned of this and so reported, by no less a person than the late President Coty. As he saw it, de Gaulle might well come back as a result of an explosion of national feeling that was slowly building up (this we knew only too well). But if that happened there would be no Popular Front for the Communists would make no difficulties at all. On the contrary, for various good reasons of their own, they might actually assist a return to power of the General. This put things in a rather new light for me and I repeat, looking back, that we had been unduly impressed by the theory of the Popular Front and had not appreciated the intense conservatism and lack of any revolutionary ardour on the part of the French Communist Party.

When, therefore, during the early part of 1958, there was increasing talk of de Gaulle we still were disinclined to go 'nap' on him in our forecasts, perhaps for the reason that when I myself saw him again in late March of that year he himself, with tears in his eyes, largely discounted his chances of returning to power. This was in reply to a straight question which I had put to him. There was almost universal belief in Paris, I said, that the existing system was weak and did not work properly. This fact had caused many to say that the only course was the return to power of General de Gaulle. Others, however, maintained that this event, if it occurred, would quickly be followed by the establishment of a Front Populaire. Could the General give his candid view on such possibilities? De Gaulle replied that since de Gaulle – and henceforward he referred to himself in the third person – had told the nation in 1946 that the Constitution of the Fourth Republic could not work, and since he had subsequently been proved abundantly right, it was evident that in the event of the regime's grinding to a halt de Gaulle would be likely to be called upon to clear up the mess. He was the only alternative to Communism. However he doubted whether he would ever have a chance to put his own schemes into operation. If he did not, then the Front Populaire, or something like it, was only too likely. And he must tell me that before the regime collapsed all the chances were that de Gaulle would be dead! This was said with great emotion and it really seemed to me that the General was near despair.

I must say I then regarded this sad event with some equanimity since once again I had the distinct impression that if he did come into power he would adopt a policy of appeasement towards the Soviet Union which would be only too likely to result in a break-up of the existing system of alliances, to say nothing of the EEC. Here I was more or less right, though I was wrong in also believing from what he said that he would probably only be able to negotiate with the Algerian rebels on the basis of some military victory. But, broadly speaking, it was with some alarm that I once again faced the prospect of his assumption of power. In any case if it was failure to predict confidently that de Gaulle would sweep into power at the age of sixty-seven and remain there for twelve years, then I frankly confess that I was a failure. In extenuation I may say that until the end of 1957 there had been a fairly widespread impression in France that de Gaulle was something of a spent force and that if he did come back to power he might be a figurehead – a sort of Neguib rather than a Nasser.

For me, in any case, the celebrated 'events' of May 1958 were non-events. The period of speculation was over and I could only send telegrams reporting the progress of the crisis. Even they were very short since everything was fully reported in the press, including the possible arrival of *les paras* in Paris. This, incidentally, was something which we by no means discounted. It was possible, technically, I was informed, for them to take over the capital but they would have to have a leader who was prepared to risk his neck. It might well have been not General de Gaulle who was going to be in command of France in a few days' time but General Massu. It was thus a relief when the man of destiny took over. After all, the democratic rules had been observed, which was a great thing. He had been duly voted into power by the Parliament. And there was no doubt that he was the person most likely to end the Algerian war which was draining the life-blood of France and might otherwise have resulted in a pro-Russian Left-of-Centre neutralist government. A Gaulist regime, I believed, would in any case be preferable to that. But I warned the Office as soon as de Gaulle had assumed power, of what was likely to be the eventual effect on NATO and on 'Europe'. Not that we could do anything about it.

Before the issue was decided we had had unofficial denials of the wilder intentions attributed to the General. He would be entirely faithful to the Atlantic Alliance, we heard, and by no means inclined to go back on the

Common Market. As for *L'Angleterre*, his respect was well-known. In any case nothing dramatic was to be expected. Yet it was only three months after he had settled down in the Matignon Palace that we were suddenly confronted by the celebrated 'memorandum' – addressed to Eisenhower and Macmillan – in which he suggested that NATO – that is to say the *Organization* of the alliance – should be drastically reformed by the establishment of what came later to be known as a 'directorate' of the three powers with 'world interests', namely the USA, the UK and France, who would jointly take all the major decisions regarding the use of the nuclear weapons. And as they would apparently take their decisions by unanimity, it was clear that the suggestion was that there should be a possible veto on all major decisions by France which was at that time not a nuclear power at all.

The 'memorandum' had only to be read in this way for it to be obvious that it could not be accepted by America, or by Britain either for that matter. It was, I think, first suggested by J.M.Tournoux, the intelligent author of *La Tragédie du Général*★ that de Gaulle always knew that this was so and only fired in the 'memorandum' in order to use its inevitable rejection, or virtual rejection, as an excuse for taking France out of NATO as soon as he could and in any case for doing a special deal with the Germans, thus 'freeing his hands'. It looks from the fourth volume of the Memoirs† as if this might have been the case, but I am not altogether convinced. It was not very typical of de Gaulle to seek excuses for what he wanted to do: he just did it. And we must recall that his first and famous interview with a suspicious Adenauer at Colombey-les-Deux-Eglises was on the very day on which he dispatched the 'memorandum'. He obviously wanted no excuse for getting together with the Western Germans; and if by any chance his 'memorandum' had found favour he would have used it as a means for weaning them away from America and towards a 'European Europe' – that is to say a Europe not including Britain – of which, in the supreme council of three, he would have been the 'European' representative.

There is however no doubt that from the moment the General walked for the second time into the Matignon, the morale of the average Frenchman shot up very considerably. The Fourth Republic, contrary to the common belief, had had a very creditable record at home and by no means a bad one abroad. The economy had been well restored: a magnificent system of social benefits had been installed; the country, under the pre-

★ J. M. Tournoux: *La Tragédie du Général*, (Paris 1967).
† Op. cit., p. 215.

fectorial system was beautifully and on the whole impartially administered and the majority of Frenchmen were probably quite content – in so far as Frenchmen can ever be content – at any rate for the first ten years of its existence. But there was no doubt that the constant changes of government, and the feeling that the same figures tended to alternate in one government and the other, none of them having really the time to take hold of their ministries before being replaced, told against the *système;* while the inability of succeeding governments to solve the Algerian question resulted in increasing exasperation on the part of the Right, who wanted the Army to suppress the rebels altogether; the Centre, who thought that some sensible and 'liberal' arrangement could be arrived at with the insurgents; and the Left, who increasingly favoured total evacuation.

The General was one obvious *deus ex machina*, but subsequent history showed how wise he was not to allow himself to be pushed into power by a rebellious army, which he might then have been unable to control, and to insist by one means or another on a perfectly legal hand-over of power. Indeed, this is perhaps his greatest claim to fame. And his first government contained a number of well-known figures of the Fourth Republic, and notably Antoine Pinay as Minister of Finance. What would have happened to France if power had been actually seized by the military and the paratroops had landed at Villacoublay is something which it is disturbing to contemplate. And it very nearly did. France might have become the equivalent of a South American Republic – unless indeed the famous 'Yugoslav' solution had emerged.

Some time after the events of May, I had a shot at predicting where the new regime was likely to take France if it managed to consolidate itself, which then seemed probable. After referring to all the past predictions – including the 'Bonapartist' one – I said that, if we wanted to be optimistic, it might well be that a combination of a successful solution in Algeria, a consequent Allied loan, and a general restoration of confidence in the country might result in the General's being assured of a long period of authority. In this case there was little reason to qualify such a period as one of 'Fascism'. There was quite a chance that with a reformed constitution and a revised electoral law the political parties might sort themselves out in a way which would permit of more than a show of democratic government. And the working classes might find themselves given sufficient representation in government institutions to render tolerable a paternalistic and authoritarian regime. If so, the General would have done his job and France would again take her proper place in a Western Europe which might then, at long last, organize itself properly. We should in that case be approaching a kind of reformed and 'liberal' Second Empire of the type Ollivier had in mind – just before the Franco-Prussian War.

But this, though it might be true enough so far as it went, was not exactly prophetic, and I would have done better, perhaps, to repeat my immediate warnings. And in that summer there was, for us, one worrying factor, more worrying than Algeria, more worrying even than the 'memorandum' – the 'Free Trade Area' conception was clearly in danger of running on to the rocks. It had been in process of doing this for some time and the reasons have been examined in the preceeding chapter, but as everyone knows, the *coup de grâce* was administered by Jacques Soustelle, then de Gaulle's Minister of Information, on 15 November 1958. That France should somehow run out of the FTA was hardly unexpected, but the flat statement in the middle of the crucial meeting of OEEC that she had no further interest in it certainly was. In a sudden flash the British Government realized what it should have realized years before, namely that Europe was about to be formed without Britain – and if without, then quite possibly against. Up till that moment we had often tended to take France for granted. Now it became clear that she might no longer be a difficult, though essentially rather subservient, partner. On the contrary a quite formidable adversary was about to emerge.

I shall never forget the ensuing scene at the reception for the OEEC delegates at the Quai d'Orsay. British indignation at French action had just been publicly voiced by Sir David Eccles;* and though he had been perfectly polite he had made no attempt to conceal his feelings. For their part Couve de Murville and Olivier Wormser – more especially the latter – were literally quivering with emotion. They looked for all the world like cats which had just survived the charge of a powerful mastiff. And well they might, for the evening was a historical watershed for their country – something which (as I have tried to explain in the preceding chapter) the mastiff himself did not as yet fully comprehend.

Soon after this watershed I had, on 12 December, another interview with the General, during which I referred, among other things, to the 'shock' occasioned by his decision on the FTA and tried to draw him on what was to be the future of Western Europe if, economically, it was seemingly to be divided into two. The General observed, very sensibly, that the Common Market was after all a quite different thing from the FTA, as epitomized in OEEC. If it were not, why had it been created? And, after

* Now The Viscount Eccles. At that time President of the Board of Trade.

all, we were ourselves largely to blame for its creation. If we had always opposed the idea of a Customs Union and had suggested some other form of close European cooperation, including ourselves, the thing would have gone through. But we had actually at one time seemed to favour the notion of a Customs Union, at least in the sense that we had done nothing to prevent it. His own attitude had been rather different. He had found it accepted when he came into office and had decided to let it come into being in so far as it was likely to improve the standard of living of all the countries concerned.

But, as he saw it, the Common Market should have no relation to international politics as such (here I must say I opened my eyes). Following on a remark of mine to the effect that Western Europe, if it were ever formed, would have primarily to be based on the industrial complexes of Western Germany, northern France and Britain, the General went further and opined that indeed a close association of these three countries was the real key to the future. Later I heard from Louis Joxe that the Quai had been much interested in this expression of the General's view which up till then had been, so far as they could understand it, more 'Carolingian' in conception. But the idea was never thereafter taken up on either side. We ourselves were far from contemplating a new political orientation in 1958; and maybe the General was himself thinking of very different solutions.

About this time I had a long talk with Mendès-France who thought that, though not necessarily disastrous economically, the exclusion of the UK and Scandinavia from the EEC would be very bad politically. For only if the UK associated herself politically with the Six and thus came into direct contact with them would it be possible to stop the emergence of a dominant Germany and the formation of what would virtually be a new *Neuordnung* on the Continent. Mendès, I may say, said this in no anti-German sense, but rather as something that was almost bound to happen by the force of things unless conscious and collective action was taken to stop it. His hope was that Britain, seeing the danger, would soon take 'some direct action on the political plane' – not necessarily in the WEU, but if not there in some other grouping. How right he was. But it was not unnatural that I should agree because I had myself been saying much the same sort of thing since 1954, and am still saying it in 1971.

We proceeded into 1959 and, with the FTA out of the way, interest was focused less on the General – still preoccupied above all with Algeria and the internal organization of France – than on the intentions of Khrushchev and the Soviet Union. At the end of the year things seemed to be coming to a head in Berlin, and notably the Berlin crisis, provoked by Khrushchev, dominated the scene. I was drawn into this because at the end of 1958 the Office asked me to come home for a while in order to prepare what might be supposed to be an independent or 'outside' view of the crisis. This I did to the best of my ability but I am not sure that when the documents are published in 1989 this will be the report of which I shall be proudest. It was not bad, in the light of hindsight, but I feel, looking back, that the General's totally uncompromising line – dictated largely, it is true, by the necessity under which he laboured to be as well disposed towards Adenauer as possible – was probably, as it turned out, the best policy in the circumstances. Not that I, as a matter of fact, was in favour of making any concessions without getting something substantial in return; but I did discuss the possibility and desirability of certain concessions. I remember also that Jean Laloy of the Quai d'Orsay, who subsequently lost his name by criticizing the European policy of the General, was in this instance strongly on the 'stay put' side: and I had a very great respect for Laloy's judgment.

Late in October 1959 I was seeing the General on some business, the nature of which I forget, and on leaving said I had brought along a copy of the third volume of his memoirs in which I hoped that he might inscribe his name. The General said he would be delighted to do so, but as I was almost in the doorway, clutching the precious volume, he suddenly pulled me back and said, 'Oh, my dear Ambassador, I have to confess that you may find this volume a little painful. As perhaps you know I describe in it in some detail an interview with your predecessor, Duff Cooper, on the subject of Syria. I can only say that when I had this interview I was completely beside myself with rage. I quite understand if your countrymen become indignant when reading my account of it.' This, I said at the time, was just about as near an apology as it was conceivable for the General to go, and I tell the story as an instance of his usually admirable manners.

In April 1960, there was the State Visit of the General to London. He had agreed to this, but I think it caused him some apprehension. After all, the British could hardly imagine that he was in favour of the system, operating since the war, whereby they had in effect run Western Europe as the 'principal ally' of America! And if they did not imagine this then clearly there was going to be, at the least, a tussle of wills, since the only way to change the system was for France to take the lead and establish the new Europe on the basis of a close alliance with Germany, or rather (as the General always really considered it) with a 'Confederation of the

Rhine', *l'Angleterre* being left to occupy herself with her Commonwealth and Empire and perhaps, if that faded out, being eventually admitted to 'Europe' as a sort of poor relation, but only after a long interval, and preferably as a kind of 'associate' with no influence on policy. Unless of course the idea was to start afresh and construct Europe on some sort of supra-national basis – a solution to which, however, the General, on grounds of principle, was unalterably opposed.

The idea that the British, or at any rate the enormous majority of them, had not seized this rather important point, and just wanted to have 'better relations' with a great man who had been on the right side in the war and who had now happily got our ally on her feet again, had probably not occurred to him. The French, of course, are much more *méfiants* (suspicious of other people's motives) than the British are; and though the General had many characteristics that were not peculiarly French, this was not one of them. Still, the British for the moment seemed to be accepting the existing situation so far as French opposition to the Free Trade Area was concerned and he himself, in the continued absence of an Algerian settlement, was not in a position to push ahead with his own policy. Perhaps, therefore, it would be worth while running the risk of a not very warm welcome in London if he could use the occasion for preparing the way for a rather new relationship with Britain. And, of course, for Britain itself he had a very great respect and even admiration.

So far as I could, I encouraged him to think that the visit would be successful. I must confess that even early in 1960, after de Gaulle had been in power for less than two years, I had, in spite of the third volume of the memoirs, not entirely appreciated the lengths to which he was likely to go in his efforts to organize a French-led 'Europe' and to transform it into a sort of Third Force lying between the Russians and the 'Anglo-Saxons' with the emphasis on the former rather than on the latter. I therefore still believed that he might be brought to accept a 'Europe' in which a kind of balance could, within the Atlantic Alliance, be struck between the French, the Germans and the British, and indeed, as I have said, at one moment I thought that he came near to accepting this basic idea. But of course even this conception involved a sort of collective leadership, and I had not as yet understood his fundamental opposition to any such idea. In any case I assured him that he was likely to be well received, not only by the Government and in the highest circles, but also by the ordinary people in the streets. He was by no means convinced.

There was also the difficulty about the exchange of decorations. He could not confer on the Queen the highest French distinction – the Grand

Cross of the Legion of Honour – because she had it already. Nor did he particularly want to be decorated with the GCB, the highest British Order that can be conferred on foreigners, apart from the Garter which by tradition is reserved for Royal Personages. President Coty had received the GCB and rightly or wrongly de Gaulle believed that he personified France in a more intimate sense than President Coty. It was a real difficulty, overcome in the first place by my own suggestion that he might confer the Order of Liberation on the Queen and in the second place by an offer on our side to confer on him the Royal Victorian Chain, a very high distinction which had been conferred on Royal Personages in the past. And so it was arranged, the General bestowing the Order of Liberation on the Queen to hold for her late father who, having presided over the nation during the war, might be deemed to have qualified. This was, indeed, a signal honour as I believe that only two other foreigners have ever held the Order of Liberation.

In the event there was no doubt about the success of the visit. Everything went off perfectly and the crowds were imposing and enthusiastic. In Westminster Hall before the assembled Lords and Commons, and in the presence of Her Majesty, he delivered one of his most impressive orations, chiefly in praise of British institutions and no doubt entirely sincere so far as it went. The text had been distributed in advance and memorized and he scarcely departed from it by a single word. But as he himself notes in the fourth volume of his memoirs* there was absolutely no mention of Europe! In various other places he said just the right thing and went all out to please. After the banquet in the Palace, the fireworks drew a huge multitude to the park; and in the middle of the reception preceding the lunch at the Guildhall he suddenly beckoned me over to his side and said *'Monsieur l'Ambassadeur, vous m'avez bien dit que ce serait un succès et je ne vous ai pas cru. Mais maintenant je constate que vous avez eu raison'*! It was a handsome tribute.

After the spectacular visits of Khrushchev to France and indeed to Britain – and incidentally after the General's official visit to the Queen in May, which I have just described – the Summit to end all Summits was agreed upon and Paris selected as the site. In preparation for this great event the Embassy was turned upside down. The Prime Minister was to have his office in the *Salon Blanc et Or*, his secretaries in the *Salon Jaune* and the upstairs dining-room, and his sitting-room in the *Salon Vert*. Selwyn Lloyd had the library and his secretaries the room next door. Meals were to be downstairs, and some of the ground-floor rooms were to be

* Op. cit. p. 250.

meeting-places and conference centres. You might have thought it was going to be a sort of Conference of Versailles. Coming in from the airport, Freddy Bishop of No. 10 had impressed on me the absolute necessity of success; even relative failure could not be contemplated.

And then the blow fell. No sooner had the rulers assembled in the Elysée than Khrushchev announced that he would take no part in the proceedings unless Eisenhower publicly apologized for the U2 incident, and said that it would never happen again. Unless this were done he would refuse to attend any Summit meetings at the Elysée. To say that Macmillan was dismayed would be one of the greatest of understatements. He was shattered. For years he had been dreaming of the moment when he and the other leaders of this world would meet together after suitable preparations and at least lay the foundations of the settlement between East and West which would prevent another world war and enable his grandchildren – who often figured in his speculation about the future – to live happy lives in an England which, with her spacious lawns and great public and private buildings, would be contentedly resting at the apex of the civilized world. And yet there was now precious little that he could do. It was impossible to urge Eisenhower to accept Khrushchev's terms. It was impossible to get the latter to abandon his outrageous position which incidentally he vigorously maintained when he was eventually persuaded to come and see the Prime Minister in the *Salon Blanc et Or*.*

Determined to stand fast, he even brought reinforcements with him. In accordance with protocol, I met our important visitor on the steps, taking him into the hall, whence Macmillan and Lloyd† could be seen coming down the stairs. But when the long, old-fashioned Soviet car drew up it was observed that on the back-seat nearest the door, in which one might have expected to see Khrushchev, was seated no less a person than Marshal Malinovski, in uniform, on his left being an interpreter, and the Ruler of all the Russias on the off-side *strapontin*! Whether this was by design or accident I cannot say, but I duly greeted the Marshal first and then seized the hand of K. as he scuttled from behind the motor-car. As we were going up the stairs in solemn silence, the atmosphere being heavy with Anglo-Saxon displeasure, K. suddenly said (through Troyanovski, who was at his elbow) 'I wanted to come and see you, Mr Prime Minister, alone; but Malinovski said you mustn't do that, Macmillan is such a

---

* He also came to say good-bye, but nothing much happened at that interview.

† Selwyn Lloyd; Minister of Defence April-December 1955; Secretary of State for Foreign Affairs 1955–60; Chancellor of the Exchequer 1960–62; Lord Privy Seal and Leader of the House of Commons 1963–4; elected Speaker in 1971.

clever diplomat that he will run rings round you.' Upon which the Marshal scowled ferociously and looked very fierce. Was it a joke? Probably not. It is more likely that there had been tremendous rows in the Soviet camp about how best to conduct business at the Summit, and indeed there is considerable evidence to the effect that the decision to blow it up by playing the U.2 card was only taken at the last minute and perhaps even at the very last minute.

The least downcast member of our party was, however myself. As will perhaps have been noticed, I had always had grave doubts about the wisdom of actually conducting affairs at the 'Summit', such meetings being left until virtual agreement has been reached between the opposing sides. I am afraid that my relative cheerfulness was not altogether appreciated in the highest quarters. I should have been wiser to have given signs of sharing the prevailing gloom. Years later Norman Brook* told me that he thought that the post-retirement job which had been held out to me by Macmillan at the beginning of the year, when I was told I was to be a Peer, would have been something connected with the follow-up work after a successful Summit. Since this was no longer a possibility there was nothing, save conceivably a job in the Government, which I could suitably do. And even if a political job had been held out I would not have taken it for reasons already given. Not that, beyond press speculations, there was any prospect of such a job so far as I knew. So after the Summit I prepared for my departure, which was ultimately fixed for the middle of September. I was sixty and a half and had been six and a half years in Paris.

I believe that in view of my rather special relationship with the General, Selwyn Lloyd wanted me to stay on but could not get round the ironclad Treasury retirement policy. This I must say has always struck me as foolish. Much better retire a considerable number of worthy but not outstanding members of the Service during their forties and fifties with an adequate pension and no stain on their characters and in return allow a successful Ambassador to stay on till sixty-five, or even occasionally till seventy. After all, Talleyrand was still a successful Ambassador when he was eighty!

I think that one of the reasons why I got on well with the General was because I was a rather unconventional type. De Gaulle was often bored by people, more especially by people who flattered him or wanted to get something out of him. Into this category probably came about ninety-nine per cent of those he met every day. First among the one per cent was,

* Secretary to the Cabinet 1947–62.

of course, Malraux, a sort of *fou du roi*, a man in whose presence the Leader could unbend and to whose prophecies he would at least listen. Then there was Mauriac for whom he had the greatest regard, though here it must be admitted that Mauriac's articles were flattering, even adulatory, and that he did indeed get something out of de Gaulle, namely the Grande Croix de la Légion d'Honneur. Still Mauriac was unusual, to say the least; you could never be certain what he was going to say.

An example of the independent type who had the courage to speak his mind was Messmer – many of the Frenchmen whom de Gaulle tolerated seem to have names beginning with M! And if he had not at one moment been a rival leader, de Gaulle would certainly have seen more of Pierre Mendès-France. There were, of course, others whose names did not begin with M., though I don't recall them at the moment. But what emerges surely is that the General had a weakness for people with strong character and independent judgment, provided always that they said things which interested and amused him and relieved the *cafard*, the black humour, which descended on him from time to time. '*Ah, Malraux*', he is supposed to have said after the latter had made a far too long and involved, though brilliant intervention at a Cabinet meeting in his often rather inaudible monotone: '*Ah, Malraux, des nuages, des nuages, mais parfois des éclairs.*' It was indeed the *éclairs* that de Gaulle appreciated. As Diaghilev said to Cocteau, so might he often have said to Malraux and the other Ms, '*étonne-moi*'.

I remember one December afternoon at the end of 1959, towards the end of my mission, I was standing in a butt at the last drive at Marly where the President had very kindly asked me to shoot since I had had to miss the official diplomatic *battue* at Rambouillet. Behind me were a uniformed loader and a marker. The pheasants were to come out of a little wood some hundreds of yards in front. They were expected, but had not yet arrived. Suddenly on the road to my right a motorcade appeared and out of the second car stepped the enormous figure of the General. Rapidly changing from his uniform, he put on a cape and a hat and strode down the line to my butt where he took up position on my left just on the other side of the marker. The butt was not very capacious and when the birds came to the left I had, as it were, to shoot round the President excusing myself at the same time for doing so. Luckily I was in form and only missed one or two. The General was delighted. His eyesight prevented him from shooting himself, but a high bird, taken properly, excited his admiration. '*Très bien, bien descendu!*' he exclaimed, as the pheasants thudded down. We went on to lunch at the little keeper's house at

Marly-le-Roi, in the very room where I had had my celebrated interview with Mendès-France.

It was hardly the moment to draw de Gaulle deeply on political matters, though I seem to remember that the name of Khrushchev did come up and we learned that he had a considerable admiration for this genial moujik, though a little preoccupied about how to treat him during his forthcoming visit. A boar-hunt at Chambord followed by a banquet in the Chateau was my own contribution. He did say, however, that he thought it not impossible that Khrushchev, for reasons of his own, probably did desire some form of *détente*. When I observed that K. would clearly do his best to divide the Allies, and that what he might want a *détente* for was in order to get a neutralized Germany, the General did not dissent but turned the conversation. He was then a little sniffy about NATO and Paul-Henri Spaak and was very properly rebuked by Aubrey Casardi, the Italian Ambassador to NATO, who observed that it was not only Spaak but surely all of us who ought to be proud of that organization. Leaving politics I asked him about the poem which he was alleged to have written as a young man, the existence of which was not then generally known. The General told us something about this now celebrated epic and the mood in which it was written and we then got on to literature generally. At one point in this discussion, though I cannot remember exactly in relation to what, I said:

Ah Dieu, l'étrange peine. Faut-il laisser un affront impuni? Faut-il punir le père de Chimène?

The President paused and looked at me rather intently 'Are you surprised,' I said, 'to hear Corneille quoted?' 'No', he replied, 'I am not surprised to hear Corneille quoted; but I am surprised to hear him quoted by you!'

There remained one final function – the farewell dinner at the Elysée. It had been intimated to me that the General had this in mind, which was in itself an exceptional honour for a departing Ambassador. But what was my surprise when the Protocol inquired which of the Embassy staff I would like to receive invitations, and indeed which of my French friends I would like to be invited too? It was evident that it was to be a grand occasion. In the event no less than 134 persons sat down at one table in the grand ballroom of the Elysée. The General himself was particularly affable. When it came to the speeches, he made some very obliging remarks about myself and Cynthia, whom he referred to as 'a great Ambassadress'. In reply, I dwelt on the theme that both Britain and France were now in much the same situation. Both were great nations who had often been great rivals but were now passing out of an imperial phase and into a new era in which they would have above all to cooperate even more closely in the narrower field of Europe. It seemed to me that we should both of us henceforward have to think of new ways to express our national personalities and I ended up quoting the great words of Chateaubriand:

Rien n'est plus vain que la gloire à moins qu'elle n'ait fait vivre l'amitié, qu'elle n'ait été utile à la vertu, secourable au malheur.

This over, and before we all got up, I said 'You will hardly believe it, *Monsieur le Président*, but I am quite *ému*!' The General thought this was very funny, and I could see that my stock, already high, was visibly rising. We parted on the best of terms.

When I got home I continued to hope against hope that the General would eventually come to some arrangement regarding 'Europe'. I even towards the end of 1962, gave an interview to Kenneth Harris of the *Observer* in which I said things which I hoped might influence him to some degree. But the veto of January 1963 seemed to me to demonstrate finally that only total opposition to his policies would be likely to have any effect, and from then on I did my best to frustrate his moves so far as it lay in my power to do so, even if this meant abandoning all attempts to influence him directly by playing on the personal friendship which had developed between us when I was Ambassador. Naturally, for a period of time it would in any case have been impossible for me to pursue this friendship, if only out of consideration for my successor. But in the summer of 1964, in spite of my many blasts against his policy, I got strong hints in Paris that the General would like to see me again and after consulting the FO I asked the French Ambassador to find out whether there was anything in them. He wrote Etienne Burin des Roziers who replied, to Courcel's apparent surprise, that a visit would indeed be welcome. All I had to do was to apply for one through the Embassy. This I did and the appointment was fixed for 4 September.

There was the same gloomy figure behind the familiar bureau, but what a difference compared to the last time I had seen the General in the flesh, at the great farewell banquet! It was quite a shock. I thought de Gaulle looked old, tired and ill. The sparkle had gone, and in a curious way he seemed to me to be less confident. Gone too was the old roguishness, the *méchanceté*, which often enlivened our serious talks. His reception of me however was kindness itself, and even affectionate, if such an adjective could be applied to the General. I was quite touched. But on the whole, though intellectually fully alert, he seemed to be lacking in vitality, and sad, sad, as if overcome by the cares of the world and the incurable stupidity of the human race. What was rather staggering, however, was his opening remark. Since my departure from Paris, he observed, he had read my articles and my speeches, and to a great extent he was in agreement with them! Was it possible that the General had not been informed of my increasingly hostile criticism of his foreign policy? How could I have given him the impression that I was, politically, on his side? But after some discussion about the *Détente*, during which he remarked that after all there would be no war and that we could go on for some time quite happily even in the absence of a German settlement, it was evident that what he wanted to talk about was the prospect of eventually arriving at some common European solution of the long-term problems confronting Britain and Europe.

I therefore seized the opportunity to say a piece about the General's attitude towards Britain. He had often told me in the past, and he had said quite recently, that Britain must at some stage join some kind of European confederation. If this was still his idea it was really no good thinking that it would be advanced by an apparent policy of carrying on without any regard for Britain at all and indeed by acting as if this rather large island had suddenly ceased to exist. Indeed, such a policy might well result in what he apparently most dreaded, namely the permanent separation of Britain from Europe and the formation of a real 'Anglo-Saxon' bloc. In any case, my firm conviction was that if it was a question of making Europe – any kind of Europe – it was impossible to do so without Britain, just as it was impossible to do so without France. It seemed to me that recent events in Europe had confirmed this thesis. I only hoped therefore that fairly soon after our elections it would be possible, if it were not already too late, to take up once again the political issue and discover exactly what kind of Europe, politically speaking, it was that France and Great Britain jointly desired. As he knew, in my view, this would not be a federal conception in the sense of setting up a sovereign assembly or electing a president of Europe. But on the other hand it must be something more definite than a mere alliance or association. If so, what?

At this point the General broke in with a longish piece about how it was true that he had said that Britain would eventually have to join a confederation (he agreed that this was a word which could be dropped, and we could call it a community if desired) and he certainly wished that this would some day come about, but he had definitely formed the impression that Britain was not ready to take this step in January 1963 economically, and certainly not from the political and military point of view either – in fact the old story about the Commonwealth, and Mr Macmillan and the final revelation of England's true policy at Nassau which we know so well and which there is no need for me to repeat, except perhaps that, in the course of it, he said that there had really been much too much exaggeration in this controversy. Mr Macmillan, for instance, had told him that if Britain were excluded from the Common Market it would be a return to the system of the *Neuordnung* or Napoleon's Continental blockade. Well, Britain had not joined the Common Market and what had happened? British exports to the Six had attained record heights and there was increased prosperity all round. Strange blockade!

When I could get in again, I said that, whatever the situation had been a year or two ago, times changed and we changed with them. The general situation after the elections in Britain and America might well be quite different, and it was to be hoped, I thought, that whatever government came into power in Britain, the question of Britain's relationship with Western Europe should be high on the agenda of any talks we might then have with the French. It seemed to me, however, if I might respectfully say so, that it could not be a question of Britain's saying she wanted to join something that was completely 'independent' of America since, for so long as the alliance lasted; the American troops were in Germany; and we were in the last resort dependent on the immense nuclear power of America, we could none of us in any real sense be 'independent' of the United States. But what we could do was to form a political Europe which might be described, if not as independent, at any rate as 'autonomous' in the sense of an organization which would somehow or other enable decisions to be taken jointly. The exact means by which such decisions would be taken could be determined once the will for political union had manifested itself. But if it did manifest itself it could be clear that something new had come about in international politics.

This was the way, as I saw it, to prevent the gradual drifting away of Germany towards Russia or, alternatively, the formation of an American-German alliance as the main prop of the Western world. If one accepted the idea of an autonomous Western Europe within the framework of the Western alliance, one could soon arrive at solutions which would not divide the alliance but would rather cause it to function properly. If one did not accept it then either the alliance would disappear or it would in practice rest on an American hegemony and nothing more. In particular, I had no doubt that if the General at some stage indicated his willingness to talk about some political union between the Six and Great Britain, most of his present difficulties with his fellow-members of the Community (he was at that time, of course, in a very anti-German mood) would vanish overnight. It would have to be evident that Britain in such circumstances would agree in principle to accept the political and economic implications of the Treaty of Rome. The General might disagree, but I personally thought she had really done so two years ago, and there was no particular reason why in certain circumstances she should not do so again. What was essential, however, was that the General himself should take the initiative (it did not seem to me very likely that Britain would do so), otherwise I thought it only too likely that events would take a course which all those who believed in the unity of Europe could only deplore. After all, France, if she played her cards well, had much to gain from a political union which included the UK. Paris could be the military and political, as it was the geographical, centre of the new formation; London the economic and financial centre; industry might be mainly represented in the Ruhr; Brussels could continue to be the administrative capital; Rome always had the Pope. It was a grand conception and I only hoped that one day the General would make it his own. He was already the greatest Frenchman; why should he not be the greatest European too?

There was a pause. I had evidently made a point. Then the General said that if there really was a genuine indication on the part of any British Government that this was its intention, the situation would indeed be changed. On the other hand, what he would never, never agree to was any sacrifice of national sovereignty. (This was said rather defensively, but with passion.) I said it was not a case of sacrificing sovereignty, but of agreeing to take certain decisions in common. All kinds of techniques could be applied to this end including that of a political commission. I could not for the life of me see why the General should be opposed to this general idea. After all, he could appoint someone like Joxe, if he liked.

De Gaulle did not dissent. There was another pause and he asked me who was likely to win the election. I said that my hunch was that the Labour Party would do so but that some of the polls gave the Conservatives a slight majority. One of the factors was that whichever party came into power with a very small majority was not likely to last for very long. Unless a party could arrange for a reasonable majority, say something over fifteen, the best thing would probably be to put the other side in. Unfortunately, this kind of thing could not be arranged and we should just have to wait and see what happened. The General said that, as I would know (I didn't know. I had indeed heard that he would prefer a victory of *les Tra-*

vaillistes), he wished 'with all his heart' that the Conservatives would get in with a reasonable majority, because after that it might really be possible, he thought, to do some business, but he was afraid that this would not happen and then it was very difficult to say how things would work out. He imagined that the majority of the Labour Party in Parliament, if Labour got in, would be predominantly anti-European? I said that I feared that his might be so, though I hoped not; but even if it were the logic of events would, in my view, after a rather longer period, result in negotiations being once again taken up for Britain's entry into Europe. That, however, was only my personal point of view and might well be wishful thinking.

Commenting on this I made a few obvious points. In the first place the General was obviously in a mood of acute disillusionment as regards Germany and would probably like to reinsure himself somehow if he could. But a separate deal with the Russians was now clearly out. Moreover, though he would block British entry he could not really hope to form a European political community based on French hegemony only. Short of becoming the 'Leader of the Uncommitted World' – for which rather thankless role he seemed to be making a bid – he therefore probably felt himself in an *impasse*. All this, in the light of hindsight, was very true but where I was not necessarily right – and certainly too optimistic – was in going on to suggest that he did not exclude the entry of the UK into some European political community in the reasonably near future – perhaps even before there could be agreement on her entering the EEC itself. He *might* even take an initiative in this sense himself – more especially if the Conservatives got back into power (and in fact he did four years later though only after his calamitous second veto). It was quite true that for so long as he was in power he would never agree to the slightest derogation from national sovereignty. But he might be persuaded that certain 'Community techniques' did not involve a derogation from sovereignty after all. And anyhow it was the first step which counted.

Whether I was too optimistic in this analysis or not the reader can himself judge in the light of subsequent events (certainly I was wrong in my estimate of his physical condition). But the advice I then gave the Government as a result of this analysis was, I am still sure, correct.

'The best line', I said, 'would seem to be to suggest to him that by arranging for us to come into some new European political community which might (if only to annoy Hallstein and Jean Monnet) be formed before we actually get into the Market, is the only way to save France, no doubt after his death, from becoming a satellite either of Germany or of America. His strong suspicion that we are ourselves merely a devoted satellite of America might be overcome by assurances that we are sincerely in favour of an "autonomous" Western Europe, though of course for so long as America has such a preponderance of nuclear weapons and the situation is such that her troops must remain in Europe we can only think of such an autonomous Western Europe as being within the framework of the Western Alliance. But this conception would have to be put over to him, no doubt by some British Prime Minister with the ability to make the necessary contact.'

It does, indeed, now appear to have been put over by a British Prime Minister to another French President and we must all hope that the move was not made too late.

Some five months after this interview I again saw the General, as it turned out for the last time. Churchill had died and Michael Stewart had appointed me his special representative attached to the President of France. After the ceremony I was asked to look in at the Embassy where I had a quarter of an hour's conversation with the great man. The General started off by saying, very amiably, that he always enjoyed exchanging views with me, but this time it was really to tell me how profoundly impressed he had been by the funeral and by the extraordinary efficiency of all the arrangements. He had moreover been delighted again to have had the honour of meeting Her Majesty, the Queen, whose reception of him at the Palace had been most gracious. And he had also much enjoyed talking to the *jeune Prince* and *jeune Princesse* about whom he was most complimentary.

Not only had he been impressed by the funeral, but also much moved. In particular the Heralds had impressed him and indeed I had noted how he seemed to concentrate on this during the service to the exclusion of almost anything else. It seemed to him that the ceremony had been symbolic of the perennial greatness of *l'Angleterre*. Here was a national sentiment which should never be extinguished: something that was part of history and would in all probability, he thought, endure. I was a European, he knew that; but whatever solution I recommended he did hope that I would not support anything which tended to diminish or blur the Englishness of England, its integrity, its identity, so to speak. He naturally hoped that France would preserve her national identity also.

I said that if I had thought that the eventual association of Britain with Western Europe would have the effect that he feared I would certainly never have recommended it. But it seemed to me that if 'Europe' by any chance could not be formed there was much more chance that both Britain and France would be merged in some larger whole that really might suppress their essential individuality. Naturally, if 'Europe' ever did emerge, arrangements would have to be made for certain decisions to be taken in common. But they would be taken as between equals, and France and Britain should, as equals, be seen to be taking the lead.

However, this was clearly not the occasion to argue the European case in detail, and the General began to tease me slightly about my joining the Liberals, which great event, he said, had been brought to his attention. I said that the Liberals were a small group in Parliament, though a considerable one in the country and that I hoped and believed that their views on Europe would become more and more acceptable. The General smiled wanly. He had, as we know, a mind above party politics. 'At any rate', he observed, 'for goodness' sake don't give away your atom bomb.' We proceeded to the airport and just as he was leaving, Burin des Roziers said that the General always enjoyed talking to me and that if I ever felt the need for consulting him in the future I had only to ring up and an interview could be arranged.

Three months later I published my first book entitled *The European Idea*. There was a chapter in it containing very severe criticism of the General's foreign policy, which, incidentally, as time went on, seemed to me to become more and more indefensible and self-destructive. Rightly or wrongly – and as I now believe wrongly – I did not send a copy of this work to my old friend. It contained, for instance, such phrases as:

It is quite possible that we are all taking the recent attitudes of the General too seriously. The apparent nihilism is principally designed to delight the more unsuspecting of the French and thus persuade them to keep the General in office. . . . Apparent contradictions or anomalies in French foreign policy cannot therefore be taken at their face value. They are *tours de force*, designed to astonish the bourgeois, performed in perfect safety to a dazzled audience over the useful safety net of American nuclear supremacy.

I thought that these would wound him, as indeed might the various stories which I was then in the habit of telling about him such as that he combined the qualities of two of the most famous of French monarchs – *l'état c'est moi, et après moi le déluge*! For the same reason I never applied again for an interview. I don't suppose I could really have influenced him very much, but it is just possible that I might have inclined him to make certain suggestions for the start of political union in Western Europe or even discussed with him the ideas advanced in my subsequent book – even more critical of his policy – entitled *De Gaulle's Europe or Why the*

General Says No. At least I could have tried. Anyhow it is seldom the things you do that you regret; it is the things you do not do. Never miss an opportunity if you can help it; always follow your own hunches and your 'star'.

On his resignation I sent an appreciation to the *Daily Telegraph*. So far as his policy was concerned this effort could scarcely be described as flattering. However just before his death I received a package from Paris and on opening it to my great surprise discovered a copy of the fourth volume of the memoirs with a quite affectionate *dédicace*. I was staggered that after the publication of my two books and the virtual campaign which I had waged for some six years against his policy the General should have made such a gesture. And slightly embarrassed too, because if he sent me his book it was clearly incumbent on me to send him mine. I therefore composed what I thought was a masterly letter enclosing both *The European Idea* and *Europe After De Gaulle* and sent it off on 26 October. The next news I had was of his death. It was considered a good story in Paris that it was my books that had killed him. But after a time a paragraph in *Le Monde* made it clear that my letter along with others from the Pope and the Shah of Iran were in the *courrier* which was on the point of being shown him by his secretary. I must say I wonder what he would have made of them. Perhaps he might even have consented to receive me once again as I had suggested in the letter. As the attentive reader will have already discerned, I was really rather fond of him.

When he did die, I paid genuine, if critical, tribute to him on 15 November in the *Sunday Times*. Nancy Mitford said it was the best that had been published about the General in either language and the very Gaullist Romain Gary liked it too. But if my considered judgment has to be summed up shortly I think I should end up with a quotation. In 1967 *Réalités* asked me to fill in a questionnaire on what changes would take place in France, in Europe and in the world if de Gaulle relinquished power. Question nine was, 'Could you state briefly what a history-book of the year 2000 might say about the influence General de Gaulle had on world affairs in his time?' To this I replied: 'He was an outstanding character who restored to the French a sense of dignity and purpose. But his contempt of any opposition, and a certain natural arrogance, led him into positions which were indefensible and to the adoption of policies which the French nation was not strong enough to carry out.' Question ten was, 'Which historical figure could be most nearly equated with de Gaulle?' My answer: 'All such comparisons are dangerous. It would be rash to compare the General to anyone save perhaps Joan of Arc.'

19

Pursuit of Europe
(1960-5)

Most politicians and higher civil servants (more particularly the latter) suffer agonies of deprivation, I believe, on leaving their comfortable offices. No more certainty of active and pleasant employment; no longer a large and dependable staff; above all, no more Red Boxes. The real world is behind one, and the end, presumably, at hand. Some, of course, adapt themselves to their new life quite easily. Others are just happy and relieved. Many occupy themselves most profitably. But all, unless they are exhausted, are left with the problem of how best to occupy their time. My own deprivation symptoms were less violent, perhaps partly as a result of the offer of employment extended by Harold Macmillan, to which I have already referred. Also, the break with my old career was less abrupt than it might otherwise have been, Alec Home, then Foreign Secretary, having very kindly put a room in the Foreign Office at my disposal for a week or two for the purpose of bringing up to date, with a view to publication, a dispatch which I had written a year or so previously on the general subject of the 'Balance of Terror', the likelihood of avoiding nuclear war and the consequences of so doing. The dispatch had been sent around the Service for comments and I embodied some of these in the final version which was eventually published in the *Daily Telegraph*. But if these memoirs are not to be intolerably long I propose to deal chiefly with what occupied by far the greater part of my time after my retirement from the Foreign Service, namely the 'Pursuit of Europe'.

It was on 7 December 1960, that I made my first speech on this subject since leaving Paris. I said that it looked as if the Government had more or less outlined their own 'sticking points', but had not as yet come to any definite decision. What was necessary now was a 'declaration that we should for our part be prepared to negotiate on the basis of the acceptance by us, and of such of our associates as were prepared to do likewise, of a common tariff'. If such negotiations were successful I believed myself that we should be better off economically. But the principal object would be 'the reaching of a political goal which might change the whole of world politics for the better'. However (I continued)

if such a spectacular advance were made . . . it could only be with the conscious intention on our part of starting afresh and of subscribing, basically, to the opposite thesis to that on which up to now we have been prepared to work. For if we do negotiate on the basis of a common tariff and if such a common tariff is eventually achieved, there will be no going back. We shall have embarked on the road which will lead, as it always has led in the past, to some form of political unification. This may take years to achieve; in the case of Europe it may, and most likely will, be consistent with the maintenance of our independent political systems and our great traditions, but come it will, provided only the initial hurdle is surmounted.

It was unlikely, therefore, that any such statement would be made until the full consequences had been carefully weighed. But if it was never made then I believed that we should in the long run be taken over by America, unless we went in for unilateral disarmament, when we should eventually be taken over by the Soviet Union. Equally, if we did take the crucial decision, and the Six still would not play, the long-term consequences might be much the same. It would be a grave decision for the Six to take since the results of an exclusion of the United Kingdom from the Continent might well from their own point of view be highly undesirable. But again if we did make a statement and the Europeans did negotiate, realizing that the United Kingdom this time was in earnest, then it would be clear that at long last the construction of a United Europe – of General de Gaulle's European confederation if you wished – was under way. It was a general declaration of faith on my part from which I have never departed. As I write it seems likely to be transformed into reality.

After this effort the Foreign Office asked me whether I would like to become the chairman of a body known as 'Britain in Europe', the object of which was to act as a centre for research into the possibilities of creating an entity in Western Europe, chiefly from the economic point of view. This job was right up my street and soon we were considering ways and means of launching out in other directions on a mounting wave of enthusiasm for the European cause.

In mid-January I had to go to Paris to attend a meeting of the newly formed Atlantic Institute, a brainchild of what was then called the 'NATO parliamentarians', then, as now, doing very useful work in pushing the general idea of Atlantic unity without in any way discouraging European unity. To my surprise I found Paris buzzing with rumours that I was to be the next Secretary-General of NATO, Paul-Henri Spaak having decided to resign. And, strange to say, the gossip was that my name had been mentioned in this connection by no less a person than General de Gaulle. Even stranger, a Frenchman fairly high up in the Gaullist hierarchy informed me that this was true. Arriving back in London I therefore inquired of No. 10 whether there was anything in the rumour, explaining that, while I was not a candidate, I could hardly refuse the Secretary-Generalship if it were offered to me. I was informed in reply that while my name had in fact been mentioned in this connection it had not come up at Rambouillet where Harold Macmillan had just (5 February) had a meeting with de Gaulle. So I assumed, possibly wrongly, that Her Majesty's Government for their part preferred the candidature of Dirk Stikker of Holland. No doubt they were right, and in any case I expect I should have found the job pretty frustrating. But I must say I wonder whether events would have turned out just as they did if I had been in a position to argue with the General, with whom I was at that time on the best of terms. No doubt we should not have remained on the best of terms for long.

A few days later I made my maiden speech in the House of Lords speaking from the cross-benches, that is to say as a member of no party. It was not on the subject of Europe, but during a debate on NATO. On this subject I think my views were pretty conventional but I presented them with a European slant. At the moment, I said, the nation simply did not know where it was going or what it wanted to do. 'The process of decolonization has left us without any very positive and generally accepted notion of our position in the world and of the role which we should play, either alone, or in conjunction with the Commonwealth and our neighbours. It looks as if our ex-Imperial nation might have to devise some new national ideology.' When Dean Acheson said much the same thing a few years later I was, however, annoyed, and stupidly so, though it is true he talked about our having 'lost an Empire' which was irritating and not altogether factual.

The next day I found myself addressing Chatham House on 'France and Europe'. For a long time, I said, the French thought there was little difference between the two expressions. *Gesta Dei per Francos* was the term used in the Middle Ages to indicate the works of God as performed by his Franks. If you excepted the Muscovites – those shadowy half-Tartar figures lurking in the background – France, after the monarchy was finally established, was by far the largest European state, and remained the largest until 1870. Twice she had attempted to unify the Continent physically under her hegemony. Once (for a short time) she had actually succeeded.

When she was in a bad way she sometimes thought, even then, of merging herself in a larger whole (witness Sully's *Grand Dessein*) but usually the idea was that the Continent should simply accommodate itself to French customs and, indeed, to French political dominance. Even after she was clearly surpassed as the leading European state from the point of view of population and production, French remained (until 1918) the sole recognized diplomatic language. Finally, the formation of an African empire, unwisely encouraged by Bismarck, gave France the feeling that, backed by her extra-continental projection and by her famous *réservoir d'hommes*, she might yet overcome the Prussian contender for the leadership title. The temporary collapse of Germany in 1918 revived these hopes. If the work of 1870 could be undone, or largely undone, France might still, with her empire and her European satellite states, be the dominant power on the continent of Europe. Had she occupied the Rhineland permanently and formed some confederation of the Rhine in association with herself, as advocated by Foch, this development might have come about.

But the effort was beyond France's power. The losses in the 1914–18 war had been too great. The opposition of the so-called Anglo-Saxon Powers to such effort was too weighty. In 1928 Briand, reverting to Sully, produced the famous French plan for a European Union – a sort of federation. This was in itself an acknowledgement that the dream of French hegemony had been abandoned. Unfortunately it was before its time and in the face of British incomprehension and, indeed, hostility, the scheme faded into nothing. In any case, the rise of Hitler dashed the secular hopes of France, and in 1940 seemed to have doomed them for ever. Ever since 1870 some French voices had been raised in favour of a Franco-German association or understanding, and after 1932 and the rise of Hitler these redoubled in intensity, gaining the upper hand in France under the Pétain regime of 1940–4. Unexpectedly England stood firm. A world coalition took shape. Once again the Reich was utterly defeated. Once again France, this time to her considerable surprise, found herself restored to her pre-war position, complete with a gigantic overseas empire. Was European hegemony really again possible? Or was the time now ripe for France to merge herself in Europe as Briand had advocated nearly twenty years before?

After the end of the first brief Gaullist experiment in 1946, it became clear that the Fourth Republic had chosen the second course. In 1948, France took the lead in negotiations for the Council of Europe. In 1950, the first real step towards union with Germany – the European Coal and Steel Community – came about. In 1950, too, the European Defence

Community – a French initiative – was first mooted. It failed, for the French themselves got cold feet and killed it; but the general tendency was apparently irreversible. 1957 saw the completion of what might well prove to be the greatest of all French achievements, the Treaty of Rome. The second Gaullist regime, which shortly followed, provoked by the failure of the Fourth Republic to cope with the problem of decolonization, notably in Algeria, might have been expected to try to reverse this trend, never accepted by the extreme nationalists, who continued to live entirely in the past. Nothing of the kind occurred. The trend towards the merging of France in Europe was actually accentuated. The entry into the Common Market was even speeded up: the remains of the overseas empire were given complete liberty; the *réservoir d'hommes* disappeared; instead of a French it became clearer and clearer that the objective of General de Gaulle was an autonomous and, if necessary in the long run, an independent Algeria. Only the decision to accelerate the manufacture of an atomic bomb and the evident desire of General de Gaulle that France should be recognized as representing 'Europe' in some three-Power directorate of the Western world, seemed to conflict in practice with the general tendency. It was, in fact, specifically stated that France, a *'puissance à intérêts mondiaux'*, was in a special category which neither Germany nor Italy had the right to enter. In other words, at the same time as the empire, as such, was liquidated, the claim was made that her overseas obligations conferred on France a special European status. How was this apparent paradox to be explained? The answer, in a word, was Britain. General de Gaulle was determined that for so long as we desired to be a 'World Power', he would also put in such a claim for France. Were we ever to abandon this position he would no doubt have to consider the possibility of admitting us to his 'confederation'. But even if he had decided in his own mind to exclude us he might find it difficult to do so before the Six had really sealed their union, and, more especially, before he had ended the Algerian war. I do not think that my seven years in France were entirely mis-spent; for this analysis to say nothing of the prognosis, is surely rather difficult to rebut.

Same theme in my second speech in the House of Lords on 9 February. There were three possible ways, I thought, in which our country might 'develop in freedom' (and I summarize very briefly). Stay as we were, trying to work the 'Three Circles' philosophy of Churchill – namely operating in the sphere of the Commonwealth and of EFTA with our 'special relations' with America and our 'independent deterrent'; ever increasing union with, and eventual absorption by the USA; or eventual entry into a European confederation of some sort. The first seemed to be

337

impossible, and if pursued would result in isolation; the second was perhaps the most likely; the third was difficult, but not impossible. Forming part of an 'Atlantic community' was not a policy, but an aspiration. I believed, therefore, that we should say we wanted to negotiate with the Six on the basis of a common tariff and of our acceptance of the political obligations of the Treaty of Rome. I did not think that de Gaulle would prevent such negotiations from taking place; and if they did take place they could not fail. (At this time I was still persuaded that we could, in the negotiations, obtain agreement on the free import of the bulk of our foodstuffs.) But if we once accepted the principle of a common tariff we should have to recognize that 'in ten years' time or sooner' we should form only a part of some greater whole – an active partner among equals no doubt, which would not be the case if we joined America but nevertheless, a part of a whole. This effort, I fear, did not appeal to all. The *Financial Times* thought it was grand, it is true, but *The Times* remarked severely that I was 'trying to stampede the nation'!

On 1 March, Roy Jenkins, for whom I have always had the greatest respect and regard, no doubt as a result of all these pronouncements, asked me to have a drink with him in the House of Commons and inquired whether I would, additionally, like to take on the chairmanship of a 'Campaign for the Common Market' which was in the process of being formed. A number of enthusiastic British 'Europeans' were behind this campaign, he said, including some definite 'federalists', though these were 'none the worse for that'. I said that I was not personally a 'federalist', in the sense that I did not believe that we could arrive at central European institutions equivalent to a Federal government on the lines of the USA for a long period of time, if ever (an attitude which, incidentally, I have never abandoned) and that it was best to go only very gradually in this direction; but I had absolutely no objection to working with federalists who believed that the British might be persuaded to go faster than I believed was possible myself. The great thing was to start. Besides, if we joined soon, we should be able to influence the progress of the Community in whichever way we thought best. The same applied in the economic field, in which no common policy, notably as regards agriculture, had as yet been established. Everything pointed therefore to an early entry; the longer we waited the more diffcult it would be. 'Certainly', said Roy, 'and that is why we must mount a Campaign to show the Government that important people in every party and in every walk of life are in favour of this. I have the impression that Macmillan wants to apply for membership of the EEC if he can get enough support.'

Thus the Common Market Campaign was started, and quite soon we had 130 signatures (there were eventually about 150, including 32 MPs, 20 Peers of all parties, and many illustrious names in industry, finance, the law, religion, the TUC and so on) of a manifesto issued on 25 May, in which we effectively said that Britain must soon decide whether she wanted to play her full part in a dynamic new power or to be increasingly cut off from the Continent. In our view the Government should now 'formally and explicitly declare their readiness to join the EEC and accept the institutions of the Treaty of Rome'. This declaration subscribed by so many members of the Establishment did have a considerable effect.

Perhaps I should add at this point that before the declaration was issued I had been producing a considerable number of articles and letters to the press reinforcing the general argument for negotiating and then signing the Treaty of Rome and in no way discounting, indeed rather underlining, all the potentially supra-national consequences of so doing. It cannot, indeed, be said with any accuracy that I failed, so far as I was concerned, to tell the public the truth. In speech after speech – most eloquently perhaps in the House of Lords on 21 June – I said that they would not only have to be prepared, on the economic front, to change their way of life to a considerable extent and accept certain short-term disadvantages and up-sets, but also that they would have to recognize that, if we came into the Community, certain decisions affecting our whole future would be taken elsewhere than in Westminster by a body on which we should, of course, be well represented but on which we should have no absolute veto.

Some of the phrases used may bear repetition. At Nottingham I informed some startled Conservatives that the path leading to the Common Market would be littered with the corpses of sacred cows. It was, I later said in the House of Lords in a debate on the Commonwealth and the Common Market, 'pathetic to oppose our entry into the EEC – and thus to pre-judice the defence of the free world against Communism – because it might in a few years conceivably put up the price of a British sausage, and not realize that if we remain divided the price of sausages may well be determined, not in Brussels, but in some place much further East.' Whether we could join would indeed 'depend upon the economic terms that we can get' but 'the political issue should by no means be pushed under the rug'. Thus, if we joined, we should not by ourselves be able to change the Common External Tariff; certain measures designed to protect our indus-tries and our balance of payments might well be the subject of a collective rather than an individual decision; we should in certain circumstances have to accept the verdict of a Court. In general, we should be undertaking a binding and, as it were, an organic commitment 'wider than and different in kind from our commitments under existing treaties'. Whether the whole thing would end up as a confederation or a federation or merely as some form of political association nobody could predict and it was useless to say 'we must know in advance exactly where we are going'.

But the risk would not be enormous since under the Treaty of Rome a supra-national parliament would (in practice) only be set up by common consent, which meant that if we came in, we ourselves, if we so wished, could veto any notable advance towards a federation. However, if we joined we should be taking at least the first step in linking ourselves with a wider European association of some kind and within a fairly short period some important decisions – it was no good blinking this fact – would take place outside our country, even though it was quite unlikely that this would happen except after long debate in Parliament and presumably with its full agreement. In any case we were approaching the moment of truth. Since the Commonwealth no longer existed as a political forum, either we should have to become a modern nation in a twentieth-century sense or we should go under. How could we achieve a new status consonant with but not overshadowed by our tremendous past? Only by combining with other ancient states, our neighbours, who were in much the same state of historical development as we were. Many accused me of being 'no politician'. But I stoutly maintained, and maintain still, that it is not only dangerous but also useless to delude the public.

We were by now in the final phase before the announcement on 31 July by the Prime Minister ('for ever amber', according to an increasingly indignant Lady Violet Bonham Carter) that we were applying for membership of the Common Market; and I see that on the day before I had been writing in the *Guardian* about 'The political commitment'. Here, while explaining quite frankly what the limitations would be on our freedom of action, I said that if we came in at the stage now reached in the development of the Community, we should have every opportunity (within a system of majority voting) of influencing its general policy and of persuading it – if that should be our intention – to become 'outward' rather than 'inward'-looking. In this effort we should have, within the Community, very powerful allies. As for the Commission, it was not something to be dreaded, but greatly to be welcomed, and our own civil servants were likely to 'take to it as ducks to water'. The parliament for its part, could not be directly elected without our consent, and the jurisdiction of the court, though real and important, should not worry us overmuch. We should also, of course, have to accept the objectives – the long-term policies – of the Community. All these were good in themselves and we should have to do our best to work towards them.

But in all these fields [I continued] it is quite evident that until we advance, of our own volition, much further along the federal road, no great state is going, so to speak, to be put in a minority of one and simply overruled by a majority. Nor is any state in practice going to tolerate, during this period, any system which would result in mass unemployment in, say, Coventry or Turin. The whole system will work by consent within the framework of the common tariff and with the wheels oiled by the patient efforts of international officials. After a time the benefits of the process will become so potent that many people will begin to wonder what the initial fuss was all about. Eventually the whole thing will no doubt end up in some form of confederation.

The question was, could this country with its old traditions accept the disciplines inherent in the common tariff? Was it still young enough to adapt itself, if necessary by revolutionary means, to current world conditions; or was it fated, under octogenarian inspiration, to be slowly stifled beneath the decaying weight of its imperial past? Somehow, with the aid of the young, we must get out of our present nineteenth-century rut and join the mainstream of mid-twentieth-century history. At much greater length I developed these points in the speech I made on 2 August in the House of Lords during the discussion of our application. The kind of European confederation to which we, together with that great leader, General de Gaulle, might legitimately aspire was something that would in no way involve our country in any *diminutio capitis*, but rather would raise it to new heights as regards its influence and standing in the world.

It will be observed in what terms I referred to the General. This was partly because I then felt that he could hardly prevent our entry if we showed our willingness to accept the political implications of the Treaty of Rome; and partly because I believed that praising him would help along the right decision. How wrong I was on both counts! But I repeat that, looking back, our effort was surely justified, and that, if it had been made six months earlier, and pushed with vigour on the political side, it might even have succeeded.

After the holidays I naturally stopped advocating and restricted my activities to explaining what might happen when and if we joined the EEC. Thus the prospects for the homologation of laws were examined before the Law Society and the trade prospects in Manchester. I also recall that, with great trepidation, I took on Manny Shinwell* at the University

---

* Emanuel Shinwell: Left-wing Labour MP; held various ministries in the post-war Labour Government, including Fuel and Power.

of London Union and in spite of the fact that the audience consisted mostly of excited socialist and black undergraduates, succeeded in defeating him by a majority of over two to one. Never have I been so surprised, not even when, six years later, I held that great tribune, Michael Foot, to a tie before the Oxford Union on precisely the same motion. Perhaps I should have gone in for politics after all? Had I misconceived my *métier*? I do recall that my old adversary, but personal friend, Yakov Alessandrovitch Malik, had once told me that William Strang was his idea of a supremely good *chinovnik* (official). Ivone Kirkpatrick, he thought, was a pretty good official too. And I myself, I rather nervously inquired? No, said Malik, kindly but firmly, 'I would not regard you as a *chinovnik*.' I took the point. I was never really cut out to be an official.

In October I addressed a dinner organized by J. J. Servan-Schreiber's father, Emile, then the proprietor of *Les Echos* at which, in the presence of my successor, Bob Dixon, I raised the question of the identity of 'Western Man' and whether 'Europeans' could be defined in any realistic way. If America was, indeed, as de Gaulle maintained, the 'daughter' of Europe, then Russia, whom he sometimes appeared to include in the family, was, in view of her quite separate cultural development, at best the 'cousin', while Britain, in spite of her record, was undoubtedly a much closer associate and might perhaps best be described as the stepmother, or possibly the mother-in-law of Europe! As for France she had for long held the most important position in that family of *la fille aînée* – the elder daughter. It was true that the title had been conferred on her by the Pope, but at a time when perhaps the Pope did speak for Europe. I also see that late in August I told Alec Home that in the view of my (Campaign for the Common Market) committee the real test to the Government would present itself in about six to eight months when the negotiations had reached the actual price we should have to pay for joining the Community 'at this rather late hour'. All the interests affected, I thought, would then try to fan up to a white heat the natural xenophobic-isolationist tendencies of our people. In the ensuing battle we hoped to be of some assistance to the Government more especially since our group was supported by a large number of Labour MPs who would in no circumstances, I believed, vote on the issue otherwise than in accordance with their principles. It is curious to think that this is something that I might very well have written to the same Foreign Secretary nearly ten years later.

As this opposition grew it seemed to me increasingly that we ought to make it entirely clear what the political advantages were in joining and, if possible, produce some scheme for political unity on our own. For not only might we, by so acting, disarm much criticism at home which was based on economic arguments only, but also give the impression abroad that we were not ourselves in favour of the Gaullist conception of a 'Europe of states', but rather of a more organic solution that really would have a chance of resulting in the famous 'confederation' of the future. At the same time it was obvious that the Government, given the strength of the opposing forces, could not lay itself open to charges of wanting to destroy our national identity and merge us totally in a greater whole. Nor was this a solution which even the great majority of 'Europeans' would favour. What, then, should be done? So it was in an address which I gave to the French Academy on 25 June 1962, that I first formulated, in a rather stumbling and hesitant way, the broad solution which I was constantly to advocate and develop during the coming years.

When explaining the general reasons that seemed even then to lead inevitably to some kind of political union in Western Europe and pointing to the great improbability of our ever establishing anything which could be as centralized as the union of the American states, I observed that it might be wiser not to speak of a federation or even of a confederation, but rather of a political community. For if we did this then we might well come to see that it was only by employing some of the techniques that had resulted in the establishment of the EEC that we should ever arrive at a meaningful political union. Thus, as it seemed to me, on the analogy of the Commission of the Treaty of Rome, we might, in the political sphere, set up a 'non-national commission'. Individual governments would naturally be able to reject any proposals put forward by such a body if they so desired, since for a long time the principle of majority voting could hardly be applied in the sphere of foreign policy. But the creation of such a commission would 'no doubt result in tendencies towards a common view being encouraged rather than discouraged in the community as a whole'. It might eventually be possible to consider such techniques in the sphere of defence also, though this was more difficult. What was certain was that if we did come into the EEC there would have to be some kind of machine which would really coordinate European defence. I did not see why such suggestions as these, if they were ever put forward by Her Majesty's Government, should be received with suspicion in France. The British, I concluded, might often be rather absurdly pragmatical, but they were not machiavellian. The Academy seemed to regard these suggestions as sensible. Even the redoubtable André François-Poncet did not appear to dissent.

And then came the veto. I had not been expecting this – any more, I believe, than de Gaulle's own government. True, I had been depressed by a talk which I had had with Couve de Murville in October, and, more especially perhaps, by another with Pompidou at a shoot of Valéry Giscard d'Estaing's in December, when he seemed unforthcoming, to say the least. But I had imagined that the idea was to spin things out until the British themselves would call it a day. And this, as the election neared, they might well have been forced to do. What the veto did reveal was the real nature of de Gaulle's policy. We no longer had any excuse for not believing that what he said he was going to do in his memoirs he was, if he could, going to do; and I therefore then and there resolved to do what I personally could to counter these designs by bringing them constantly to the attention of Parliament and of the public. De Gaulle was admittedly a great man. But great men before him had pursued disastrous policies, and there was no reason why Britain should acquiesce in plans not only to exclude her politically from the Continent but also to undermine the one hopeful and creative experiment in international relations which had taken place since the Second World War.

As he (General de Gaulle) sees it, apparently, the new Carolingian Empire will rest solidly on a French *force de frappe*; on well-trained German infantry (with French backing and presumably under French command) recruited from the new Confederation of the Rhine; on patient Italian camp-followers; on the *braves Belges;* and on the reluctant, but inevitable support of the solid burghers of Amsterdam. The object of this imposing machine will (we understand) be to restore complete independence to ancient Europe; to rid it as soon as possible of any tiresome 'Anglo-Saxon' presence; to transform it into a largely self-sufficient Third Force, the equal of America and the Soviet Union; and, this done, to negotiate a separate deal with the USSR in which the 'Anglo-Saxons' will not have any say, thus creating, in the General's chosen phrase, a bloc extending 'from the Atlantic to the Urals'.

What could we do? Little at the moment beyond making it clear that the break was for political reasons. And then? Well,

'even if Britain's destiny should not be apparent to the French Monarch, it might be possible that the consequences of dividing Western Europe, and perhaps leaving it defenceless, would gradually dawn even on the mesmerized Chancellor in Bonn.'

So, three days after the Elysée veto, I expressed myself in the *Daily Telegraph*. Not many, then, I think, altogether believed me; but what I said was true. The General did in fact try to do everything which I predicted he would. Luckily, he failed. The solid Dutch refused to play his game in Britain's absence; the parliament of the Confederation of the Rhine flatly disclaimed, in a specially drafted Protocol, the treaty he had signed with the mesmerized Chancellor; and, finally, the Russians made it clear that they wished to talk business with America and not with France. After the occupation of Czechoslovakia in 1968, the whole Gaullist foreign policy collapsed in ruins. And, though some have still not grasped the fact, it became as clear as daylight that, in the absence of a Western political entity of some kind that would include Great Britain, the beautiful Gaullist conception of '*détente, entente et coopération*' (with the Soviet Union) was a myth.

How should we best react, however, to what was clearly a major threat to our own interests, if not to world peace? Before the negotiations were actually broken off I had already prepared my own scheme. As I saw it, we should not simply sit back and do nothing, thus allowing the General to go ahead with forming 'Europe', if he could, in his own way. A bold move on our part might snatch the political initiative from him and in any case demonstrate that it was we, rather than he, who were in favour of constituting some valid European entity. I suggested, therefore, that we should summon a conference in London to consider ways and means of creating fuller Western European unity in the sphere of foreign policy and defence, and at that conference produce a scheme for a council of ministers with four permanent and three non-permanent members (as in the Security Council of the United Nations) which would take decisions, to start off with at any rate, by a majority of five, including the votes of the four permanent members. There would also be provision, of course, for an independent (advisory) commission and certain additional powers for the European parliament. One of the chief functions of this new machine would be to consider the whole question of the defence of Western Europe within the Western Alliance and the role of any European nuclear force (or forces). I believed that in this way we could at least regain the initiative and make it clear that it was in any case not we who were holding up the construction of Europe. Nor was I the only one to urge such a policy on Her Majesty's Government. Others with some knowledge of 'Europe' made very similar proposals.

I need hardly say that in the general mood provoked in governmental circles by the veto, such ideas did not catch on, though to some extent they did make progress in the European movement. But strange to say the proposal for a restricted council of ministers plus an independent commission found considerable favour in France where it was elaborated in a major speech I made in Paris in May 1963: '*Le Plan Gladwyn pour l'Europe*', (as the Paris press termed it). It was indeed even hailed by some Gaullists as a great step in advance. 'If' said no less a person than Maurice Schumann, 'the plan put forward by Lord Gladwyn had been proposed by the British Government, all the difficulties which now presented themselves would have been easily solved.' Blocked on the economic front, I cannot see why we should not at least have made an attempt to progress in the sphere of foreign policy and defence. Suitably approached, it might even have been that the General himself would have found this acceptable. Conceivably, he might have done so after his rebuff by the West German Parliament when it was clear that the chances of his own proposed alternative were extremely dim. At the very least he would have found it difficult to reject entirely any such proposal by Her Majesty's Government. And had he done so his own position in the EEC would have been correspondingly weakened. It is therefore rather difficult to understand what we thought we should stand to lose if we acted as suggested.

Meanwhile our Campaign,* which was shortly to be merged in 'Britain in Europe', tried to pick up the bits. We endeavoured to look at the veto in perspective and to think of ways and means of keeping the European spirit alive in Britain. In several speeches at home and abroad I showed how a Gaullist Europe could not possibly work, and how only the extension of the EEC so as to include Britain made any political sense. I also extended my field of activity to include not only the Atlantic Institute – in which I quickly found an ally after my own heart in Kurt Birrenbach, the brilliant Christian Democratic Union (CDU) deputy and one of the heads of Thyssen – but also in the Atlantic Treaty Association which was to elect me its president (for three years) at its assembly in Ankara in August.

All through this period I also attended many debates, both in the European movement proper and in many of its allied organizations on the perpetual dispute between federalists and pragmatists and tended to take a middle line. On the one hand I had always felt, almost instinctively, that any union of our ancient European nation-states could not be on the lines of the United States of America with an elected president and a congress based on universal suffrage. In particular the 'Monnetist' insistence on the creation of a 'United States of Europe' always struck me as rather misguided. Whatever might happen at the end of the century it seemed to me that we could hardly, before then, contemplate the virtual abolition of our countries and the creation of a 'European man' whose primary allegiance would be to a Central European government and who would

---

* Of which Peter Kirk, Martin Maddan (Conservative MP) and Norman Hart (a prospective Labour candidate) were the moving spirits.

only feel himself to be an Englishman, a Frenchman and so on in the same way as a modern American feels himself to be a Californian or a North Dakotan. On the other hand, if there was to be any union at all, then obviously it had to be something more than a mere alliance, or even than a confederation in the usually accepted meaning of the word.

I therefore developed and refined my general 'political' thesis which was that in all the matters not covered by the Treaty of Rome, namely foreign affairs, defence, and indeed 'culture', we should not have to wait until the EEC was extended and gradually formed these necessary institutions within itself, but there should be new machinery established among the Seven, who would then act as a 'nucleus' round which further unity could be built. And since it would be necessary, in this sphere, to proceed slowly, the best thing might be to graft such new machinery on to the Western European Union, which might even be extended so as to include Norway and Denmark, both members of NATO and both obvious candidates for the EEC as well. Then, using the same techniques as those employed under the Treaty of Rome, we could advance towards the point at which, the EEC having been extended, all the European institutions, notably, of course, the Council of Europe and WEU, could profitably be merged.

After being aired in, and partially approved by the European movement meeting under Professor Hallstein in Rome, my views were elaborated in an article in *Encounter*. Briefly we should seek to form a European political community which, in minor categories of questions, would take decisions by some form of majority vote in which not even a large Power would have a veto, but on all matters of great importance, such as nuclear matters, would have to take decisions by some form of majority involving unanimity between the four larger members. It should be for such a European political community, aided by an impartial commission, to whom such grave questions would be submitted for study and report, to decide itself on the exact roles within the Western Alliance of the British or potential French deterrent and what measure of coordination should exist between them. With other governments in power in the various countries concerned, it might conceivably be found desirable to suppress these deterrents altogether. Alternatively, and perhaps preferably, they could be given some joint role to perform in agreement with the Americans. They might even be amalgamated or increased if that was the common desire. The great thing would be that the nuclear policy, whatever it was, of Western Europe, should first be decided by common consent among the four greater Powers concerned. Conclusions, when reached, should be discussed with the Americans and Canadians. Out of such negotiations a genuine common strategy might well be born.

The general conclusion which I drew at the end of 1963 as a result of all my expeditions was that if we wanted to reserve the 'lead' for ourselves in Europe at any rate – and we must always remember that if de Gaulle disappeared tomorrow, or shortly, we could if we played our cards right, effectively still have that lead – we should avoid if possible the temptation to wrap ourselves in our Union Jack, boasting that our possession of a dwindling four per cent of the nuclear striking force of the West enabled us in some way to exert leadership' (but whom exactly are we to lead?) and put us in a special, exceptional and highly desirable position as the indisputable number two power of the Western World and the special partner of America. For such a posture would indeed encourage the spread of Gaullist conceptions on the continent of Europe and cause our many friends to despair of our ever willingly entering any genuinely European political association. General de Gaulle was, after all, in a stronger position to pursue a Gaullist policy than we were. He already had his veto trump. We could only defeat this by playing the Community card – that is, if we wanted to. Unfortunately we might be left with it in our hand.

I don't know if these candid remarks were ever brought to the notice of the General, but as the reader may have gathered from Chapter 17 it is not impossible that they were. Anyway in speech after speech, in articles, in letters, I continued during 1963 and 1964 to advance and to elaborate on these general ideas. I developed them in lectures in Frankfurt, in Düsseldorf, in Loccum, in Hamburg, in Rome, in Luxembourg, in Brussels and in The Hague. I talked to Paul-Henri Spaak, who seemed to be rather despairing of British entry; with Hallstein who seemed to share my views to some extent; with Professor Courtin, once a passionate Gaullist and now bitterly anti de Gaulle; with Couve de Murville and with many other European and 'Atlantic' personalities. My position as president of the Atlantic Association gave me a forum in which to argue that the only sure way of pressing the alliance was to form a political Europe and then form a real partnership with the USA. I invariably concluded that a purely national policy on the part of any one Western European democracy would be disastrous. One of the great advantages of my proposed independent political commission would be to examine methods of coping with what was often nowadays only a legal fiction, namely the alleged total independence of states which were actually in a state of anarchy.

Eventually I consulted the High Priest of Europe himself, Jean Monnet. There was no uncertainty here. Monnet had in no way changed any of his views as the result of the events of the previous year (1963). The Common Market was taking shape according to plan: the time-table would be duly observed; eventually the parliament would be directly elected and we should enter into the federal European paradise. This accomplished, the Atlantic Community would gradually take shape; there would be some economic association of the Western world; and we should spend our time organizing the under-developed countries and resisting the forward march of Communism. Nothing that General de Gaulle might do could alter this predestined course of events. A political Europe was, of course, a necessity, but it must duly emerge from the existing organizations such as the Brussels Commission. On no account should the British try to get it organized outside the potentially federal Brussels machine. This would upset the workings of destiny (and up to here in our conversation this was the only point on which my old friend showed the slightest agitation). It was intellectually possible to argue, he continued, that the British might perhaps – in the event of a Labour Government with a large Left-wing majority – go neutralist to some extent, though he himself did not think this was likely. But any idea that they could join up with the Americans as it were in opposition to Europe could be dismissed; the Americans just would not fall for such a thing. In particular the Labour Party would get nowhere with the idea that they might be accorded some special position as regards nuclear policy and decision-making in return for scrapping the British 'Independent Deterrent'.

But supposing, I said, General de Gaulle disappeared tomorrow and there was a period of uncertainty in France during which our association with Europe might be re-negotiated? Monnet jumped out of his chair and began touching pieces of wood. What was I saying? That was a thing that must never happen. We must hope that the General would be with us for a long time yet. He could not, even if he would, now prevent the full development of the EEC, and that being so, his continued presence en-sured stability. One thing, I thought, was certain: Monnet would not himself be prepared to welcome us into the EEC unless we accepted the full federal thesis. He was further persuaded that that was something which we were bound to accept in the fullness of time.

In April 1964 there was a fascinating, if rather chilly, meeting of the Anglo-German *Königswinter* group in Christ Church, Oxford and I was asked to sum up. I divided the participants into two. There were those who thought the only real solution of our difficulties was first to form Western Europe and then establish the 'partnership' with America, and those who believed that we should now forget about European unity and

349

go for some new 'Atlantic Community' in which Britain and the Commonwealth would play an important and individual role. I was rather hard on the latter. The idea that we could remain the centre of a political and economic Commonwealth was 'pure nostalgia', and if the Atlantic Community enthusiasts really thought that we could maintain ourselves as a medium-sized individual state by ignoring the Europeans (whom we did not understand) and playing cricket with the Fuzzy Wuzzies (whom we did) they would have to think again.

In July I see that I was (no doubt unduly) concerned with the success of Barry Goldwater in the American primaries and made, in the House of Lords, a vigorous attack on the whole principle of nationalism – a virus injected into our system by the General which now showed signs of spreading. Even in Britain 'British Gaullism' was making considerable progress.

It might be defined (I said) as 'going it alone', on the basis of our Commonwealth and our independent deterrent and not taking much notice of the views of foreigners. I believe our Gaullists are only waiting for a patriotic leader of real talent who knows how to formulate and give eloquent expression to our frustrations and our subconscious desires. Who knows, the British leader of the future may perhaps be in Your Lordships' House this afternoon although I daresay he might equally be found in another place! But the point I am making is that it is nationalism which is primarily responsible for our exclusion from the Common Market; that nationalism is undoubtedly catching; and that it may well spread in the Western world.

Well, that was only seven years ago and the bacillus is still very much with us. At any moment, I fear, the disease may become endemic. Certainly a potential leader is now present in the House of Commons.

In November, after the Labour Government and the new administration of President Johnson had both come into power, I was, in the same place, lamenting the unfortunate state of the Alliance.

The fact remains that the debris created by the catastrophic end to the negotiations in January 1963 has not yet been cleared away, and that, instead of the great European conception which we thought would emerge, we now see, to our dismay, moving through the fog, the shapes of old tattered nationalisms, the gravediggers of the last war and the harbingers of the next. Here in this country, after happily living beyond our means for about a year, we have suddenly woken up to the fact that, unless the foreigner temporarily bails us out by accepting our goods while agreeing to restrictions on his own, we are obviously once again confronted with the depressing old 'Stop and Go'. But it is becoming increasingly clear that, dependent as we are to such an enormous extent on exports, we are the last country who ought to go in for nationalism of any kind – and, indeed, for protectionism. The same applies, I think, to many of the nations of Western Europe. Therefore some wider conception of our destiny is necessary for this country and, indeed, for them. In 1961 we thought, or some of us did, that we had found it: but 'Where is it now, the glory and the dream?'.

Could not the new Labour brooms get busy on the debris and at least try out the conception of a new form of political community on the French, later entering into wider discussions with the other states concerned? For 'You must, indeed (I said) get agreement between France and this country first; otherwise you will never get anywhere.' There should be a joint statement by the two governments of the desirability of setting up some kind of political association in Western Europe which would include all the members of EEC and those countries which in the last two years or so applied for admission to it, namely, the United Kingdom, Denmark, Norway and Ireland. Secondly, it should be admitted – and this was vital – that such a union could be established only within the framework of the Western Alliance. Even General de Gaulle said he accepted the Alliance; what he disliked was the NATO organization, not the Alliance. Thirdly, it should be the declared object to arrive, in agreement with the Americans, at arrangements for the coordination and association, or even the eventual merger of the present nuclear strike forces of France and Britain. Unless, indeed, they were going to be abolished, both must have a future of some kind. The role in war of these two strike forces should be agreed with the Americans, and determined by the political association itself. And, fourthly, the statement should include acceptance, in principle, of my own well-known and oft-repeated political proposals.

The silence that greeted this renewed suggestion was once again deafening, and on 22 December I see that I was bordering on despair.

I must confess (I told a rather bored House of Lords) that sometimes in the small hours of the night I have a nightmare. Perhaps it is a nightmare which some of your Lordships may occasionally share. It is the idea of the emergence, soon perhaps, of a rather down-at-heel, but quite complacent Britannia living 'on tick' under the nuclear umbrella of the United States: indulging in quite unrealistic day dreams; keeping up all her ancient traditions, such as tea-breaks, restrictive practices, football pools, meiosis and the Changing of the Guard; massaging her battered pride by maintaining a few bombers East of Suez; playing the Lady Bountiful with inadequate means in Indonesia, and indeed in Africa; and, in a word, trying to fill the role of a World Power without either the will or the capacity to do any such thing.

But the new administration showed even less interest in my ideas than their predecessors. Preoccupied with the need for new socialist reforms, possessed by the notion of developing a new inter-racial Commonwealth, they were, on the face of it, completely indifferent to 'Europe'. When de Gaulle came over for Churchill's funeral it was rumoured that the new Prime Minister, meeting the Great Man for the first time, had told the General how much he admired him and his various policies. The General was alleged to have been delighted by this intelligence and on his return to Paris was reported to have said, '*Il*' (Harold Wilson) '*est tres intelligent – mais il a beaucoup a apprendre.*' In Britain, it was the nadir of the European Idea. The future seemed to belong to Nationalism – and perhaps to National Socialism.

One comforting feature was the extent to which the London press during this gloomy period kept the European Idea alive. *The Times* did its best. *The Daily Telegraph* (which was the paper which came closest to sharing my own views on the dangers of Gaullist policies) was usually splendid. But, in a way, the greatest credit must go to Cecil King and the *Daily Mirror*, who never failed in their enthusiasm for 'Europe', in spite of the fact that, with their mass, largely working-class circulation, they probably had the most to lose.

20

Hopeful Liberal
(1965-71)

The change of government at the end of 1964 had, so far as I was concerned, one important effect. For it freed me from what I conceived to be my duty to sit on the 'cross-benches' in the House of Lords (i.e. to be politically neutral) for so long as the Tories were in power. It would have been improper – though not unprecedented – for a civil servant, recommended by the Prime Minister for promotion to the peerage, to join the official opposition to the administration of that Prime Minister or even of his immediate successor. But on the departure from power of the Conservatives, it was open for me to join the political party of my choice. I did not want to join the Tory Party. I had never really got on with what after the war became for some reason to be known as the 'Establishment'. Nor does the Tory Party usually take kindly to idea-merchants. Its great influence lies in its conformity and in a sort of herd-instinct. When the bell-wether turns, they all turn. I was too old to insert myself into a great machine with any prospect of getting high employment, and in any case it was not the prospect of office that tempted me. Employment of some kind under any government was one thing; office in it another. The Labour Party did not attract me either, partly for the same reasons and partly because I could not honestly have subscribed to certain fundamental doctrines. But there remained the Liberal Party, which was a different thing.

I have never regretted joining the Liberal Party, which in 1964 was the only party wholly committed to the 'European Idea'. Not only do I believe that, with the great emphasis that it lays on the freedom of the individual, it stands for something that must more and more be treasured in our urban civilization, but it comprises people who are the salt of our society – intelligent, high principled and humane. That there are such people in all parties is undisputed. But the proportion of them in the Liberal Party is, I believe, much higher than in the other two. And this is not just because the Liberal Party has no reasonable chance of forming an administration – anyhow by itself. It is because the ancient tradition of self-respect and plain decency which was the basis of the old Liberalism has been handed on in certain families and is still the dominant note at Liberal gatherings. In any case, the causes that were dear to the Liberal Party were dear to me, and, whatever the chances of the Liberals themselves, there is always hope that one day some Left-of-Centre government may be found consisting of the progressive Tories, the Right-wing Labourites and the Liberals – which is probably what three-quarters of the electorate would desire.

One great additional advantage of the Liberal Party from my point of view was that, apart from the support of an excellent machine, I was eventually able to be the Liberal representative on the parliamentary delegations to the WEU and Council of Europe assemblies (the Liberals are allotted one representative out of a total delegation of 18). This means that I could intervene in the international debates in Paris and Strasbourg on the great European issues in which I was interested; take part in the preparation of the reports; interrogate ministers and so on. And seeing that I had been the official negotiator of the Statute of the Council of Europe, to say nothing of the Brussels Treaty, of which the WEU was the direct offspring, and our representative for two years on the Brussels Treaty Organization in London, it was obvious that I had a rather special knowledge of the background. Also, in Parliament, I could speak from the Liberal front bench in the House of Lords. More advantageous still, I could, when I became Deputy-Leader some two years later, usually speak Number two or Number three in the Lords' debates.

I actually joined the Party at the end of January 1965. The pleasure of the Bonham Carter clan in my joining them seemed to be almost as great as mine. In particular, Lady Violet had always been very indulgent towards me and I had the greatest admiration for her; while with her brilliant son Mark I nearly always, politically, saw eye to eye. On 8 April I made my first speech as the Liberal spokesman on defence. It was a strong plea to reverse entirely our existing defence policy 'East of Suez', and to evacuate as soon as possible all our bases in that area, which seemed to me, for reasons which I developed at some length, to represent an appalling waste of money and reserves. Aghast, Lord Carrington inquired whether this really represented the official policy of the Liberal Party? Later, Lord Chalfont said that I was proposing to hand over vast areas to 'anarchy'. Who could have imagined that within three years my suggestion was to become the official policy of the one, and a little later, of the other of our major political parties?

After what Harold Wilson had said during the Election campaign ('we must always be able to buy our food in the cheapest market', etc.), nobody in 1965 expected that much progress would be made during the Labour administration in the direction of closer relations between Britain and the EEC. The talk was all of the Commonwealth and of the great role which Britain, as the leader of this vast and democratic association, could play in the development of the poorer nations, thus mitigating racial feeling and atoning, in some degree, for her imperial past. The thesis was particularly dear to the Left wing of the party who were always suspicious of the EEC, allegedly run by Catholics, capitalists, trusts and faceless bureaucrats. Nevertheless, as the year wore on, to their great surprise, British 'Europeans' noted that the atmosphere in the Labour Party, to say nothing of the country generally seemed to be changing, and a motion which I had at the end of February, with the approval of my new Liberal colleagues, put down in the House of Lords urging Her Majesty's Government to 'make plain their intention to join' the Common Market may have had a certain impact. As time went on this was elaborated and became known as a 'declaration of intent'. On 18 March I explained to the Federal Trust that it was not a legal conception but simply a suggestion that Her Majesty's Government should say (a) that it still wanted to sign the Treaty of Rome if possible before the 'third stage' was reached on 1 January 1968 and (b) that it would regard the interim period as a transitional one during which it would do anything possible to adapt the British economy to the system which would have to be applied when it did enter the Community. Clearly such a statement would be taken as meaning that Britain was ready to sign the Treaty as it stood, subject to certain transitional arrangements for, for instance, British agriculture and some overseas interests, notably those of New Zealand.

At the end of April 1965, when our resolution came up for debate in the Lords, I repeated these arguments and also enlarged on the need for HMG to make a corresponding declaration on its political intentions, in other words to outline the kind of political community which it would wish to join. All this seemed to fall on deaf ears, though it may well be that it hastened the Labour 'conversion' to 'Europe' which then began to take place fairly rapidly. But it seemed to me – and it still seems to me – the greatest of pities that when de Gaulle, a couple of months later, went on his famous 'strike' and temporarily abandoned the EEC, we should not have come forward with some such scheme. For we then really had the ball at our feet. In a long letter to the *Daily Telegraph* immediately after the French withdrawal I urged some declaration on our part which would at least rally the Five. Why should we not at least say what we, for our part, stood for? And could we not initiate talks between the Five and EFTA with a view to harmonizing the tariffs between the two groups?

Then, when France gets bored with glory, as one day she will, a new negotiation could be set on foot . . . Embarrassed and speechless, our present masters gaze at the European drama from the wings, trying to build such little bridges to Europe as the General may agree to and spending hundreds of millions of pounds a year on the defence of Aden and Singapore. How much better if they demonstrated that, contrary to the general belief, it is we who are in favour of a genuinely united and democratic Europe, and that we still propose to assist this process by all means in our power.

At the end of July I renewed my appeal in the House of Lords, and at Scarborough in September, at the Liberal Assembly, I did so again.

What this country would clearly go for, if only it had a foreign policy, is the achievement in Western Europe of a genuinely supranational community with a common economic, foreign and defence policy; this community to be in association with the present neutrals and eventually perhaps even with certain Eastern European states; the whole constituting a valid partner of America in some revised 'Atlantic' system.

The Government would no doubt not be able to progress in this direction because it did not want to face this issue. But they should. We are informed, in effect (I concluded)

by the ruler of France that the British people will not accept any community solution which transcends the bounds of the present nation-state. Who, I respectfully ask, is the ruler of France to tell us what we shall accept or not accept? In his own country he may hold up progress towards a real community, though I believe that even there the necessity of creating Europe will prevail over an archaic nationalism which, in an age of Super-Powers and super-bombs, is about as relevant to our modern problems as the arquebus or the First Crusade.

In Rome, at a meeting of the Atlantic Treaty Association; to the NATO parliamentarians; in the University of Sussex; before the Kensington Liberals and over again in the House of Lords, I developed the same thesis. It was all no good. De Gaulle's bluff was not called. The Five did not sufficiently believe in the European convictions of the Labour Government to take any risks about the Community. They made it up with the General in the sorry compromise of Luxembourg. The second opportunity was at this point lost. After the 1966 election, when the Labour Party, under the influence of George Brown, was largely converted (though never to the extent of coming out in favour of a meaningful political and defence community) the position of the General was much too strong and he had no difficulty in throwing out the boarding-party even before they managed to parley on the ship.

Nevertheless there was in the first few months of 1966, an undoubted revival of the European Idea in Britain and it seemed to come from the bottom rather than the top, Already in February, I had come to the conclusion that about half the Parliamentary Labour Party would then be in favour of joining the EEC 'provided only that we could negotiate transitional periods in agricultural matters, not ruin the economy of New Zealand and obtain the willing consent of our EFTA partners', while some seventy or eighty would probably even subscribe to the doctrine that, having joined the EEC, we should seek to build up on that foundation some democratic and parliamentary political community of the future. As for the Tories, the great bulk of them were for joining the Community on conditions and a large number accepted the political thesis as well. There were welcome signs, too, that 'European' ideas were penetrating the Ministry of Defence. 'Like so many great personalities of our time with a Marxist background [I told Their Lordships] Mr Healey carries a Marshal's baton in his knapsack', and we must hope that he would impose himself and clear out of the Indian Ocean, and this in spite of Mr Wilson who, fairly recently, had declared that 'our frontier was on the Himalayas'.

After the 1966 election I was duly appointed the Liberal member of the parliamentary delegations to the assemblies of the WEU and the Council of Europe and in midsummer I found myself addressing the former in Paris. I must say, looking back, that this, as a 'maiden' might well have been thought to be too 'severe', as the French have it. But it must be remembered that it occurred just after the French had declared that they no longer were prepared to remain in NATO and that all non-French military establishments in France must forthwith leave the country. On the assumption that this would not amount to a *renversement des alliances* we should, I said, not take the recent moves of the French Government too tragically, if only because we could not really take them seriously. It looked as if they had been made to prepare the way for the President's visit to Moscow, from which great results were apparently expected. But what could these possibly be? France had already said that she was still bound by the Brussels Treaty commitment which was much more binding than under the North Atlantic Treaty. She was also proposing to keep her troops in Germany, and it was to be supposed that she would continue in the Berlin contingency planning machine. She could not therefore possibly give the Russians what they no doubt chiefly wanted, namely French neutrality in the event of a show-down. Even a deal on rockets or space techniques was most unlikely. What would the Russians get out of that? True, the French could recognize the DDR. But that would be a major blow for the Federal Republic. Indeed any significant uni-lateral gesture towards the Soviet Union by France could only result in a tight Anglo-American-German bloc, which would be the one thing pre-sumably, that France would wish to avoid, and this would have as a corollary the repression of all 'liberal' elements in Eastern Europe. What then would be likely to happen? Nothing, in all probability, save a rather meaningless communiqué and agreement to co-operate in general. This was precisely what happened in the event.

But it was now the moment, or so we thought – that is to say the group of 'Europeans' with which I was then associated, namely Peter Kirk, Chris Mayhew, David Harlech, Martin Maddan and many others, assisted as Secretary by Roy Hattersley – to make it clear that a clear majority in Parliament and in the country was in favour of what we called a 'political Europe', that is to say the entry of the UK into a genuine economic and political community in which decisions were increasingly taken in com-mon by an agreed democratic procedure and who therefore did not favour our entry into a 'Europe of states' which, owing to the necessary acceptance of the principle of a national veto, could only function, if it functioned at all, on the basis of the hegemony of one of the partners. In the same way as in the 'Campaign for the Common Market' (see p. 339) a large number of MPs, peers and distinguished people put their names to the declaration.

In the Lords I next said that the essential thing, on which everything else depended, was for the governments concerned to agree to be bound by a formal system for taking decisions in common, not only in the economic spheres but also – gradually, of course – in the spheres of foreign policy and defence as well. When this happened a sort of mutation would have taken place. Out of a number of things one thing would have emerged. Admittedly this would take a long time to develop, but the new thing would at least have been born, and that ancient promoter of wars, the nation-state, conceived in Europe after the Reformation nearly five hundred years ago, would have been tamed, not by conquest, as had so far been thought the only way in the troubled history of Europe, but by the exercise of human reason. It only needed an inspired leader to produce a conviction among us that really would change the face of international politics and lead us away from our ridiculous nationalist bickerings and towards genuine co-operation for the construction of a new society in the West of Europe which, once established, would enable the Americans to go back to America and the Russians to Russia and thus contribute, as nothing else, to world peace, to the reduction of tension and to the solution of all the major political problems of our time.

My main point was the necessity for France and Britain to agree on some means of harmonizing their general policies. Now that the General had apparently returned empty-handed from Moscow, surely thought should be given to this essential objective. The French Government could hardly now be totally oblivious of the clear political advantages of Britain's join-ing the EEC and of the grave dangers for France of some struggle, as it were, for the soul of Germany between the so-called Anglo-Saxons and the French in some rather improbable association with the Russians. The great thing was for Britain to come out with some ideas of her own as to how this political co-operation could best be achieved, whether in a reformed WEU or otherwise.

All this time I had been working on my report to the WEU assembly on 'The Problems raised by the possible accession of the UK to the Euro-pean Community' which after it had been blessed by the General Affairs Committee, I presented to the assembly in December. Passed almost unanimously, the report (which contained an analysis of British public opinion, including the great advance in the thinking of the Parliamentary Labour Party) recommended 'that without waiting until Britain feels able to make a second formal application to accede to the Treaties of Paris and Rome, the Council should at once begin co-ordination of the main lines of a common European foreign and defence policy'; and that it should examine the best procedure, should Britain apply, for getting agreement on only the major outstanding issues, the details being gradually worked out with British co-operation in the institutions of the Community during the necessary transitional period. And in my introductory speech I hinted that the only reasonable way of settling such 'details' would be by the acceptance by all concerned, in the last resort, of the principle of 'qualified' majority voting. Mine was, I need hardly say, only a contribution to the great head of steam which was at this time being created by 'Europeans' in Britain of all parties in favour of a new effort to break into the Common Market, and I would like at this point to pay tribute to the unfailing efforts in this direction of Duncan Sandys. Lone wolf though he is, unacceptable though his attitudes may be to some people at some moments, this rock-like figure has throughout been indefatigable in his devotion to the Euro-pean Idea, and as he is by nature an organizer it is largely due to him that the central issues have been brought squarely before parliamentarians both here and on the Continent over the years.

After the publication of my first book, *The European Idea*, it was with growing enthusiasm that I developed early in 1967 my ideas in Brussels and in an animated debate with Maurice Schumann himself in Lille, which is always appreciative of British ideas and where the coverage was consequently excellent. An article which I had previously contributed to *The Times* was, I found, widely appreciated in France, especially perhaps by Jean Monnet who told me that if Her Majesty's Government accepted my advice he did not see what could prevent an eventual entry into the EEC though it was true that de Gaulle would do his best to block this. However we could rely on the Germans, he thought, to resist any such efforts on the part of the General. Willy Brandt was a very strong character, he said.

But a shadow was quickly creeping over all this hopeful activity. It was clear to me that though the Government as a result of their journeys all round Western Europe, would probably now officially apply for membership of the EEC, the General would in that event either see to it that negotiations once more ran into the sand, or even go so far as to prevent them from even taking place at all. This view was not shared by the Government. But I suggested to them privately that, in common prudence, rather than just firing in an application for membership, it might be better to announce that HMG wished to sign the Treaty of Rome subject only to prior agreement on the length of the various 'transitional periods'; a broad arrangement covering the interests of New Zealand and the sugar-producing ex-Colonies; and the necessary 'adjustments' consequent on the entry of any new member, and proposed that this decision should be considered by the Six among themselves with the object of discovering whether it would provide a suitable basis for negotiations. (It will be remembered that in the spring of 1967 the Six were nowhere near agreement on the financing of the Common Agricultural Policy.) For various, I suspect internal, reasons this ingenious scheme was not acceptable. I repeated my belief that the General would fairly shortly veto any negotiations. But on 4 May the Government duly sent our formal application in.

The Lords had a debate on the day of our application, which I nevertheless welcomed officially on behalf of the Liberal Party. Lord Chalfont teased me by saying that the Liberal Party were guilty of 'suggesting that anybody embarking on enlightened and imaginative policies' was accepting Liberal advice, a habit which, he continued, enabled the Liberal Party 'to propose ideal solutions for any problems, however unrealistic . . . or irrelevant . . . to current political realities'. But I asked what he expected the Liberals to do in this particular case? Nobody could deny that they had for years pushed various governments in the direction of Europe. Should they now apologize for having supported 'unrealistic and irrelevant policies'? Should they say that they were staggered by the speed of the Government's conversion? Liberals certainly did not have a monopoly of wisdom, but really were entitled, on this occasion, to just a little self-praise.

The fatal year of 1967 wore on, and after a further appeal (in *The Times*) to the Government to take some political initiative, I made (in June), a rather desperate suggestion that we should now contemplate what I called a 'delayed entry'. This was because, being persuaded that a French veto was inevitable if we simply went on pressing our application, it seemed to me that we would be well advised to prepare ourselves for considerable delay and to avoid the possibly fatal effect of another veto on the whole European Idea. This well-intentioned, even if misguided, effort had the distinction of being immediately and officially repudiated by the Foreign Office as an unacceptable form of British 'association' with the EEC. Whatever its demerits, this it certainly was not, since it would at least have provided for full membership after a defined period. It was also understood not to appeal to the Leader of the Opposition. But the press on the whole welcomed it as a 'second-best' solution, greatly preferable in any case to indefinite exclusion from the EEC as the result of some arbitrary, and indeed illegal, veto by the President of France.

The impending veto, however, continued to cast a gloom over the scene. At the beginning of November I made a last effort, in the House of Lords, to persuade the Government of the advantages of (a) some 'political' initiative and (b) the proposal for a 'delayed entry'. I subsequently inveighed, in *The Times*, against the 'Bonapartist bombast' of de Gaulle and drew attention to the grim future for France, if he had his way, in developing as a sort of Soviet satellite. If the Five were able to call his bluff, France would be compelled to pursue the alternative course of forming 'Europe' with her present partners and the UK. 'Two points should be grasped. First, by the irony of fate, de Gaulle nearly always achieves the opposite of what he apparently desires. Secondly, he never knocks his head against a brick wall: The Five stuck together in 1965 and France eventually returned to the fold. If they stick together this time she will not leave it.' However, they did not. In spite of the fact that at the assembly of the WEU in the middle of December we passed a 'Declaration of Paris' signed by the presidents of the political groups there represented – Christian

Democrats, Socialists and Liberals – deploring the illegal pre-judgment of the situation made by de Gaulle in a press conference (the effective veto) and calling on the Council of Ministers – i.e. presumably the Five – at its forthcoming meeting to open negotiations on the basis of Article 237 of the Treaty of Rome, they did nothing of the kind. The de Gaulle myth was still too strong, and we had to wait six months before it was gravely undermined and yet another year before it was finally shattered.

But de Gaulle's policy seemed to me to become more and more dreadful as one pondered over its probable effects. So during the first few months of 1968 I conducted a regular campaign against the disastrous attitude of the French Government, ending up with my new book (published at the beginning of the following year) entitled *De Gaulle's Europe, or Why the General Says No*. In letters, in articles, in speeches, I denounced this policy, and even carried the war into the largely Gaullist territory of Liège. Likewise I spent some time refuting the validity of the other 'alternative', namely closer association with the Communist states of Eastern Europe. The critics were all at one in denouncing those who believed that our only course still lay in demanding entry into the EEC as 'static'. If you supported a new 'Western' or a new 'Eastern' policy, you were 'dynamic'. But it was even easier to demonstrate the absurdity of advocating association with the EEC of e.g. Eastern Germany (still less membership) than it was to prove the impracticability of the North Atlantic Free Trade Area.

So we staggered on until the 'events' of May in Paris when de Gaulle tottered and very nearly fell. I was in Paris at the beginning of these 'events', which by then were taking the form of disturbances in the Sorbonne, and was a witness of the extraordinary change of tone among the Gaullist deputies whom I met, to say nothing of the *monde*, who appeared to have no longer any Gaullists left among them. In spite of the General's recovery, I did not think he could remain in power for very long, for the myth had been destroyed, and after the occupation of Czechoslovakia in August by the Russians, it was evident to all that his foreign policy was in ruins also. In ruins rightly, because it was not a policy but a pursuit of dreams, or rather of 'prestige-opportunism' as I called it, in my second book which I was by now actively engaged in composing.

When, in addition to all this, the French had to pay for the May 'events' and devalue the franc in the process, I took advantage, in November, of a House of Lords debate to try to draw conclusions from the extraordinary happenings of the last six months dominated, as I saw it, by two major political events: the social and economic upheavals of May and June in France and the occupation of Czechoslovakia in August by the armed forces of the Soviet Union. The first called in question the French Government's ability to conduct a totally independent and nationalistic foreign policy; the second involved the end of the so-called *détente* and the consequent collapse, for a long period at any rate, of the European policy of General de Gaulle and his devoted lieutenant, Chancellor Kiesinger. There was also the possibility of another thunderstorm in the spring, and in the circumstances France could hardly be a very satisfactory member of the European Community. But the last thing we should indulge in would be *Schadenfreude*. We must hope that fairly shortly the French Government would see the error of their ways. And so it did.

Going through the old papers, I think that my general attitude during this last phase of Gaullist rule was best expressed in the assembly of WEU. In a way, this became my favourite forum. Not because what you say in that rostrum of the rather ugly palace on the Place d'Iéna makes much immediate appeal. Such deputies as are present (most are usually in committees or busy elsewhere) often tend to concentrate on *Le Monde* or the *Neue Zürcher Zeitung*. Over half cannot really follow rapid, idiomatic English and have to listen, if they listen at all, to a hasty improvisation called a 'simultaneous translation', usually wonderfully good in the circumstances, but scarcely conveying all the nuances. But the great bulk of the deputies are nevertheless sincere and able men among whom genuine 'European' spirit is usually uppermost. They read the record of important speeches next day and discuss them behind the scenes. You do feel, therefore, that you have some opportunity of influencing opinion in the seven capitals. Even the ministers and 'permanent representatives' on the front bench of the 'hemicycle' occasionally open an eye at some telling phrase – not that, in spite of their protestations they attach much importance to the utterances of the 'parliamentarians'. But you can sometimes have a certain *succès d'estime*, and it is certainly here that the general European Idea is best kept alive in times of difficulty.

On this occasion 'We seemed', I said, 'to be approaching another turning point in the affairs of Europe.' For the last ten years or so there had been *two major tendencies* observable in the west of our small sub-continent. One had been the concept of European union in some sort of confederation, which would preserve the basic inviolability of the sovereignty of the nation-state; the other had been that of a community of nations in which, in all fields, but to begin with in the economic field, decisions would increasingly be taken in common by some agreed means other than unanimous vote in a council of ministers, increasing attention also being paid to a European parliament that would eventually be elected by direct universal suffrage. There was a whole world of difference between these two concepts. One was an idea of the past; the other an idea of the future.

The truth was, I repeated constantly, that if the nationalist concept was adopted, the only conceivable form of European union was a system in which one of the members effectively took the lead and all the others followed. And if anything was obvious it was that, whatever Germany and Italy might choose to do, Britain was a country which was just not prepared to play the role of 'brilliant second' to a state which was certainly no more significant than she was as regards population and production and, more generally, in her influence on the course of events. Consequently, under the Gaullist concept, she could not possibly qualify for membership – unless indeed she did accept French hegemony which it was quite clear she would never do. All the economic arguments against British admission, valid though some might be in the short run, were secondary to this over-riding consideration. It was not a question of suddenly deciding to establish a kind of federation on the American model, as the nationalists, whether in France or in Britain, always asserted. A system devised nearly two hundred years ago for uniting a few small rebellious colonies, all of whom spoke the same language, and for the most part were of the same race and religion, was not necessarily suited to a union of the ancient nation-states of Europe, all with their long, separate, cultural and historical traditions. It was rather a question of discovering the best means of arriving eventually at majority decisions on all really major issues, and first of all starting to apply the new system in fields where the so-called 'vital interests' of the partners were not directly engaged. As it seemed to me, therefore, it rested largely with the UK Government whether a fresh impetus could now be given to the general idea of Western European Union. We could only hope that a new Phoenix would arise out of the ashes of our post-war dreams, and that leaders would forthwith emerge with the necessary ability and inner fire to impress the sheer necessity of unity on all the peoples of Europe.

Pending the expected Parisian 'thunderstorm', we did our best in the Campaign for Europe to prevent the European Idea from fading out in Britain or (more probably) turning sour. More especially I denounced the 'British Gaullists', that is to say those in both parties who now seemed drawn towards the General and his unfortunate notions just at the moment when they appeared to be going to be discredited by events. One of the ideas launched to the end of keeping the European Idea in the public eye was that of a new 'Messina Conference' of the Six and the Seven, and the reasons for this were fully exposed in the Lords on 4 March in a short debate, provoked by me, on the so-called 'Soames Affair' in regard to which I more or less sided with the Government in that I believed that the substance of the Ambassador's interview with the General should have been communicated to our allies, though the way in which this was actually done was no doubt not above reproach. But it was the presumed intention of de Gaulle in making his advance which was the really interesting thing. And I suggested a converse to the 'Soames Affair' in a sort of 'Courcel Affair'! Why not send for the excellent French Ambassador and explain our own plan to him? Why always leave the initiative to the Great Man in Paris? Perhaps things have changed for the better now, but it can hardly be said that for the last decade or so our governments have given much evidence of imaginative thinking. A rather grim, provincial mediocrity still haunts Westminster. Certainly it seemed to prevail in the spring of 1969.

It was said, I knew, that even if Her Majesty's Government did give a lead in the direction I wanted, the course of continental nationalism, notably in France, would not necessarily be arrested. But it very well might. A great crisis was impending in Europe and after the German elections at the end of September, it would materialize when the whole agricultural policy of the Six would have to be re-negotiated before the end of the year. If at that time it was clear that Britain was prepared to enter a new form of European union that would be both effective and democratic and capable of giving expression to a common will, then the whole international horizon would be far less black. No doubt, under the pressure of our 'technological' civilization the Western European nations were destined to come together one day: but the real question was how? Willingly, or unwillingly; in freedom, or not? The Romans, as usual, had a phrase for it. The Fates, they said, lead the willing man, but drag the unwilling. We should try, if we could, to be the masters of our destiny.

And then, quite suddenly, de Gaulle resigned. 'The great oak' I then wrote – anticipating Malraux* – 'has fallen, and the French political forest now consists of many strong and healthy, but comparatively equal trees.' Was its crash due to mistakes on the General's part, or was it an inevitable event that might have occurred earlier? Perhaps the answer to these questions might throw some light on the probable future of Franco-British relations. After tracing briefly the General's spectacular career, I noted that his performance over Algeria had been so welcome to the French nation that, instead of returning him to grass, as had been confidently expected, they actually gave him a large majority in the parlia-

* André Malraux: *Les Chênes qu'on abat'*, (Paris 1971).

mentary elections at the end of 1962. 'Flattered, and perhaps even surprised, the General, not unnaturally, proceeded to embark on his long-term political schemes', his first act being the original 'veto'. It was also the moment when he began the process which led some six years later to his political downfall. The temptation to pursue unrealistic policies was irresistible. Not only had he been brooding on them during his twelve-year period in the 'wilderness', but he possessed a personal magnetism, a power of expression, a degree of unscrupulousness and a sheer ability unparalleled among contemporary statesmen.

I listed these well-known and deplorable gestures, all designed to put France on the map and prepare the way for some eventual French European hegemony. It was possible that de Gaulle really knew that this was a myth without which his beloved France, under the influence of the fickle and ungovernable French, would be only too likely to savour the delights of *la douce anarchie*, in other words revert to being a simple parliamentary democracy. But perhaps he just felt obliged to obey his 'voices'. The trouble was that the General's projects were too expensive. Rich and intelligent as the French were, they simply could not carry out a policy daunting even for a Super-Power. So Nemesis finally struck and the pent-up discontent of the students, the teaching profession and the workers exploded with such force that the regime practically collapsed, and would have done so but for the total disunity of the Left. And then there was Czechoslovakia, which revealed the policy's absolute bankruptcy. What was really rather extraordinary was the extreme ability with which the Emperor, then clearly shown to be without any clothes, was able to play on the desire of the new American administration to put an end to 'bad relations' with France and to obtain a virtual certificate of good behaviour from President Nixon. Enormous play was made with this during the campaign for the spring referendum. Indeed had General de Gaulle once again triumphed – and I never subscribed to the idea that the referendum was the result of a sort of 'death wish' – his victory might well have been ascribed to the support of the American President. Mercifully, as we might suppose, the Gods thought differently.

De Gaulle had often hinted that after him there would be anarchy. I did not believe in anything of the kind. I thought that there was likely to be a reasonably stable parliamentary regime applying the 1958 Constitution, which, though subsequently modified for the worse, was neither unreasonable nor unworkable. Since another Gaullist autocracy was impossible, power would, however, I thought, gradually shift from the Elysée to the Matignon and the nation, with luck, might emerge as a strong and united member of the European family. (I was wrong, or rather I have so far been wrong, about the shift of power, but otherwise the prediction was not a bad one.) Anyway, we must hope that, now that the reign of the man who whatever his faults, at least restored their confidence to the French, was over, our two nations, forgetting both the vetoes and Waterloo, would come together as equals in the construction of a veto-less, vigorous and autonomous Europe. That would be the best tribute we could jointly pay to the fallen giant.

But the moment had almost come when the creation of 'Europe' would once again present itself – perhaps for the last time. In the debate on the Queen's speech at the end of October 1969, I consequently reverted to my well-known theme. All three political parties, I said, were still firmly committed to the proposition that we along with Scandinavia and Ireland, should now seek to negotiate our way into the EEC with the general object of forming some new kind of union which would be both demo-cratic in character and capable of maintaining, or rather restoring, the old influence of European countries. But nobody wanted to join a union dominated by one member, and, if so, then all of us must, logically, be prepared to accept some collective leadership or control. Equally none of us wanted to lose our national 'personality'. Therefore we had to seek some democratic association of a completely new and modern kind. So far I hoped everybody would agree.

In our English way, we no doubt thought we could avoid taking sides in the battle between those on the Continent who favoured a 'community' and those who wanted to revert to a 'Europe of states', but it really would be deplorable if we simply shuffled backwards and blindfolded into Europe. Before the negotiations started we ought to make our general point of view clear. If we did not, many of our friends on the Continent would assume that de Gaulle was right and that all we really wanted was to come into the EEC in a Trojan Horse for the purpose of destroying it from within. The 'terms' for our entry were already obvious (I outlined the three points on which we should have to have some satisfaction in almost exactly the same terms as those employed by Geoffrey Rippon eighteen months later). But the main message I tried to convey in this speech was, on the assumption that the negotiations, when they did take place, were likely to be 'long and acrimonious rather than satisfactory and short', the desirability of making parallel progress on the political front. Why not, after the German elections and the proposed 'Summit' Meeting of the Six, come forward with the idea of a conference of the Common Market countries and the candidates to consider ways and means of making progress in this direction? The possibilities here were obvious and had already been widely canvassed. Surely HMG could make them their own? Lord Chalfont was not unsympathetic. I had made a closely reasoned speech of great value containing, however, suggestions 'with not all of which HMG would wish to go along'. Nobody else took them up. Possible progress on the political front seemed even to be regarded with marked distaste. 'I will not try', said Lord Gore-Booth, fresh from running the Foreign Office, in his excellent maiden speech, 'to go down the institutional road taken by the Noble Lord, Lord Gladwyn'. And another ex-diplomatist, Lord Trevelyan, said he would not propose to 'emulate my prophetic flights', not that, so far as I was aware, I had made any prophecies.

It always seems to be thus in this country. It is quite in order to discuss the formation of 'Europe' if you limit the discussion to what might be supposed to be the advantages (or disadvantages) for this country in joining an organization called the EEC – usually referred to however as the 'Common Market'. But if you try to get discussion moving on how exactly you would want the Community to operate and what objectives – economic or political – you ought as a Government to seek to achieve, and thus at any rate to define, you are treated as a sort of dreamer, worse still, as an 'intellectual'. Anyway there was no support among my colleagues for my suggestion during this debate, or indeed at any time to my knowledge.

However, the subsequent Hague Conference raised hopes for a new deal in Europe and I hailed it as such in the assembly of WEU – a body less allergic, as I have said, to ideas than the Palace of Westminster. Indeed I over-hailed it – if that is the right expression – as implying a reversal of the external policy of General de Gaulle. It is true that it would never have happened if the General had still been in the Elysée. But it is also true that the constructive proposals in the communiqué were only very partially applied. In particular the European parliament was only, in the event, given control (after 1975) over a tiny fraction of the Community's common budget, and the prospect of progress towards a common European defence and foreign policy resulted in the clearly inadequate arrangements for mutual consultation among the Six themselves and the 'candidates' contained in the so-called 'Davignon Plan'. The near-revolutionary undertaking in respect of a monetary union did produce the Werner Paper which was then promptly emasculated. Progress towards an economic union also looked as if it would be very slow in the event.

Still I think I was justified in remarking that the truth was at last now dawning that in the first place no European community, or union, could possibly function without the willing adoption by all concerned of certain elementary techniques which were in fact supra-national, even if it was tactless to refer to them in such a way; and in the second place, that it could not function at all for so long as the whole industrial complex of the Western half of our continent was divided by an arbitrary and quite indefensible line, for which, of course, my own country was originally responsible, even though about eight years ago we tried, in principle, to repair this error on our part. One would have thought therefore that the Six would begin to apply the rules of the Treaty of Rome, notably in regard to majority voting, but in fact these were still largely disregarded. It was no good saying that such disregard might well be acceptable to the British. It very well might. But even the British might have doubts about joining at great expense a club which was not working. However the great thing admittedly was that negotiations for the enlargement of the EEC would now apparently start.

Early in the New Year of 1970, the famous Government White Paper on the likely economic effects of joining the Common Market appeared and I criticized this in detail chiefly as laying the main emphasis on the situation likely to be produced on the worst possible hypothesis. In any case, the actual conclusions, namely that the cost of joining the Market might represent a burden on the balance of payments from anything between a hundred and eleven hundred million pounds, showed that the whole study was pretty useless. It had, I suggested, been prepared by two gangs of civil servants, those from the Ministry of Agriculture and Fisheries, and no doubt the Board of Trade and Treasury being largely 'con' and those from the Foreign Office (led by Sir Con O'Neill) being presumably 'pro'. And no doubt in their discussions on the political side, the only 'Pro' was 'Con'!

A little later I find I was doing battle in the *Daily Telegraph* with Neil Marten,* who had congratulated me on my efforts to get people to 'face the real issue', but naturally, for the wrong reason, since he suggested that any form of supra-nationalism must equal the dreaded 'federation' and result in the probable abolition of our Parliament and even of the Queen. It could not be repeated too often, I said, that this was *quite untrue*. Like all new conceptions the creation of a democratic 'community' in which certain decisions, in certain carefully defined fields only, are taken in common by new techniques that give the fullest co-ordination to national sentiments and interests, takes a long time to sink in. But it really should

* Conservative MP; leading Anti-Marketeer.

be grasped before we joined a body which had now (at The Hague) definitely accepted the community principle. It was perfectly true that having joined the Community we could not legally abandon it. It was also true that if a member really wanted to secede it could. Nor would secession be in the least likely to lead to a civil war. But I believed that the long term advantages of joining, both economic and political, would be so tremendous that no question of secession would ever arise. It was only if we did *not* join that I thought our great legal concept of 'The Queen in Parliament' might be in some danger. If we were, owing to economic pressure, forced to accept some highly directed economy all democratic institutions might be swept away by some 'providential man'. There were people consciously working towards such a breakdown of our institutions. It would be a pity if Neil Marten turned out to be Mr Brezhnev's poodle!

In June, in the WEU assembly I see I was partly gloomy, but, as I said intentionally, hoping to persuade the leaders on both sides of the Channel that some action was necessary without delay. The effect was *nil*, or rather a minus quantity, since the new Tory Government, which I had suggested might make some advance, seemed to be even more frightened of supranationalism than their predecessors. In particular the new Foreign Secretary, while agreeing with his colleague Mr Barber that we should actually work towards a monetary union (which of course presupposes something equivalent to a central government), declared flatly that he was opposed to any kind of political union whether it was called integration, federation or anything else. 'Europe' would indeed in his view have to 'make a response' to an American demand that she should assume a greater share of her own defence, and 'Britain would have to make her response as part of the European reaction'.

But 'Europe', I told the House of Lords, did not exist. It was, alas, either a geographical expression or a figment of the imagination. It could only exist if there was an institution which personified it, even if only in a rudimentary way. According to Sir Alec Douglas-Home it would only be when it had been possible to 'identify an area in which it would be advantageous to the partners to take common action' that a suitable institution might be set up. Though he did admit that, for instance, the question of a 'European Security Conference' might be discussed in the WEU, which, after all, was an institution of some kind even if so designed as to be quite incapable of collective action. I said I thought we must be blind if we could not 'identify' Western Europe as an area in which it was now essential for certain democratic states to take common action, notably on defence, if they were not to lose, but rather to preserve their famous 'identities' and indeed their whole way of life. The Foreign Secretary was, I suggested, mesmerized by the very word 'federation'. If the Government really could not contemplate the emergence of a new form of European community they would do better to wrap themselves in their Union Jack, stop talking about 'Europe' and adopt the scarcely very successful nationalist policy of 'free hands', advocated and practised until his downfall by the late President of France. But could they not even say they approved of the recent proposal of the Prince de Broglie, once a Gaullist minister, and now president of the Foreign Affairs Commission of the French National Assembly, for what was in effect the exact equivalent of my famous independent political commission? No, that was really asking too much. It was a very interesting suggestion said Lord Lothian, the new Tory Under-Secretary in the Lords.

But it is time to end these recollections which, after all, are chiefly recollections and not a major contribution to a debate on a great issue which will presumably have been decided by the time that they appear in print. I will therefore only say that throughout the remainder of 1970 and in 1971 I continued my campaign and played my part in the collective effort of the European movement now well directed by David Harlech with the powerful aid of Ernest Wistrich, an organizer of genius whom I personally recruited for 'Britain in Europe' in 1967.

From my point of view General de Gaulle had always been the great adversary. I can only say that I hope that my crusade against certain conceptions of this great man was in the nature of what he would himself have called *une grande querrelle*. This quarrel, to which I have devoted almost all my time since my retirement from the Foreign Service, will, I have no doubt, persist and be conducted in the future, so far as the critique of a narrow nationalism is concerned, by figures much abler and more important than myself. It will, I believe, continue irrespective of whether the present negotiations are successful. But if the supra-national thesis is to prevail it needs as an exponent a man of power who can, as I could never hope to do, capture, when the time is ripe, the imagination of the people. It is in the hope that this chronicle may to some degree serve as a quarry for the arguments that may then be developed by such a leader that I end it believing, as I have so often said to myself in moments of gloom, that finally, the truth will prevail – *magna est veritas et praevalebit*.

21

Final Reflections

The greater part of my already fairly long life has been devoted to policy-making. And yet I often ask myself whether this process has had any real effect on the march of events.

The nation-state, most regrettably, refuses to respond, as often as not, to the intelligent promptings of the experts, the students of politics, the forecasters, the *Weltverbesser*, such as you and I. *Tout s'arrange, mais mal*. The older he got the more Oxenstierna was impressed by the folly which governed international relations. The 'Old Adam', Lord Vansittart came to believe, was incorrigible – a sort of brainless anarch who at intervals kicked over the green baize tables of the civilized diplomats. Even the profoundest revolution comes full circle, and the disgusted revolutionary sees 'Kings crawl out into the light again'.

Thus I began my address to Chatham House on 28 March 1965.

But perhaps the important thing is that people should believe that the expert has some influence. Two incidents in recent years gave me some slight encouragement. The redoubtable Enoch Powell, for instance, whom I had met at dinner some seven years ago and found to be a delightful neighbour, called off at the last moment a lunch with me at my club – arranged a long time ahead – on the grounds (explained by his secretary on the telephone) that 'quite frankly he could no longer afford to be seen with Lord Gladwyn in public'! The second incident was when the agreeable editor of the *Sunday Express* solemnly informed me that I was 'Enemy Number One'. I must say I was quite pleased by these unconscious tributes.

Whether I have personally had any influence on events matters, however, very little. What is more interesting is why I have always been fascinated by speculation about the future. It is I suppose possible occasionally to discern what is to come. Anyhow there is every advantage in knowing what ought to happen. Because it is only if a nation has a clear idea of what it wants that it is likely to get it – provided it has a first-class leader who can interpret and represent the broad national mood. There were moments, too, during the last forty years when the future could certainly have been affected by a British decision. Stresa in 1935, the Rhineland in 1936, Munich in 1938, the guarantee to Poland in 1939, if the British attitude on all these occasions had been different the whole face of Europe would have been changed, even if the long-term outcome might not have been vastly dissimilar. Our future is indeed shaped in advance by forces which no government can control, even though it is possible within certain limits, as it were, to deflect the course of the stream of history. A tempered determinism must, therefore, in practice be the philosophy of our men of action. Thus few would now dispute that the British Empire, that strange thalassocracy which dominated the world political scene in the nineteenth century, was by its nature destined to disappear in the twentieth. Seen in perspective, its chief function was no doubt to extend the process of industrialization – first initiated in Britain – throughout the world in what was, on the whole, an orderly fashion. When this process, for many years regarded in Asia and Africa as the magic of the White Man, was understood, in other words as education spread, the peoples under the sway of Britain were bound to assert their independence. The astonishing thing was that the system existed for so long and even survived the Second World War in which, however, it received its death-blow, chiefly at the hands of the Japanese. After the independence of India in 1947, the stage was set for its disappearance.

The Commonwealth had been invented by far-seeing Englishmen before the First World War primarily as a device to arrest the inevitable decline of Empire and enable it to be gradually dissolved without major campaigns that would in all probability have further weakened the metropolis while in no way preventing the spread of independence. And this particular object it achieved so far as the 'Old' Commonwealth was concerned. But the sad fact was that the mere existence of a Commonwealth of some 750 million people (Black and White, 'new' and 'old') spread the illusion that it was, in itself, a great source of strength to the metropolis, whereas in point of fact it was probably, on balance, a liability. For had it not existed, and had the successor states, more particularly the 'new' Commonwealth countries, while maintaining friendly links with the 'Mother Country', become totally independent, each concluding some special economic arrangement with the latter that it deemed to be in its own best interests, the whole preferential, and indeed the Sterling Area might have fairly quickly vanished and Britain by the force of things would, very soon after the war, have been obliged to form, in Europe, that economic association which, at long last, she is now trying to achieve. It would have been a wrench, but it could have been done. If Germany could triumphantly survive her defeat, so would we triumphantly have survived our victory.

But for a decade at least the maintenance of the old, traditional markets prevented the reorganization and modernization of much of British Industry, while the necessity of upholding the 'prestige of sterling' as a 'world currency' was partly responsible for the perpetual stops and gos of the British economy. Politically, too, the British people came under the illusion that the mere existence of the vast area of which the Queen was the titular head meant that they were a Power far superior to the neighbouring Continental democracies. This was shown to be a fallacy at the time of Suez, but it was only demonstrated conclusively to the British people in the sixties when, for instance, South Africa seceded, Russia arbitrated between India and Pakistan, Rhodesia rebelled and the African successor states mostly accused us of neo-colonialism, and even of genocide, suggesting that the best service we could render the Commonwealth would be to resign from it.

Still, it may be said that, Britain being a democracy, no Government could have explained to the electorate what the real situation was until it was apparent for all to see. And it may be – it will be if the present negotiations for entry into the EEC are successful – that finally the destiny of these islands will be accomplished in accordance with what many believe to be the irresistible tendency of the age. If not now, then certainly later. What is hardly predictable is what may then happen. What is certain is that any Government which has a clear conception of the 'role' of this country in the world is far more likely to be successful in governing it than one which says, for instance, that the first object of HMG is to preserve peace and ensure close co-operation with other friendly democracies in the United Nations and bromides of that sort.

But governments, like individuals, have only a limited freedom of manoeuvre. If they are democracies, they cannot disregard public opinion or indeed the promises which they make on assuming power. Even if they are dictatorships they must make some estimate of what is possible and impossible. Whatever they are, governments must make some appeal to the emotions of the governed who can often, as in war, put up with appalling physical conditions if only they feel that they are suffering in a great and worthy cause. It may be true that, in general, the public wants to be deceived – *vulgus vult decipi* – but only in the sense that they like to be assured that things are really better than they think they are.

The British respond to good leadership and all their best qualities emerge when the nation is thought to be in real trouble.

Would this apply to the younger generation many of whom, I am informed by all those who know, could not care less about Britain, or, for that matter 'Europe', being only concerned with pollution, or urban poverty, or the miseries of the two-thirds of humanity who are said to be undernourished, everything else (including, no doubt, the whole of this book) being dismissed as 'irrelevant'? As a matter of fact, I rather suspect it would. For a little reflection will show that none of the great ills that concern us all can possibly be alleviated to any considerable extent by action other than governmental. Certainly they would not be alleviated at all if there was chaos. So the only real question is what sort of government should we have? And this brings us back to politics. It is possible to believe, for instance, that nobody under thirty should be in the government (often, as a matter of fact, the result of a real revolution); or that nobody should be in it who has had any experience of government at all; but these beliefs could only be put into practice by organized action, in other words, by forming a party and thus entering the political arena. In this sense, it is surely Herbert Marcuse himself who may be dismissed as 'irrelevant', since while he denounces, as he very well may, the ills of modern industrial society, his only apparent solution is to recommend that his supporters, and more especially his student supporters, should contract out of society altogether.

In any case the anarchistic purpose of destruction for its own sake – because if you destroy the existing order something new will have to take its place even though it is totally impossible to say what – will not, I predict, have any more success than it did in the nineteenth century, when, even in the case of Bakunin, it was usually combined with some kind of collectivist schemes for the post-revolutionary organization of society. The danger seems to be rather that the state may be taken over by violent men with a clear idea of what they want to do in order to secure the interests of one section of society or another. It is not at all impossible, if things should go wrong, that some 'inspired leader', elected by perfectly democratic means, should, with the aid of television, perpetuate his rule and make use of enthusiastic and beshirted young people for this purpose. Whether he was technically of the Left or the Right would probably make little difference in practice. There would be a directed economy of some kind; and even if the virtual dictator did not himself last for very long, it would be difficult, after his disappearance, to revert to anything like our present democracy.

Evidently, if our 'standard of living' is more or less maintained, such political developments are unlikely; though it is undoubtedly true that there is a serious *malaise* among the most intelligent of our younger citizens who do not see much point in our modern industrial society. And it is possible that some of these would be only too glad to join some organization in which they would be told what to do and at any rate have the impression that they were engaged in profitable activity. Of course it might be profitable; but more likely in a non-democratic society the activity would be regarded by many citizens as not profitable at all. For instance, a simple solution for much discontent might be to put a large number of young people into the armed forces and the police. It is true that large-scale war (other than a nuclear holocaust) now being virtually impossible, the bulk of this force would probably have to stay at home. But within the British Isles a non-democratic government might well find this helpful for its own purposes.

It is partly to provide against such unpleasant possibilities – which some may regard as unimaginable, though not I – that I have always advocated the formation in Western Europe of some wider democracy which might well temper the system of nation-states by greater emphasis on regionalism. Indeed I have often reflected that this may be the only sure way to provide for the very continuance of democracy, that is to say representative government of any sort. The Italians are convinced of this already. Only by making a success of the European parliament (in which the Communists would probably be in a minority of some ten per cent) will they obtain the necessary backing for their regional and social policies. A good many people in France besides the controversial J. J. Servan-Schreiber, are arriving at the same conclusion; and before very long it may be that it will dawn on us as well. For many years now it has been the broad Liberal conception. It is certain, too, that British MPs would bring a whiff of fresh air to Strasbourg, even during the period before the Assembly is directly elected.

My own convictions were reinforced in 1965 at a conference organized by the University of Harvard. Harvard's idea was to have a discussion on 'Conditions of World Order' conducted by the representatives of various 'disciplines' not usually associated with this idea. There had been enough discussion on this subject, so they thought, by politicians, strategists, military theorists, historians and so on: what was now needed was some vision of the future in the light of contributions by biologists, sociologists, planners, philosophers, economists and even physicists. The result was embodied in a special edition of *Daedalus* and is well worth looking at, especially the summing up of the *rapporteur*, Professor Hoffmann of Harvard. Raymond Aron's chairmanship was superb. No agreed conclusions were reached, but the debate was fascinating.

I mention this Areopagus chiefly because of my own denunciation before it, of the 'nation-state' as the chief obstacle in the way of some better 'world order' of the future. Not the abolition of nations, as such, but some agreed and defined limitation on the complete liberty of action of the only basis of international society hitherto recognized. The thesis whereby small or medium nation-states might, before the end of the century, come together in 'groups' which could settle many problems among themselves and, for the rest, negotiate with existing Super-Powers more or less as equals, perhaps in a reformed Security Council of the United Nations, met with a good deal of sympathy, though with considerable scepticism. Most of the assembled great brains seemed, indeed, to think that before such a triumph of reason could be achieved there would have to be what is known as a 'mutation on the brink' – i.e. that the imminent danger of some appalling nuclear catastrophe, or even the explosion of one or two nuclear bombs, might be the only force capable of transmuting the national atom and thus deflecting the sum of human energy into a more profitable course. But in default of any other apparently tenable thesis as regards the development of international society my conception was accorded by the chairman a *préjugé favorable*. This qualified approval struck me, I must admit, as being in the nature of a Nobel Prize of a minor order!

A few months later I developed the notion at much greater length in a series of lectures at Columbia University, and the result was published in book form under the title *Half-Way to 1984;** the idea being that instead of that dismal *dénouement* – namely perpetual 'conventional' wars between vast and similar mindless monsters, to which we had advanced some way since Orwell wrote his book in 1948 – we might form a new order based on the existing Super-Powers and on equivalent 'regions'. An essential part of my whole thesis was that one of the main long-term reasons for endeavouring to construct some kind of 'group' or 'entity' in Western Europe was because of its stabilizing effect in international politics and in the hope that it might give rise to similar attempts elsewhere to limit the complete freedom of action of nation-states. There was no reason why these separate entities should not continue to flourish and to organize themselves as happy and like-minded communities. It had also to be admitted that all attempts to form federations or confederations after the war had failed and that the nation consequently still remained the only

* Columbia University Press 1967.

basis of organized international society. But the notion that, if it were to remain vigorous, the nation-state would have, by the force of things, to seek to expand at the expense of its neighbours, seemed to me to be fundamentally vicious and, in the age of the fission bomb, to have been repudiated by the logic of events.

On the whole I was comforted by the Serbelloni conference. Nobody there really seemed to think that the human race was doomed. Certainly they did not act as if it were. All put forward their own projects for the future. The Pandit Pant, the head planner of India, even believed that the Indians would fairly soon master their population problem. He placed tremendous faith in 'the coil', a contraceptive device then in process of being distributed to the women of India. Perhaps there was too much optimism, but without optimism the human race is no doubt doomed anyway. That there was indeed cause for alarm all would have admitted. Nowhere has this cause for alarm been better analysed – even if the work is now to some extent outdated – than in Raymond Aron's *Le Grand Débat* (in which, among other things, he demolished the Gaullist case for a totally independent French nuclear deterrent); while his *Guerre et Paix entre les Nations* remains, in my view, one of the classics of our time. Besides, the whole history of the human race, and more especially of the 'white' race, has been so ghastly during the twentieth century that nobody can deny the possibility of some *Götterdämmerung*. And yet, instinctively, nobody seems to believe that this will really happen. It is quite true that, though we all know that we shall die some day, this does not normally prevent us from acting as if we were immortal. So it might be argued that the human race, though aware, logically, of its impending demise, continues with its daily tasks as if this were inconceivable. And indeed, what else can it do?

It is quite true also that even if the human race escapes the alternative doom predicted by those who point to the effects of pollution of the environment and over-population the future may not be too rosy, even supposing that my own political and regional solutions are ever applied.

Shall we really be better off or happier, [I inquired of Their Lordships on 12 March 1969] when we are hurled about the world at supersonic speeds; when everybody can see and hear what is happening at any moment of time in any corner of the globe; when all our factories are automated; when, thanks to computers, we no longer have to read or write; when there is no more countryside; when our roads will be impassable; when we can all live to be about two hundred by buying other people's organs; when babies are produced in test-tubes; when romantic love between the sexes is regarded as a sort of infantile disorder; and when we can spend days and months in hopeless and encapsulated boredom on our way to the uninhabitable planets or even to the dreadful, desolate moon? I must say I doubt it. But still, if that is to be our fate, we cannot do much to prevent it. It is something which is, apparently, inherent in our modern type of society. We might, I suppose, in so far as we British are concerned, desperately try to avoid it by breaking up all the machines and becoming a nation of Luddites. But that might be even worse. The thought of the British in the year 2100 or so becoming something like the Navajo Indians, practising their curious old customs in native reserves and gazed at from their helicopters by rich tourists from overseas, is hardly encouraging. Yet, exaggeration apart, this is something that could begin to happen by the end of this century if we do not look out.

But it is equally possible that our civilization is on the edge of a great breakthrough and that a kindly providence has obliged us to construct the Nuclear Bomb precisely in order to force us to co-operate. Logically, as it has always seemed to me, the first area in which this breakthrough may be accomplished is that situated in between the potential cross-fire of the two existing Super-Powers, namely Western Europe. But if this is to happen it is not only the peoples concerned who will have to be convinced of the necessity of unity; it is above all the leaders. And in democracies it is not always the men of vision who emerge from the party struggle or who possess the necessary powers. I admit that in 1965, and subsequently, I developed a theory of the reform of government in the United Kingdom whereby less power would devolve on the Prime Minister, who should, as I saw it, be obliged to pay more attention to standing committees of a (reduced) House of Commons which would provide fewer ministers than at present but at the same time have a greater opportunity of influencing governmental decisions at an earlier stage. But I have never denied the desirability of having a strong personality as Prime Minister, and, indeed, under my scheme of reform he would be less dependent on his actual cabinet colleagues than he is at present. But in foreign policy, and especially as things are now, Prime Ministerial leadership is essential. And our leader must also be capable of explaining to the people the long-term goal that he wishes to attain and inspire the enthusiasm necessary for attaining it.

This is naturally more difficult in peace-time than in war-time. The great war leaders – Churchill, Roosevelt, Stalin – had only one objective – the winning of the war. It was to this end that they successfully harnessed the united efforts of their peoples. Though they did manage to agree during the war on the main lines of a world organization, their individual peace aims were usually either unattainable or unattractive. Stalin in any case virtually killed the peace by his imperialist external policy and his unspeakable internal repressions. To rouse a nation in peace-time and harness it to a definable goal is much more difficult. De Gaulle did it, but unfortunately his objective was a will-o'-the-wisp which dis-appeared with himself. Mao may be doing it for all we know. Kennedy might have done it. But since the war I do not myself feel that the British have yet had a leader who could tell them what ought to be their real 'role'. The formulas of 'you have never had it so good' and that of a 'techno-logical revolution' (subsequently replaced by an appeal to the 'spirit of Dunkirk') were, I believe, misconceived. Curiously enough, the quite un-charismatic Clement Attlee may have come nearest to rallying the nation to constructive effort by his emphasis on sacrifices in order to construct the 'Welfare State'. Certainly no rallying cry since then has embodied any real sense of national purpose.

Unfortunately, it could well be that such a rallying cry might be found in a simple appeal to national sentiment. There is nothing like fear for getting people to work together, and it is entirely possible for them to combine against some external, or, more probably, perhaps, against some alleged internal menace. 'Freedom from domination by foreigners' would naturally be the principal slogan; but the reduction of our coloured popu-lation to the status of second-class citizens can certainly not be ruled out as an objective as well. In such a campaign of 'Britain for the British' the old cry of 'rootless foreigners in our midst' would no doubt also be raised – and we all know what that means. Should the European Idea really collapse, there is indeed good reason to suppose that some 'providential man' will pull all these skeletons out of their cupboards. If by any chance, in addition, the economic situation gets much worse than it now is, I have little doubt of his eventual emergence.

Even if the European Idea prevails, it will no doubt be a long time before the same confidence is placed in common institutions as is now placed in national ones. The idea that British and French, for instance, will feel 'European' before everything else, in other words that their first loyalty will be to Europe and only in the second place towards their own country, is certainly not for this generation. And it seems equally unlikely that the central institutions, which will, of course, include a parliament, will during this time be dominated by some overwhelming figure who may by himself act as the famous 'federator'. The new machine, when it gets run in, is much more likely to work in the same way as the Swiss Confederation, that is to say without fireworks – though that is not a real comparison since France will not resemble the Canton of Vaud nor Germany the Canton of Bern. A great deal will therefore depend on the national leaders who will have perpetually to explain to their peoples what the long-term goal is and what they are meant to be working for. This may be difficult, but if the international situation is at all dangerous it should certainly be possible – provided always that the council of ministers contains men of energy, and even of genius, who are determined to work together in a conciliar administration.

What therefore is now wanted, I repeat, is someone, and preferably someone in their thirties, who can fire the imagination of at any rate one of the major nations of Western Europe, and preferably all of them. Men of the Monnet generation are now, alas, too old, and in any case too many are steeped in a rather utilitarian or Benthamite tradition which does not seem to make much appeal to the young people of today. Machiavelli spent his life looking for a 'Prince' who would unify Italy and save her from the barbarian. I do not say that we must now seek out some modern Cesare Borgia; we cannot, as I have already said, imagine some physical 'federator' of Europe; but we can see some figure emerging who would produce the right formula for the central conciliar administration that we need. In the early stages of the French Revolution young Frenchmen very nearly unified Europe by preaching the new idea of Liberty. So long as the French armies stuck to this central idea they might well have founded a new society that could have endured. Unfortunately Napoleon, carried away by his genius, embarked on what was really a career of pure conquest. When this was seen to be such, and though many of the reforms of the Revolution persisted, the great French effort failed. You have only to read the memoirs of Chateaubriand to see why.

That some new philosophy is now essential: that it will probably not be produced by the men who were influenced by the last World War; that it may strike the older generation as crude, all this, I believe, is undeniable. But we do not yet hear the new note which will surely some day be struck. What we of our generation can do, however, is to provide the right framework, the right kind of elementary institutions, in which these new ideas can be gradually put into practice. For it is probably only in this wider area that they can come to fruition. The small and medium nation-state is not suitable for large-scale experiments. New attitudes towards unemployment – which increasingly may be seen as the problem of leisure – new conceptions of authority, new ways of eliminating boredom in industry, new and ruthless plans for countering pollution even at the expense of production, all these problems could be far more easily solved in a unit, however flexible to start off with, than in governmental parleys between totally sovereign states.

And so, I take leave of the reader, always supposing that he has persevered as far as this. So far as I can, I have tried to acquaint him, frankly, with my state of mind over the years and with the political reasons for my actions. I have not, so far as I know, maligned or traduced anyone, but that perhaps is only because I have never entertained any very hard feeling against anybody – if you except Hitler and his sub-human Nazi gang. It may be that I am by nature too optimistic and cannot comprehend the essentially destructive nature of 'Western Man'. Possibly Dr Steiner is right when he maintains that the collapse of religion in the Western world has merely resulted in Hell coming up from below into our urban existence and in the defeat of the ideas of Voltaire by those of the Marquis de Sade. Perhaps we really are now in a sort of 'Post-Culture' not far removed from absolute barbarism. But unless all human life is eliminated hope can never be destroyed; and I continue to believe that, though there are many dangerous people around nowadays, it should be possible, given the right touch and the right cause, to rally the great army of the happy and the good. More particularly should this be possible in Britain, where political passion has seldom consumed the nation and where the harmonizing effect of the old religion still runs deep. The fears that invest us are often illusions. The worst, as the French say, is not certain. Death, indeed, is certain, but if we live courageously and joyously, and to paraphrase Catullus, *mors est perpetua una dormienda* – it is only a perpetual sleep.

Appendix

Extracts from Sir Gladwyn Jebb's Speeches in the Security Council on Korea in 1950

I

I am sure we all welcome the return of the representative of the Soviet Union to the Council table after his long absence. I hope this portends that the Government of the Union of Soviet Socialist Republics has come to regret its desertion of the Council last January, and that we can in the future count on its sincere collaboration in the Council's proceedings. I cannot suppose that our President has failed to keep himself informed of the Council's work since his withdrawal. He will no doubt be aware that the item under which the council has so far considered the Korean question is entitled 'Complaint of aggression upon the Republic of Korea'. Now, the item which the representative of the Soviet Union in his capacity as President has placed upon the provisional agenda is entitled 'Peaceful settlement of the Korean question'. The difference in wording seems to me, as it seems to my United States colleague, to be significant. If we were to adopt the formula of the Soviet Union, all reference to aggression would disappear. Yet it is the act of aggression which is responsible for bringing this matter before the Council, and it is the main factor with which we have to deal.

The wording proposed by the representative of the USSR might also be held to imply that up to now the Council has made no attempt to settle the Korean question by peaceful means. This is a manifest travesty of the facts, since the first action of the Council in its resolution of 25 June was to call for the immediate cessation of hostilities and for the withdrawal forthwith of the North Korean forces to the thirty-eighth parallel. The flagrant disregard of the North Korean authorities for the will of the United Nations is the one thing which has prevented and still prevents the peaceful settlement of this question. I therefore feel that, while we are dealing with the Korean question, we should do so under the item which has appeared on our agenda for the last five weeks. This will, of course, in no way prevent the representative of the USSR from suggesting means for a peaceful settlement, and we shall be the first to rejoice if he were to come forward with concrete proposals for a solution of the question which will be consistent with the principles of the United Nations on which the Security Council so far has acted.

In any case, I note that in his speech yesterday the President said that it was 'not by chance that he' – that is to say the United States representative – 'fears the words "peace" and "peaceful settlement".' The implication of this remark was, of course, that the United States and those nations associated with it wanted a warlike settlement. This is an instance, if I may say so, of the queer upside-down language which always seems to be employed by USSR propaganda. If the side favoured by that Government attacked its neighbour, as in this case it has, then that is not an act of war; it is an act of peace. It would follow that the right settlement which, of course, would be a 'peaceful settlement', would be that it should defeat its neighbour and attain all of its objectives. Peace would then be established, and any action on the part of anybody else to interfere with the 'peaceful' moves on the state or authorities concerned would be a warlike act inspired by capitalists and imperialists intent on world domination. Moreover, quite apart from this, the very words 'peaceful settlement' in the mouth of the USSR representative are sufficient to cause a certain anxiety. So far as I remember, there was a 'peaceful settlement' in Czechoslovakia in 1938 and again in 1948 – 'peaceful' in the sense that on those occasions not a shot was fired. The only doubt in the minds of other countries lay in the settlements themselves, for in the course of both those 'settlements' freedom died. This is not the sort of settlement which at any rate fifty-two nations desire to see established in Korea and the overriding point is that it is a settlement which they are determined to resist.

Another instance of the 'upside-down method' occurred when our President stated that 'the resolution submitted by the United States representative is aimed at continuing and intensifying that aggression' – that is, by the United States Government – 'and extending its scope.' If, however, the United States resolution is actually read, it will be found that it is specifically aimed at localizing the conflict. We really do seem to be living in a rather nightmarish Alice-in-Wonderland world.

In conclusion I should like to make one general remark. The whole object of the United Nations and more particularly of the Security Council is to maintain peace not only by mediation and conciliation and other methods laid down in the Charter, but also in the last resort by banding together to resist those who break the peace. This is a simple proposition which is understood by the common man all over the world, and though it may not be accepted by genuine pacifists who object to the use of force in any circumstances whatever, the overwhelming majority of mankind can conceive of no other method whereby peace can be maintained. However great the attempt may be to assert the contrary on ideological and propaganda grounds, the fact is that the North Korean authorities attacked the Republic of Korea and that the situation must be restored in accordance with the Charter. No other issue must be allowed to cloud this cardinal fact, and that is why I shall continue to insist that the complaint of aggression against the Republic of Korea be placed as the first substantive item on our agenda.

II

482ND MEETING, 3 AUGUST 1950: PROCEDURE

Mr President, we have now had a very protracted debate in which, as I quite admit, many members have followed your example in straying from the main point at issue, which is the agenda itself, but in the course of this debate it has become absolutely clear that what almost all the members of the Council want, as far as I can see, except the President, is that we should have a simple vote on the American amendment which is before us now. If this is carried, the 'Complaint of Aggression upon the Republic of Korea' will be established as the first substantive item. Should you then wish, Mr President, to put to a vote the two items which you have proposed, I cannot imagine for a moment that there would be any objection. This, in fact, is the only solution of the agenda problem to which I, and, I suspect, the large majority of my colleagues are prepared to agree, and until you are prepared, therefore, to allow the vote on the United States motion to take place in the first instance, I fear that the debate on the agenda is likely to go on for a considerable time. This would be, no doubt, unfortunate in some ways, but it would, I think, be preferable to our consenting to a procedural device which is only being resorted to for propaganda purposes.

[Later] I want to explain the vote which I am about to cast, now that we are proceeding to the vote on the two following items on the provisional agenda. The long, gratuitous, offensive and, indeed, irregular speech to which the President treated us this afternoon makes it completely clear that his Government is determined to maintain what is the reverse of the truth, namely, that the Americans and not the North Korean authorities are the aggressors. No amount of photographs of Mr Dulles in a trench – and I only wish there had been more trenches – no suggestion that he himself first rushed across the frontier; no repetition of arguments which a child could refute or, indeed, anybody who is not a 'partisan of peace', that aggression cannot apply to wars between peoples of the same nationality, can obscure the patent fact that it was the North Korean troops who, in large numbers and heavily armed, crossed the frontier on 24 June last and overran the territory of a government which had been established by the United Nations.

III

486TH MEETING, 11 AUGUST 1950: SOVIET TACTICS

It is, I fear, only too true that the refusal of our President [Mr Malik] to admit the representative of the Korean Republic and his insistence on inviting a representative of the North Korean authorities raise most important and, indeed, basic matters of principle, some of which, but not all, have already been alluded to in the long debate which we have now had on this subject. I do not think that this debate has been entirely wasted, because it is gradually bringing into evidence real differences which divide us here. That is at least my impression. Perhaps it may help to overcome the reluctance of our President to abide by the rules of procedure – and, incidentally, by the views of almost every member of this Council, besides himself – if I urge him, if only in his capacity as the representative of the Soviet Union, to take note of the following considerations.

The Soviet representative's basic intention, as I understand it, is based on the premise that what we are dealing with in Korea is a civil war. He proceeds to argue that, as is indeed natural, there are two sides to most civil wars and, therefore, two sides to this one. Consequently, if we invite the representative of one side to be present, we are bound in logic and in equity – and, indeed, I think he said in accordance with the dictates of common sense – to invite the representative of the other side also.

This would all be very obvious were it not for the fact that the Soviet representative, in his desire to impress public opinion with the rightness of his cause, has omitted to draw attention to the fact that the Government of the Republic of Korea has already been declared the lawful government by the United Nations; that United Nations observers were stationed on its *de facto* northern frontier; and that, therefore, the whole state was, as it were, existing under the mantle of this great international organization. The Government of the Korean Republic was, however, attacked – and I will not here proceed to demonstrate that it was attacked or to counter

Soviet propaganda to the effect that it was Mr Dulles and Mr Muccio who attacked the Northern Koreans first – incidentally, I must apologize for omitting to refer to Mr Muccio previously, since clearly Mr Muccio's presence doubled the total number of the interventionist force – since that is so obviously absurd that it is hard to think that it can be swallowed even by the automata who listen to the Moscow radio. It was attacked, I say, by soldiers coming under the authority of a rival Korean government, not acceptable to the United Nations, and established at Pyongyang. It is quite true that the soldiers I refer to were Koreans, and therefore were, so to speak, blood brothers of the people whom they attacked; but to argue that this fact in itself constitutes a civil war or that it necessarily in itself puts both sides on an equal footing is patent nonsense. The President made what he thought were some very telling observations regarding the American Civil War, but they would only have been relevant if he had gone on to show that in 1861 either the northern states or the southern had been recognized by an international organization, which he could not do for the simple reason that no international organization existed at that time.

Moreover, whatever the version of history current in Moscow may now be – and I understand it is rewritten from time to time so as to blot out uncomfortable facts from any public memory – the fact is that England, though it could have done so, did not intervene in the war between the states. Indeed, as is well known, my fellow-countrymen, and particularly the working class, suffered great privations by not intervening.

Quite apart from this, there is absolutely no reason to suppose that wars between people of the same race, even if they do not involve a government which has been set up under the ægis of the United Nations, are necessarily exempt from the decisions of the Security Council. A civil war in certain circumstances might well, under Article 39 of the Charter, constitute a 'threat to the peace', or even a 'breach of the peace', and if the Security Council so decided, there would be nothing whatever to prevent its taking any action it liked in order to put an end to the incident, even if it should involve two or more portions of the same international entity. Indeed, Article 2 (7) of the Charter so provides. This reads:

Nothing contained in the present Charter shall authorize the United Nations to intervene in matters which are essentially within the domestic jurisdiction of any state or shall require the members to submit such matters to settlement under the present Charter; but this principle shall not prejudice the application of enforcement measures under chapter VII.

You will see that the last few words make it quite clear that the United

Nations has full authority to intervene actively in the internal affairs of any country if this is necessary for the purpose of enforcing its decisions as regards the maintenance of international peace and security. I do honestly hope that, for the reasons given, we shall hear no more of this civil war argument from the mouth of the Soviet Union spokesman.

It is equally true that under the Charter the Security Council might be unlikely to make a recommendation or a decision under Article 39 in regard to another such incident as the present, since such action could and no doubt would be vetoed by the Soviet Union. But when the Security Council very properly decided that the Government of the Republic of Korea should be defended against a brutal attack, and decided on the appropriate measures to that effect, it did so unanimously, and no permanent member present at this table objected in the slightest degree or even made any reservations. On the contrary, they were all horrified at the outrage which had occurred and the Council machinery therefore worked smoothly and easily and in entire accord with the purposes and principles of the Charter. Nor can the fact that one of these permanent members represents a government not recognized by a minority of members of the Security Council affect the issue at all. This point can only be decided by a majority; and if this is disputed – as it is disputed – it is difficult to see how the Security Council can function. For how can it decide anything, except by a process of voting?

Finally, it may also be said, and indeed is said by my Soviet colleague, that he himself was not present when the decision to resist aggression was made. Perhaps he regrets the fact that he was not present now. That may be. But to maintain that the Security Council must be powerless because one member in a fit of pique simply boycotts it, is really to admit that the Security Council and, indeed, the whole of the United Nations can only function if it functions in accordance with the wish and even at the behest of one individual permanent member.

Valid though I myself believe the theory of Great Power unity to be, in the sense that the United Nations can never work properly, for so long as the Great Powers are at loggerheads, and can therefore only proceed in the long run on the basis of unanimity, I cannot conceive that any rational being would admit that the theory ought to be abused in such a way as this, more especially since all the Great Powers, along with the small ones, have entered into a solemn obligation to abide by the purposes and principles of the Charter.

This, indeed, brings us to what is really the chief trouble with the Soviet Union, and – as I know well – has been the chief trouble since the beginning of the United Nations. Having now been, most of them, brought up from infancy on a doctrine of state infallibility, it seems almost impossible for any member of the Government of the Soviet Union to believe that the Government could in any circumstances be wrong, and, indeed, for any member of the Soviet Union not to believe that his Government is always, as it were, divinely inspired. Indeed, under the peculiar, long-outmoded deterministic philosophy to which they subscribe, the rulers of the Soviet Union are forced to maintain that everything works in accordance with what the major Soviet Union prophets have foretold. If, therefore, some canonized professor declared in, say, 1848 that it was inevitable that at some stage the imperialist Powers would band together to overcome any country in which socialism had been established then – and of course begging the question whether socialism is, in fact, the kind of regime now established in the Soviet Union – such an imperialist war becomes inevitable and therefore an obsession which haunts the minds of perhaps otherwise sane Soviet Union citizens, the great bulk of whom are fundamentally, of course, as decent and honourable a body of men as are to be found anywhere in the world. And yet, there is no reality in their nightmare. All that the non-Communist Powers are in fact doing is to take steps to see that the repressive and old-fashioned philosophy to which I have referred is not imposed by force on states which it does not suit and which have no desire to live under it. All they would ask of the Soviet Union Government is that they should not become the slaves of their own theories – that, as the poet has it, they should 'drain not to its dregs the urn of bitter prophecy'.

However, the draining of the urn which has been proceeding now for many years ensures that any action taken by any body or state which subscribed to the particular philosophy of the Soviet Union must, in the opinion of the Soviet Union, be right, provided only that such action is taken in accordance with the interpretation of the philosophy which is prevalent at Moscow at the time. Thus, if such a state attacks another one, that is not, and indeed cannot be, according to the Soviet Union point of view, aggression. It can only be an effort to repel an attack by the imperialist Powers. Imperialist Powers, good gracious me! Are we really to believe that the boys from Iowa or Colorado who are now sitting in foxholes near Ching-ju doing their best to defend democracy as they know it, and longing for the day when they will get back to Denver or Sioux City, are we really to believe that these people are out, like Genghis Khan, to enslave the world? Show me any one of these United States soldiers, Mr President, who would rather reign in Outer Mongolia than go back to

Seattle, and I will gladly concede your point about 'Imperialist America'. Until then, no; I prefer to rely not on Marx but on the judgment of my own eyes and ears.

Anyhow, basing himself on this false premise, the representative of the Soviet Union is now engaged, as we have seen, in an effort to ensure that representatives of the Korean Republic and the North Korean authorities appear before this Council table at the same time. The point of this last manoeuvre is simply to get an opportunity of arguing that both sides in Korea may to some extent be to blame, that the great thing in any case is to let Koreans settle the matter themselves, and that consequently the only real solution is for the 'foreign devils' to leave and so allow the Communization of Korea to take place on well-established lines. We all know what this now means. It means the elimination of all those sufficiently intelligent to dispute anything that some Man-God may from time to time assert; the 'liquidation' – as the pleasant phrase has it – of anyone who could be described as belonging to the *bourgeoisie;* and the establishment of a centrally-trained and largely non-indigenous bureaucracy who regard the transformation of sentient human beings into machines as the chief triumph, and indeed the main purpose of what is agreeably referred to, I understand, as 'social engineering'.

Up to now it has always been pretended that countries which have undergone this terrible experience have undergone it by some process of law. On the face of it the constitutional forms have been preserved, whatever the grim realities below the surface. It has thus invariably been proclaimed that the 'people' have decided on their own destruction and that 99·9 per cent have voted in favour of a regime under which usually at least fifty per cent have been condemned to slavery or death. But there is not even a pretence that the South Koreans voted for slavery; on the contrary, whatever the representative of the Soviet Union may assert, the fact is that they showed in their elections – observed by the United Nations – that they did not care for Communism of the Soviet type in the least. They dared indeed to register, by a perfectly free vote, that they were in favour of democracy. Not upside-down democracy, which is, of course, dictatorship, but real democracy, blundering perhaps, inefficient possibly, but nevertheless a regime under which spiritual progress was at least possible for the simple reason that thought was free.

Faced with this situation, the rulers of North Korea decided that their brethren in the South must be given a lesson. The existence of a free regime on their very doorstep was naturally anathema to them. They planned a crime which, in the circumstances, it is true, could hardly have been carried out undetected, but which they thought they could get away with because the policeman's back was turned. However, the policeman, though perhaps somewhat off his guard, was not indifferent. Though jumped on, he blew his whistle and a number of other policemen are now coming to his aid. The argument that all the policemen ought now to be called off, leaving the victim to the tender mercies of the attacker is not one which is likely to find much favour, if only for the fact that, if this were done, it would be only too likely that the incident would soon be repeated, and that Asia would once again be the scene of the crime.

Yes, Asia would once again be the scene of the crime. Here is the vast arena in which, repulsed in Europe, it is now clear that the dark forces of Communist imperialism are concentrating for the kill. All the new emergent Asian states are affected by this, and they know it. There is no secret at all. In Burma, the Communists are in arms against the recognized Government. In Indonesia, so soon as it became clear that Hatta and Soekarno were consolidating their authority, the Communist, Moeso, was sent to destroy them if he could. In Vietnam the emergent Government has had to wage active war against the Communists. The Communist, Hukbalahap, is similarly in arms against the Government of the Philippines. Even in India, the greatest of all the new Asian democracies, the Communist resort to armed violence in Hyderabad was a deliberate attempt by an armed minority to assert its power. Yes, it is not for nothing that the great statesman, Pandit Nehru, said as lately as 22 June –

Communism is sheer pure terrorism and the Communists in South-East Asia are automatically weakening themselves by turning against nationalism. The strongest and growing urge in South-East Asia is the nationalist urge, plus the urge for social justice.

That is what he said on 22 June.

Perhaps it is true that the Western Powers have not always heeded or sufficiently recognized this urge in the past. But if anything is certain it is that Communist imperialism, if it is allowed to get under way, will recognize it far less in the future. Here is a field, indeed, in which Western Europe and Asia seem to have much in common; and, whatever their relations in the past, they are likely both to be lost unless they both realize the danger and concert to meet it.

For this purpose what has happened in Korea simply must not be allowed to occur again. The immediate necessity is, as I think I have said before, for the North Korean authorities who are responsible for the outrage, to say that they will do what this Council has told them to do before they can come to us and put forward any constructive proposals, that they may then have, for a solution as regards the future of Korea as a whole.

Nor is it any use for the Soviet Union Government to try to make out that it is only the United States which is insisting on this, the proper and obvious course. Irrespective of race or creed, fifty-three of the free nations of the world are insisting on it, too. Though it may be the most powerful, the United States is not even the largest state which is insisting on such a course, and this for the simple reason that any person who is capable of forming a rational view at all and does not have his thought imposed upon him by dictatorship, is convinced that conformity with the various resolutions passed by this Council is a prerequisite for the settlement which we all hope will shortly be achieved.

In short, whatever solution is finally established, one thing comes necessarily first, and that is, that the invading forces in Korea should go back whence they came. Then there might be a period, during which some body representing the United Nations could establish contact with the North Korea authorities and report to the Security Council. Only then, I suggest, could we think of inviting representatives of the North Korean authorities to this table, with the object of enabling the United Nations to consider and carry out a scheme establishing a really independent and democratic Korea, which, of course, it is in the interest of all of us, including the Soviet Union Government, to achieve.

This is what I would call the United Nations way – a way totally at variance with the solutions based on force which, unfortunately, at present seem to be approved by the Soviet Union. It is in pursuing this way, which discards force except when it is necessary to meet aggression by force, that we can hope to create a world community consisting of free nations, obedient only to law, which must in the final count be based on the will of a majority of the human race. Imperfect though the United Nations undoubtedly still is, slow though the progress towards the ideal must inevitably be, wrong though it may be to precipitate changes too suddenly, with consequent risk of chaos and the breakdown of society as such, still it is true that the United Nations is the only present basis for a possible world community other than some centrally controlled world despotism which must be at variance with all the purpose and principles inscribed in the Charter itself.

Even if it is admitted – which, personally, I would not admit – that in theory the productive resources of the twentieth century would best be organized for the purposes of humanity by some centrally controlled bureaucracy in the slave-like conditions which such a system would inevitably impose upon about ninety-nine per cent of the human race, those conditions would undoubtedly render it odious to humanity at large. With the world in its present state and with opportunities for contact so greatly enlarged, there must be a great constructive effort to reconcile divergent national philosophies, to raise the standard of living of under-developed peoples not only in their own interests but in those of the developed peoples as well, and gradually to achieve peace and prosperity on a scale totally impossible in the past. The United Nations way is perhaps not the only way to achieve this end because in human affairs everything is possible, but it is the only way which the common man can at present see for improving his lot. And one thing is certain. This hope will be destroyed and the way will be lost if we do not now succeed in dealing with aggression as it should be dealt with, and by ensuring that the barbarous and old-fashioned methods of former centuries are not repeated in this.

IV

489TH MEETING, 22 AUGUST 1950: SOVIET POLICY

Mr President [Mr Malik], after twenty-one days of your presidency, and nine days of debate, during which, according to my calculations at any rate, no less than seventy-six pages in the English text of the verbatim record have been filled by yourself – what the score is now I am afraid I do not know – twenty-five pages by the representative of the United States, sixteen by the representative of China and, I regret to say, twenty-one pages by me, it is still uncertain – I repeat, it is still uncertain – whether everybody has appreciated exactly why we cannot, at any rate for another ten days, proceed at all in this Council on the subject of Korea. I should therefore like to seize the opportunity, while we are marking time in this way, to explain once more why we are marking time and why, during this period, it is not possible for us – in the opinion of my delegation at any rate – even to consider peace aims and still less to do anything effective in the way of ending this terrible, if happily still limited, war.

The immediate reason for the *impasse*, of course, is your refusal to agree to the presence at this table of the representative of the victim, the Republic of Korea, or more accurately perhaps, your refusal to agree to his presence unless there is a simultaneous appearance of the representative of those who let loose the war, namely, the Communist authorities of North Korea. What is still not generally understood, I think, is the immense importance of this attitude of yours which is not, of course, shared and is indeed bitterly opposed by no less than nine of your colleagues on the Security Council. Behind the dreary debate which we have had on procedure there looms indeed a question of vast significance, and one which, as might have been expected, has brought the proceedings in this body to a complete, if only temporary, stop. Let me explain.

Your whole thesis, Mr President, which, as you have so obligingly and at such length explained, and to which your latest effort has contributed absolutely nothing, is as follows:

(1) The forces of the Republic of Korea, headed by Mr Dulles, attacked North Korea at the instance of the United States and other 'imperialist' Powers.

(2) Nevertheless, and to some extent despite this argument, the war in Korea is a 'civil war' in which, whatever the Charter may say, the United Nations should not intervene.

(3) However that may be, the whole thing is a 'dispute' to which there are two sides, and the obvious thing is to get representatives of both sides together in order that the Security Council, by exercising mediation, should arrange for what is described as a 'peaceful settlement' of the whole affair.

(4) By 'peaceful settlement' is meant some arrangement whereby the fighting stops, the United Nations forces retire, and the Communists are, by one means or another, left in ultimate possession of the field.

(5) All that is required, therefore, to achieve peace in the first instance, is for a representative of the Communist authorities in North Korea to be invited to this table, along with a representative of the Korean Republic.

That is the thesis. Now as regards (1), we all know here that this foundation of the whole case is a gigantic falsehood; but what we do not perhaps all realize is that in propaganda the bigger the falsehood the better the chance it has of being believed. Perhaps I should repeat therefore, once again, that the patent fact of aggression was verified by the United Nations Commission on Korea itself. It is useless to throw mud at this body and to say that it was 'prejudiced' for the reason that it did not include a Soviet representative, since it was the Soviet Government itself which has boycotted the Commission from the start. Why did they boycott it? Because they feared that it might find out what was really happening behind the Iron Curtain in Korea; why a million people – I suppose they were the *bourgeoisie* – fled the country; what the conditions, forced on the majority of the unfortunate population, were really like; how the army of aggression composed of specially selected and tough young fanatics was being formed; and generally what the whole plot was about. It may be impossible to keep 'social engineering' on this scale altogether dark; but to say that the United Nations were incapable of observing the crime when it was committed because they were prevented from observing it when it was in preparation is really too blatant even for the faithful on this side of the Iron Curtain. On the contrary, the mere fact of their exclusion is in itself pretty good evidence that the Communists in North Korea were engaging in some form of activity which would revolt any non-Communist spectator.

As regards (2) – the 'civil war' – I have already said what I feel about this in my speech of 11 August, and I concluded my remarks by saying: 'I do honestly hope that for the reasons given we shall hear no more of this "civil war" argument from the mouth of the Soviet spokesman.' We have just heard some more, and unfortunately we still continue to hear about it; and in default, apparently, of other support, no less a person than Professor Krylov, Soviet Judge on the Permanent Court of International Justice at The Hague, has, I see, been mobilized to reinforce the Politburo's thesis which has been so ably expressed by the President. I will not now go into the question whether an international judge with a proper sense of his duty should plunge into political controversy in this way. Astonishing though it may appear, Professor Krylov relies largely in his argumentation on Article 2, paragraph 7, of the Charter, which you may remember, I quoted in full in my speech on this subject. But Professor Krylov does not even quote it in full, merely saying – unless press reports are inaccurate – that it provides that nothing in the Charter authorizes the United Nations to intervene in matters which are essentially within the domestic jurisdiction of any state, which, so far as it goes, is perfectly correct. The final words of this Article, as I pointed out the last time, are those at the end which read: 'but this principle shall not prejudice the application of enforcement measures under chapter VII.' It is not difficult, perhaps, to see why the learned judge did not allude to this awkward passage in his statement.

Quite apart from this, however, the civil war argument simply does not make sense on general grounds. First of all, you divide a state into two, then you organize a special government in one part of it, not allowing anybody else to see how this government is formed or what it is doing. You give it full governmental powers and you recognize it, even though most states have recognized the other government. Then the government organized in this way, possessing *de facto* authority over half the territory, attacks the lawful government of the other half which has been set up under the international protection of the United Nations. Nobody, however, is allowed to interfere with this process on the grounds that it is a 'civil war'. The result, of course, is that, in defiance of international authority, you get control of the whole country and you get what you want. It is quite easy to think of other cases in which this interesting, if rather sinister, theory might be applied.

This brings me to (3), the argument of the 'two sides', as I will call it. Here I believe, in contradistinction to the first two arguments I mentioned, a certain impression has been made by what our President has said. There are indeed a number of fair-minded persons in the free world who have been brought up in the great traditions of Roman and English jurisprudence and who consequently believe that 'both sides should be heard'. Now, this would be perfectly correct if the Council were now dealing with the case as a dispute, but, as I think my Norwegian colleague has already pointed out, we are dealing, on the contrary, with a violent attack by one party on another in which the Security Council has already found that attacker to be in the wrong. Transferring this to the field of common law it would mean that there should be no question of hearing a man who has committed a violent crime until he has either surrendered to the police or the police have caught him. When he has surrendered, he should, indeed, be given a fair trial, and it is then, no doubt, that he can state his own case and explain what were the pathological reasons which lay behind his action, or even, conceivably, who inspired it. But until then, a 'hearing' of the party concerned in this particular instance would be, broadly speaking, equivalent to going and asking the criminal for a statement of his views when he was still actively engaged in prosecuting the crime.

If we conclude that (3) is also a completely specious argument, therefore we are left with (4), which simply means that we must have a 'peaceful settlement' at all costs. This, of course, is also begging the question: nobody wants to have a 'warlike settlement', nobody wants the fighting in Korea to go on for a moment longer than necessary. But if by 'peaceful settlement' is meant anything except a demonstration that aggression does not pay and that Communist governments must not indulge in this kind of violent activity any more, it will not be a settlement which will bring peace to our troubled world. Perhaps now, therefore, I might say a few words on the general subject of peace, a subject which, incidentally, was not excluded, I think, from the President's last intervention.

For well over a year now the Soviet propaganda machine has been harping on one theme, namely, that the world is divided into two camps, the camp of 'imperialism and aggression' led by the Western countries and notably by the United States, and the camp of 'democracy and peace,' led by the Soviet Union, with the help of the Communist Parties all over the world. Now, of course, the various catch-terms which are employed by the Soviet propaganda machine have, as I think I have suggested before, a real meaning which is the reverse of the actual meaning, and if you apply this simple test, then, of course, you will observe that what the Soviet propaganda machine is saying is that the world is divided into two camps, the camp of democracy and peace, led by the Western nations – and notably by the United States – and the camp of imperialism and aggression, led, of course, by the Soviet Union with the help of the various Communist Parties of the world. But it is perhaps no good for me just to assert this, though many would believe it, some also would be misled by the wonderful propaganda device of calling white black and evil good. To these, therefore, it may be of some interest to know that it is a fundamental article of Communist belief that the aims of the Party can, in the long run, only be achieved by force.

We are living not merely in a state, but in a system of states, and the existence of the Soviet Republic side by side with imperialist states for a long time is unthinkable. We or the other must triumph in the end, and before that end supervenes, a series of frightful collisions between the Soviet Republic and the bourgeois states will be inevitable. . . .

This was originally said by Lenin in 1919 and is quoted in Stalin's essay, *On the Problems of Leninism* (first published in 1926). But if we want something rather later, we need only turn to the leading periodical of the Soviet Communist Party, *Bolshevik*. In July 1948, this magazine said –

Communism teaches that the violent overthrow of the exploiting classes and the establishment of the dictatorship of the proletariat is a general law of the Socialist revolution.

The same journal goes on to say –

Communism is incompatible with opportunistic ideas to the effect that the transition from capitalism to Socialism can be carried out peacefully on the basis of parliamentary voting.

You will see that, in accordance with this doctrine, and even if the Soviet thesis that the Korean war is a civil war is accepted, it would be perfectly in order for a Communist minority to turn out a democratically elected government by force of arms, provided only that it had the opportunity to do so. This, indeed, is exactly what happened, except that the North

Korean authorities first organized themselves effectively as a separate state and then seized upon what they thought was the right opportunity. Whether it will be the right opportunity remains, of course, to be seen.

Still, it may conceivably be questioned whether the Soviet doctrine of violence applies necessarily to relations between states. In *Problems of Leninism*, which is very properly required reading for all Communists everywhere, Stalin himself explains that the Russian Revolution resulted in the establishment of the 'first proletarian dictatorship', which he described as 'a powerful and open base for the world revolutionary movement'. Now, a state which admittedly regards itself in this light is hardly likely to pursue a peaceful and cooperative foreign policy, since it must necessarily take every step to weaken and undermine every other government which it regards as opposed to the world revolutionary movement. In other words, the bleak fact is that it is really impossible for any non-Communist government – and even difficult for some Communist ones – to be on terms of real friendship and intimacy with the Soviet government. It is, indeed, this messianic urge which leads to the Soviet attitude towards war, conveniently defined as it is in the *Short History of the Communist Party*, which is also 'must' reading for Communists all over the world. This is as follows:

There are two kinds of war –
(a) *Just* wars, wars that are not wars of conquest but wars of liberation, waged to defend the people from foreign attack and from attempts to enslave them, or to liberate the people from capitalist slavery, or, lastly, to liberate colonies and dependent countries from the yoke of imperialism; and
(b) *Unjust* wars, wars of conquest, waged to conquer and enslave foreign countries and foreign nations.

Whether the Soviet Government approves or disapproves of a particular war depends, therefore, on which of these categories they decide fits the war in question. The decision is ludicrously simple. Any war in which they or their clients are engaged must be a just war of liberation, whereas any war in which the non-Communist countries are engaged must be an unjust war of conquest. As the Western countries cannot possibly engage in a just war, it is logical to demand their disarmament or, at the very least, to prevent their using the one weapon with regard to which they enjoy superiority. On the other hand, it is equally logical to exempt the Soviet Union from all real control in this field, for that country is by definition capable of waging only just wars 'of liberation'.

All this is, of course, behind the peculiar Soviet attitude towards the war in Korea, in which, as we all know, the Northern Koreans are engaged, in the opinion of the Soviet Government, in a desperate struggle against the aggressive forces of 'imperialism'.

Imperialism – That is perhaps the best catch-word of all with which to delude peace-loving people all over the world, including many, no doubt, in the Soviet Union itself. But what exactly is imperialism? If it means the period of the expansion of Europe on the basis of new ideas, formulated about the time of the Renaissance, which came to a head in the industrial revolution of the late eighteenth and early nineteenth century, that at least is comprehensible. Most periods of expansion of any Power or group of Powers – and with reference to what Dr Tsiang said on this subject last time I would like to point out that on many occasions such expansion came from Asia and had Europe as its object – most of such periods of expansion I say were based on new ideas and new techniques. It was not just a case of evil intention or lust for conquest, so much as the possession of some 'know-how' which other nations did not have and could not get for a considerable period.

But one would have thought that almost anybody could now see that the period of European, as opposed to Russian, expansion is over, the last physical manifestation of it being perhaps the bursting out of the Germans under Hitler, which incidentally the Western Powers, now described as imperialists, did quite as much as the Russians to resist. Any government, indeed, which is not about forty years behind the times, and thus cut off from modern thought and developments, could presumably see that, for instance, those nations of Asia who were placed in an unequal position by their lack of the necessary techniques have now largely acquired them, and that the old system, which was essentially based on the idea of teacher and pupil, has now been changed into one of cooperation and partnership, if indeed the original roles are not eventually reversed.

Though there may be some continuing stresses and strains resulting from this vast change in human relationships, the fact does still emerge that what was denounced by Marx in 1848 as 'imperialism' now no longer exists, except as a bogey by the use of which certain despotic oligarchies are enabled to keep themselves in power. Applied to such bodies as the British Labour Government or the American Administration it would indeed be funny, if it were not so sad, and how even Marx would explain why the stock market goes down when there are rumours of the conflict spreading, and up when it is thought it will be localized, is perhaps only explicable after a life-long study of the Soviet classics. In short, all this stuff about imperialism which pours out from the Moscow radio is really nothing but an attempt to conceal the fact that it is not America, but quite another Power which is trying to clamp down a despotism on the world as a whole.

What is actually happening in the Soviet colonies – I beg your pardon – republics of Central Asia I frankly do not know. You said, Mr President, that the paradisial conditions there prevailing were not hidden. But this is precisely what they are, since no representative of the free world – so far as I know – is allowed to penetrate into this worker's Eden.

And so, Mr President, I resume my thought on the real reasons why our unfortunate *impasse* has been reached during the month of August (I repeat during the month of August), as follows. Peace propaganda, whether it takes the form of signatures for an ambiguous declaration of proposals for getting 'both sides' to agree on a 'peaceful solution' in Korea, is essentially only a means for securing aggression and making it even more successful in the future. Peace propaganda, in fact, is itself part of the very preparation for aggression. It is principally designed to prevent, or at least to hinder, other people from coming to the victim's aid. In the official *Soviet History of Diplomacy* these tactics are analysed with great clarity and shrewdness. In volume two there is a discussion about what the book calls 'the concealment of predatory ends behind noble principles'. Among the ways of doing this are listed 'the exploitation of disarmament and pacifist propaganda for one's own purposes'. The book goes on to say 'From time immemorial the idea of disarmament has been one of the most popular ways of dissimulating the true motives and plans of aggressive governments.' An interesting side-light is a statement of the Communist Minister of Defence in Hungary, Farkas, who wrote on 12 April last:

A certain pacifism has made itself felt within the ranks of our party, particularly lately. Slogans like 'we want no more wars' are very significant of this pacifism. First of all, therefore, we have to overcome this feeling of pacifism within our own party in order to be able to fight it down in the masses . . . a considerable feeling of pacifism is reigning among our people, particularly among our women and peasants. . . .

That is what the Hungarian Minister of Defence said.

In any case, the Soviet Union rulers have always had some peculiar views about aggression, no doubt owing to the strict application of the outmoded doctrines to which they persistently adhere. Stalin himself, you will remember, said on 29 December 1939:

It was not Germany who attacked France and Britain, but France and Britain who attacked Germany, thus assuming responsibility for the present war. The ruling circles of Britain and France rudely declined both Germany's peace proposals and the attempts of the Soviet Union to achieve the earliest termination of the war.

If Stalin himself subscribed to this remarkable analysis of aggression in 1939, who is going to believe Soviet theories of aggression in 1950?

The truth is that unless these mad deterministic ideas are abandoned, peace cannot be final and the possibility of war must always be there. The ideas need not, of course, be explicitly abandoned, but perhaps they can in practice not be applied. Perhaps we can draw at any rate one conclusion. If the fifty-three nations on which you, Mr President, pour so much scorn, can remain together, these ideas will not be applied in practice because in practice it will be impossible for the Soviet Government to achieve by violence, direct or indirect, those ends which at the moment they seem determined to secure. This, I suggest, is the plain truth and the root of the matter.

V

493RD MEETING, 31 AUGUST 1950: SOVIET PROPAGANDA

As regards the torrent of abuse which we next heard in connection with item five on the provisional agenda ('The Unceasing Terrorism and Mass Executions in Greece'), let me just say this: For the representative of a country which maintains millions of its own compatriots in slave-labour camps in unspeakable conditions, which has frequently transported whole populations in cattle trucks to Siberia, whose whole way of life is based on recruiting slaves for the labour force by means of the secret police, for the representative of such a government to denounce other governments for alleged misdemeanours as regards political prisoners is just about as nauseating a spectacle as that of Satan rebuking sin.

VI

497TH MEETING, 7 SEPTEMBER 1950: SOVIET PROTEST AGAINST BOMBING

The President (Sir Gladwyn Jebb): I should like to say just a few words in my capacity as the representative of the United Kingdom. The Soviet representative in his speech made much play with the name of Hitler and said on several occasions that the strategic bombing of Korean objectives, which the United Nations Air Force has been compelled to undertake, was a barbarous and Hitlerian technique. The Council may remember, as I pointed out on 22 August 1950, that Generalissimo Stalin declared, substantially, in 1939 that it was not Hitler who had attacked France and the United Kingdom but rather France and the United Kingdom which had attacked Hitler. Generalissimo Stalin's present view appears to be, unless I am mistaken, that it was not the North Koreans who attacked the Republic of Korea last June but rather the United States, together with some Korean allies, which attacked the authorities of North Korea. Nobody outside the Soviet Union – and even there there may have been a little surprise – believed Generalissimo Stalin in 1939, and nobody outside the Soviet Union believes him now.

The fact is that Hitler and his Nazis set the world ablaze in 1939 and that the North Korean Communist warlords took the same incendiary action in 1950. But it is the same old story. When Hitler let loose the dogs of war, he did not expect himself to be bitten by those dogs – in other words, he did not expect that the German people would suffer by reason of his abominable act. Nor did the North Korean Communist warlords believe that the horrors of war would descend upon their unfortunate country as a result of their disgraceful decision. And yet both Hitler and the North Koreans were wrong. Modern war is a horrible business, and in my own country we have a pretty fair conception of how horrible it is. But there is only one way to escape these horrors, and it is after all a very simple way. Governments in fact, however dictatorial, should not commit acts of aggression. If they do, a great many innocent people will suffer, as they are now suffering in Korea. But the responsibility for such suffering can only lie with the people who caused it, namely, the North Korean leaders. If they really want to stop it, they can do it to-morrow: simply by complying with the various resolutions of the Security Council.

Index

Compiled by Norman Knight, MA, and Valerie Chandler, BA., ALAA

For reasons of space the author's name in the index has been abbreviated to 'G'. Similarly Sir Winston Churchill is referred to as WSC, De Gaulle as 'D Ge' and the Foreign Office as 'FO'. 'q' stands for quoted.

Reference nos. in bold type denote substantial allusions.

Laniel, Joseph (French premier), 269, 270

Laski, Harold, 177

Law, Richard (later 1st Baron Coleraine), 182; Minister of State for Foreign Affairs (1942–3), 115, 118

Law Society, examines prospects for homologation of laws and EEC (1961), 341

Lawrence, T. E., 13

Layton, Walter (later 1st Baron), 142

Leadership, **379–80**

League of Nations (1920–46), 43, 74–5; dominated by Britain and France (1923), 16; G attends Assembly (1929), 40–1; Mussolini's criticism of, 46; Italy broke her obligations under (1935), 47, 60; could not by itself maintain the peace, 54, 60, 65; Economic Committee, of, 64; could it be resuscitated?, 113; WSC's wish to replace it by 'instrument of European Government', 122; winding up of (1945), 174

Leeds, D'Arcy Osborne, 12th Duke of, 33

Leeper, Reginald (Counsellor, FO), 59, 60, 63, 97; controversy with, 96; embarrassing appointment as Head of SOI, 102; relations with, **102** bis

Leith-Ross, Sir Frederick ('Leithers'); Economic Adviser, G attached to (1936), 64; negotiates in Washington on post-war requirements (1941–5), 111

Leloy, Jean (adviser Quai d'Orsay), 2

Lewis, (Percy) Wyndham, *Time and Western Man*, 33

Liberal Party: author joins (Jan 1965), 331, 353–4; speech on Western Europe at Liberal Assembly (1965), 356; policy for Britain and Europe, 354, 360–1

Libya, discussed at Peace Conference (1946), 193, 194

Lie, Trygve, first Secy-Gen. of UN, (1946–51), 182, 186, **256–8**

Litvinov, Maxim (Soviet diplomatist), 78

Lloyd, Geoffrey (Chamberlain's PPS), 81

Lloyd, Selwyn (Foreign Secretary, now Speaker): appointed Minister of State (1951), 253; defended against criticisms of Acheson, 253; but for diffidence of, Suez disaster might have been averted, 253; and his 'Grand Design', 292, 294, 296, 297; at Summit Meeting (1960), 320–1; wants G to stay as Ambassador to France (1958), 322

Lloyd George, David (later 1st Earl), q. on meaning of 'Gladwyn', 5

Lodge, Cabot (US representative at UN), 254–5

London Conference (1954), 273, 274

London University Union, debate between G & Shinwell on EEC, 341–2

Longmore, Air Vice Marshal, 132

Loraine, Lady (née Louise Stuart-Wortley), 23

Loraine, Sir Percy, 12th Bt, British Minister in Persia (1921–6), 21–2, **23**; reprimanded by 'Ponderous Percy', **24–5**; relations with, 26

Lothian, Marquess of, (FO Under-Secy in Lords), on independent political commission (1970), 371

Loxley, Peter (of FO), death of, 152–3

Lumley, Roger (later Earl of Scarbrough), 13

MI (R), War Office Intelligence, 101

McArthur, General Douglas: and the Korean War, 242, 243; his position in 1951, 249; dismissed by Truman (1951), 250–1, 263

McCarthy, Senator Joseph, organises anti-Communist witch-hunt in US, 255–6

MacDonald, James Ramsay, 43, 48

McDougall, Frank, chairs unofficial committee (1938), 63, 65; q. on Dalton, 105

Maclean, Donald, 215–6, 277

Macmillan, Harold: 'convinced summiteer', 276; at 1960 Summit, 320–2; and Bulganin-Khruschev visit to UK, 279; repair work after Suez, 289; attends Anglo-American Conference (1957), 300, 311; attitude to EEC; apprehensive in 1960, 305; in 1961, 338; 'For ever amber', (1961), 340; on Britain's exclusion from EEC (1963), 327; offers G post-retirement job, 322, 333; apparently prefers Stikker to G as Secretary-General of NATO, 335

McNeil, Hector (representative at UN), 194, 204, 236, 241; passed over for Foreign Secretary, 251

Maddan, Martin, 338

Makins, Sir Roger (now Lord Sherfield), 59

Malaya, war against insurgents had to be continued, 252

Malenkov, George, 277, 278

Malik, Yakov Alexandrovich (Russian Representative on Security Council),